EDDIE MAC
EDDIE MAC

Life and times at Chelsea under Eddie McCreadie

presented by

EDDIE MCCREADIE'S
BLUE AND WHITE ARMY

Eddie Mac Eddie Mac: Life and times at Chelsea under Eddie McCreadie

CONTENTS

ACKNOWLEDGMENTS... 1

FOREWORD 2

IT MIGHT BE COLD TOMORROW 10

RELEGATION AND RECESSION 12

HARD TIMES 37

PROMOTION AND PUNK 61

EDDIE MCCREADIE 84

SMITH AND THE KID 162

CASH FOR CHELSEA... 206

EDDIE'S PLAYERS.. 214

COMPENDIUM OF RESULTS... 396

ACKNOWLEDGEMENTS

Eddie McCreadie's Blue and White Army (Kelvin Barker, David Johnstone, Mark Meehan, Neil Smith, Mark Worrall) wish to thank the following people for providing their valuable time, wisdom and assistance. Without their contributions, *Eddie Mac, Eddie Mac* would have remained just a beautiful idea to tell the greatest Chelsea story never told.

Eddie McCreadie, Linda Crouch McCreadie, Omid Djalili, Julie Carr, Neil Barnett, Martin Knight, Chris Mears, Ashley Rolfe, Max Rolfe, Nicholas Tilt, Ian Britton RIP, Charlie Cooke, John Dempsey, Micky Droy, Steve Finnieston, Ron Harris, David Hay, Tommy Langley, Ray Lewington, Gary Locke, Teddy Maybank, John Phillips, Steve Sherwood, John Sparrow, Garry Stanley, Kenny Swain, Clive Walker, Steve Wicks, Graham Wilkins, Ray Wilkins.

This collector's edition of *Eddie Mac, Eddie Mac* was published to coincide with a benefit evening held at Stamford Bridge on 20 May 2017 to celebrate the life and times of Eddie McCreadie and commemorate the 40th anniversary of Chelsea Football Club's remarkable 1977 promotion season.

FOREWORD
Omid Djalili

It's almost incredible to me now that back in 1975 when I was ten years old my parents let me go to Stamford Bridge all alone. Being immigrants they didn't technically know I was watching football at Chelsea with thousands of other fans.

My Dad recently told me when I said I was 'going to Chelsea' he thought I meant I was going for a kick about in Kensington Gardens (in the Royal Borough of Kensington & Chelsea). Little did he know I was spending every other Saturday at Stamford Bridge either inside the stadium sitting politely between adults screaming all sorts, or loitering outside the ground waiting for the 80 minute mark when they'd open The Shed gates and let you in for free, or on the roof of my own block of flats listening out for the odd roar of the crowd that would somehow reach my ears a full two miles away in Kensington.

I first went to Chelsea in 1972 when I was six years of age. Chelsea 1 West Ham 3. That first game always burns into the memory. But it was the Eddie McCreadie years that I remember so well, purely because he had a charisma that shone over the club like a beacon, even in days when the media covered only a fraction of what they cover now. He became manager just before the 74/75 season had ended. We were struggling all season and got beaten by Spurs which almost sealed our fate. It meant we had to beat Everton at home on the last day of the season to stand any chance of staying up. I was at home watching the teleprinter that Saturday glued to BBC1 Grandstand. In those days the latest scores would flash up by someone typing them out on the bottom of the screen while the horse racing was on.

Finally it came up on the screen:

Latest scores:

Chelsea1 Everton 0

I even heard the intense roar of the crowd out the window of our flat on that mild May afternoon moments before it flashed up on TV. The feeling of hope and jubilation it raised in me was indescribable. I stood by the window listening out for the crowd with eyes on the TV hoping and praying for the score to turn to 2-0. I didn't hear any more cheers. Ominously the teleprinter started typing:

Final score:

Chelsea 1 Everton 1

They equalized. Oh my goodness. My heart sank. I watched the screen for more news. The final whistle had blown and they were beaming live pictures from Stamford Bridge showing Chelsea players walking around in a daze. John Motson was saying that Chelsea had been relegated. I had no idea what to do. I had to do *something*.

My brother's moped, barely bigger than a bicycle, was parked in the hallway. The helmet was dangling over the seat so I picked it up and started throwing it randomly around hallway, the only way I could express my anger at Chelsea's fate. My father came in from the kitchen to restrain me.

"What's the matter with you?"

"Chelsea have been relegated!"

"What does that mean?"

"You mean… you don't know?"

"No. What is it?"

I immediately ran out of the house shouting, "You don't know my life!"

I was so upset. Chelsea being relegated to the Second Division was a big deal in 1975. I was absolutely gutted. But Eddie McCreadie was going round each player patting them on the back as if promising we would be back. There was hope. A small but tangible hope, a real sense if anyone could turn things around it was Eddie.

The following season there was such a wave of optimism at the club that I started going regularly to games. A bizarre feel-good factor stemmed directly from our glamorous Eddie even though we were playing the likes of Bristol Rovers and Crewe Alexandra. It wasn't all plain sailing. The next season, apart from a great November when we won four games on the trot, Chelsea were decidedly average and finished mid-table.

I must have had some real courage as a child as I went on my own from the age of ten and had no fears. I loved being at grotty, run down old Stamford Bridge. I saw us lose more games than we won but no matter, I was there supporting my team.

Once when walking home from a game a posh lanky bloke came up to me and asked, "Have you been to the Chelsea game?" I said yes. "What was the score?" I told him we'd just lost and he said theatrically, "Oh my goodness, no! We always lose! What's happened to us? This is just terrible!" and he walked off upset and angry gesticulating to himself. I thought "what are YOU upset about? You weren't even there. Tell you what, things are looking up. But you wouldn't know, would you, because you're a posh ponce who gets the results off real supporters like me!" Of course I was too young to articulate all this and just walked off in the opposite direction. But the sense that Chelsea was my club, my cause, my pride was ingrained in me very early.

Going to live games gave me a real sense of belonging. I usually sat in the East Stand, lower or upper tier. Sometimes it was even middle tier, it didn't seem to be as exclusive as it is now. The odd time I went up seven flights of stairs to the top floor of a block of flats that used to exist on the Fulham Road right next to Stamford Bridge. There would be a huddle of four or five of us watching the game from a vantage point where only two thirds of the pitch was visible. The others were boys around my age who went to a primary school in Fulham called Ashburham. They were proper cockneys and I remember saying very little fearing my Kensington accent would alienate me from the group. When my school played them in football we didn't speak, just nodded acknowledgments before kick off as a code of honour that we were part of a renegade hard boys' club. Only without the honour. Or being hard. Ultimately we were just boys who didn't have enough money that week to get into the game.

Eddie McCreadie embodied everything about Chelsea. The big sunglasses, the sheepskin coat, he looked like a faded rock star who'd come back to help his old band, a rock 'n roll image in keeping with Kings Road hipsters and anything that was deemed 'cool' back then; and Chelsea Football Cub was somehow associated with it: film stars, rock stars, punk rock, you name it. Eddie seemed to be in tune with the cultural pulse of the age. It was the 1970s and Eddie Mac was our 'sexy' Commander In Chief by popular choice. And all that optimism continued all the way through to Tommy Langley scoring away at Wolves to win us promotion in the 76/77 season.

One of my earliest memories of that season was when we beat Cardiff 2-1 at home in early October and Ray Lewington scored the winning goal. It was a tremendous left foot volley into the right hand corner of the net. The whole crowd was going mad about this little red head called Lewington. He was some player.

I met Ray recently at an event and he was very impressed that I could remember that goal against Cardiff City. It wasn't difficult to remember, he hardly ever scored, and when he did it was spectacular (think Claude Makelele away to Spurs a few seasons back).

I described his goal to him blow by blow. He said that it was the first time someone had ever spoken to him about that goal and was impressed by the detail. He declared me, "A proper football bloke with forensic knowledge of the game." I beamed with pride. Though if I'm honest I also worried about my youth, which was clearly hugely misspent.

Chelsea had an entertaining team back then with a great midfield. Ian Britton (now sadly passed away), Brian Bason (who could play) and Garry Stanley (looked like a pop star). All good players – it was the dawn of a new era at Chelsea, and central to that was our beloved Ray Wilkins.

Probably the best game I saw him play was at home to Oldham when we won 4-3. We went 2-0 up, Oldham came back to 2-2 but we ran out winners. Wilkins was involved in everything that day and one particular goal he scored seemed to prove a point.

Wilkins was an England player by then and during the week there was a piece in the Daily Telegraph (my parents had the Telegraph delivered and I read the sports pages avidly) about whether he was good enough to play for England and even question marks about his left foot. As Chelsea supporters we knew that, like Glenn Hoddle, Wilkins was both footed. He took all our corners with his right foot and left foot on both sides of the pitch as in-swingers. The Oldham game was the first game after the article. Wilkins took a corner with his so called 'weaker' foot and it curled straight into the net via the near post over the defender's head. It was a fabulous moment as few of us had seen a goal go in straight from a corner before. His celebration referenced his left foot that it was "on purpose" and not a fluke. His eligibility for England was put to bed soon after.

It was a great time to be in the Second Division back then. Crowd figures alone were impressive and as big as anywhere in the First Division. I remember being at Stamford Bridge when 55,000 turned up against Fulham who had two old boys in their team called George Best and Rodney Marsh, the only time I saw them play live. 40,000 showed up against Southampton in the League and then over 40,000 again in the FA Cup when they beat us 3-0 after extra time. Though Peter Osgood was playing for them at that time which may have inflated the numbers somewhat.

Football COULD be scary for a ten year old in the '70s. I remember a fifth round FA cup tie versus Crystal Palace who had Peter Taylor playing for them, a brilliant winger who tormented us. Palace were in the 3rd division and with 50,000 fans at Stamford Bridge it was shocking to see violence was kicking off left, right and centre. There was even fighting in The Shed but I wasn't sure if it was our supporters fighting with Palace fans or just Chelsea supporters fighting each other. David Carradine was in a TV series called Kung Fu then and there seemed to be blokes in flared trousers practicing high kicks on each other in the north stand. Palace won the game 3-2 and it was very tense. But there was never an issue for me being a little foreign-looking kid being amongst it. I was aware of some racist chanting, aware of the edge of violence that bubbled under the surface when we played the likes of West Ham and Millwall – sometimes seeing the violence with my own eyes. But no one ever had a go at me. There was a real edge to that Palace FA Cup tie, and yet I still felt safe.

Because of the way things were in the 1970s I'm never sure if I felt safe at Chelsea because I trusted responsible adults would step in if things got nasty or if I was just used to witnessing violence. Certainly seeing the odd punch up was more commonplace then than it is now.

The one time I was subject to violence myself was after a benefit game in 1977. Peter Houseman, a much loved winger who played in the FA cup final in 1970, had tragically died in a car crash aged 31 along with his wife. The club put on a benefit game for his orphaned children shortly after and about 17,000 showed up. The game itself was Chelsea 1970 v Chelsea 1977

7

which Chelsea 1977 won 3-0.

I was walking home after possibly the most good natured game ever played at the Bridge, still reeling from the death of one of our heroes. At the top of Finborough Road I became aware I was being followed. I looked behind and saw it was a tall guy, about 17, a good five-years older than me, and he seemed to be following me with real intent. There was no one else around. Suddenly we both broke into a sprint, as if a gazelle was chasing its prey. He caught up with me and with one blow smacked me to the ground and, after the briefest of struggles, he managed to snatch away my Chelsea scarf. Again, with no powers of articulation, I simply picked myself up and ran in the opposite direction. But as I lay on the ground watching him run off I remember thinking very clearly, "For goodness sake, if you wanted my scarf all you had to do was ask me! We're all Chelsea mate. If you'd asked nicely I'd have given it ya!"

And that was Eddie McCreadie for you. Or rather what he gave to the club. He gave us a real sense of unity. And hope. And it's lasted with me all my Chelsea supporting days. Important values we need as supporters as well as in our lives. "Love, hope, unity and having fun" as one song went. I wouldn't be joking if I said as a society we need them more now than ever before.

Omid Djalili

London 2017

IT MIGHT BE COLD TOMORROW
Eddie McCreadie

Shall we? Yes.

Let's fly to the moon.

What the hell if we hurt later,

Let's touch the stars while we can,

And blue skies be our ground to walk on,

Let's equal the warmth of the sun

With our hearts,

It might be cold tomorrow.

Let's see flowers where there wasn't any,

And be happy when we shouldn't.

Do you remember the times

When we were the only two people in the world?

EDDIE MCCREADIE'S BLUE AND WHITE ARMY

We were afraid then!

Let's go back again,

This time with courage

It might be cold tomorrow.

Let's say words to each other,

This time with our true feelings,

Where before

It was silent insinuations from our hearts,

Words like:

Let's not break each other's hearts,

Too soon,

I've never felt so happy

And yet sad,

I love today,

It might be cold tomorrow.

RELEGATION AND RECESSION
1974 - 1975

Wednesday 1 May 1974. *It Might Be Cold Tomorrow,* a poem written by Eddie McCreadie, found its way into the pages of the programme published for a testimonial match granted in recognition of his epic 410 match career as a Chelsea player which had concluded the previous October. Manchester United, surprisingly just relegated from England's top flight, provided the opposition for the game that took place at Stamford Bridge at the end of the 1973-74 season.

Despite their woes, the Red Devils were still good enough to beat a Blues side skippered by Eddie. A crowd of 6,437 cheered and thanked their hero for his sterling service to the club and applauded teammate John Hollins for successfully slotting home a 15th minute penalty... but one goal wasn't enough for Chelsea, and United, managed by former Blues boss Tommy Docherty, prevailed 2-1. Way back in April 1962 it had been Docherty who'd signed precocious left-back McCreadie for Chelsea for £5,000 from East Stirlingshire so there was an eerie sense of symmetry about the circumstances which saw the two men reunited once more.

The title of Eddie's existential poem, along with the result of his testimonial, the curtain call on a miserable Chelsea campaign, was uncannily appropriate in the context of what was about to happen to the football club. Equally, *It Might Be Cold Tomorrow* would have been a fitting forecast for the ills embracing the wider world.

*****

At the start of 1974, Great Britain, in the grip of rampant inflation, had entered its first post-war recession. In an earlier bid to arrest the problem, the Conservative Government, headed by Prime Minister Edward Heath, had capped public sector pay rises, thereby invoking the wrath of powerful trade unions whose members' wages could no longer keep abreast of price rises.

A backlash was inevitable. The National Union of Mineworkers (NUM), whose members worked in the coal industry that provided fuel to generate the nation's electricity, had been locked in futile negotiations with the government for months. With NUM members required to work-to-rule, coal stocks became depleted – worse still, the 1973 Oil Crisis had forced up the price of imported coal.

In December 1973, in an attempt to conserve coal stocks and lower electricity consumption, Heath announced a number of measures including the Three Day Week that came into force on 31 December and restricted the commercial consumption of electricity to three consecutive days each week.

By late January 1974 NUM members, having rejected a 16.5% pay rise, voted to strike. The following month, a desperate act of brinksmanship saw Heath call a general election. "Who Governs Britain?" asked the Conservatives of the electorate... Labour would be the eventual reply. A hung parliament would see leader Harold Wilson returned to power in a minority government and the normal working week was restored in March.

Against a background of deepening austerity, although the adult world was mired in doom, power-cut gloom and despondency... the younger generation were having a laugh. Slade's Christmas 1973 Number One saw everyone singing, *"So here it is Merry Christmas... everybody's having fun"* while *Match of the Day* took on a new meaning as candles lit up living rooms, and conversation replaced television as the main source of entertainment. Having said that, the following winter's baby boom suggested grown-ups had also found a (re)productive way of passing the blackout hours.

By summer, while the ills and chills of winter had largely been forgotten, the actions of extreme political parties and organisations became a constant and deadly reminder of the deep-seated problems inherent in British society.

A National Front march through central London on 15 June led to a 21-year-old man, **Kevin Gately**, being killed during violent clashes between the NF, police and anti-fascist protestors.

The average weekly wage had crept up to almost £50 for men (£30 for women) and affordable package holidays made Spain a popular destination for many Chelsea-supporting families, whose football-obsessed members had seen their vacation plans wrecked by England's failure to qualify for the 1974 World Cup Finals held in West Germany, which commenced in June.

Sunburns, sangria hangovers and papier-mache donkeys replaced kiss-me-quick hats and sticks of rock as souvenirs of choice, although postcards from Germany sent by gleeful Scottish relatives found waiting on many a doormat were a painful reminder of what might have been.

As stories abounded of Spain's sunshine and senoritas in string bikinis, envious late bookers who subsequently opted for the Costa's over the likes of Canvey Island would soon be in for an expensive shock. August saw the collapse of Court Line Aviation and its subsidiary tour operators Clarksons

Holidays and Horizon Travel, meaning over 40,000 holidaymakers were left stranded abroad with no means of getting home and as many more out of pocket with failed bookings. Suddenly that £78 fortnight in Benidorm wasn't quite so cheap and cheerful after all.

Men wanting to drown their sorrows as a result of the Court Line debacle found a pint of Heineken, advertised on TV as being able to reach the parts that other beers could not reach, a reasonable option at 15p. Ladies meanwhile were seduced into drinking Babycham by heartthrob actor Patrick Mower.

Sitcoms were a popular draw on the small screen with *It Ain't Half Hot Mum* and *Happy Ever After* drawing large audiences. At the cinema, *Chinatown* starring Jack Nicholson, and *Death Wish* featuring Charles Bronson pulled in the crowds.

Summer 1974 saw the first Knebworth Festival take place in July, with 60,000 mostly long-haired, denim-clad gig-goers gathering to watch headline act The Allman Brothers Band.

Best-selling albums included *Diamond Dogs* by David Bowie, *Caribou* by Elton John and *Band on the Run* by Paul McCartney & Wings, which topped the charts for seven weeks from July through to September. The singles chart was dominated by an American country and western singer called Harold Ray Ragsdale… better known as Ray Stevens. Stevens' smash hit *The Streak* was a musical ode to the worldwide, attention-seeking craze of disrobing in public.

Earlier in the year, Australian Michael O'Brien had written himself into the history books when becoming the first streaker at a major sporting event. O'Brien ran naked onto the pitch at Twickenham during a game between England and France, and was eventually apprehended by PC Bruce Perry, who covered his genitals with his police helmet.

There is no evidence to suggest that streaking was a reaction to wearing impractical clothes, though looking back at the predominant clobber of the day, long since consigned to the dustbin of fashion history, it's not hard to understand the urge to undress.

Away from the music mainstream, Northern Soul had reached the peak of its popularity with all-nighters at Wigan Casino and Blackpool Mecca drawing in the crowds clad in sew-on-patch-adorned sports vests and high-waisted wide-hemmed trousers who would spin, flip, karate kick and backdrop their way across talcum powder-covered dance-floors to obscure Tamla Motown tracks.

Interestingly enough, the genre had originally been christened northern soul in London record shop *Soul City* run by music journalist Dave Godin. Godin had noticed that when northern football fans were in town following their teams, many would make a beeline for *Soul City* where, rather than ask for the funkier sounds of 70s US soul, they were seeking mid-60s Motown-influenced tracks. Godin advised sales staff, "If you've got customers from the north, don't waste time playing them records currently in the U.S. black chart, just play them what they like – Northern Soul"

Across London, rock group called The Strand, whose members included a couple of vagabond Chelsea supporters, singer, Steve Jones, drummer, Paul Cook as well as bassist Glen Matlock and guitarist Wally Nightingale, began rehearsing in earnest in an old BBC studio in Hammersmith. The Strand were devotees of a clothes shop *SEX* co-owned by Malcolm McClaren. Previously called *Let It Rock* and *Too Fast to Live, Too Young to Die*, the shop at 460 King's Road, a decent free-kick from Stamford Bridge, was an outlet for clothes designed by McClaren's then girlfriend Vivienne Westwood. Jones had persuaded McClaren to help out The Strand by paying for their rehearsal space.

Elsewhere in the Capital, Pub Rock became increasingly popular with

Islington's *Hope & Anchor* putting on gigs by leading proponents of the genre Kilburn and the High Roads who featured Ian Dury on vocals and the outstanding Dr Feelgood fronted by singer Lee Brilleaux and manic guitarist Wilko Johnson.

There may have been a recession on, but there was no skimping on going to gigs or the material that made up the clobber many music fans wore out... be they boy or girl. Quite simply there were acres of the stuff... wool, cotton, corduroy, nylon, rayon... you name it. Man-made fibres? More like Martian-made. Wide collars on shirts were complemented by wider lapels on 'bomber' jackets... and flared trousers that billowed gaily at feet mounted on gravity-defying, platform-soled shoes.

At football matches, the 'look' would be complemented by scarves (silk optional) tied at the wrist, while some supporters eschewed platforms in favour of more practical footwear such as the boots designed and marketed by a former German army doctor called Klaus Martens.

MAKING HAY WHILE THE SUN SHINES

5.45pm Saturday 22 June 1974. In Frankfurt's Waldstadion the final whistle has just blown on Scotland's World Cup hopes. Britain's only representatives at that summer's footballing Mondial, the Scots leave as genuinely plucky losers, unbeaten and unbowed. Their group included a Brazilian team which, if a pale imitation of their triumphant line-up four years earlier, remained a worthy opponent, and a powerful Yugoslavia side. The whipping boys were Zaire, and it would ultimately be the Scots' failure to capitalise on the Africans' naivety which would prove their undoing. Scotland beat Zaire 2-0, Yugoslavia put nine past them. Scotland drew with both the Yugoslavs and the Brazilians, but would miss out on qualifying for the next stage on goal difference.

The Scotland squad included some outstanding footballers. Peter Lorimer and Billy Bremner were key components in the midfield of England's strongest club side, Leeds United, while Joe Jordan was a magnificent battering-ram of a striker for the Yorkshiremen. In defence, the Tartan Army were represented by solid and reliable old-firm defenders Danny McGrain and Sandy Jardine, while Jordan was joined in attack by an ageing but still capable Denis Law, who had only recently back-heeled his beloved Manchester United to the brink of relegation in the colours of their local rivals City. But most observers picked out a lesser-known player, a versatile schemer who plies his trade in the green and white hoops of Celtic, as Scotland's outstanding player in Germany. As 26-year-old David Hay packed away his boots and headed to Cyprus for a well-earned holiday, he did so having caught the eye of a number of top clubs.

In the balmy south of England, as the sun beat down on an unusually warm summer, Chelsea Football Club were preparing for a new campaign. A top three side at the start of the decade, the Blues had accumulated two cup trophies in the first 18 months of the 1970s and had reached another Wembley showpiece in 1972, only to slip to a surprise defeat by Stoke City in the League Cup Final. Chelsea's goal that day in a 2-1 defeat was scored by Peter Osgood, who was sitting on his backside as he prodded the ball home. It was a fitting position for a club which was about to hit the skids in spectacular fashion.

As the 1974-75 season approached, the swanky west London club had lost plenty of its renowned swagger. The previous season had been a traumatic one, summed up by a Boxing Day defeat by West Ham at Stamford Bridge which had seen the Blues blow a 2-0 half-time lead and concede four goals without reply in the second period. The repercussions were swift. Manager Dave Sexton and his two star players, Osgood and Alan Hudson, fell out publicly and before the campaign was over, Osgood and Hudson were plying their trade elsewhere. Chelsea finished in 17th place in Division One, three places but just one point above relegated Southampton.

Early in the decade, club chairman Brian Mears had unveiled ambitious plans for a complete renovation of Stamford Bridge. All four sides of the ground would be redeveloped and the entire stadium moved northwards. However, after a shortage of materials and a builder's strike - with other nationwide crises of the mid-Seventies exacerbating the problem - costs escalated out of control, plunging the club into debt. The only stand which would ultimately be redeveloped during Mears' tenure was the imposing East Stand, which was due to be opened for the first time at the start of the 1974-75 season.

The ground redevelopment was intended to cement Chelsea's place as one of England and Europe's premier clubs. It was no coincidence that the plans were announced at a time when the club's stock was high. The relegation scare of 1973-74 focused minds, and with a huge debt to service now, a drop into English football's second tier was simply unthinkable.

The Blues' bean counters had estimated that regular crowds in excess of 30,000 – at a time when few clubs could confidently assume such a number of punters coming through the gates on a Saturday afternoon – would be needed in order for the club to meet its repayment obligations. But even in this climate of financial concern, the Board took the brave decision to bolster their squad by spending a club record £250,000 to sign David Hay, keeping him out of the clutches of a host of other top English clubs.

AUGUST 1974

David Hay would make his Chelsea debut on the same day as the new East Stand, when newly-promoted Carlisle United would visit. The Cumbrians had sealed an unexpected promotion three months earlier but now, in August 1974, were everybody's favourites for relegation. Whipping boys was the general term used.

Hay, the East Stand and £50,000 winger John Sissons would all get their first Stamford Bridge run-out on 17 August 1974, on a glorious day which was befitting of the start of a new era. The team ran out in front of 31,268 supporters, most of whom expected to see their heroes in blue put paid to any suggestions that the previous season's tribulations were anything other than a short-term blip.

At 4.40pm Dave Sexton's new Chelsea team walked down the tunnel of the new East Stand, back into their state-of-the-art changing room with the catcalls of the majority present ringing in their ears. A 2-0 defeat, albeit in a game dominated by the Blues, would set the tone for the season ahead. Four days later, the Stamford Bridge faithful – and there were already 8,000 less of them being faithful – witnessed another horror show, as Chelsea surrendered a 3-0 half-time lead to share the points with Burnley. Trusty stalwart Peter Houseman, beginning what would prove to be his last campaign in SW6, gave the Blues an early lead which Bill Garner and Charlie Cooke added to, but a win was not to be.

One point from two home games was not the start envisaged for this new era. It was clear that the previous season's issues had not been swept away that summer – they had just been swept under the carpet.

The first win of the campaign came at Coventry, where the Blues' wide men Sissons and Cooke provided the thrills in a 3-1 victory which saw young right-back Gary Locke get his name on the score sheet for the first time, with Cooke and Garner again also finding the net.

In keeping with the rather odd tradition of the time, Chelsea and Burnley completed their League head-to-head for the season when the Blues travelled to Turf Moor six days after their first meeting and secured a 2-1 win. The brave but unfortunate Ian Hutchinson returned from his latest injury to turn the game on its head from the substitute's bench, creating an equalising goal for Garner and then firing the winner himself with just six minutes remaining. However, a comprehensive 3-0 humbling by Liverpool at Stamford Bridge brought August to a disappointing end, even if the near 40,000 crowd gave the Chelsea hierarchy something to be grateful for.

*****

The third annual Windsor Free Festival held in Windsor Great Park scheduled to last nine days, was controversially broken up on the sixth day by baton-wielding officers of the Thames Valley police force who took issue with the herbal / chemical lifestyle choices of various tribes, sub-societies, religious groups, anarchists and liberals that had gathered in the 'Queen's back garden' to enjoy themselves and the music of iconic hippy bands like Hawkwind and Gong.

On the opening day of the football season, while top-flight Chelsea were slipping to that surprise home defeat in west London, Manchester United's Red Army invaded east London to watch the Red Devils contest a Second Division fixture for the first time since 1938. United beat Orient 2-0 at Brisbane Road, but the day would be remembered for an outbreak of lawless hooliganism in and around the ground and on the Capital's public transport services.

The Osmonds *Love Me For A Reason* toppled The Three Degrees *When Will I See You Again* from the summit of the singles chart.

SEPTEMBER 1974

Ian Hutchinson's return to Chelsea's starting XI continued to reap dividends when he earned the Blues a point at Middlesbrough at the start of September, before fellow striker Chris Garland took centre stage with a hat-trick as Newport County were beaten 4-2 at Stamford Bridge in front of a meagre 13,322 in the League Cup.

The crowds returned for a goalless draw with Arsenal which left Chelsea in

13th place in the table, but a 2-0 defeat at injury-hit Ipswich ended the Blues' unbeaten away record for the season. The Suffolk side's goals were scored by future England players Brian Talbot and David Johnson, but it was a man who would one day wear the blue of Chelsea – albeit briefly and disappointingly – Colin Viljoen, who ran the show for the home team.

The limp showing at Portman Road was followed up by a 4-1 hammering at The Baseball Ground, home of a Derby County side which would be crowned champions at the end of the campaign and, when the first full month of the season concluded with a 1-0 defeat at the hands of Wolves in front of just 23,073 hardy Stamford Bridge souls, Chelsea found themselves precariously perched in 18th position in Division One.

*****

Ceefax was launched by the BBC and soon became a popular way of checking live football scores.

Niki Lauda finished third in a Ferrari at the Italian Grand Prix at Monza. The result saw the Austrian crowned Formula One World Champion with a race to spare.

Porridge starring Ronny Barker was first screened by BBC1 and proved an instant ratings winner. ITV fought back with Leonard Rossiter in *Rising Damp*.

As football fans were battling on the terraces, Carl Doulgas was *Kung Fu Fighting* at the top of the singles chart. Mike Oldfield's follow up album to *Tubular Bells*, *Hergest Ridge*, was the best selling album.

Notable birth
Tennis player, Tim Henman 06/09

OCTOBER 1974

When the internal strife had surfaced during the previous season, Chelsea's Board had backed their manager, Dave Sexton, and allowed their two star players, Peter Osgood and Alan Hudson, to leave the club. However, the defeat by Wolves would prove to be Sexton's final match in charge. Sacked after a successful, trophy-winning seven-year spell at the helm, the likeable manager was replaced by his assistant, the popular Ron Suart, who had enjoyed a spell as caretaker manager previously after the dismissal of Tommy Docherty in 1967.

Suart's first game in charge saw his side travel to Maine Road to take on Manchester City. A fiery affair which saw City's Asa Hartford and Chelsea's Steve Kember both sent off, the Blues sealed a well-earned point thanks to yet another Ian Hutchinson effort.

The magnificent 'Hutch' took his goals tally for the season to six with a brace of controversial strikes in a 2-2 League Cup draw with Stoke City – the first being adjudged to have crossed the line by a linesman, and the second after bundling both ball and goalkeeper over the line; before a John Hollins penalty earned a 1-0 win at home to Spurs.

The League Cup replay with Stoke saw the sides play out another draw – 1-1 after extra-time – at the Victoria Ground, with Ian Britton scoring on his first appearance of the season, as the Blues came within 10 minutes of a surprise victory. Another draw followed in a tempestuous affair at Everton, where Charlie Cooke's goal was equalised by a controversial penalty awarded by a referee, John Yates, who booked six Chelsea players and coach Norman Medhurst, before sending off John Dempsey for protesting after the final whistle had blown.

Unbeaten since Sexton's dismissal, a coin-toss sent Chelsea back to Stoke for the League Cup second replay where they found themselves four goals behind by half-time, two of the goals being headed past their own goalkeeper, John Phillips, by Micky Droy and Ron Harris. By the time the visitors found the net, Hollins scoring midway through the second period, the Potters had run up a cool half-dozen, and the 6-2 final score brought Ron Suart's honeymoon period to a crushing end.

By a strange quirk of fate, October's league fixtures concluded four days later with Stoke travelling to Stamford Bridge. Buoyed by their midweek humbling of the Blues, the Potters again found their shooting boots, but despite taking the lead on three occasions, the home side levelled each time, with Ian Hutchinson sealing a 3-3 draw in injury-time. In scoring Chelsea's first, Micky Droy exacted some measure of revenge for his midweek own-goal, while Chris Garland also notched for the Blues.

*****

The Provisional IRA detonated bombs at two pubs, the *Horse and Groom* and *Seven Stars* in Guildford, Surrey. Five people were murdered in the atrocity. The attacks were the first in a year long IRA active service unit campaign on the British mainland.

The second General Election of the year resulted in a narrow, three-seat victory for Harold Wilson's Labour Party. Having rejected an offer to stand as a candidate for the National Front, controversial former Conservative MP Enoch Powell returned to Parliament as Ulster Unionist MP for South Down.

The UKs first McDonalds restaurant opened in Woolwich, London.

The Rumble in the Jungle took place in Kinshasa, Zaire where Muhammad Ali knocked out George Foreman in eight rounds to regain the World Heavyweight Title he had been stripped of seven-years earlier.

Texas Chain Saw Massacre saw Leatherface scaring kids who had somehow smuggled their way into cinemas for this Certificate 18 horror.

Ken Boothe stormed the singles charts with *Everything I Own* while the Bay City Rollers *Rollin* and *Smiler* by Rod Stewart regularly exchanged places at the top of the albums charts throughout October and November.

Chelsea births
Neil Shipperley 30/10
Muzzy Izzet 31/10

NOVEMBER 1974

Despite Peter Bonetti being recalled to the team for the visit to Birmingham City at the start of November, and with the home side shorn of the emerging talents of Trevor Francis, the Blues surrendered meekly to a 2-0 defeat. With Garner and, once again, Hutchinson on the injured list, Chelsea turned to 16-year-old reserve striker Tommy Langley a week later and the young, enthusiastic front man took his bow in front of almost 24,000 spectators as Leicester City travelled to SW6. Not surprisingly, he was unable to make any real mark on a dreadful match which finished goalless, and saw the Blues slip back into 19th place, just one above the relegation places.

In need of both points and turnstile clicks, a mere 11,048 watched a midweek clash with Coventry City. On a wet night in West London, goals from the fit-again Garner and his strike partner Chris Garland saw the Blues overcome the concession of an early goal from the visitors, but by half-time it was all square at 2-2. A long-range screamer on the hour mark from Charlie Cooke put the home side back in charge, but a late leveller from Scottish World Cup winger Tommy Hutchison sealed a point for the Sky Blues. Chairman Brian Mears did his best to hide his disappointment after the game, but there was a telling sting in the tail of his statement to the press: "The gate was as much as we could expect on a night when the weather was so miserable... but of course we can't survive with these sorts of gates."

It was gates of a different kind – floodgates – which had the chairman panicking three days later, as Newcastle United struck five second half goals past Peter Bonetti as Chelsea slipped into the relegation zone for the first time, which is where they stayed following a 2-0 defeat at Leeds United a week later.

*****

The Provisional IRA detonated bombs at two pubs, the *Mulberry Bush* and *Tavern in the Town*, in Birmingham. 21 people were murdered and 182 injured in what was the worst mainland terrorist atrocity of the Troubles. Shortly after, the government outlawed the IRA in the UK and passed the Prevention of Terrorism Act.

Lord Lucan disappeared without trace following the murder of his children's nanny Sandra Rivett.

Silver-tongued West Ham fan David Essex, christened plain old David Albert Cook by his parents, had a Number One single with *Gonna Make You A Star*.

Notable birth
Actor, Leonardo DiCaprio 11/11

DECEMBER 1974

There was some seasonal cheer at the start of December, as second half goals by Hutchinson and Kember sealed a comfortable victory over bottom club Luton Town, and when two John Hollins goals were enough to avenge the opening day defeat by Carlisle United, the Blues were hitting the heady heights of 18th place again. However, a late Bobby Gould strike for West Ham which equalised another Hutchinson effort saw Chelsea drop a point and a place in the table on the final weekend before Christmas.

As Santa dropped gifts with an aplomb which was matched only by the Chelsea defence, chairman Mears would have noted with some dismay that the attendance for the West Ham game was just the fourth occasion on which the break-even mark of 30,000 spectators had been breached before Christmas.

Boxing Day saw Chelsea win 2-1 at Arsenal to leapfrog the Gunners, who found themselves in the incredible position of fourth from bottom after Chris Garland struck twice at Highbury, but 1974 ended with a comprehensive 3-0 home defeat by Queens Park Rangers... the Shepherds Bush minnows now managed by none other than Dave Sexton.

*****

The Provisional IRA bombed the London home of former Prime Minister Edward Heath. The leader of the Conservative Party was out at the time, but returned just 10 minutes after the bomb had been detonated.

Former government minister John Stonehouse was arrested in Australia by police who thought he was Lord Lucan! The previous month, Stonehouse had faked his death when leaving a pile of clothes on a beach in Miami and travelled down under where he planned to start a new life with mistress and secretary Sheila Buckley.

The BBC screened the final episodes of *Monty Python's Flying Circus*, *Whatever Happened to the Likely Lads* and *Steptoe and Son*.

Tom Baker made his first appearance as *Doctor Who*.

At the cinema, *Godfather Part II* was the main box office draw.

Heavyweight soul crooner Barry White topped the singles charts early in December with *You're the First, the Last, My Everything* but Mud had the festive Number One with *Lonely This Christmas*.

Elton John's *Greatest Hits* compilation was the best-selling long-player.

JANUARY 1975

The turn of the year did little to improve the mood of all associated with Chelsea Football Club. It started well enough when the Blues recovered from an early penalty miss by John Hollins and a two-goal deficit to clinch an unlikely 3-2 victory over Sheffield Wednesday in the third round of the FA Cup. Micky Droy, who had conceded the penalty from which Wednesday took the lead, was the unlikely goal scoring hero as his brace sandwiched a Chris Garland strike, the three goals all coming in the last 15 minutes.

The return to league action came with a visit to Luton, who had been brushed aside comfortably a month earlier. This time however, Chelsea were grateful for a lucky rebound off Steve Kember which saw them take a fortunate point from a 1-1 draw, before old enemy Leeds United coasted to an easy 2-0 win at Stamford Bridge.

The FA Cup dream ended with a tame 1-0 defeat at home to Birmingham City, the winning goal being scored by the visitors' centre-forward Kenny Burns. The ferocious Scot would end the decade as a European champion and Football League Player of the Year, playing as a converted centre-half.

*****

Heiress Lesley Whittle was kidnapped from her home in Highley,

Shropshire by Donald Neilson. Dubbed the 'Black Panther' by the British Press because of the black balaclava he wore during raids on post offices, Neilson, who at the time had already committed three murders and over 400 robberies, demanded a ransom of £50,000.

The Sweeney premiered on ITV.

Status Quo topped the singles charts with *Down Down*.

Notable birth
Thomas Bangalter aka Daft Punk 03/01
Chelsea birth
Danny Granville 19/01

FEBRUARY 1975

Another visit to play one of the three teams below them in the table, Leicester City, ended the same way as the Luton game had. The Foxes scored through ex-Chelsea man Keith Weller with their only effort on target in the game, and again it was Steve Kember – soon to be plying his trade permanently at Filbert Street – who struck late to give his team a share of the spoils.

It was boys' own stuff a week later as some measure of revenge was taken with a 2-1 win over FA Cup conquerors Birmingham City. 18-year-old Ray Wilkins, an increasingly regular face on the team sheet, fired the home side ahead with his first goal for the club. Prolific striker Bob Hatton replied for the visitors before half-time, before boyhood Chelsea supporter Tommy Langley replaced the injured Gary Locke for just his second Blues appearance. Celebrating his 17th birthday that day, the youngster rifled home a cracking shot with 14 minutes remaining to get the party started early. Less fortunate was, as usual, fellow striker Ian Hutchinson. Given a pain-killing injection to allow him to play with a broken toe, Hutch joined

Locke on the sidelines when he was forced off with a broken finger.

Chelsea could consider themselves unfortunate a week later, when Sheffield United struck twice in four first-half minutes at Bramall Lane to clinch a 2-1 win. It was a game dominated by the visitors, who were left to rue a host of missed chances, including a John Hollins penalty, and left with just Bill Garner's 90th minute consolation to their name.

February drew to a close with another five-goal battle with Newcastle. This game, however, was somewhat more even than the humiliating 5-0 defeat the Blues had suffered the previous November. With Ron Suart's line-up featuring five players aged under 20, the Chelsea manager would have been overjoyed to see one of that group, Steve Finnieston, score his first goal for the club to give the Blues a 36th minute lead.

Charlie Cooke struck soon after to send the home side into the break with a two-goal lead, and seconds after the prolific Malcolm Macdonald – scorer of a brace against the Blues earlier in the season – had halved the deficit, Hollins fired home a penalty to restore the two-goal lead. Two minutes later John Tudor found the net for the Geordies, before the visitors were awarded a spot-kick of their own. Up stepped Macdonald to strike with his trusty left-foot... straight at home goalkeeper John Phillips.

Despite a few late jitters, Suart's young team held out to clinch a win which saw Chelsea rise to 16th place in the table, an unlikely two places above Arsenal and three above the Gunners' north London rivals Spurs.

*****

A southbound train travelling on the Northern City Line operated by London Underground failed to stop at Moorgate Station terminus and crashed into the wall at the end of the tunnel killing 43 people.

Metropolitan Police officer PC Stephen Tibble was murdered in London by Liam Quinn a member of the Provisional IRA.

Margaret Thatcher defeated Edward Heath in the Conservative Party leadership election to become the party's first female leader.

British coalminers accepted a 35% pay rise offer from the government.

England won the sixth and final Ashes test of the 1974/75 series played in Australia. It was cold comfort for the 'Poms' though as they lost the series 4-1 with one test drawn.

The film *Slade in Flame* starring glam-rock band Slade premiered in London.

January by Pilot hit the top of the singles charts in February but was deposed after three weeks by Steve Harley & Cockney Rebel's sublime tune *Make Me Smile (Come Up and See Me)*.

Engelbert Humperdinck's selection of *Greatest Hits* replaced those of Elton John at the top of the album charts.

Notable birth
Actress, Drew Barrymore 22/02

MARCH 1975

The Chelsea kids continued to make headlines as winter gave way to early spring. A 2-2 draw at Liverpool was a commendable result, made even more so by the fact that the Blues twice took the lead with goals scored by the youthful Ian Britton and Steve Finnieston. Indeed, a rare win on the red side of Merseyside was in their grasp, only to be snatched away by a last minute leveller.

The feel-good factor was dimmed somewhat when champions-elect Derby County won 2-1 in front of just 22,644 spectators at Stamford Bridge; and the lights were then firmly put out by Wolverhampton Wanderers. Quite how the Blues could be so competitive at Anfield only to fall to a 7-1 hammering at Molineux is almost inexplicable, but perhaps the clue is in one of the following day's newspaper headlines which read: 'MASSACRE OF THE INNOCENTS'.

A midweek visit to Loftus Road to take on Dave Sexton's QPR ended in a 1-0 defeat, but there was some measure of satisfaction to be had from the fact that despite conceding a goal after just two minutes, Chelsea's youngsters had the better of the game. Roared on by the vast majority of the 25,324 crowd – many of whom spent much of the night fighting with the local police – only the width of a goal post and some excellent saves by home 'keeper Phil Parkes thwarted the visiting side.

A third consecutive defeat came at the hands of Middlesbrough, who won 2-1 at the Bridge despite having former Leeds defender Terry Cooper sent off early in the second half. Chelsea's goal came from teenage left-back John Sparrow, and had David Hay scored rather than struck the post when well placed, the Blues might have escaped with a fortunate point.

A much needed two points were secured courtesy of Micky Droy's diving header at West Ham, as the giant, talismanic defender returned from a six-week injury absence at Upton Park, before March ended with a tepid 0-0 draw with Ipswich on Easter Monday, in front of an impressive 35,005 Stamford Bridge spectators.

*****

The body of Lesley Whittle was discovered in the underground drainage shaft of a reservoir in Kidsgrove, Staffordshire.
Actor Charlie Chaplin was knighted by the Queen.

The film version of The Who's rock opera Tommy premiered in London.

Lollipop sucking televison detective *Kojak*, aka Telly Savalas had a number one single with *If*.

Physical Graffiti by Led Zeppelin was the best-selling long player.

APRIL 1975

A second comprehensive beating of the season at Stoke City's Victoria Ground – the Blues falling to a 3-0 defeat – saw Chelsea slip back into 19th place on the first Saturday in April; and the following weekend's home defeat by Manchester City proved to be the final game in charge for Ron Suart. With Carlisle rooted to the bottom, but only a point keeping Chelsea out of the other two relegation spots, currently occupied by Luton Town and Tottenham Hotspur, it was time to act. The fact that a visit to White Hart Lane was on the horizon, only added to the anxiety.

With three games remaining, Brian Mears and the Chelsea Board turned to a past hero to help revive their ailing club's hopes. Eddie McCreadie, a Blues stalwart of the past 13-years, and a key component in three Cup triumphs during his Stamford Bridge playing career – including scoring the winning goal in the two-legged 1965 League Cup Final against Leicester City – was asked to step up from his coaching role into the managerial hot seat. He accepted, and Eddie McCreadie's Blue and White Army was formed.

McCreadie's army put its boots on the ground – literally – for the first time at White Hart Lane on 19 April 1975. With Carlisle already relegated and Luton strong favourites to join the Cumbrians in taking the plunge, the final place in the relegation shake-up would almost certainly be taken by the loser, if there was one, of the clash in north London. Incredibly, McCreadie's first move as manager was to install 18-year-old midfield wonder-kid Ray 'Butch' Wilkins as captain.

The magnificent Wilkins, a player of sublime ability who was clearly on his way to the very top, took the role in his diffident stride. McCreadie, who was keen to show he was as brave off the pitch as he was on it, followed the lead of his predecessor and put immediate faith in some of the youngsters he had guided through the ranks previously as Chelsea's reserve team manager. For the crucial match with Spurs, the erudite Scot dropped a number of his very experienced, previous team-mates – John Hollins, Marvin Hinton, Steve Kember and Peter Houseman – and replaced them with the youthful John Sparrow, Ian Britton, Teddy Maybank and skipper Wilkins, who's last start for the Blues had come a month earlier at QPR.

On a violent day when marauding Chelsea supporters, locked out in their thousands, caused havoc on the Seven Sisters Road while kick off was being delayed inside White Hart Lane due to supporters fighting on the pitch, two second half goals by the home side virtually consigned Chelsea to relegation.

A draw at home to Sheffield United the following midweek – youngster Maybank scoring the Blues' goal – saw the Blues drop below Luton into 21st place and another draw at home to Everton the following Saturday left them there, confirming relegation in the process. If there were any chinks of light coming through on that dreary late-April day, they came in the shape of three key figures: a young captain who had scored Chelsea's goal that day, a young manager who held the confidence of supporters and players alike, and a near 30,000 crowd of loyal Blues who waved goodbye to an old era and said hello to a new one.

*****

The Vietnam War ended with the fall of Saigon.
Unemployment in the UK exceeded one million.

Badfinger lead singer Pete Ham, co-composer of Nilsson's global smash hit *Without You* committed suicide.

The Good Life premiered on BBC1.

Monty Python and the Holy Grail opened at cinemas.

The Godfather Part II wins the Oscar for Best Picture at the 47th Academy Awards.

Ritchie Blackmore played his final show with Deep Purple leaving to form Rainbow.

'Rollermania' was in full swing as tartan-clad teenyboppers couldn't stop buying the Bay City Rollers single *Bye Bye Bye Baby*. Edinburgh's finest – Les McKeown, Eric Faulker, Stuart 'Woody' Wood and brothers Derek and Alan Longmuir topped the charts for six weeks and the track goes on to be the year's best-selling 45.

Tom Jones became the latest crooner to have a *Greatest Hits* package top the album charts.

MAY 1975

West Ham United won the FA Cup beating Fulham 2-0 in the final at Wembley.

Bayern Munich beat Leeds United 2-0 in the European Cup Final at Parc des Princes, Paris. Leeds fans rioted when a Peter Lorimer goal which would have given their side the lead was ruled offside. The Yorkshire club was subsequently banned from European competition for four years, reduced to two years on appeal.

*****

The worst ever road traffic accident in the UK occurred at Dibbles Bridge in North Yorkshire. Brake failure on a tour coach led to the deaths of 31 women pensioners as the driver who also died lost control of the vehicle that careered off a bridge near Hebden.

Led Zeppelin played five sold out shows at Earls Court.

Tammy Wynette topped the singles charts in the UK with *Stand By Your Man* seven years after she had done so in the USA!

Rollermania showed no sign of slowing down as the Bay City Rollers stormed the album charts with *Once Upon A Star.*

Notable births
Footballer, David Beckham 02/05
All Black rugby union legend, Jonah Lomu 12/05
Chef, Jamie Oliver 27/05
Spice Girl, Mel B 29/05
Chelsea birth
Aleksey Smertin 01/05

HARD TIMES
1975 - 1976

The summer of '75 was the warmest summer since 1947, and while coastal waters heated up, they weren't quite tropical enough to attract a great white shark like the one featured in blockbuster movie *Jaws* that premiered in London in June. Directed by Steven Spielberg and based on Peter Benchley's novel, *Jaws* broke box office records the world over and would go on to become the highest grossing movie of all time – well at least until *Star Wars* was released two-years later.

Wannabe pop Svengali Malcolm McClaren, back in London having spent time in the USA managing the New York Dolls, refocused his attention on The Strand.

Talking Heads performed their first show at CBGB in New York.

Having being fired by Hawkwind in May, bass-player-come-vocalist Ian Fraser Kilmister, better known as Lemmy, formed Motorhead.

West Indies won the inaugural Cricket World Cup defeating Australia by 17 runs at Lords in the final. Australia remained in England to play a four test Ashes series which they went on to win 1-0 with three matches drawn.

Don Estelle and Windsor Davies, stars of the popular sitcom *It Ain't Half Hot Mum,* topped the charts in June with novelty hit *Whispering Grass.* 10cc eventually replaced them with *I'm Not in Love,* but it was the unstoppable Bay City Rollers who would have the summer's biggest hit with *Give A Little Love* which was *Top of the Pops* in July.

Venus and Mars by Wings traded places several times with *Horizon* by The Carpenters at the top of the album charts

Notable births
Comedian, Russell Brand 04/06
Actress, Angelina Jolie 04/06
Rapper, 50 Cent 06/07
Chelsea birth
Hernan Crespo born 05/07

AUGUST 1975

'In spite of all our efforts towards the end of last season to avoid the drop into the Second Division, it was not to be and we look forward to a speedy return to the First Division.'

Chairman Brian Mears, writing in the programme for the opening home fixture of his club's first Division Two campaign since 1962-63, spoke confidently about the 'good blend of youth and experience' in Eddie McCreadie's squad, and in thanking the departing Steve Kember, John Hollins and Peter Houseman for their 'fine service to the club', he alluded to a clear change in policy. Yes, the blend between youth and experience was there, but it was clear that Eddie McCreadie and those at the helm of the club would be entrusting the future of the club primarily to the impressive crop of youngsters which had risen through the ranks. This was reflected in the first team selected by McCreadie that season, for the opening day trip to Sunderland where a Blues side featuring Graham and

Ray Wilkins, John Sparrow, Garry Stanley, Ian Britton and Teddy Maybank slipped to a 2-1 defeat. Bill Garner, who had joined from Southend earlier in the decade, gave the Blues the lead at Roker Park, but future Chelsea striker Bryan 'Pop' Robson equalised after an error by stand-in 'keeper Steve Sherwood, before Dennis Longhorn fired a second half winner for the home side.

A goalless draw with West Bromwich Albion at the Hawthorns gave McCreadie's men their first point of the campaign, but with the home side reduced to ten men in just the 16th minute, it felt like a point dropped rather than one gained. Nevertheless, there was some merit in claiming a draw against a team which would be promoted at the end of the season, and which featured the likes of Johnny Giles, Geoff Hurst and Tony Brown amongst its number.

The first win of the new season came when Carlisle United were the first visitors to the Bridge for the second successive season. This time there would be no repeat of the previous fixture's horrors, as buoyed by a tremendous two-goal performance from livewire 18-year-old striker Teddy Maybank, and an outrageous long-range shot from yet another young starlet, Brian Bason, Chelsea ran out 3-1 winners. Just under 20,000 were at Stamford Bridge to witness the opening home game – not ideal, but confidence remained that the fans would return just as soon as the Blue bandwagon picked up momentum.

Sure enough, just four days after the impressive victory over Carlisle, just under 23,000 showed up for another 3-1 win at the Bridge, as Oxford United were beaten by the same score. This time it was another 18-year-old, Ray Wilkins, who helped himself to a brace, with Kenny Swain, signed from non-league Wycombe Wanderers, notching the third. Peter Houseman, who had moved to the Manor Ground in the summer, returned to Stamford Bridge in the colours of his new side and helped create the visitors' early goal, but it was the young breed from SW6 who took away the spoils and joined Southampton and Sunderland at the top of the division.

With the plaudits from two excellent performances ringing in their ears, and the bookmakers' short odds on a Chelsea promotion being endorsed by a wealth of match reports drafted by impressed journalists, there was an air of inevitability about the way in which August ended. A 3-0 defeat by Luton at Kenilworth Road sent the Blues down to sixth, and a broken leg suffered by Graham Wilkins only added to the woes of the day. The game ended in unruly scenes both on and off the pitch, with visiting supporters running amok inside the stadium, and the home side's John Aston being sent off for lashing out at Ian Britton. Aston's noble post-match comment that, "I deserved to be sent off. I was stupid and I should have known better," is possibly the last recorded incidence of a footballer admitting an indiscretion.

*****

The 'Birmingham Six', Hugh Callaghan, Patrick Joseph Hill, Gerard Hunter, Richard McIlkenny, William Power and John Walker are sentenced to life imprisonment for the Birmingham Pub Bombings. Their convictions would later be declared 'unsafe and unsatisfactory' and quashed by the Court of Appeal in March 1991. The six men were later awarded compensation ranging from £840,000 to £1.2 million.

The campaign in which the slogan *George Davis is Innocent* was widely sprayed throughout London reached a climax when Headingley cricket ground was vandalized by lobbyists seeking the armed robber's release from prison.

Having engineered Wally Nightingale's departure from The Strand who around this time had adopted the name QT Jones & his Sex Pistols, Malcolm McClaren's protégés, with Steve Jones moving to guitar, were on the lookout for a new frontman. Among those approached were Slik singer / guitarist Jim 'Midge' Ure and Kevin Rowland later of Dexys Midnight

Runners.

McClaren's long time friend Bernie Rhodes spotted King's Road habitué John Lydon wearing a Pink Floyd t-shirt with the words *I HATE* handwritten above the band's name and an audition swiftly followed. Lydon was in. Shortly after, Jones rechristened him Johnny Rotten apparently because of the singer's appalling dental hygiene – and with their name shortened to the Sex Pistols, the band were ready to take on the world.

Genesis lead singer Peter Gabriel left the band.

Progressive rock merchants Yes headlined the prime Saturday slot at the Reading Festival where a weekend ticket for the event cost £5.50. Further down the bill are the excellent Heavy Metal Kids fronted by showman extraordinaire Gary Holton. Holton, who would go on to become a household name playing Cockney carpenter Wayne in the hit TV series *Auf Wiedersehen Pet*, would die tragically young of a heroin overdose a decade later.

Barbados by Typically Tropical jockeyed for the Number One slot in the singles charts with *I Can't Give You Anything (But My Love)* by The Stylistics.

SEPTEMBER 1975

September began with a dreadful 0-0 draw against Brian Clough's Nottingham Forest. Micky Droy missed a late opportunity to clinch both points, heading over the bar from point-blank range when it seemed easier to score, but the deadlock remained unbroken. A solitary point looked a disappointing return at the time, but the hindsight which allows us to note that the visiting team included six players who would pick up European Cup winners' medals later in the decade, suggests that this was a solid performance from the home side.

Of more concern than the draw with Clough's men was an early departure from the League Cup at the hands of Crewe Alexandra, a Fourth Division 'motley crew' according to one reporter, most of whom 'played with their shirts hanging outside their shorts'.

Defeat by a bunch of scruffs at Gresty Road was compounded three days later, when Oldham Athletic tucked in their shirts and tucked away both points with a 2-1 win at their Boundary Park headquarters. That loss saw the Blues plummet to 11th in the division, but despite being held to a 1-1 draw a week later by Bristol City at Stamford Bridge – Bill Garner both scoring and then being sent off later in the game for a foul on City's 'keeper – they actually rose to 9th by virtue of picking up a point.

Another 1-1 draw, this time at Portsmouth where Garner – yet to begin his suspension – scored again, left Chelsea still searching for their first away win of the season; and this remained unchanged when Fulham won 2-0 at Craven Cottage to send the Blues down to a humiliating 14th place in Division Two.

*****

The London Hilton was bombed by the Provisional IRA, two people were murdered and a further 63 injured.

Fawlty Towers aired for the first time on BBC2.

Pink Floyd released one of the all time classic rock albums *Wish You Were Here* which eased its way to the top of the charts the following month.

Rod Stewart dominated both the singles and albums charts. *Sailing*, taken from long-player *Atlantic Crossing*, remains Stewart's best-selling single to this day.

Notable births
DJ, musician, and record producer, Mark Ronson 04/09
Crooner, Michael Buble 09/09
One half of Ant & Dec, Declan Donnelly 25/09

OCTOBER 1975

York City – resplendent in their maroon and white shirts with a 'Y' logo on the front, and enjoying a rare and brief flirtation with the upper half of the Football League – were the first visitors to Stamford Bridge in October. An almost unthinkable league fixture just a season or two earlier, the visitors rode their luck to such good effect that they left SW6 with a point from a goalless draw. Ray Wilkins, the maestro in the middle for Chelsea, missed a first half penalty as the Blues failed to win for the eighth game in succession.

Noting the almost absurd situation which saw Chelsea v York City not only become a league fixture but one that the visitors emerged unscathed from, former Charlton and England goalkeeper Sam Bartram wrote in the following day's Sunday People: 'Only 15,000 there yesterday for the first visit of a team who not so long ago were only a name on the pools coupon to the glamour boys of the First Division. And those days of wine and roses begin to seem light years away as Chelsea's erratic stars and callow youths turn in a series of disappointing performances, seemingly designed to turn that magnificent new stand into the most expensive tombstone in football.'

A Southampton side managed by Lawrie McMenemy and inspired by Chelsea icon Peter Osgood and Mick Channon proved far too strong for a more experienced than usual Blues side a week later. Chelsea remained competitive until the latter stages, but conceded three goals in the last 20-minutes as they fell to a 4-1 defeat. A fuming McCreadie exclaimed afterwards, "I knew I had a great deal of work to do at Stamford Bridge, and today it was made very clear there is still a lot to be done." The manager's mood wasn't helped by an incident which took place with the Saints still only a goal to the good. A shot by Micky Droy caught Southampton defender Mel Blyth full in the face, and as he fell to the floor, a team-mate picked up the ball in the home penalty area, apparently and wrongly thinking a free-kick had been awarded. However, instead of awarding a penalty to the visitors, the referee restarted the game with a drop-ball... on the halfway line! "That's not in my book of rules," stated McCreadie.

The winless run was ended at the tenth time of asking, with an uninspired but nevertheless very welcome 2-0 win over Blackpool at Stamford Bridge. It took 78 minutes for the breakthrough to come, Ray Wilkins this time converting from the spot, before Tommy Langley sealed the win in the last minute. The game was notable for the return to the starting line-up of experienced goalkeeper Peter Bonetti, who had failed to don the gloves all season despite his replacement, Steve Sherwood, making a handful of errors. The former England custodian was brought back into the fray just as other suitors were beginning to circle, Southend United having tried to lure the 34-year-old to Roots Hall earlier that week. Bonetti kept his place for the visit to Blackburn, where he turned in a man of the match performance as an Ian Hutchinson goal clinched a draw which saw Chelsea end October in twelfth place.

*****

The IRA exploded a bomb outside Green Park underground station in London murdering one person and injuring 20 more.

The 'Guildford Four' were convicted of murder and other charges relating to the Guildford pub bombings and sentenced to life imprisonment.

Peter Sutcliffe who would achieve notoriety as the Yorkshire Ripper committed his first murder.

Muhammad Ali beat Joe Frazier in the *'Thrilla in Manila'* to retain the WBC and WBA World Heavyweight titles.

Rock group Queen released *Bohemian Rhapsody*. At the time it was the most expensive single ever recorded.

Happy Hammer, David Essex, had his second (and final) number one single with *Hold Me Close*.

Notable birth
Actress, Kate Winslet 5/10
Chelsea births
Michael Duberry 14/10
Henrique Hilario 21/10

NOVEMBER 1975

November was less than a day old when bad habits from earlier in the season resurfaced. Facing a Plymouth Argyle side far closer to the bottom of the table than the top, the Blues raced into an early lead courtesy of an Ian Britton strike, which they doubled soon after half-time with a spectacular Ray Wilkins diving header. Seemingly coasting to a second consecutive home win, the Blues inexplicably switched off and allowed Argyle to draw level with two goals in five minutes scored by future Ipswich, Arsenal and England striker Paul Mariner.

Spirits were lifted a week later when Chelsea came from behind to beat Hull City 2-1 at Boothferry Park, Britton capitalising on a goalkeeping error to equalise, before Hutchinson scored his second important goal in three games as he continued yet another brave comeback from a litany of injuries. From the pit of despair after the Plymouth debacle, the Blues finally clicked into gear. There was perhaps some good fortune to thank for a 2-0 win over Notts County which came as a result of a Garner goal which may have been scored from an offside position, and a Wilkins penalty which was harshly awarded. Nonetheless, there was no need for County manager Ronnie Fenton to bitterly refer to Chelsea as "the poorest side we've played" when he could just as easily have put his dummy back in and given his rattle a shake.

A third successive victory came when McCreadie's young starlets clinched a league double over Blackpool by beating the Tangerines for the second time in a month. This was a performance to warm the manager's heart, as his youthful charges showed they were adding nous to their natural enthusiasm. Allowing the hosts the majority of the ball, the visitors soaked up the pressure and struck twice on the break, Droy and Maybank scoring late in each half to clinch a 2-0 win. Seven days later, the November fixtures ended with a fourth consecutive win, Maybank and Garner scoring the goals as Chelsea edged a bruising encounter with Bristol Rovers at Eastville. For the second time this season, the temperamental Garner was sent off in a game in which he had also scored, whilst Rovers' skipper Alan Warboys left the pitch on a stretcher following a challenge by Ian Hutchinson. As December approached, Chelsea's promotion push was back on track, with the Blues eighth in the Division Two table.

*****

Ross McWhirter, co-founder of the *Guinness Book of Records*, was murdered by the Provisional IRA who shot him dead for offering reward money to informers.

Double Formula One World Champion Graham Hill was killed along with five members of the Embassy Hill motor racing team when a light plane piloted by the 46-year old crashed in foggy conditions near Elstree Airfield to the north of London.

The Sex Pistols played their first public gig supporting Bazooka Joe in the top-floor common room of Saint Martin's College in London. Playing bass guitar for the headline act was Stuart Goddard who would go on to find fame and fortune as Adam Ant.

David Bowie enjoyed his first Number One with *Space Oddity*. The track had previously been released in 1969 when it reached number five in the charts. Queen's *Bohemian Rhapsody* reached the top slot on 29 November. It remained the best-selling single for a phenomenal nine weeks.

Notable birth
The other half of Ant & Dec, Anthony McPartlin 18/11

DECEMBER 1975

Unbeaten in seven, the Blues took to the field against Bolton Wanderers in buoyant mood. The visitors had reason of their own to be pleased with their season to date, as they sat third in the table. Like Chelsea, Wanderers had an impressive mix of youth and experience in their side, with young talents such as Peter Reid and Sam Allardyce complementing the skills of former Liverpool winger Peter Thompson and grizzled skipper Roy Greaves. In goal they had a renowned penalty stopper in Barry Siddall, whose record in keeping out spot-kicks was unparalleled at the time.

It took Bolton just 15-minutes to edge ahead at the Bridge, when Greaves tucked away a rebound following good work by Thompson. Micky Droy then picked up a yellow card which triggered a three-match suspension for the giant defender.

With two-minutes remaining, a period of extended pressure on the Bolton defence saw a goalbound shot handled on the line, and referee Roger Kirkpatrick – a rotund and jolly figure, befitting of the time of year – awarded a penalty. Ray Wilkins, who had missed from the spot against York two months earlier, and also in a pre-season Anglo-Scottish Cup clash with

Fulham, showed courage beyond his years and insisted on taking the kick. Siddall, however, guessed right and dived to his left, keeping out Wilkins' kick and follow-up. With that chance went Chelsea's unbeaten home record, and ended a run of seven games without defeat.

Chelsea's skipper made swift recompense for his Bolton lapse when he gave his team the lead at Carlisle a week later, after good work by Teddy Maybank. Unfortunately, though, despite a man of the match performance, young Maybank was unable to match his goal scoring exploits against the Cumbrians earlier in the season, and the home side bounced back to exact revenge for their August humbling by consigning the Blues to a second consecutive defeat.

Next up for McCreadie's team were top of the table Sunderland. The previous match programme, for the clash with Bolton, had implored the supporters to turn up in their droves for the big match with the Wearsiders. In what was becoming an increasingly regular and somewhat desperate appeal to get bums on seats – Chelsea also took the highly unusual step of advertising their home games on TV in 1975/76 – the programme editor asked, "How about a 40,000 attendance to see the leaders toppled?"

On the last Saturday before Christmas, a day when crowds were traditionally kept down by the need for last-minute Christmas shopping – no option to do it online back in those days – Chelsea fell almost 18,000 spectators short of their 40,000 target. However, those present did receive the one Christmas present they most wanted, as Ian Britton's goal midway through the second period earned a win for the Blues, in a game which marked Ron Harris' 500th league appearance for the club.

The festive cheer gained from a win over the league leaders was replaced by gloom before the New Year had been reached. Two London derbies in two days, a trip to Orient on Boxing Day followed by a visit from Charlton Athletic the next afternoon, saw the Blues hit by consecutive defeats. In east London, Orient struck twice in the last eight minutes to secure a 3-1 win, while Charlton won by the odd goal in five at the Bridge. The game at Brisbane Road saw a pitch invasion from visiting supporters, which was becoming an increasing trend, particularly at games where the Blues were falling to defeat.

As 1975 drew to a close, Chelsea found themselves 13th in Division Two. Sunderland, Bolton and Bristol City occupied the top three places, with third-placed City fully eight points clear of the Blues at a time of just two points for a win.

*****

The Balcombe Street siege, a terrorist incident in London that involved members of the Provisional IRA, two hostages and the Metropolitan Police, played out in front of a television audience of millions. Lasting from 6th to 12th December , the siege began following a chase through the capital as police pursued four members of the IRA. The terrorists took two hostages in a council flat in Balcombe Street adjacent to Marylebone Station, and a six-day standoff followed before the gang surrendered. The hostages were released unharmed.

Donald Neilson was arrested on suspicion of being responsible for the 'Black Panther' murders.

New Wave of British heavy metal pioneers Iron Maiden formed in London.

A Night At the Opera by Queen deposed Perry Como's *Greatest Hits* from the top of the album charts.

Notable births
Snooker star, Ronnie O'Sullivan 5/12
Golf legend, Tiger Woods 30/12

JANUARY 1976

There was further evidence of Chelsea's desperate financial plight when the Football Association agreed to allow the club to bring forward by 48-hours their FA Cup third round clash with Bristol Rovers. By playing the game on New Year's Day, the club reckoned on maximising the gate receipt and so it proved. Despite the tie appearing unglamorous, more than 35,000 people were at Stamford Bridge to witness a 1-1 draw, with Bill Garner earning a replay with a first-half equaliser. That replay, played just two days later on what was the actual third round day, saw Kenny Swain score a late winner when he tapped home after a Maybank header had come back off a post.

A good run in the FA Cup was the money-spinning dream of the Chelsea Board, and it became even more of a priority when the Blues slipped to 15th place after a dreadful mauling by Oldham Athletic. A paltry crowd of 16,464 – almost 20,000 down on the previous home attendance – witnessed a shambolic performance, as the visitors romped to just their second away win in 34 attempts. The gulf in standard between the clubs, if not the teams, was represented in the fact that this was Oldham's first visit to Stamford Bridge in 45 years, a statistic that only added clarity to the dreadful state of affairs prevalent in SW6 at the time.

Much lost pride was regained a week later, when Charlie Cooke turned back the years to inspire his side to a magnificent 3-1 win at Nottingham Forest's City Ground. The portents hadn't been good when Ian Bowyer put the home side ahead early on, but Bill Garner quickly restored parity, and the win was complete when first Ray Wilkins and then Ian Hutchinson struck in the final 10 minutes to earn a well-deserved win. That was followed by a comfortable 2-0 win at York – Garner and Hutchinson again finding the net – which saw Chelsea through to the fifth round of the FA Cup and a home clash with Malcolm Allison's Division Three giant-killers Crystal Palace. Brian Mears was certainly happy, the chairman announcing, "It will be a 50,000 sell-out. Our bank manager will be pleased – he'll probably somersault all the way down the King's Road."

January ended in controversy, as West Bromwich Albion stole both points from a Stamford Bridge battle which saw Ian Britton head Chelsea into the lead after just two minutes, and Hutchinson score what appeared to be a valid 86th minute equaliser after the visitors had turned the game on its head. However, the referee thought otherwise and Hutchinson's 'goal' was ruled out, leaving the Blues languishing in 14th place.

*****

Members of a group calling itself the South Armagh Republican Action Force murdered 10 Ulster Protestant workmen near the village of Kingsmill in Northern Ireland.

12 Provisional IRA bombs were exploded in London's West End. Several started small fires but fortunately only one person was injured.

The first commercial Concorde flight took off from London's Heathrow Airport bound for Bahrain.

Korean cars were imported into the UK for the first time as Hyundai launched its appropriately-named Pony model.

Having sold over one million copies, *Bohemian Rhapsody* by Queen was finally replaced at the top of the charts by ABBA's *Mamma Mia*.

Notable birth
Spice Girl, Emma Bunton (Baby Spice) 21/1

FEBRUARY 1976

With more than one eye on the following week's huge Cup clash, Chelsea fought out a 1-1 draw with Oxford at the Manor Ground, where Bill Garner capitalised on an error by former team-mate Peter Houseman to give the Blues a lead which was cancelled out by a goal direct from a controversially awarded free-kick. Worse was to follow, with the news that the in-form Garner was a doubt for the Cup match having pulled a hamstring in the Oxford game.

On the day of FA Cup fifth roundclash, Garner was pronounced fit. Managed by the flamboyant Malcolm Allison, Palace had belied their lowly status by beating mighty Leeds United at Elland Road in the previous round. They arrived at Stamford Bridge as the darlings of the media, and there was no doubt that the game had captured the imagination of the entire football public.

On Valentine's Day 1976, but with little love in the air around SW6, Allison wallowed in the spotlight as he strolled around the pitch before the game. All fedora, fur coat and full of himself, the Palace manager predicted a 3-2 scoreline to the boys in the Shed, turning his two fingers to them to raise their hackles; while at the other end of the ground, home supporters mingled happily – OK, not exactly happily – with the visiting fans who had been brave enough to make the short journey to the Fulham Road.

The bank manager may have been happy with the near-55,000 crowd packed into Stamford Bridge that afternoon, but it would prove to be the last big pay day of the season. The two sides engaged in a cagey first half of football which saw the visitors score twice in the closing minutes to go into the break 2-0 ahead. The second goal sparked a riot on the North Stand terrace as Chelsea supporters attacked their Palace counterparts, while dozens of police and nine horses sought to restore order. A kung-fu kick delivered by a Chelsea supporter was dissected that evening on *Match of the*

Day.

In need of a retort, the home side piled forward at the start of the second half. Just after the hour mark, Stamford Bridge rose to acknowledge a fine Ray Wilkins strike which the young skipper celebrated with a two-fingered salute in Allison's direction; and when young defender Steve Wicks headed home a corner to bring the Blues level 10 minutes later, the old stadium reached fever pitch. However, as the home fans implored their heroes to go in for the kill, future England winger Peter Taylor – the architect of the opening goal and scorer of the second – curled a sensational free-kick past Peter Bonetti to give victory to Allison's men. Chelsea exited the competition in despair, while Palace would ultimately fall to eventual winners Southampton in a semi-final which was played at Stamford Bridge.

Four days after the Palace epic in front of more than 54,000 spectators, came a turgid 0-0 draw with Hull which was watched by little more than 10,000. Who knows what the attendance would have been had Chelsea been lifted by progressing to the last eight of the oldest competition, but the attendance for the Hull match was Mr Mears' worst nightmare coming true. It was the lowest crowd of the season by fully 5,000, many of whom booed and chanted for their money back at the final whistle.

To add insult to injury, three days after the Blues were held by Hull, they threw away a lead not once but twice at Notts County, as they fell to a 3-2 defeat. County manager Ronnie Fenton, who bitterly ridiculed the Chelsea team when his side were beaten at Stamford Bridge earlier in the season, suddenly found himself telling the press: "It was great to win against a side of such tremendous skill."

Back into 15th position after the defeat at Meadow Lane, some relief was found in consecutive home wins in the final week of February. Two stalwarts of better days, Charlie Cooke and Gary Locke, were the unlikely scorers as Portsmouth – stranded at the bottom of the table and already in need of a miracle to avoid relegation – were beaten 2-0 in front of 12,709 spectators. For both men it was their first goal of the season. Three days later, almost 15,000 were there to see Blackburn Rovers dispatched 3-1, Ray Wilkins scoring twice as the Blues bounced back in style from the concession of an early goal.

*****

The Queen opened the National Exhibition Centre in Birmingham.

John Curry became Britain's first gold medallist in skating at the Winter Olympics held in Innsbruck, Austria.

Popular sitcom *Open All Hours* starring Ronnie Barker was screened for the first time by the BBC.

The Sex Pistols supported Eddie and the Hot Rods at London's *Marquee* and gained their first review in the weekly music newspaper *New Musical Express*. The review in which Steve Jones declared, "actually we're not into music, we're into chaos," was read by Howard Trafford (Devoto) and Peter Shelley, two students at Bolton Institute of Technology who subsequently travelled down to London to watch the Pistols. Influenced by what they had seen and heard, on returning north they set about forming their own group, Buzzcocks.

Slik, still featuring singer / guitarist Midge Ure, topped the singles charts with *Forever and Ever*. US Country and Western star Slim Whitman's *Very Best of* compilation was the best-selling long player.

MARCH 1976

Having dropped a point and a clanger when lowly Plymouth visited the Bridge earlier in the season, Chelsea made surprisingly light work of beating Argyle on their own pitch at the start of March. A bumper Home Park crowd of more than 20,000 was swelled by hordes of Londoners, who made their presence felt inside and outside the ground. On the pitch, goals by Garry Stanley, Ian Britton and Kenny Swain clinched a comfortable 3-0 win.

With a promotion push still looking an unlikely prospect, Brian Mears would have been pleasantly surprised to see more than 29,000 people through the gates for the visit of Southampton. The Saints, preparing for their FA Cup semi-final with Crystal Palace, were one of the stronger Division Two sides, and the presence of Peter Osgood in their line-up certainly helped swell the gate. However, the raucous atmosphere did nothing to improve a tedious game in which Mick Channon gave the visitors the lead on the hour mark, only for Steve Finnieston to head the Blues level seconds later. Osgood left more impact on his old mate Peter Bonetti than he did on the game, with a late challenge that left the Chelsea custodian in a heap, while Southampton manager Lawrie McMenemy told reporters: "I was bored stiff, so I can't imagine what the public felt."

A 0-0 draw at home to Bristol Rovers was notable only for the booing aimed at Eddie McCreadie after he substituted the influential Kenny Swain late in the game, but that was nothing compared to the catcalls which greeted a 2-1 defeat at Bolton seven days later. Ahead thanks to an Ian Britton goal early in the second half, Chelsea slipped to defeat courtesy of two clumsy own goals, David Hay heading past Bonetti from a corner before Graham Wilkins – playing his first game in two months – inexplicably guided a back pass beyond his 'keeper to gift Wanderers a late winner.

*****

The 'Maguire Seven' were convicted of handling explosives used in the Guildford pub bombings. Sentences ranged from five to 14 years.

Direct rule of Northern Ireland from London via the British Parliament was introduced.

Harold Wilson announced his resignation as UK Prime Minister.

Anita Roddick opened the first branch of the *Body Shop* in Brighton.

Paul Kossoff, former lead guitarist with *Alright Now* rockers Free died aged 25 from heroin-related heart problems.

One Flew Over The Cuckoos Nest won the Oscar for Best Film at the 48th Academy Awards. Jack Nicholson and Louise Fletcher were named Best Actor and Best Actress in the same film.

I Love to Love (But my Baby Just Loves to Dance) gave Tina Charles, whose previous credits included backing vocals on Steve Harley & Cockney Rebel's smash hit *Make Me Smile (Come Up and See Me)*, her only Number One single.

Denim-clad rockers Status Quo topped the albums charts with *Blue For You*.

APRIL 1976

Only a handful of Fulham fans made the short journey to Stamford Bridge for another goalless draw, one which was enlivened only by a hissy fit thrown by visiting goalkeeper Peter Mellor when a ball boy refused to release the ball as the Cottagers' keeper looked to initiate a quick counter attack. A more notable draw followed when Kenny Swain and Garry Stanley scored the goals to earn a point at promotion-bound Bristol City, and a third consecutive draw came on Good Friday, when Chelsea shared four goals with Luton Town at Stamford Bridge. David Hay and Steve Finnieston found the net against the Hatters, but many of the plaudits went to Bill Garner, after the burly striker replaced the injured Bonetti in goal after the veteran stopper dislocated a finger. Garner donned the gloves for almost the entire second period, conceding just once in that time.

John Phillips, recovered from a broken leg suffered in the previous summer, made his first start of the season as Stamford Bridge hosted its second game in 24-hours with the visit of Orient. Prior to the game, Brian Mears took to the pitch and, acknowledging that promotion was no longer a possibility, told the supporters present: "We will make a really determined effort to get promotion next season, and we will not, definitely not, be selling any of our players." The cheers that greeted the chairman's words had barely abated when the visitors began to exert their dominance. On a warm and sunny spring day, Orient belied their position in the lower reaches of the division. Inspired by young winger Laurie Cunningham, who gave Graham Wilkins a torrid time throughout, the visitors secured both points with a comfortable 2-0 win.

Easter Monday saw thousands of Chelsea supporters descend on Charlton Athletic's Valley ground, to give the south-east London side their biggest crowd of the season. The home side were indebted to their young goalkeeper, Jeff Wood, for thwarting numerous efforts by a dominant Blues side which was eventually grateful for a clumsy own-goal by Charlton defender Les Berry, as the game finished in a 1-1 draw.

Almost inevitably, the season finished with another draw on the final Saturday in April. Relegated York City gave their once-illustrious visitors an almighty fright, soaking up Blues' pressure and twice hitting them on the break. Ian Britton's penalty was sandwiched between the home side's two goals, and Chelsea were eventually grateful for Steve Finnieston's 88th minute leveller.

Chelsea's first Division Two campaign in more than a decade saw them finish in 11th place. Sunderland, Bristol City and West Bromwich Albion took the promotion spots, while the likes of Notts County, Charlton and

Blackpool finished above a Blues side which just five years earlier had been crowned 'Cup Kings of Europe'.

Many bookmakers' promotion favourites at the outset, an inconsistent campaign which saw numerous flashes of brilliance offset by a number of disastrous performances, demonstrated clearly that Eddie McCreadie's young team remained a work in progress. But confidence remained high at Stamford Bridge, as noted by the final paragraph of the last matchday programme editorial of 1975/76:

'The summer can be used for a welcome break and a "recharging of the batteries" as we all look forward to an all-out push for promotion next season. The foundations have been well laid, so August really can't come quick enough for the club.'

*****

Apple was formed by Steve Jobs and Steve Wozniak

James Callaghan succeeded Harold Wilson as UK Prime Minister after defeating Roy Jenkins and Michael Foot in the contest to become leader of the Labour Party.

Sid James, comedy star of the *Carry On* series of feature films died on stage at the Sunderland Empire Theatre after suffering a heart attack.

The Sex Pistols supported the 101'ers at London's *Nashville*. 101'ers frontman Joe Strummer (John Mellor) was impressed. Shortly after the gig, Strummer was approached by Bernie Rhodes and Mick Jones, guitarist from the group London SS, who wanted to form a group similar in outlook to the Pistols. Given an ultimatum by Rhodes, Strummer would soon leave the 101'ers and join Jones, bassist Paul Simonon, drummer Terry Chimes and guitarist Keith Levene and The Clash were born.

Brotherhood of Man won the Eurovision Song Contest with *Save Your Kisses For Me*. The single topped the UK charts throughout the month.

Led Zeppelin's *Presence* was the best-selling long player.

MAY 1976

With Chelsea's season already over, True Blue eyes re-focussed themselves keenly on Wembley and the FA Cup Final where fellow Second Division side Southampton, featuring Stamford Bridge legend Peter Osgood in their starting XI, caused a major shock beating Manchester United of the top flight 1-0 thanks to a late Bobby Stokes goal.

If Ossie winning another FA Cup winners medal was a fillip for Chelsea supporters, three days later there was more good news when Liverpool came from a goal down to beat Wolverhampton Wanderers 3-1 and win the First Division by a point from Queens Park Rangers. The result condemned Wolves to relegation alongside Sheffield United and Burnley.

Blues of a truly spiteful nature were chuckling once again the following day as West Ham United were beaten 4-2 by Anderlecht in the European Cup Winners Cup Final which was played at Brussels Heysel Stadium.

Staying in Belgium, Liverpool brought the curtain down on the season drawing 1-1 with FC Bruges at Bruges Olympiastadion in the Second Leg of the UEFA Cup Final. The Reds won the trophy courtesy of a 3-2 First Leg victory at Anfield.

*****

Jeremy Thorpe resigned as leader of the Liberal Party.

David Bowie, who had earlier in the year been quoted as saying, "Britain could benefit from a Fascist leader", was photographed waving to fans at London's Victoria Station in a Mercedes convertible. Caught mid-wave, Bowie's gesture resembled a Nazi salute. The photo was published in the *New Musical Express*. Bowie would later attribute his comments and behaviour during this period to drug addiction and the *Thin White Duke* character he was portraying at the time.

Fernando saw ABBA re-acquaint themselves with the top of the singles charts. The Swedish songsters *Greatest Hits* compilation went to the top of the album charts and stayed there for nine weeks.

PROMOTION AND PUNK
1976 - 1977

Britain sweltered from mid-June to the end of August as a record-breaking heat wave brought scorching temperatures and a severe drought to the nation.

For 15 consecutive days, 23 June–7 July, the temperature reached 32c (90f) or more. At Wimbledon, where Sweden's ice-cool tennis superstar Bjorn Borg won the first of five consecutive men's singles titles, umpires were permitted to remove their jackets for the first time since the tournament began 99-years previously.

'Save Water Bath With A Friend' was a popular t-shirt slogan prompted in response to the National Water Council drought warning that implored people to not only limit bathwater, but share it as well.

Watneys Party Seven was the beer can of choice for summer revellers. Having succeeded in doubly piercing the can, usually with a screwdriver or Swiss Army knife, seven pints of liquid refreshment awaited. Cherry B wine would also be on offer for more sophisticated palates at social gatherings.

David Steel was elected the new leader of the Liberal Party

Ford launched the Fiesta.

The 1976 Olympics took place in Montreal, Canada. The games were opened by Queen Elizabeth II on 17 July. The former Soviet Union topped the medals table ahead of the former East Germany with the United States in third place. Great Britain was ranked 13th winning just three gold medals. Swimmer David Wilkie was Team GB's star performer winning gold in the 200 metres Breaststroke and picking up silver in the 100 metres version of the event.

Cult Martin Scorsese movie *Taxi Driver* starring Robert De Niro as disaffected Vietnam veteran Travis Bickle was the summer's must-see film.

The Clash made their live debut supporting the Sex Pistols at the *Black Swan* in Sheffield.

Two diverse singles, The Wurzels novelty record *The Combine Harvester (Brand New Key)* and *You To Me Are Everything* by The Real Thing, traded places at the top of the charts. The Beach Boys compilation *20 Golden Greats* reflected the summer vibe reaching the top of the album charts and staying there for 10 weeks.

Notable birth
Actor, Benedict Cumberbatch 19/07

AUGUST 1976

As Britain baked, Chelsea Football Club's bankers were sweating for a different reason; the Stamford Bridge coffers were as parched as the nation's reservoirs. The Blues' financial plight was so severe that with the club now £3 million in debt, the forthcoming season was 'promotion or bust'.

Staying true to his word, Brian Mears refused to sell any of his in-demand young players, and backed Eddie McCreadie to lead them to promotion. The club did, however, lose the playing talents of the experienced and ridiculously brave Ian Hutchinson, albeit that the Stamford Bridge playboy did remain at the club in as 'Promotions Executive'.

The season began at Orient, against a team which had cantered to a league double over the Blues in the previous term. This time, though, there would be no such outcome. A tempestuous affair which saw the home side's Laurie Cunningham targeted with some tough tackling, was won at the death by Steve Finnieston, starting the new season as he had finished the old.

If chairman Mears was happy with the result, his Orient counterpart Brian Winston was less so. Having seen away supporters celebrate victory on the pitch, damaging a concrete wall in the process, Winston complained bitterly: "That wall will cost up to £4,000 to repair. That means the difference of a player's wages for a year." Then, banning McCreadie from the director's room after the game, the excitable O's chairman stated: "You can't hold a club responsible for their supporters – even if some of them act like animals – but you can blame a manager for his team. If someone doesn't take a stand against play like we saw today, players will become gladiators and the game will degenerate." No Chelsea players were sent off by the referee, and no home players were injured or killed as a result of that production.

The draw specialists of 1975/76 opened their home campaign in familiar style, a late Ian Britton header securing a point against a wily and experienced Notts County side. Carlisle United – again early-season visitors to SW6 – were then dispatched 2-1 as Chelsea soared to the top of the table. Buoyed by the unbeaten start, Brian Mears was further enthused when he received the news that a group of season ticket holders were in the process of raising £100,000 to gift to the club at the end of the season, while the official supporters club had identified fund raising schemes which would mirror that amount. A grateful Mears said: "This, with the economies we are going to make, could save us."

*****

100 police officers and 60 revellers were injured during riots at London's Notting Hill Carnival. 66 people were arrested in clashes at the carnival that drew an estimated total crowd of 150,000.

If David Bowie's alleged right wing sympathies weren't enough to contend with, during a concert at Birmingham Odeon, Eric Clapton interrupted his set to advise shocked fans to vote for Enoch Powell and then went on to repeat the phrase "Keep Britain White". His outburst prompted photographer Red Saunders to write to several music papers to remind Clapton about the origins of the music he played. Saunders concluded his letters with the declaration we urge support for *Rock Against Racism* that led to the formation of a movement of the same name.

10,000 Protestant and Catholic women demonstrated for peace in Northern Ireland.

A dispute at the Grunwick Film Processing Laboratories in Willesden, North London led to a two-year strike that at its height resulted in serious and often violent confrontations between Trade Unionists and the police.

Mechanical failure stopped Big Ben as metal fatigue exacerbated by searing temperatures took its toll.

Reigning Formula One world champion Niki Lauda suffered near fatal injuries when his Ferrari was engulfed in flames following an accident during the German Grand Prix at the Nurburgring.

Elton John and Kiki Dee's duet *Don't Go Breaking My Heart* topped the singles charts throughout the month.

Chelsea births
Mineiro 02/08
Bolo Zenden 15/08

SEPTEMBER 1976

'A show that defied belief' – that was how one reporter described Ray Wilkins' performance as the young captain led from the front, scoring twice as Sheffield United were beaten 3-1 in a League Cup tie. Already on the brink of an England call-up, Wilkins was proving to be the leader of a group of players that his manager described in a post-match interview as being: "The beginnings of Chelsea's greatest ever side."

Such plaudits were a long way from anybody's lips when, three days later, McCreadie's young team showed all of its naivety in falling three goals behind at Millwall before half-time. As violence flared all around them, Wilkins and his boys melted away before coming to terms with matters after the break, and carrying out a damage limitation exercise to keep the score down to 0-3.

Top spot had been spectacularly surrendered at the Den, with Chelsea slipping to ninth, but they rose up the table again with a 3-2 win at Plymouth, where Ian Britton, Kenny Swain and the increasingly prolific Steve Finnieston got their name on the scoresheet.

On the day that supporters announced a new initiative whereby they would pay the club £750 for every point earned throughout 1976/77, Bolton Wanderers arrived at Stamford Bridge in top spot. The visitors, who had completed the double over the Blues a season earlier but had narrowly missed out on promotion, discovered that their opponents had a new found vigour. Roared on by a boisterous crowd of almost 25,000 – as the home supporters increasingly impressed with the way in which they took their young heroes to their hearts – Chelsea took the lead when David Hay headed powerfully home from a Garry Stanley cross. Midway through the second period, Stanley doubled the lead with a 25-yard blast which was deflected past goalkeeper Barry Siddall. A last minute consolation for the visitors did little to quell the enthusiasm of the home fans, as the final whistle blew on a result which saw Chelsea leapfrog their opponents and settle in behind Wolverhampton Wanderers at the top of the table, with only goal difference separating the two sides.

Two more goals from Steve Finnieston saw Chelsea into the fourth round of the League Cup at Huddersfield Town's expense, and it was the same man who fired the only goal at Blackpool to bring September to a successful conclusion, with Chelsea rising above Wolves to top the table as the month ended.

*****

A peace march in Derry calling for a halt to the violence in Northern Ireland attracted 25,000 people.

ITV screened ratings winners, *George and Mildred* and *The Muppet Show* for the first time.

ABBA achieved their third number one hit of the year with the single *Dancing Queen*.

Chelsea births
Junior Mendes 15/9
Andriy Shevchenko 29/09

OCTOBER 1976

Even in the pit of despair, Chelsea had never been far from the headlines. Now though, as autumn set in, Eddie McCreadie's young team found themselves being talked about for all the right reasons. A crowd of just under 30,000 greeted the visit of Cardiff City on the first Saturday of October, as did the *Match of the Day* cameras, as the TV boys decided it was time the whole nation saw what was beginning to unfold in SW6. They weren't disappointed either, as Kenny Swain and Ray Lewington struck spectacular goals to give the Blues another two points, and another £1500 from their generous fans. Cardiff manager Jimmy Andrews was certainly impressed, saying "Chelsea are good and they'll get much better", while Match of the Day's Jimmy Hill stated "This young Chelsea side are a team in every sense of the word."

A 2-1 defeat at Bristol Rovers, where visiting fans showed their disappointment by rioting and smashing the changing room windows, did nothing to alter the Blues' position at the top of the table, and although for the second time in the year Chelsea conceded three goals at home to Oldham Athletic, this time there were no recriminations as they scored four of their own to secure both points from a mid-October thriller.

Steve Finnieston took his goals tally for the season into double figures when his brace was enough to clinch a 2-0 win at Blackburn, and he was on target again a week later, as Southampton's fine team were blown away 3-1 at the Bridge despite taking a fortunate lead with only 18-minutes remaining. As the supporters rose again to acclaim his players, McCreadie was at pains to stress how proud he was of the way his team had responded, while visiting manager Lawrie McMenemy said he believed Chelsea had everything needed to get out of Division Two.

Perhaps the Blues' triumph over the Saints was given added kudos as it came in the wake of a hurtful League Cup defeat at Arsenal three days earlier, where the home side's Irish defender Sammy Nelson put two Chelsea players on a stretcher. Gary Locke's injury was ultimately diagnosed as nothing more sinister than severe bruising, but young midfielder Brian Bason would never return to the Chelsea team after the broken leg he suffered that night.

*****

InterCity 125 trains were introduced by British Rail.

British racing driver James Hunt became Formula One world champion.

Kids show *Multi-Coloured Swap Shop* hosted by Noel Edmonds and featuring Keith Chegwin and John Craven aired for the first time.

Stiff Records released *New Rose* by the Damned. The first single to be promoted as punk rock made little impression on the charts failing to reach the Top 40. With plenty of punks adding a splash of colour to the Shed terrace at Stamford Bridge on match-days, a couple of months later an advert for *New Rose* found its way into the Chelsea v Wolves programme.

Dutch pop act Pussycat headed the singles charts with Mississippi. Canvey Island's finest export, Dr. Feelgood, were catapulted from rocking in pubs to concert halls when they topped the album charts with *Stupidity*.

NOVEMBER 1976

Former England man Terry Paine, who had officially retired from playing just three weeks earlier, returned to the Hereford side to give a midfield master-class in a 2-2 draw at Edgar Street. Chelsea led twice – Finnieston again scoring both goals – but the home side, managed by former Chelsea player John Sillett, fought gamely to ensure the Blues came away with just one point.

In the programme for the home clash with Charlton Athletic, Mike Eaton of the now-defunct News of the World was quoted in the aftermath of the Southampton game as saying, "Crowds of this size belong in the First Division. So do Chelsea." A little under 43,000 had witnessed the Saints clash, and equally impressive was the near 40,000 who turned out for the midweek battle with the Addicks. And the vast majority of them went home happy, too, as Chelsea's Swain and Stanley fired the goals that took their side to another win.

A 1-1 draw away to Brian Clough's high-flying Nottingham Forest was a fair return from a tough game, which had been delayed during the first-half as rival fans fought on the pitch. Forest's legendary manager, who had praised the Blues before the game and announced them as the best team in the division, reiterated his admiration afterwards when he said: "They are really good and I'm satisfied with a point."

November drew to a close with a 2-1 win over Burnley courtesy of goals by Ian Britton and Steve Finnieston. The increasingly inspirational McCreadie was unhappy with his side's profligacy in front of goal – "We should have scored six" – but also noted: "I still think we were terrific. It must be like capital punishment to play against us."

*****

Amid much hype, EMI released the Sex Pistols debut single *Anarchy in the UK* but it was American adult orientated rockers Chicago who dominated the charts with *If You Leave Me Now*.

Despite the arrival of punk, it was established acts that continued to sell records in quantity as Led Zeppelin proved when their live set *The Song Remains the Same*, recorded at New York's Madison Square Garden, gave them a second album chart topper of the year.

Chelsea birth
Mario Melchiot 4/11

DECEMBER 1976

A goal by former Blue Ian 'Chico' Hamilton gave Sheffield United a 1-0 victory at Bramall Lane, as December opened in disappointing style. The game was played on a freezing Friday evening, and the icy pitch contributed to Graham Wilkins conceding the 68th minute penalty which Hamilton duly converted.

Wolverhampton Wanderers were the next visitors to Stamford Bridge, in what would be the most significant test yet for the new blue dawn. Wanderers went into the game five points behind the Blues, having played one game more. However, their squad included the likes of Steve Daley – a future British transfer fee record holder – Kenny Hibbitt, Bobby Gould, Alan Sunderland and prolific goal-getter John Richards. It was certainly a game that caught the attention of the public, with ITV's *The Big Match* covering it and their cameras picking out the American Secretary of State, Dr Henry Kissinger, in the posh East Stand seats, surrounded by bodyguards and with other 'protectors' scattered around the ground in various strategic vantage points.

What the American contingent thought of the game is anyone's guess, but the only thing that came under severe threat that day was Chelsea's precious unbeaten home record. On another icy pitch, the two teams slugged out a memorable battle in which Richards scored first, only for Ray Wilkins to nod home a close range equaliser just two minutes later. Former West Ham man Gould then put the visitors back in front prior to the break, and Richards extended that lead further with a clinical finish.

Faced with their sternest test of character yet, the home side responded in style. With just 10 minutes remaining, little Ian Britton rose highest to nod home a Wilkins corner in front of the Shed; and with just three minutes left on the clock, Steve Finnieston did similarly to spark scenes of delirium around Stamford Bridge. Hilariously, as 36,000 spectators rose to wildly celebrate the late leveller, Dr Kissinger's assorted henchmen panicked as they lost sight of the politician they were there to protect. Thankfully for them, no triggers were pulled and no call was made for Chelsea's notorious North Stand mob to 'do their job'.

The Blues had to rely on a last minute Ian Britton strike to secure a point at Hull City in the last game before Christmas, before future Chelsea manager Bobby Campbell brought a Fulham side featuring George Best and Bobby Moore across SW6 to the Bridge. In front of a baying crowd of 55,003, the illustrious Best and Moore could do little other than admire their opponents. A lively match with both teams thundering into challenges – Best had the misfortune to be flattened by Micky Droy at one stage – was decided by two late goals, Droy heading the first from some way out, before Kenny Swain beat future Chelsea loanee Gerry Peyton at the death to clinch a 2-0 win.

The year ended ignominiously for the Blues, with a crushing 4-0 defeat by Luton Town. This notwithstanding, McCreadie's boys ended 1976 top of Division Two, but with a chasing pack of Bolton, Wolves, Blackpool and Nottingham Forest all within touching distance, and all with games in hand on Chelsea.

*****

The Sex Pistols achieved instant notoriety on 1 December when they were guests on Bill Grundy's live and uncensored Thames Television show *Today* which aired daily in the London region at 6pm. Grundy goaded several members of the band, in particular Steve Jones, into swearing after the presenter had said 'let's meet after' to Siouxsie Soux who had appeared on the show as part of the Pistols entourage.

Leicester Teddy Boys Showaddywaddy were *Under the Moon of Love* at the top of the singles charts for much of December, but it was crooner Johnny Mathis who had the Christmas Number One with *When a Child is Born*. American country music star Glen Campbell topped the album charts throughout the festive period with his *20 Golden Greats* compilation.

JANUARY 1977

1977 could barely have got off to a better start. Hereford United were the visitors to Stamford Bridge on New Year's Day for a genuine top versus bottom clash. The gulf in class was apparent from a mere glance at the league table, and it widened further within three minutes when Kenny Swain headed the Blues into the lead. Garry Stanley doubled that lead midway through the first half, but the day's highlight came just before half time, when Ray Wilkins collected a poor kick out from the visiting goalkeeper, and duly dispatched it back over his head and into the goal. The scoring was completed in the second half when Steve Finnieston and an own goal sandwiched a consolation strike by Terry Paine.

Drawn against holders Southampton in the FA Cup third round, a rare Gary Locke strike secured a replay at the Bridge, but an extra-time capitulation on a mud-heap of a pitch, saw the Saints run riot at the death to eventually win 3-0.

Before the home clash with Orient, the financial woes engulfing Chelsea were brought back into the spotlight by Financial Director Martin Spencer. Announcing a rare mid-season hike in prices, Spencer said that the new break even attendance figure for the club was 40,000 spectators per game. Seeking to assure supporters of the need for the rise, Brian Mears said: "People may say we are cashing in on our position as promotion candidates, but this isn't so. We must do this because of our financial position." Effective from the next home game, adults would pay a minimum entrance fee of £1 to attend Chelsea games.

EDDIE MCCREADIE'S BLUE AND WHITE ARMY

On a pitch described as 'diabolical' by McCreadie, Orient took an early lead against the Blues, which was equalised before half time by Garry Stanley. The visitors' goal scorer, Alan Whittle, made the point afterwards that the poor pitch could potentially be to the advantage of visiting sides, less talented than the Blues: "That is the worst pitch we have played on away. It's nearly as bad as our own! When we saw it we thought we could win. Chelsea have some good players, but they could be in trouble if they have to play too many games on that."

*****

Under political pressure and intense media scrutiny, following the Bill Grundy *Today* show debacle, EMI terminated the Sex Pistols record contract.

The Provisional IRA exploded seven bombs in London's West End. Thankfully there were no fatalities or serious injuries.

Gary Gilmore was executed by firing squad in Utah, the first execution since the reintroduction of the death penalty in the USA. Later in the year, punk band The Adverts released a single entitled *Gary Gilmore's Eyes*, a song written from the point of view of a patient who has just had an eye transplant and finds out he has been given Gilmore's eyes.

Jimmy Carter succeeded Gerald Ford as the President of the United States.

The Clash headlined the opening night at Covent Garden, London music venue *The Roxy* and signed a record deal worth £100,000 with CBS Records.

Having made a name for himself as the *Hutch* half of popular US TV detective duo *Starsky and Hutch*, David Soul further enhanced his showbiz credentials with a Number One single when his ode to giving love another

73

chance *Don't Give Up On Us Baby* topped the charts. Far from practising what he preached, Soul, who to date has been married five times, would also later be arrested and jailed for assaulting his third wife Patti Sherman, seven months pregnant at the time.

Queen long-player *A Day At The Races* headed the album charts.

FEBRUARY 1977

A late Kenny Swain goal was enough to secure the points at Carlisle, but the gloss was taken off the win with the news that the prolific Steve Finnieston had picked up a fractured jaw in a clash with Bobby Moncur. With 15 league goals to his name already, this was a serious blow to both player and team.

Fabled Chelsea groundsman George Anstiss was working on the pitch from 4am on the day that Millwall were the visitors to Stamford Bridge. Eddie McCreadie deemed the pitch unplayable, but the referee felt otherwise and with the new entrance charges in place, almost 35,000 spectators saw the London rivals play out a 1-1 draw. Chelsea's goal, scored by Garry Stanley, had a large element of good fortune about it, as the midfield heart-throb found the net past stand-in goalkeeper Dave Donaldson, as the visitors' full-time custodian, Ray Goddard, received treatment after a collision with the colossal Micky Droy.

Despite slipping to a 2-1 defeat at Notts County, Ray Wilkins scoring for the Blues, Chelsea remained in top spot. A 2-2 draw with Plymouth thanks to goals from Kenny Swain and Ian Britton did nothing to change the order at the top, despite the Blues having dropped five points in the last five games; and they remained top of the table as February drew to a close with another 2-2 draw, the returning Finnieston and another Swain strike seeing the Blues come back from a two goal deficit against a Bolton side that would have leapfrogged them at the top of the table had they held on to their lead.

*****

Sex Pistols bass player Glen Matlock was sacked by the Sex Pistols, allegedly because he liked the Beatles. The Pistols most obsessive fan John Beverley, aka Sid Vicious, replaced Matlock despite not being able to play bass guitar.

Fleetwood Mac released their best selling album *Rumours*.

Don't Cry For Me Argentina, a track written produced by Tim Rice and Andrew Lloyd-Webber for their concept album *Evita* and recorded by Julie Covington topped the singles charts. Popular instrumental combo The Shadows compilation *20 Golden Greats* dominated the album charts hitting the top slot and staying there for six-weeks.

MARCH 1977

March began with the top of the Division Two table showing:

	Played	Points	Goal Difference
Chelsea	29	38	+10
Bolton	27	36	+15
Wolves	26	35	+30
Blackpool	28	34	+13

With all the teams below them having games in hand, Chelsea could ill afford another month like February, but March began with another point dropped in a 2-2 draw at home to Blackpool. Kenny Swain and Steve Wicks scored the Blues' goals.

The winning habit finally returned at Cardiff, where the Welsh side were well beaten thanks to an inspired final half hour by the visitors. They had the energetic Ian Britton to thank for breaking the deadlock on the hour mark, before Kenny Swain fired home to double the lead. The home side pulled a goal back late on, but Garry Stanley had the final word in the very last minute.

"These were the two points we needed, we're now out of our bad run." Those were words of Eddie McCreadie following the Cardiff game, and he would feel vindicated as his side followed up that win by comfortably beating Bristol Rovers 2-0 at Stamford Bridge. An own-goal and a rare Steve Wicks effort secured the points in a game which could at best be described as humdrum. However, celebrity attendee David Soul thought otherwise, announcing that he had never seen a better game... an observation that prompted some Chelsea supporters to question if the American heartthrob, who was on a UK tour to promote his pop career, fully understood football. They would get their answer some years later when nice guy Soul emigrated to the UK, set up home in London... and declared he was an avid Arsenal fan.

The warm glow of the returning winning feeling was quickly tempered the following day, when news broke of the horrific and senseless death overnight of 1970 FA Cup hero Peter Houseman. The quiet man of Dave Sexton's maverick side, 'Nobby', as he was known to his teammates, was held in high esteem by Eddie McCreadie and his fellow players, even if he at times was less warmly received by the supporters.

Houseman, aged 31-years, who had been playing for Oxford United for the past two seasons was returning home from a fund-raising event when the Hillman Avenger saloon he was travelling in with his wife Sally and family friends Allan and Janice Gillham was struck by a Maserati sports car being driven at excessive speed along the A40 Oxford-Witney road by Bartholomew Evan Eric Smith.

The son of a former Conservative MP, public school educated 22-year-old Smith, who had three previous convictions for speeding and another for failing to obey a road sign, was found guilty of four charges of causing death by dangerous driving but acquitted of drink-related charges despite arousing the suspicions of a hospital doctor who examined him following the fatal incident.

Six children were orphaned as a consequence of the totally avoidable tragedy that cost four innocent lives. Smith, who had the temerity to deny all the charges, avoided a custodial sentence and was fined £4000 and banned from driving for 10-years.

On 29 March, almost 17,000 spectators attended a special benefit match at Stamford Bridge and saw the current Blues side defeat a Chelsea 1970 XI 3-0. All proceeds from the event went to the dependents of Peter and Sally Houseman and Allan and Janice Gillham.

*****

The Centenary Test marking the 100th anniversary of the first test played between Australia and England took place at Melbourne Cricket Ground. Remarkably, as had been the case in 1877, Australia won the test by 45 runs.

A&M Records signed the Sex Pistols in a ceremony in front of Buckingham Palace. The contract was terminated less than a week later following the band's misbehaviour at A&M's offices.

Soccer fanatic David *'Hutch' Don't Give Up On Us Baby* Soul played back-to-back shows at The Rainbow in London's Finsbury Park. The following evening, 18 March, punk rock met glam rock when The Damned supported Marc Bolan's T-Rex at the same venue.

The Clash released their first single *White Riot*.

The Manhattan Transfer top the singles charts with *Chanson D'Amour*

Notable birth
Coldplay singer, Chris Martin 02/03

APRIL 1977

A trio of successive wins was secured when Wicks netted again to open the scoring against Blackburn Rovers, before Steve Finnieston helped himself to two more goals as the Lancastrians were beaten 3-1 at the start of April. However, a comprehensive 3-1 defeat at Fulham on Good Friday was cause for concern. The following day, all was good in the world again as Finnieston and a 30-yard John Sparrow screamer – 'Sparrow's Arrow' screamed the Sunday papers – saw the heavy defeat at Luton earlier in the season avenged, but two days later, on Easter Monday, Chelsea's angry followers were building bonfires on the terraces as Charlton put four past the Blues without reply at the Valley. To make matters worse, Wolverhampton Wanderers overtook Chelsea at the top of the table as a result of that day's results.

In need of old heads to help his team over the line, Eddie McCreadie recalled Peter Bonetti and Charlie Cooke for the visit of an improving Nottingham Forest side which was making a late push for promotion. A little more surprising was the decision to replace Kenny Swain with the enthusiastic Tommy Langley, but McCreadie's actions would prove to be perfectly thought out. Despite the well-organised visitors taking the lead through Martin O'Neill's low shot, a second half fightback saw Ian Britton level before Steve Finnieston, looking half a yard offside, turned to fire a late, late winner.

A 0-0 midweek draw at Oldham saw Chelsea edge back into top spot, albeit with just a point more than a Wolves side which had played two games less. Turning back the years in the way in which McCreadie hoped he would, Peter Bonetti received all the plaudits for a man of the match performance at Boundary Park. Sadly, though, Bonetti was unable to stop an 85th minute strike at Burnley the following Saturday which cost Chelsea top spot again, a position that Wolves would not relinquish a second time.

With pressure heaped on shoulders young and old, the Blues ended April with a 4-0 destruction of Sheffield United which all but secured their promotion. The confidence which came flooding back during an exceptional display was a joy to witness, as was Tommy Langley's face when he opened the scoring after just 15-minutes. The game's outstanding performer, Ray Lewington, quickly doubled the home side's lead, and when Ray Wilkins struck the purest of volleys past the visiting keeper early in the second period, it was carnival time in SW6. Steve Finnieston scored the game's last goal in the closing stages, and with two games to play – the first of those being away to the only team above them in the table, Wolves – Chelsea were four points clear of the two Nottingham clubs in third and fourth place. They now needed just a single point to be certain of promotion.

*****

National Front marchers clashed with anti-Nazi protestors in London.

Red Rum won the Grand National for the third time.

CBS Records released the debut album by The Clash imaginatively entitled *The Clash*.

Taken from the album of the same, Polydor Records released *In The City*, the debut single by The Jam.

ABBA were back at the top of the singles charts with *Knowing Me Knowing You*. The track was taken from their fourth studio album *Arrival* which also topped the charts and stayed there for nine weeks. *Arrival* went on to be the best selling album of the year.

MAY 1977

In light of the serious misconduct of the Chelsea fans at Charlton on Easter Monday, the FA decreed that the Blues' clash with Wolves at Molineux would be an all-ticket affair, with no terrace tickets available to away fans. A small allocation of seats went to season ticket holders, but by and large this was a punishment which was designed to stop the anticipated thousands of Blues making the journey to the Black Country. Furthermore, the 'football specials' trains which ferried many thousands of travelling fans around the country every Saturday would not be running from London to Wolverhampton and back that day.

While the Lancaster Gate based Football Association tie-and-blazer brigade were pompously patting themselves on the back, huge numbers of Chelsea supporters were busily making their own arrangements to ensure their heroes got the reception they deserved when they ran out onto the Molineux pitch at 2.50pm on Saturday 7th May 1977. Various scams, blags and strokes were pulled – and when Ray Wilkins led his men and boys out onto the turf, somewhere between 6,000 and 8,000 Chelsea supporters rose to acclaim the away team. The magnificent Hugh Johns, ITV's football commentator for the Midlands region, told *World of Sport* viewers in almost reverential tones that the Chelsea boys had turned up in their droves. As he did so, the cameras panned around the ground to show thousands of blue and white scarves being held aloft.

Boyhood Chelsea supporter Tommy Langley had the pleasure of scoring the goal which would ultimately clinch promotion for Eddie McCreadie's Blue and White Army. John Richards equalised with little more than 10 minutes remaining, and with the home side needing only to keep parity to win the title, and the visitors knowing that promotion would be assured if the score remained the same, the final few minutes proved to be little more than a training ground exercise.

As the final whistle blew, the Molineux pitch was invaded by supporters of both clubs. In the aftermath of the game ending, there were 111 arrests and 18 people taken to hospital. Heaven knows how high those figures might have been if one side or other had lost the game.

Eddie McCreadie, by now acknowledged as one of the finest young managers in the game, and with his legendary player status amongst the Chelsea fans further cemented by his achievements off the pitch, bullishly announced: "My magnificent boys will enhance football in this country. Once we have consolidated ourselves, I think in the season after we will terrorise the First Division."

The final game of a memorable and magnificent 1976/77 season saw Billy Bremner's Hull City cast in the role of Cinderella as a monumental party took place at Stamford Bridge. It was announced during the week prior to the game that McCreadie would be taking to the pitch before kick-off and introducing his players one by one to the crowd, before leading them on a lap of honour. This he did, and amidst incredible, raucous scenes, the players were joined on their trot round the pitch by hundreds of ecstatic supporters who had ripped down the flimsy fences skirting the pitch in order to take part in the festivities. There was no aggravation, no hooliganism, just sheer, unadulterated joy.

When the game kicked off, it was almost an afterthought. Almost 44,000 fans were present, all dotted around various parts of the ground, having taken their place wherever they found it following the pre-match shenanigans. It is well known that there were grinning supporters sitting amongst the photographers who were huddled behind the Hull City goal.

These were the first supporters – the first of many hundreds – to join the players in celebrating Steve Finnieston's first goal of the afternoon.

A goal to the good at half-time, as the players prepared to kick off the second half, a young skinhead raced across the pitch in the direction of where Ray Wilkins was standing. As the Chelsea skipper took a startled step back, the fan produced a bunch of flowers which he handed to his hero, before dropping to his knees and kissing Wilkins' boots.

Three more goals followed in the second period. After Ian Britton had joined Finnieston on the score-sheet to put Chelsea 3-0 up, the prolific Scot having earlier doubled both his and his team's tally for the day, the referee announced that he would abandon the match if there were any more pitch invasions. McCreadie took to the microphone for the second time that day and implored the fans to stay off the pitch. The referee then awarded a penalty in the closing seconds, which was converted by Finnieston for his 26th goal of the season... and the fans stayed where they were until, seconds later, the final whistle blew. Chelsea were back, with a team of young stars and a fantastic, talismanic miracle worker of a manager at the helm.
What could possibly go wrong?

*****

Her Majesty Queen Elizabeth II toured the UK as part of her Silver Jubilee celebrations.

Virgin Records announced that they had signed the Sex Pistols.

Rod Stewart's double-A-side single, *I Don't Want to Talk About It / The First Cut Is the Deepest* topped the singles charts.

Chelsea birth
Mark Nicholls 30/05

SUMMER 1977

Queen Elizabeth II Silver Jubilee was marked by a public holiday on 7 June with street parties held the length and breadth of the UK to celebrate her 25 years as monarch. The Sex Pistols performed their new single *God Save the Queen* on board a pleasure boat that was cruising the River Thames. Police intervened forcing the boat to dock and several arrests were in the ensuing scuffles.

16-year old shop assistant Jayne McDonald was found battered and stabbed to death in Leeds. Police believed she was the fifth victim of the 'so called' Yorkshire Ripper.

214 people were arrested and 56 police officers are injured during violent clashes in South East London between the National Front, anti-NF demonstrators and the police in what became known as the Battle of Lewisham.

Playing on home soil, England won the Ashes for the first time since 1972, defeating Australia 3-0 in a five test series.

Eddie McCreadie left his post as Chelsea manager.

EDDIE MCCREADIE
in his own words

I always thought it was an interesting statement that football was a working man's sport as opposed to cricket and rugby, which were perhaps viewed as sports for the upper-class. It was most certainly a true reflection of my own background.

I was brought up in the rat-infested tenement slums of Glasgow, Scotland, and most days we had very little to eat. The buildings we lived in were old and filthy and should have been condemned. There were three floors, ground, middle and top, with three families on each floor. There were six of us, my mum and dad, my two brothers, Jim and Jack, and my sister, Esther, in one room, perhaps not much bigger than 12ft x 10ft. There was one 'outside' bathroom on the ground floor with just a toilet which we had to share with the eight other families. Did I realise at that time we were so poor? Not really, because most people we knew that lived around us were living the same way. I just thought that all people lived like we did. Was I unhappy? Not in the least.

When I was around 11-years old all I could think about was playing football in the streets with my friends. Was I any good? I had no idea. All I can tell you is that I loved to play and would play all day if I could. There were many times we didn't have a ball, so we would roll up old newspapers into a ball and tie it up with string. We were always able to get a few hours playing before our makeshift ball was shredded. I guess there was an indication at that time of how good I was that I never thought much about. My two older brothers, Jack and Jim, and their friends who were in their teens and their twenties would always invite me to play with them in their games, but not any of my friends.

My favourite professional team was Partick Thistle at this time. They played their games at Firhill, their home ground. I won't try, but I feel sure I could name every player by name right now if I had to. Every Saturday I would walk five or six miles just to see them play and sometimes, if I had any money, I would catch the bus. Most of the time, I didn't have any money so on occasion I would ask some older folks if they would lift me over the fence. I don't think I'll ever forget watching the players running onto the pitch in their yellow and orange shirts and the beautiful contrast they made against the green grass. To me, every one of them was a hero. My favourite player was Johnny McKenzie, a right-winger. He was such a great player and so fast. One day, after one of their games, I was walking outside the stadium when several of the players came out and I was standing there just looking at them. And, there he was – Johnny McKenzie! I wanted to go up and ask for his autograph but I was very shy and didn't. I always wished I had.

But, even at this time, I never imagined for a second that one day I might become a professional footballer like them. It was the furthest thing on my mind. They were so far above anything I had ever seen in my life, and I was just a kid who couldn't wait to get back to the streets and kick a ball around with my friends. I'd shout to them when our games started that I was Johnny McKenzie so look out!

I was asked to join a boys team in Glasgow called Drumchapel Amateurs. From there, I was asked to sign for a semi-professional team, Clydebank

Juniors and I played there for a couple of seasons. At this time, I was just happy to be playing football anywhere. Then, out of nowhere and to my surprise, I saw my name in our local newspaper for the first time and, to my amazement, it said that East Stirling of the Scottish Second Division, and Fulham Football Club who were then in the English First Division and perhaps in the best league in the world were showing some interest in Eddie McCreadie, the centre-forward of Clydebank Juniors.

I was absolutely flabbergasted and could hardly believe it. I remember running home as fast as I could, I just couldn't wait to tell my parents. I was so terribly excited when I got to our house. My dad was there and I started to tell him about the article and how happy I was to perhaps join Fulham in the English First Division. My excitement was not to last very long. My dad asked me, "What about East Stirling?" I told him if it turns out they both want to sign me then obviously I would prefer to go to London. He answered me with perhaps the most disappointing words I had ever heard in my life. He said, "I know you will make up your mind as to your decision, but you are only 19-years old and there are things you don't know and are unaware of." His next words stunned me, "If indeed both teams want you, you need to sign with East Stirling."

"Why would I want to go to a team who are at the bottom of the Scottish Second Division when I might have the chance to join Fulham and perhaps play in the best league in the world?" I said. Again his answer left me speechless.

"I am not an expert," he said, "but it is my opinion that you are not good enough yet, even though that might come. But more importantly you are not physically strong enough. All you have known up till now is semi-professional football. If you go to Fulham, you will get hurt, and maybe badly. I don't think you know how to take care of yourself physically. This league not only is the best technical league in the world, but it is also one of the most physical leagues in the world and they have players there that you have never ever come across before. Players who will attempt to break your leg and not even blink an eye doing it. Not only are they hard, tough and mean, but they also know how to do it. I am not suggesting you are afraid physically, but you don't know how to take care of yourself or defend yourself against these kind of players. And I believe that you need to go into the Scottish Second Division where they perhaps might not be as smart, as the kind of players I am talking about, but it is a very physical league and it will help to toughen you up." I was devastated by his words and I just walked out of the house.

A week later he was in the house when I came home. "Have you made any decision regarding what we talked about?" he asked. "I have," I said, "East Stirling have asked me to sign for them, and I have told them I would."
I played for East Stirling for the next three years and although I enjoyed playing for them, I just couldn't get Fulham out of my mind. In these three years, no other clubs had shown any interest in me, and I truly felt I had lost my opportunity – perhaps the only one I was going to get in my life. It also made me think that I wasn't perhaps good enough anyway. We had a home game one night at East Stirling. It was raining hard and there were probably about 200 people there. As I was walking off the field at the final whistle, the most amazing thing happened to me which was to change my life in a way I could never have imagined.

The East Stirling owner, Jack Steedman, who ran the club with his brother Charlie, came up to me and told me that Tommy Docherty was in his office and wanted to speak to me. Tommy Docherty was a very famous player and was the new manager of Chelsea. I still don't remember to this day how I got to his office, whether the walk took me two-minutes or ten-minutes. I was in a complete daze and really had no idea what Tommy Docherty would want to talk to me about.

When I entered the office, still wearing my kit which was drenched, there he was with several people standing around. He was sitting in a chair, larger than life. I recognized him immediately. He got up from his chair and walked toward me and warmly shook my hand. "Hello, Eddie," he said, "It's nice to meet you. My name is Tommy Docherty." (Did he really think I didn't know who he was?) At this time, I really didn't know what was going on. I thought I might be dreaming everything. His next words to me were, "Eddie, I believe you have a future and I want to take you to London and sign you for Chelsea Football Club. What do you think, Eddie?"

I remember looking around the room and everyone was looking at me waiting for me to answer. I could hardly speak. I really couldn't quite believe what I was hearing. Then he added, "Eddie, I have to fly back to London tonight. I have a contract with me for you to sign if you agree to these financial terms." You can tell I haven't said a word yet? I was a nobody and here was Tommy Docherty representing one of the most famous clubs in the world, Chelsea Football Club, saying all these things to me. "Mr Docherty," I said, "I don't have any interest in what's in the contract. I would like to sign now, sir, if that would be alright with you." And that was it, I certainly didn't realise what was to be ahead of me, but it was to take me on the fastest rise to fame I would ever have dreamed possible.

It was a completely new and different world to me. It is not my intention to dwell on my background but as I have said we had very little to eat most of the time and my mother had to pawn any decent clothes we had to feed us. And, it wasn't until I got a little older that I realised how desperately embarrassed and ashamed my mother was in having to do such things. I'm telling you these things in order to help you understand the change and differences I was to encounter in my new life.

After flying in an aircraft for the first time in my life – it was also the first time I'd ever been away from home – I arrived at Heathrow Airport and was met by two Chelsea officials. One of them said, "Mr McCreadie, we have a private car waiting for you and our instructions are to take you to your hotel in London and make sure you get settled in." This was definitely a first. I knew what a hotel was, but I had never stayed in one. It wasn't one of the larger hotels in London, but it was very private and definitely 'five star'. They introduced me to the owner of the hotel who personally showed me to my room. When he opened the door, I walked in and it was beautiful. "Mr McCreadie," he said to me (that was the second time anyone had ever called me "Mr McCreadie"), "we have been instructed by Chelsea Football Club that absolutely anything you might need in our hotel – dinner, breakfast, transport, anything, sir, should be charged to Chelsea Football Club. Your signature will be sufficient, Mr McCreadie." There was that "Mr. McCreadie" again.

I unpacked and rested a little and then I decided I was getting hungry so I went downstairs to the restaurant to see what they might have. I felt pretty sure they wouldn't have haggis on the menu. What's 'haggis you might ask… I'll tell you what haggis is. It is oatmeal, various meats and spices cooked inside a sheep stomach membrane. I've actually tasted it; it's really quite delicious. "Yeah right," I can hear all you English people right now, "See, I told you these Scottish people were savages?" I sat down in the dining room and a waiter brought me a menu and left me there looking at it. I couldn't understand most of what was on there as it was in French. But I sure noticed the prices. My mum could have fed us for several days on the price of one dish. Anyway, I had a wonderful meal and retired for the evening to my beautiful room. The following morning I was picked up and driven to Stamford Bridge where, although I was not to know it at this time, would provide me over the next 15-years as player and manager an incredible career filled with an assortment of emotions most of which I had never experience before in my life – fear, excitement, tension, glory, anxiety, happiness, disappointment, loneliness, pressure, nerves and fame—that I never dreamed of, and perhaps suitably last – heartbreak.

The stadium was huge and empty. I stood on the pitch and looked around me and thought to myself, 'My goodness, is all this really happening to me?'

The dressing rooms were so very impressive – baths, showers, medical room, recreational rooms for the players. There were ground staff, electricians, engineers, office staff, sales staff, physiotherapists, doctors and Harley Street specialists. Unfortunately, over the last few years of my playing career, I would personally keep them busy.

The most surprising impression I got after a few days was what the priority was at Chelsea. It was the players. Everything was structured around the players. It was enormously flattering. I was quickly beginning to realise that by becoming a Chelsea player, what went with it was immediate status. And I was aware already that people were treating me differently and looking up to me in a way I hadn't experienced before and I hadn't even kicked a ball for them yet. My life was surely changing quickly and it was quite confusing to me. My wife, Linda, who obviously knows about my upbringing, jokes with me sometimes and says that for sure at some time in my life I was spoiled and she would be absolutely correct.

Everything was done for us with the idea in mind that in our preparation leading up to games, nothing would be on our minds except our opponents and the game itself. There were never any thoughts about losing. We were to give everything we had to win – everything. This was the highest level in the world. They would take care of our luggage when we travelled. If we were playing overseas, they would take care of our passports. Every time we would travel it was first-class. Every hotel we stayed in was first-class. Before games, we would be on certain pre-game diets and would eat in private dining rooms in every hotel. When we didn't have to have a diet meal, we were allowed to order absolutely anything we wanted in the best restaurants and the best hotels all over the world regardless of cost, the price was never questioned.

The Club treated the players with such respect and caring, over and above our salaries, we were also given 'per diem' money every day to spend when we were on the road. Perhaps you might be imagining life wasn't just changing for me, it was changing dramatically. People would now look at me and treat me differently from other people for the rest of my life.

The Club also had the best tailors in London make every player, every year, made-to-measure suits and blazers with the Chelsea crest on them along with the Chelsea tie and dress shirt. It was Club policy that they would be worn every time and everywhere we travelled, whether it would only be across London or a 20-hour flight to Mozambique in East Africa. I have to admit to you how proud I felt when I wore the Chelsea suit or blazer. I had never been dressed so smartly in my whole life and that part of my wonderfully exciting new life was very easy to accept. But other things were not quite so easy, as I was about to find out.

At East Stirling, I was a part-time footballer and trained only twice a week. I was about to find out that that part of my life was about to change again, drastically. Remember, I had only been at Chelsea for about a week and the Club is about to prepare for the new season which was only six-weeks away and pre-season training was getting ready to start. I had no idea what my status was at this time, but I was told to report with the first team squad to Chelsea's training ground along with eight other players from our reserve team. I had very few social skills at this time because of my background and here I was about to mix with some of the most elite Chelsea footballers who represented one of the most famous clubs in the world. I was driven to our training ground. It was a Monday morning and when we arrived in the car park, several other cars were arriving also. I saw a few guys get out and walk toward the building which housed the players' dressing rooms.

"Who are they?" I asked my driver.

"You will be introduced to them soon," he answered.

"First team players?" I asked.

"Yes, most of them are,"

"But they are so young," I said. "I am 22-years old and they look younger than I am."

"Most of them have come through as apprentices and have been with the

Club since they were 16-years old," he said. "They're the future of Chelsea Football Club and are very highly rated."

"Are they driving their own cars?" I asked.

"Yes, most of them do. I expect you will be buying one too very shortly," he said.

As we were walking towards the dressing rooms where all the players were, I suddenly felt very nervous and asked myself 'Why am I here? Am I good enough to be here?' These players are obviously the best there is or they would not be at Chelsea. I wasn't very much looking forward to entering the building.

I was unsure of myself with people I didn't know. As I entered the room, there must have been at least 20-players there, some of them getting changed into their training kits, a couple of guys on the treatment tables getting medical aid, there was also a lot of laughing and joking amongst them. Most of them looked at me as I walked in but didn't pay me much attention. I didn't know at the time I was the only Scottish player at the Club. Everyone was English except for Graham Moore who was Welsh. I was taken over to a couple of players and introduced to them. Then one of the trainers shouted, "Hey you, guys, listen up, this is Eddie McCreadie our new full-back we signed from East Stirling in Scotland." I know somebody said, "Who?" And another said, "From where?" and everyone in the room howled with laughter. And then the most wonderful thing happened to me. All the players came straight over to me individually and warmly shook my hand. "Good luck, Eddie, Welcome to Chelsea Eddie. Happy you could join us mate," etc.

"Thank you, I'm a bit nervous," I said.

"Did you hear him?" somebody said, "I hope he can play because he can't speak English!" Again, the room erupted in laughter.

I had 'arrived' but still had to prove myself. Nevertheless, I experienced something in that room with the players that I had never felt before. All the kind words of welcome to me from these players were the warmest I have ever known and they all meant it. I was accepted so quickly, it seemed that the fact I was a Chelsea player was enough for them. It became very clear to me that I had joined something very special. There was an undeniable pride amongst them that they were representing Chelsea Football Club.

So far everything was going wonderfully. "Okay, you guys, I want you outside on the track in 10 minutes," shouted Tommy Docherty. When they said 10-minutes, they didn't mean 10-minutes and 10-seconds. If you were late, you were fined. I thought at this time, I was a pretty good athlete and never had any problem training.

Every player had his own special number on every item of his training equipment. I was given number 8 and it was stamped on everything that was mine – towels, bathrobes, boots, shorts, and socks, etc. This was for hygiene purposes so no one else could use your gear. I got out there in plenty of time, not wanting to make any mistakes. Everything was so highly organised and I thought this must be what the army is like. I was very curious to see the other players in action, and I knew for sure they were going to be checking me out also. Everything was new to me. I didn't know what to expect. Again, I felt very nervous. 'Whatever they ask you to do, don't mess up' I told myself. They started us off with warm up stretching on all parts of our bodies and especially our legs.

At East Stirling, we never warmed up and would just kick the ball around. They kept us at this for about 20-minutes. 'Piece of cake,' I thought to myself, 'got that over with. "What's next," I asked the guy next to me, "Do we get to kick a ball around now?" He looked at me and said, "Yeah, maybe in six or seven days if we are lucky." He then told me I'd probably find the games ahead of me easier that what was ahead of me the next three-weeks. Well, I have to tell you that he wasn't lying to me. Without going into too much detail, we went from 10am to 12pm without stopping with some of the hardest and most demanding sprints, short, medium and long-distance running I had ever experienced in my life.

I got through it, but I was absolutely exhausted and turned to someone and said, "Wow! I'm glad that's over!"

"Over?" he said, "We have an hour break with a salad lunch and we have to do the same thing again this afternoon!"

"We train twice a day?" I asked.

"For the next three weeks," he said smiling at me, "welcome to Chelsea, Eddie!"

Most of my new teammates had been through pre-season training before and knew what to expect. I hadn't and it completely drained me. I was exhausted and hurting all over my body. The heels of both my feet were bloody and torn. There was no skin there anymore. I never dreamed it could be this hard. Day after day, this went on and I was beginning to realise that there was an enormous price to be paid to play football at the highest level and to be a Chelsea player.

There were two weeks left before the season would start and having been relegated the season before, Chelsea would face Rotherham away in the Second Division for their first game of the season. We had played some practice matches at the training ground the two previous weeks. Mostly, the first-team against the reserves and I was so excited to be chosen for the reserve team. I was actually playing against the Chelsea first-team players. This was an amazing change for me as, only two months ago, I was playing in the rain for East Stirling in front of 200 people. As I have said, I had no idea what was ahead of me, but I was more than willing to play in the reserve team for a couple of years in the hope that they might give me an opportunity to play in the first-team. I was starting to feel better and stronger than I had ever felt before. All the brutal training was beginning to kick-in. The medical staff had worked on me and had taken care of my heels and they were healing well. We were told to report to Stamford Bridge a week before the game at Rotherham for light training. Both squads were there, the first-team and second-team. I remember we were told to gather behind the goal at the Shed End and to sit on the ground. Tommy Docherty and the Chelsea coaches walked over to us. The squad was so young and it was a new team that Tommy Docherty had decided would have to take us back to the First Division. It was a huge task.

Again, I couldn't believe that here I was sitting on the ground at Stamford Bridge as a Chelsea player and that I was part of a group Tommy Docherty was talking to. "Listen up!" he said, "The team that will travel to Rotherham to kick off our new season will be as follows: Peter Bonetti, Ken Shellito, John Mortimer, Frank Upton, Eddie McCreadie" etc. etc. 'What?' I thought to myself. Did he really just say my name? No sooner had he named the team than everyone was on their feet hugging and congratulating each other and as shocked and surprised as I was, I wasn't celebrating like everyone else. I don't know if you can understand this, but I was instantly experiencing something I had never felt before. I believed I had just become a 'man'. Nobody had had ever put such responsibility and trust on my shoulders and believed I could hold my own at such a high level. It gave me a confidence in myself that I never lost. I was nervous, but I wasn't afraid any more, and whatever was ahead of me now, I was ready for it. My incredible journey and career was about to take off.

When we were on the road, some of our instructions were as follows:
The first team will meet at Stamford Bridge on Friday morning at 9am in your club suits with, of course, collar and tie, Gentlemen. We will proceed by private coach to King's Cross Railway Station where we have private first-class reservations and lunch will be served to you on your journey. Upon your arrival in Rotherham, you will be transported to your hotel where you will be given keys to your rooms. You may order dinner in your rooms if you wish or in the hotel dining room. We do not expect to see any Chelsea players out of their rooms after 9pm. Gentlemen, on Saturday morning you may have cereal and toast for breakfast in your room if you wish. Kick-off against Rotherham will be 3pm, Saturday. We will meet in a

private dining room at 11.30am in the hotel where we will have our pre-match meal. Your only choice, Gentlemen, will be steak accompanied by one side of toast only, or if you wish, boiled chicken. After lunch, we will have a pre-match meeting where we will discuss tactics for the game and, of course, the opposition. You will then return to your rooms, get dressed and gather in the hotel lobby with your luggage as we will be returning to London immediately after the game. Thank you, Gentlemen.

Not wanting to make any mistakes, I made sure I was on time. When I stepped out of the lift in the hotel lobby, everyone was there and what a sight it was to me. The whole team were in their Chelsea blazers. They looked so athletic and tanned and I was one of them. We were Chelsea. I felt proud to be where I was. When I got on the coach, some guys were laughing and joking. A couple of them were reading, some just sitting quietly and looking out the window. Everyone had his own way of dealing with their nerves and the pressure they were feeling. I decided to sit by myself near the window. I wondered what my next emotion might be in my new life. It seemed that I was experiencing something different every couple of hours. We had a 20-minute drive to the stadium and I was surprised how calm I felt considering that in less than two-hours, I would be stepping onto the pitch wearing the colours of Chelsea Football Club for the very first time.

Suddenly, there was an incredible roar of, "Chelsea, Chelsea!" I looked and the bus had slowed down and was surrounded by, it seemed, thousands of people in blue and white scarves and also carrying Chelsea banners, waving to us, blowing us kisses. I smiled and waved back to them and they went crazy jumping up and down. We had arrived at the stadium. I suddenly felt very nervous and my stomach was turning over.

We went straight to our dressing room after pushing our way through the crowds. When I walked in, all our kits, boots had been laid out ready for us. The backroom and medical staff had already been there for two-hours preparing everything for us. I looked and there was my number three shirt hanging up waiting for me. I suddenly felt sick to my stomach and immediately went to the toilet but I couldn't bring anything up so I went back to my place and was just looking at my teammates getting ready. I had no idea what might be ahead of me when I started to think about the game. I also wondered how good our team might be and, more importantly, would I be good enough at this level.

One of our medical staff came over and sat down beside me. "Is there anything I can do for you Eddie?" he asked.

"No, thank you, "I said, "I'm just feeling a little bit nervous but I'm alright, thank you."

"Eddie," he said, "All of us are nervous. It is something you will have to learn to deal with leading up to every game, especially when you are representing Chelsea Football Club."

"Can I ask you something?"

"Of course Eddie, anything," he replied.

"I'm not sure how I am going to perform, but I just wondered about the rest of the guys. They seem so young."

"Eddie, we all know you have a great deal to contend with today, what with it being your debut, but you couldn't be in better company. These young men are the very best of this Club and I can assure you, they know how to take care of themselves."

Those he was referring to included Bobby Tambling, Terry Venables, Barry Bridges, Graham Moore, Frank Blunstone, Frank Upton, Bert Murray, Ken Shellito, Peter Bonetti and John Mortimer. Most of them would become legendary in our Club's history.

"Good luck Eddie!" he said. I started to get changed and began to put on my kit I took my shirt off its hook and pulled it on. Oh my! What a feeling it gave me. I could hardly believe it was me. Again my mind raced back to East Stirling where I'd been a mere ten-weeks ago and here I was about to play for Chelsea.

We were then given our pre-match instructions which lasted about 15-minutes. I listened intently for what I was expected to do. My priority as the left full-back was to mark their right-winger. Their wingers were normally the fastest players, and I was instructed as a priority to 'contain' him as best as I could defensively.

"Are you ready Chelsea?" was the call. "Are you ready to go?" Everyone rose to their feet and began shaking hands and hugging each other. My heart was pounding but I couldn't wait to get out there. There was no doubt in my mind that I was ready. I was representing Chelsea and whatever I had I was going to leave out there.

It was a small ground but it was packed to the rafters. When we walked onto the pitch, the noise was deafening. I learned something afterward that whenever Chelsea visited other teams, people would come out in the thousands just to see us. We were one of the biggest attractions in the country. Both teams lined up and they kicked-off and the game was on. My first ever game for Chelsea had begun. We'd been playing for about 20-minutes and it was so fast, much faster than I thought it would be. And, my Chelsea teammates, as young as they were, were fantastic. They were fast, aggressive, confident, demonstrating skills I'd never seen before. Their passing was amazingly accurate and every pass was hitting its mark. I had never seen football played this way before and we were all over the opposition.

I was personally doing okay I thought. I was pushing forward offensively and was causing their defence some problems. My passes to my team-mates were also finding their target. Everyone was encouraging each other constantly. The team spirit was something I had never experienced before. It was happening – I was in the middle of it. I was playing for Chelsea. The winger I was supposed to mark suddenly decided to take me on. I think he wanted to find out if he could take me for speed. He picked up the ball on the halfway line wide and he was fast. I moved out to him quickly and stayed inside of him and showed him down the line, he hit the ball ahead of me toward our goal and went past me fast. I let him go and let him get about a yard ahead of me. After about 20-yards, I picked up my pace and closed him down where I wanted him and tackled him hard, very hard, taking the ball from him and also making considerable physical contact across his knees and ankles at the same time. I believe everyone in the stadium heard his scream as he went down. A couple of my teammates looked at each other and raised their eyebrows. When he recovered, the winger stayed away from me for the remainder of the game. His game was over. He didn't want any more, but I gave him some more anyway. My three years at East Stirling was paying off early.

Terry Venables, our midfield general, was all over the place, coming to get the ball from our defence at every opportunity, constantly pushing us forward against them with pinpoint passes to our two forwards, Barry Bridges and Bobby Tambling, up front who, incidentally, were giving the Rotherham defence nightmares. I had never seen players like them with such strength and speed. Their defenders couldn't cope with them and eventually Bobby scored the goal that gave us a 1-0 victory for our first win of the season.

It was over. My first game for my new club was over. When I went into our dressing room everyone was going crazy, jumping up and down and congratulating each other. I can't remember ever feeling so wonderful. I had just played for Chelsea and more than held my own I felt. I just sat down. I was exhausted. I took my shirt off and quietly tried to wind down. I surely in all my life had never been so high before and I needed to come down again. And then some of my new teammates were coming over. "Eddie, you did great, you played really well!"

Then Tommy Docherty came over. "Are you alright, son?"

"Yes sir," I said.

"You did good Eddie, you did good!" he said.

"Thank you," I replied.

In 1965, Chelsea beat Leicester City in a two-legged game to win the League Cup Final. I'll tell you one thing for a start, to my knowledge they never got my goal on television. Man, how is my luck? I think I only scored about five goals at Chelsea. The goal I scored against Leicester should have been in the running for goal of the century. I'm joking of course. But c'mon, you must admit it was an unbelievable effort. I ran about 90-yards in heavy going nearly the length of the pitch. When I think of it now, it makes me tired just remembering it.

I remember before the game our manager Tommy Docherty came to me and told me that Barry Bridges our centre-forward was injured and that he was going to play me there in his place. Did I have any problem with that? "No, that's fine," I said. I had played centre-forward for East Stirling several times but this was a considerably different standard. So, I'm getting ready in the dressing room and I start to think about what Leicester players would be marking me. They had two centre-backs and one of them, Graham Cross, I'll never forget! He made Billy Bremner, Norman Hunter and Jackie Charlton look like pussy cats! Man, this guy was rough and tough. He would just run over the top of you. He didn't take any prisoners. Now I'm starting to get a little bit concerned because the conditions were real heavy and pretty muddy. I thought I could beat them for speed, but the heavy conditions would surely slow me down to their pace. Anyway, the game starts and I don't remember if it is the first-half or second-half, but things are okay and I'm doing alright. Although the both of them had tried to nail me a couple of times, but the last time I looked down, my legs were still there.

Anyway, we had just defended a corner and I had come all the way back to just outside our 18-yard box and our goalkeeper Peter Bonetti got the ball in his hands and threw it straight to my feet. I controlled it and turned quickly to face their goal. Now don't forget I'm still about 80-yards from their goal. I went around one of their players pretty fast and now I'm on my way to the halfway line and, like I said, the pitch was really heavy anyway I picked up my pace and left a couple of their players behind me. Now I'm about 15-yards from the halfway line and I look up and you might have guessed it. Here he comes… Graham Cross along with one of his accomplices. I saw their faces and they weren't coming to invite me for a beer after the game. And I thought to myself, 'Oops, this could be painful.' They are just about on me, about 15-yards away and coming fast and I noticed just at the last second that they were both square to each other with about five or six-yards between them leaving a gap. I thought to myself, 'I've got to go for it. If I can pick up my pace I think I can make it between them and get through because there was no one else behind them, except their goalkeeper who was still about 50-yards away.' You know they say when you are dying, your life flashes in front of your eyes? That is probably an exaggeration about my circumstances in these last few seconds, but there was no doubt in my mind that if I didn't make it through there was going to be one almighty pile up and the odds were that I was going to be at the bottom of it. I've got to tell you I kicked my legs into gear and went through between the two of them like the Devil himself was chasing me and, as I was going by them, I could practically feel them trying to kick my legs away from me. Now I was on my way toward their goal with half of their team still chasing me. I got to their 18-yard line with only Gordon Banks, their goalkeeper to beat. (I have to throw this one in as it's great for my ego…) Gordon was rated at this time perhaps as the best goalkeeper in the world. Anyway, he came off his line to narrow the angle, I was absolutely exhausted by the time I had got this far and really didn't have enough energy to have a decent shot at goal. So, as Gordon came out, I just leapt toward the ball and managed to get my toe on it and it slowly trickled over the line behind him. Goal, making the score 3-2 to Chelsea! I've been telling people for years that if Gordon had stayed on his line, he could have thrown his cap on it and prevented it from going in. We played the second-leg at Leicester the following week and drew 0-0. So my goal, I guess, won the League Cup for Chelsea and again sadly, it wasn't even on television.

I think now might be an appropriate time for me to direct some words to my first manager Tommy Docherty. As we moved forward through the years, our relationship became very intense and on several occasions, I made my feelings known to him in no uncertain terms, as he did to me. To say the relationship at times between us was contentious might be an understatement. My next few words are directed to you sir. "Thank you Boss! Thank you for everything you did for me. I never got the chance to tell you that. If it hadn't been for you, I might never have got the opportunity that you alone gave me. It was you who had the courage and confidence to give me my first start. I shall always be grateful to you, sir. It was you also who very forcibly pushed the Scottish Football Association and told them – if I remember correctly – that they must be blind that you had one of the best full-backs in the world playing for you at Chelsea and they still hadn't chosen me to play for my country for the first time. I learned a great deal from you as a coach, and especially how to be a coach. There is no doubt in my mind that part of you was surely with me when I faced the difficult task of trying to save our Club in perhaps its darkest moments, as you yourself did in 1962, my first season as a player. I want to now describe to you, sir, if I may, my accomplishments because of you – 400 games for Chelsea, never having lost my place once. I also went on to represent Scotland 23 times against some of the top countries in the world and to also follow you and become the manager of one of the greatest football clubs in the world, Chelsea Football Club. I shall always be indebted to you. Thank you, Boss."

I must also tell about a very interesting thing that happened to me which I hope you might enjoy. As I have already told you, I saw my boyhood hero Johnny McKenzie outside the Partick stadium after one of his games and I was very shy and was afraid to ask him for his autograph. After several years and after I'd established myself as a Chelsea player and as a Scottish international player, I was invited by the Scottish Sports Writers Association to be their guest at their annual dinner in Scotland. I flew up from London and, at some point during dinner, I left my table to go to the toilet. As I was washing my hands, another gentleman stood at the sink beside me and started washing his hands.

He turned to me. "Eddie… Eddie McCreadie?"

"Yes," I said.

"Eddie, my name is Johnny McKenzie and I am a huge fan of yours and have watched you play for our country many times and I just wanted to say hello. I hope that's okay with you."

My mouth, I think, fell open. I looked at him in astonishment. I couldn't believe my eyes. Yes, it was him. Johnny McKenzie. I recognized him immediately. "Do I mind you talking to me," I said. "I am going to tell you something that you are never going to believe." He looked at me with a certain amount of puzzlement on his face.

"Really, what would that be Eddie?"

"You are my hero. I watched you play when I was a young boy. Playing with Partick Thistle, I thought you were the greatest player I had ever seen and here you are talking to me. I am so proud to meet you. This is wonderful," I told him.

"Are you serious Eddie?" he asked.

"I am absolutely serious!" I told him.

"This might be the best compliment I've ever had Eddie. Thank you," he said.

We talked some more then said a warm goodbye to each other.

There were many memorable matches, but two in particular perhaps stand out. In 1967, I was picked for Scotland to play against England at Wembley. There were 100,000 people there and, if I remember, correctly, the press had told us that nearly 30,000 Scots had travelled down from north of the border to cheer on their country and support our flag. It was 1967 and just after England had won the World Cup by beating West Germany 4-2 which was a great and historic achievement and so very well deserved I thought. They had many very talented players and were coached by Sir Alf Ramsay. Their victory was huge and not something my own country could have achieved but, because of our respective history, the Scotland players didn't need much motivation to play against England and I believe the English team would rather play West Germany twice than face Scotland.

Our incentive to play against England might be described as being somewhat similar to Mel Gibson's enthusiasm in the film 'Braveheart.' So having the opportunity to play against England in their own backyard and perhaps having the chance to beat them when they were World Champions was a unique opportunity we weren't about to pass up. I've already mentioned how nervous I was when I made my Chelsea debut and that never changed from my first game to my last and, when I was getting ready for the game against England. I was extremely nervous. Representing my country against England was huge. When you're representing wearing your country's colours, making a mistake is unthinkable – letting Chelsea down would be bad enough but can you imagine letting your country down?

We faced England that day and were fortunate in that we beat them 3-2. I shall never forget the individual performances of every one of my countrymen that day. The energy and will they displayed was amazing and it was a truly outstanding victory for us, and it was still only four seasons since I had walked off the East Stirling pitch in the rain.

Before I move on to my second most memorable game, let me tell you about one other game I played for my country. I was selected to play for Scotland against Italy in Naples in a World Cup qualifying game which was, perhaps, one of the most important games in my country's history. If we could just get a draw against them, Scotland would go through to the World Cup finals for the first time in their history. We were told our whole country was listening to it on the radio. Ten-minutes from half-time we were doing well and were drawing 0-0. The Italian left-winger crossed a very hard low ball to our far post where I was marking their right-winger. We were both ten-yards from our goal line and I was the last defender. I moved forward to try and clear it. I misjudged the flight of the ball and it went under my foot and straight to their right-winger. He immediately controlled it and kicked it into the goal to make the score Italy 1-0 Scotland. It stayed that way to the end of the game. We were out!! I played the rest of the game with my head up and played harder than I think I have ever done in my life, but if it were at all possible I thought my heart would surely break. I had let my country down and all of my fellow countrymen. In the dressing room after the game, two or three of my teammates came over to where I was sitting still wearing my country's shirt. "Eddie, it's over. Try not to think about it. It could have happened to any one of us." I nodded to them, but there were no words that could console me. I felt totally humiliated and ashamed of myself.

I guess the second most memorable game that perhaps stands out to me is the FA Cup Final replay at Old Trafford against Leeds United in 1970. We had drawn with them at Wembley and had to play them again the following week. It was over 40-years ago but not a game I will ever easily forget. Leeds were, perhaps, one of the best club teams in Europe at that time and we had played against them a dozen times in the previous seasons, but they also had other abilities that were not in any football book I had ever read.

Being a Christian, I am not about to judge anyone but it is my hope that God might understand and smile perhaps when He hears my description of the Leeds team and forgives me when I try to describe them to you. Do you remember the advice my father gave me as to 'certain players' I would encounter if I moved to English football? Leeds United, and they knew it and wanted every other team to know it too, that they were the hardest, toughest, meanest, dirtiest team in the league and they used that reputation to intimidate every team in the league. And, it worked except for one team. Yes, Chelsea. We were also intimidated but not at any time were we prepared to give in to them.

Let me explain something about my own physical approach to my opponents before I describe Leeds tactics to you. Perhaps you will forgive me if I talk about myself in these terms, but there was a difference between them and me. When I tackled opposing players was I trying to physically hurt and intimidate them? Yes. Would I continue doing that to them until they were very scared for their own safety? Yes. Did I enjoy it? Yes. I was not afraid whatsoever of hurting myself when I challenged other players physically. Every opponent I played against knew all of the above about me. I believe it took away most of their ambitions before the game even started. As far as I was concerned, football was a physical game and I intended to play it that way. I was playing against the best wingers in the world most of the time and I wasn't about to let them get the upper-hand against me.

Leeds had at least seven players out of their 11 who would 'go over the top of the ball' forcing their boots into their opponents' legs. That was the description of this type of 'tackle'. If successful, the player on the receiving end would run the risk of having his leg broken anywhere from the ankle up to the shin or, if performed higher, the knee. If it didn't break your leg, it could severely injure you and tear you up good. As prepared as I was physically when I joined Chelsea, I still had some lessons to learn but I learned quickly.

My first lesson was in my first season. We were playing Middlesbrough away from home. "Listen, Eddie, when you get out there, be careful," I was told, "They have some players in their team who will kick anything that moves, and they have one guy in particular and his name is Ray Yeoman – he's a veteran and he will 'go over the top'." I think it may have been Tommy Docherty, who was no angel himself when he played, who told me that. It was about 20-minutes into the game against Middlesbrough and there was a 50-50 challenge between Yeoman and myself. It is in the middle of both of us, we are each about 10-yards from the ball and, for sure, there was going to be some physical contact between us. I thought to myself, 'Okay, let's see how tough this guy really is.' I was ready and went in with everything I had. The next thing I remember I was going down hard and then slowly trying to get myself up on one knee and in considerable pain. And I mean in 'considerable pain' and holding my right leg. He was on his feet looking down at me smirking. When I got to the dressing room at half-time, there was blood running through my sock and when they gently rolled my sock down, there were three holes in my shin-pads from his studs. When the pads were removed, there were three holes in my shin and, just to top this story off, Tommy Docherty walked over to me, looked at my leg, and said, "Maybe, now you'll learn something," and walked away.

I learned quickly after that and, together with one of my teammates in defence – Chopper Harris who didn't get his nickname for nothing – I was earning a reputation as a player who didn't take any prisoners. So any time we would play Leeds, it was a war. They would kick our forwards viciously and would go over the top with them every chance they got. Our two centre forwards at this time were my friends, Peter Osgood and Ian Hutchinson. Both were six-feet tall and brave and would never give in to them.

The story goes that Ossie was asked how bad it was to be kicked by the Leeds defenders. His answer, I believe, was that it wasn't any fun, but at least he could look back at our own defence now and again and get some pleasure watching Eddie and Chopper putting some serious pain on the Leeds forwards. He was also supposed to have said, "I think I'd rather be kicked by the Leeds defenders, than those two."

Before I get to that Cup Final replay, there was one match against Leeds at Stamford Bridge I remember. They had two midfield players, Billy Bremner and Johnny Giles. They were both great players but, were famous for going over the top of the ball. I never respected anyone who would go over the top. I thought it was a cheap-shot and cheating. They had both on several occasions gone over the top with several of my teammates and I hadn't forgotten. This game at Stamford Bridge had been going about half-an-hour

107

and Giles came at me with the ball at his feet attempting to take me on. I showed him inside and he surprisingly took it. I closed him down quickly to where again I wanted him and came across his knees and ankles with more than a 'tickle'. He would not be playing any more in this game. They took him off on a stretcher with badly torn knee ligaments which kept him out I heard for three-months. I just gave him a small taste of what he had been dishing out to everyone else.

The replay against Leeds at 'Old Trafford' was huge. After drawing 2-2 at Wembley, we faced each other again – another 'war' to decide who would win the FA Cup. I also managed in this game to give Giles accomplice, Billy Bremner, a pretty dangerous tackle to the head with six studs which can be seen on YouTube. It was a cracker I promise you. I actually thought at first I might have killed him. But Bremner, being a Scotsman, also got up again after a few minutes. Like I've said many times before, we Scotsmen are as tough as nails, not only that, but we also eat haggis.

Personally, I didn't need another game or any replay. I had been diagnosed two weeks before the first game with a hernia. I was in considerable pain with it. Dave Sexton, the manager and his medical staff asked me if I thought I could play one more game. I told them that if I didn't have to do any training leading up to the game, I was willing to have a go at it. And being the hero as you can tell I am making myself out to be (I'm joking; I'm joking) I played the game and got through but it was really quite difficult for me. We played the game and I guess it was in the second-half and I believe it was 1-1. It was a hard fought game with neither team giving much away. One of the greatest strengths Leeds had was their strength of staying together and never giving up and would always give everything to the final whistle. I personally was beginning to tire when we got to the second-half and had definitely lost about a yard in speed and was beginning to experience some discomfort again. I remember Ossie scoring a great headed goal off a pass from Charlie Cooke. The Chelsea supporters went crazy. All the players were jumping all over Ossie. I don't think I moved from wherever I was when he scored. I really didn't have very much left. We then went 2-1 up with about 15-minutes to go to the final whistle. I thought we must make it now. We have to. It was then that I noticed something about Leeds that I had never ever seen before. It had been an exhausting game for both teams, but I noticed two or three of their players were dropping their heads. I saw it for the first time ever. They were giving up. We had worn them down and were beating them in every aspect of the game. My Chelsea team-mates were magnificent that day. I found a bit more myself and started to push every one forward verbally as Chopper was doing also. We had them on the run. The referee blew the final whistle. We had won the FA Cup. What a great feeling it was for all of us. We had run Leeds into the ground and they knew it.

On our arrival back in London, two things happened. First, there were thousands and thousands of supporters welcoming us back to London. People were lining the streets as we slowly passed by on our open-top double-decker bus. Secondly, I was immediately taken to hospital where the following day, they successfully operated on me for my hernia. I told you I was a hero.

In 1975, I was appointed manager of Chelsea but, first of all, I should tell you I was already a qualified coach. I took the course at Lilleshall with Terry Venables and we were the only two players to pass with 'distinction'. But I have to tell you that if you are going to be a successful manager, there is far more needed to accomplish that. Half-a-dozen different degrees wouldn't have been enough to help me with the problems I had to face at Chelsea at this dreadful time. It would be difficult for me to explain to you what I had to face and contend with when I took over as manager of Chelsea in without question the darkest time in their history. After I stopped playing because of my many injuries, Dave Sexton appointed me as coach of our reserve team. After Dave left, Ron Suart took over and I had Dario Gradi as first-team coach. I had taken our reserve-team to the top of their league, and I Ron asked me to move up to the first team with him, and put Dario back in charge of the reserves. I accepted the position as Ron was having a tough time and the team was in deep danger of relegation. I was now in charge of all coaching with the first-team, but I was not given any input whatsoever in team selection, which became very frustrating for me. Ron Suart was a gentleman and a fine man and I liked him a lot and respected him, but Chelsea were dying in front of our eyes and relegation looked certain and we continued to keep playing players that I felt were not going to help us. I told him we needed to talk and we did. I told him it looked as we were going down to the Second Division and we immediately must start bringing more of the younger players in gradually and start building for the future if indeed there was going to be one.

I think he was personally at the end of his time and really couldn't cope anymore with our terrible situation and the pressure of it, he didn't disagree with me about anything. In fact, he thought my vision about the young players was correct. Let's just say we both agreed he should step down and decided we should go to the board where he wanted to personally recommend to the directors that he felt it would be in the best interest of Chelsea that I should replace him as manager immediately and explained to them why. The Board immediately appointed me as manager. They were in a desperate situation at this time. The Club was bankrupt and couldn't even pay their bills. Most of the supporters blamed the directors for putting us in this dismal situation. I was told that there was absolutely no chance of my buying any new players to strengthen the squad and would have to make the best of what I had and if possible could I see my way clear to sell some of our players to other teams. The money was needed to pay our debts and salaries. The situation at the Club was dreadful. It was so bad the directors had to bring in a controller, Martin Spencer, and they were told by him, I believe, that under any circumstances they would not be allowed to sign even a cheque for £20 pounds without Mr. Spencer's approval and signature.

This was a great come down for our directors who had always called all the shots at the Club. They were used to making all the important decisions. The board consisted of our Chairman who was Brian Mears, Viscount Chelsea, Sir Richard Attenborough, George Thomson and Leslie Mears. As I said, most people held them responsible for the Club's situation.

So there it was. We played the last few games unsuccessfully and we went down. We were relegated. As I have stated before, the atmosphere at the Club was depressing. We had no team that even our Chelsea could get behind. We were relegated, we were bankrupt, we couldn't pay our bills, we were millions in debt. I was asked by the board if I would personally talk to every Chelsea player and ask them to take a cut in their wages, which I did. We were also a losing team. The outlook was grim and depressing and everyone knew that Chelsea, as big as the Club was, could not survive financially in the Second Division. I was once asked by my 'friend', well known Chelsea journalist Neil Barnett (don't let that statement go to your head, Barnett! You're still a sassanach and an Englishman), "What did you think would have happened to Chelsea had you not been successful?" I thought for a moment then answered, "I have no idea."

What was I thinking at this time? I looked around to see where I might get some help but there was none. The Board was non-existent and absolutely dependent on what I could do for the Club. For sure, this was the most desperate time in Chelsea's history to date.

Getting relegated was a terrible feeling. But if that was to be our fate and it was, I personally had to get over that in a hurry. I have already explained the Club was dying. We had nothing. The atmosphere was dreadful. Nobody really knew where the Club was going. If Chelsea Football Club was going to have a future, then I had better get going, and quick. The decisions ahead of me were many. I was torn between two immediate things which I believed had to be my first priorities.

My first priority had to be the team if we were to survive. It was absolutely essential that I build a winning team. One that would take us back to the First Division in as little time as possible.

The second priority was even at the risk of perhaps selling the wrong players which I might need to take us back to the First Division. I had to sell players in order to keep the Club running. So, I decided to take a long hard look at my playing staff, individually and choose the players that I believed would take us back to the First Division. As I have already stated I had spent a couple of months with the reserve-team and that had given me the opportunity to assess the younger players at our Club.

I continually questioned myself, would my judgments be correct as to which players might be my strongest squad. I had to get this right. Our whole future depended on it. It was my intention to build a "new" team using most of my young players coupled with several of my senior experienced players, but which ones? I couldn't keep them all and this was very difficult for me. I was still only 35-years old and all the experience players I had at the Club were my friends. Some of them had been at the Club as long as I had. None of them wanted to leave Chelsea.

But, unfortunately, I had made my list of the players I had decided I would have to let go. I had made my choices and transferred many of them to other teams which brought in monies which was essential to keep our Club afloat.

At this time I want to make something very clear to all. I brought every one of these players into my office individually and told them directly to their face that I was letting them go. And they would have to leave Chelsea. And you can take my word for it, it was without a doubt one of the most difficult things I have ever had to do. They loved Chelsea just as much as I did. They were my friends and I had to tell them words to the effect that their time at Chelsea was over, and that I was moving on without them. As difficult as that was for me, let me again be very clear, if I had to do the same thing again, the next day and the day after that, which I had to, I would do it again and again. I know that sounds hard and cold and as much as I felt their pain and I did, I knew also that if Chelsea were to survive, this enormous responsibility was mine and mine alone. No one was more important than our Club, not even me and if it were at all possible I was not going to fail and everyone else and everything else would be second in my priorities. Chelsea, our fallen Club would be first from now on in all of my decisions. Its welfare and future became my first priority.

Before our first season began, I had my first press conference. As usual the press did not pull any punches. "This is serious, Eddie, the Club is in big trouble. They have no money. You can't buy any new players. You can't pay your bills. You haven't been a manager before. How do you intend to cope with this? The team has been relegated to the Second Division and you know as well as we do, a Club as big as Chelsea can't survive there financially. How long do you think it is going to take you, if it can possibly be done, to take them back to the First Division?"

"I will return the Club to the First Division in two seasons," I said. "I will need the first season to prepare and evaluate my squad and to find our strengths and weaknesses and I will take us back the following season." They all looked at me as though I were crazy. And I left the conference.

If you are all asking yourselves, did I believe this? I did. I did believe it but most importantly I needed to say it even though I was aware I was bringing considerable pressure on myself. I needed to be bold and confident. The Club was dying. I could tell that the directors and Chairman Brian Mears hadn't very much hope anymore. I could tell by their faces. The people who worked at the stadium, secretaries, ground staff, the ladies who did all the laundry, engineers, medical staff – there was nobody smiling any more at Stamford Bridge. Although my priority was to build a new team and take us back to the First Division and, as if that wasn't enough, I also believed I had to stimulate people at Chelsea and get them to believe in the Club and the team again. There was no time to be negative any more and I was not going to allow it anywhere at the Club. I was determined to move Chelsea forward at any cost. To say I never contemplated failure would be lying to you. It was constantly with me. But, I had an enormous drive inside me, I loved our Club and I kept telling myself, you can do this. You can do it, as you can probably imagine we had an enormous task ahead of us. We had our pre-season training prior to our 'first' season and I truly felt good about my playing squad. I knew what my senior players were capable of and what I felt was a great advantage for us was the wonderful attitude of my young players who varied in ages from 17 to 18, 19 and 20-years old, most of them had played together before in our apprentice system or our reserve team. They were all, it seemed, good friends and I felt they brought with them the team attitude and atmosphere I wanted and was looking for. They were what our Club needed at this time. They were young and exciting and they laughed with each other a lot and they seemed to be getting on fairly well with my senior players, who I can assure you gave them a considerable ribbing at time. But, more importantly, they were highly professional and highly talented young men.

Regarding my own attitude at his time, I tried not to be too serious and tried to keep our atmosphere light and relaxed and have some fun, especially around my players. It was important to me that they were loose and not thinking too much about the pressure that was surely over them, and perhaps through them and their future performances they would eventually lift up the spirits of everyone connected to the Club. These young players were on the threshold and starting line and about to take on the awesome responsibility of saving this great but fallen Club at the most tragic and devastating time in its proud history. We were now getting close to our first season starting and I had two very important decisions to make: one, who would be the team captain, and two, what playing system I was going to use.

Strangely enough, Ray 'Butch' Wilkins at 18-years old was to be equally involved in both my decisions. Let's take the captain's position first. Whoever was going to be my choice for captain had to be someone who I felt was going to be a regular in the team. One who was going to play every game. At this time, I couldn't honestly tell you who was going to be a regular on the team. Just about everyone was on trial. There was nothing more important to me than these two decisions, if indeed, we were going to save our Club. It was going to be on the field, as I have told you. I was a qualified coach, but that in itself would not possibly allow me to accomplish what we did. My next task before I get back to the choice of captain and system, was to evaluate and appraise everyone on my playing staff and determine if I thought they were going to be good enough to achieve what I believed was ahead of us. My statement when I said I would bring the Club back in two seasons. If that sounded outrageous to most people, and I know it did, it didn't to me. When I looked at my squad, the experienced and the inexperienced players, I liked what I saw, untested I know, but I felt excited about them. Now you might ask yourselves, how could he possibly evaluate all these players and especially the young players and get it right as to their strengths and weaknesses with just a coaching degree? That would be a good question. Let me answer it in this way if you would allow me.

I was blessed and fortunate to have played with some of the greatest players in our Club's history including Terry Venables, Peter Osgood, Bobby Tambling, Alan Hudson, Peter Bonetti, Frank Blunstone to name just a few. I hope my former colleagues will forgive me if I haven't mentioned them also. I also had the privilege and honour of representing Scotland 23 times against the players of some of the best and strongest countries in the world and also had the opportunity to study their many playing systems. Other players I played against? Bobby Moore, Geoff Hurst, Bobby Charlton, Denis Law, George Best, Pele were just a few of the big 'names'. Although I was a 'rookie' manager, I had a considerable amount of knowledge which up to now had never been asked for.

You may be interested after I have mentioned all the legends named above, who I thought was the best I ever played against. Pele was a handful for sure, but not my choice. I played against him at least a dozen times, his name was George Best. He from Northern Ireland and I thought he was the greatest player I had ever seen and had played against. And If some of you disagree, I couldn't care less because I was the one who was always delegated to mark him, not you.

I enjoyed immensely the many duels we had against each other and I always had got the distinct impression I was far from being his favourite opponent. Perhaps because he knew I was going to unload all the physical abilities I had on him. But I have to tell you, he was tough and would come back for more. I not only admired him, but I respected him, too. We had never met socially off the field. Perhaps you will allow me to tell you a very interesting story which I hope you might enjoy. Not long after I resigned from my position at Chelsea, I accepted the position of head coach for the Memphis Rogues of the then new North American Soccer League in Memphis, Tennessee. Our season was just starting in Memphis and Fort Lauderdale was one of our first games at the Liberty Bowl Stadium.

Perhaps you might remember George Best had just signed for them. It was the morning of our game which was to start at 7.00pm, I was in my office and the phone rang. I picked it up and my secretary said, "Coach, there is a gentleman in my office who is asking if he could see you."
I said, "Really? What did he say his name was."
"Hold on, Coach and I'll ask him... Coach, he said his name is George Best."
"George Best? Are you sure?" I said.
"Yes sir, that's what he said."
"Send him in," I told her.

George was the 'fifth Beatle'. He had film star looks and the ladies were lining up for him. He was constantly in the press and couldn't go anywhere without being recognized. Muttering "George Best" to myself, I got up from my desk and walked towards my door when it suddenly opened and, low and behold, the man himself walked in with a wonderful smile on his face.

"Hello, Eddie," he said. I couldn't believe it and I immediately moved forward to grasp and shake his outstretched hand. "George, how are you?" I asked. "How wonderful to see you! I must admit to you I am totally shocked you are perhaps the very last man in the world I thought would come and see me."

"Now why would you think that?" he said sarcastically but with a smile on his face. We both laughed. "To tell you the absolute honest truth, Eddie, I hated your guts. I knew every time I had to play against you that you were going to kick me black and blue."

I laughed a little and said to him, "George, I really am very sorry. It certainly wasn't personal. You were just so great, and I had to slow you down the best way I could. You have absolutely blown me away what a wonderful gesture you have made in coming to see me. I have to tell you George, it is one of the nicest things that's ever happened to me. Thank you."

We sat down and we laughed and talked about several things. He was one of the nicest guys I think I had ever met and I was amazed how much we seemed to like each other. "Listen, George, when are you flying back to Ft. Lauderdale?" I asked.

"We were going to fly back straight after the game, Eddie, but they changed it and now we are flying back in the morning, why do you ask?"

"That's great George, I wonder if you would do me a favour?"

"Sure, Eddie."

"After the game tonight our players always go over to a bar where they meet our fans and sign autographs for them. I know all my players and especially my American players would love to meet you and I wondered if you might stop by briefly and say hello to them?"

"Absolutely Eddie, I would be happy to do it." We talked more for a while and then he got up to leave and warmly shook my hand. "I am really glad I came to see you Eddie!"

"I am too, George. Thanks once again."

He came over after the game as he promised. I watched him and how he was handling himself with my players. He had a drink with them and talked to nearly everyone I think. They were so impressed with him and he signed everything that was put in front of him. I was very impressed with him and liked him a lot.

My players were thrilled they never imagined they would get the opportunity to sit down and talk with the best footballer in the world.

We said a very warm goodbye to each other and I left and as I was driving home, I had the strangest thought. We had had this bitter physical war against each other for ten-years and had never met and I was thinking how much I liked him and really felt that had we both been able to spend time with each other, not only would we have become friends, but I believe we would have become close friends. I feel very sad at this moment as I am writing this and there are tears in my eyes, I don't mind telling you. We had both ended up on a similar path in our lives. We both became alcoholics. I was more fortunate than my new friend. I found my faith and became a Christian and because of our Lord Jesus and my new found faith in Him, I was able to find the strength I needed to stop many years afterward. I read that George didn't make it. After several attempts to save his life, I heard he was told by his London physicians that he must stop drinking immediately. He couldn't. He didn't. I was told he died.

Writing my part in this book has become more difficult than I imagined. Regarding my choice for skipper; I had a ready made captain on my playing staff at this time. Ron Chopper Harris, who I personally felt did an outstanding job for our Club during some of our wonderful successes in the past and have no doubt if I had called on him, he would have stepped forward for me. But this was another time. He had served this Club honourably it was a time for our young players and it was my intention to build the team and our system around Butch Wilkins and although he was only 18-years old I sensed and believed strongly that he had exceptional abilities, not only as a player but I firmly believed also that he had leadership qualities and if given some encouragement they would grow.

Regarding my decision to make Butch captain, I knew everyone would probably think I had already lost it and was beginning to show some measure of the pressure I was perhaps under, and these people would probably be the press, the Chelsea Board, the supporters and, of course, my senior players. But with respect to the others, my senior players especially were my main focus. I believed very strongly that given time, Butch would very quickly and naturally take over the role as leader on the field. But I also realized that at the beginning this might prove difficult for him, perhaps for instance giving orders to my senior players on the field. So what I did was to call Butch and Micky Droy into my office. Micky was a huge gentleman and one of our centre-backs. He was six-foot four and not someone you wanted to be tackled by. Up until now he hadn't been given any responsibility at the Club and I had a situation and if I could solve it quickly, it would allow me to concentrate on the many other things I had to deal with.

The situation I am referring to was that more than anything, let me repeat that more than anything, I had to have the best possible relationship between my senior players and my young players. I knew as I have already told you, that if we were to have a chance of saving our Club, it was going to be on the field. It was my focus and my priority and I needed it to be theirs. We had to be 'one' not two different camps. If we were indeed to go on the field with less, we would fail.

"Hi Micky, Hi Butch, please sit down," (I can't remember the exact conversation as it was many ago so Michael and Butch please forgive me if it is not as accurate as perhaps it should be.) "Micky, as you already know I have appointed Butch as the team captain of this Club. That means when he is on field, he has my full confidence and the authority to change things quickly if he thinks it is necessary. But under normal circumstances, he will check with me first before he makes any decision. Micky, I am going to appoint you as Club Captain. I want you to be our go-between all the players and me. If any of my players wish to see me privately, I will take care of that myself, but if any of our players have a problem or a team problem and you think that it is important enough that I should deal with it, I want you to tell me." Basically what I was doing here with Micky was giving all my players a voice. We had always had a team captain at Chelsea, but never a Club captain.

It was important for me at this time that my players were happy and if they had a problem whether it was an individual one or a team problem at least now they would know they could take it straight to Micky. If any of you are wondering why I chose Micky Droy to be our first Club captain, I will tell you. It was quite simple, I didn't know Micky terribly well, but I liked him and the fact that I appointed him Club captain for Chelsea Football Club should also tell you that I trusted him. The important thing for me though, was that I knew that if he had something he had to tell me, he wasn't going to pull any punches and he was just what I needed at that time. There was plenty of traffic coming through my office door and it was mostly problems. Sometimes having to face five or six every day it seemed, but I was very conscious of the fact that there were very few players beating down my door. I could only assume that my appointment of Micky Droy was working. The atmosphere at the Club was getting better especially among my players and I felt Micky's presence at that time was a considerable help to me.

In addition to my conversation with Butch and Micky, I believe I also told

Butch that if he had a problem on the field and he wasn't sure how to handle it, then he could discuss it with Micky and between the both of them I felt sure they would work it out.

Because of my own playing career, I had a front row seat watching the best players in the world and also taking note of each of their country's playing systems. Every team needs a playmaker, someone who is able consistently to get your offense started and this player is normally a midfield player as you know and when I studied Butch he obviously fitted the bill for that position. I was especially impressed with his vision and his passing abilities, short and long, and his composure on the ball. He also had an ability to test the opposing goalkeeper with shots at goal from pretty far out. In short, I thought he was a very gifted young man and felt very strongly that I could build my system around him and for sure someone who could consistently get the attack going with a wide variety of passing abilities. But when I thought about the teams in the Second Division that we were about to face, they were tough and tackled very hard, especially in their midfield. Butch had a great deal of ability but I felt there was one thing he lacked. I thought he was very competitive when the opposition had the ball and would try to win it back, but he wasn't going to win many tackles for me in midfield nor did I want him to. I felt there must be a better way for me to use him and take full advantage of his exceptional skills. I thought long and hard about it. But I couldn't quite get it worked out in my mind it was taking me some time. I knew I wanted to get him away from midfield, away from the physical part of the game if possible. I also knew I wanted to push him forward where I felt he might be a considerable threat to the opposing defences with his obvious abilities and still be in a position to dominate, but where? I wanted also at the same time if possible, to create some problems for opposing defences and perhaps give us some type of advantage where it might be confusing for them as to who was going to pick him up. After some time, it came to me. I decided to play two centre-forwards who would obviously be picked up by their two central defenders and I placed Butch just in front of these two centre-forwards and behind 'their' midfield, where

I tried to 'hide' him. This not only gave us an advantage where Butch was nearer their goal, but it would also give the opposition a considerable problem as to indeed who was going to pick him up.

The choices I was giving the opposition were these. I knew they couldn't leave him unmarked. If they did, that would certainly be to our advantage. So their choices as I saw it were these: they would have to bring in one of their full-backs to pick him up, which would leave them very open down one side and give us a considerable advantage to exploit the space where the defender would normally be. The only other alternative I thought they had and I was leaving for them was to drop back their central-midfield player to pick up Butch which if they had done might probably have given us a three to two midfield advantage. Either way, I felt that his presence there would cause some considerable problems for our opposition. And it did. I also believed that with Butch being in that position that if one of my centre-forwards would make a diagonal run and pull one of their centre-backs out wide, it would leave a considerable "hole" there in the middle of their defence which would give him an opportunity to get behind them and put him in shooting range of the goal very quickly. It worked exceptionally well for us and I could see that opposing coaches were having several problems trying to figure it out?

Nevertheless, I still wasn't fully satisfied with it. There was more to the system I felt. For one thing, I was losing width and the fact that I had decided to play two centre-forwards meant I needed to get them service into the opposition's defence with crosses. Relying on my overlapping full-backs was not going to be anywhere near acceptable to me. I will elaborate further on this problem later for you and how we solved it.

I am not going to dwell too much on our first season except to tell you how very important it was to me personally and obviously for my players also. It now gave them a measure of knowledge of what was going to be ahead of them going into our second and most important season. It was the season I needed personally to evaluate everything and everyone and what we quickly discovered was that it certainly wasn't going to be any easy task. It was imperative for me in particular. I had no knowledge of other team's players or their systems in the Second Division and if I was to ask and demand everything from my players, it was extremely important that I provide them with the absolute best possible knowledge of every team we would meet game by game if indeed I expected them to succeed and I believe I did that. We set up a scouting system which I truly felt was invaluable to us. Ron Suart had suggested to me before our first season started that he knew someone who could cover every team we had to face every week and provide me with knowledge I certainly needed. He said his name was Eddie Bailey, who he said had been associated with West Ham United for a number of years. I told Ron to get him aboard immediately and send him a copy of our fixture list and to send him to the game of our next opponent and to explain to you how we did that. If, for instance, Wolves were on the road playing and we had to play them the following week or even the week after at Stamford Bridge, he would scout them to watch their tactics when they were playing away from home and that would give me a pretty good idea of how they played and what system they used or again, if they were playing at home he would watch them there, where again, their tactics and system might be different.

I would get Eddie Bailey's report every Monday morning and it was very detailed. It would explain to me the system they played and where their players would be if they had a corner against the opposition for example or indeed where their players would set up when defending a corner or free kicks for and against. He would make comments to me for example that their right winger was very fast and would most certainly be testing my left full-back. All in all, there might be 20 to 25 different observations and details he would explain in his report.

I would sit in my office for hours and study his notes for several days until I felt I knew their tactics as well as I knew my own in order to give my players the very best information I possibly could.

Before every game in our own dressing room, I would meet with our players. Every member of our team knew exactly where they were supposed to be if we were defending a corner or a free kick, or if we had a corner for us in just about every set play that would occur in the game. They knew pretty much where I wanted them to be. I would also use our blackboard and put the opposing team up there, their formation their names and shirt numbers. I would instruct my players individually who I wanted them to pick up at corners and free kicks, etc and, during the game, exactly which opposing player I wanted them individually to mark. I would also discuss with them where I thought we might be able to get some success against them. Generally speaking also what I thought their strength and weaknesses might be so overall we were pretty well organized ourselves.

I made the statement that I would take our Club back to the First Division in two seasons and that I would need the first season to prepare for that. As you know we finished that very important season in the middle of the table. Was I disappointed? Absolutely not! In fact, if someone had offered me the middle of the table before the season started I would have taken it gladly. Let me explain that to you if I may. I had to be realistic there was no chance we were going to go up in the first season. We had a lot of players but we didn't have a settled team. I had to build a completely new team. Let me say it again. I had to build a new team. The first season I was about to face was in many ways just as important to me as the second season where I said I was going to take us back to the First Division. I want all of you to keep this in mind. What I couldn't afford to have in our first season was a bad season. That would have destroyed all of my players' confidence in themselves and they wouldn't have been in any position to achieve what was so importantly ahead of them in our second season. I needed to steady the ship in this first season, and also at the same time select and build a new team. How was I supposed to do that? I knew in my heart that the majority of the team I was going to build would consist of my young players, but there was something troubling me. If I were to put too many young players in too quickly then I would be running the risk of them being perhaps defeated badly in a couple of games. Maybe even losing 5-0 or even 6-0, which I really felt like I said might ruin their confidence in each other. It was too much of a risk I decided. There was so much I had to learn about my players in this first season after giving it a great deal of thought I decided the team had to consist early with the majority of my senior players plus three or four of my young players and that is exactly what I did and if I felt we were holding a steady course and not getting blown away, I would in the last 10 or 15 games throw in four or five more of my younger players where I could evaluate them. Whatever young players I would choose, I knew one thing – I was convinced that their enthusiasm, their pace and their individual abilities were going to cause considerable problems for all of the teams in the Second Division.

At the end of our first season, I felt I had all the knowledge I needed to prepare and select what I believed was the team and squad to take us back to the First Division. Some of the things I found in that very important season for us, you might be interested in hearing, before I make any comments as to some of the things I knew we had to improve on if indeed we were to be successful. Let me say this, every Chelsea player that played in the first season gave 110% for our Club. I never had to say one word to any of my players regarding their effort. It was already there from all of them. They delighted me when I saw how professional they were and how much they were willing to give for their Club.

I felt very happy with our goalkeeping situation. I thought that Peter Bonetti and John Phillips were more than up to the task of what I might require from them. I also felt confident in the quality of our full backs, Gary Locke, Graham Wilkins and John Sparrow. We were very strong at centre-back I felt with Micky Droy, Stevie Wicks, David Hay and Ron Harris. So, in general, I felt good with my defence. In midfield, everybody was working their tails off, but we weren't winning enough tackles and that was a problem for me. I felt, nevertheless, the players I played there were hugely talented and never ever let us down. Garry Stanley, Ian Britton, Charlie Cooke and Ray Lewington who I brought into the team late in our first season if I remember correctly.

I had no problem with what I saw with Butch Wilkins in our new system. It was definitely causing problems for the opposition and considering how new it was to him I felt he did an excellent job and would only get better. But up front, I was having some problems at centre-forward with my two strikers. I used several players there and I just felt we were not scoring enough goals. I had used Ian Hutchinson, Bill Garner, Kenny Swain, Teddy Maybank, Jock Finnieston, and Tommy Langley and just couldn't find what I wanted because we weren't scoring the goals I felt we needed. I think I played too many centre-forwards in trying to find the solution. On reflection, I believe I should have stuck with two of them and given them an extensive run and that in effect is what I would eventually do and it worked.

Concerning Butch again, the system was working well, but was lacking width and I needed to set him up with more passing options. But we solved that too. Ian Britton and Garry Stanley, our two outside midfield players, must have been the two most hard working wide midfield players in the history of football. Not only had they to get back defensively and win balls in midfield, but when we got the ball they also had to play like wingers to give us the width I needed for Butch and also supplied us with crosses into the box for our strikers. The other two players who made up our squad were Brian Bason and Clive Walker, both wingers. So I really felt we accomplished many things in that first season. In the last eight to ten games, I had five or six of my young players in the team, and I made a positive move by playing Kenny Swain and Jock as my two strikers who not only scored goals for us, but gave us more movement up front with more diagonal runs, which would give Butch more passing options. If I remember correctly, we scored around 20 more goals in our second season than we had in our first. I also solved my midfield problem. I found the young man I was looking for. Someone to compete physically with the opposition there, someone who I believed would stop the flow of their midfield players from getting through easily and questioning my back four. He didn't have the skills of Butch Wilkins, but he was a 'tank'. His name was Ray Lewington. He was the difference I needed and lacked; we were ready.

The 'second' season was now upon us. The talking was over. Could I deliver on my promise to take us back to the First Division in this season that was now ahead?

The stakes were higher than anything I had ever experienced in my whole professional life up to this time. The survival perhaps of Chelsea Football Club was in my hands and in my players' hands as well – whoever they might be.

After much thought, I decided that due to the majority of my senior players in our first season, they had steadied our Club which gave me the platform I desperately needed and wanted and my decision was made.

The responsibility of taking our Club back to the First Division I decided would be given to our young players. I named eight of them for our first game with only three senior players in the team. If anyone might be curious about what was going through my mind at this time, how was I feeling and perhaps what I was thinking. I will do my best to try and explain. I truly felt they could do it. My preparation in building and shaping our new team, plus our new playing systems were complete. I felt very confident that we were ready to go. Was there pressure on me? Did I feel it? Yes, of course, it was around me every day. But I knew what pressure was. I had lived with it for 12-years as a player but this was different. It seemed I wasn't to be allowed to get away from it for any length of time. There was so much we could lose. But no pressure, no matter how bad it might get was going to deter me. I must sound very dramatic right now.

But these words are coming from my heart. I loved Chelsea Football Club, and it is my hope that you might understand my words to you now. I am glad it was me that was there at this time in our history. My love for our Club has never changed, even as I am writing these words to you now. You see, I wasn't alone, far from it. I had a great love for my Club that was driving me forward and a 'determination' to succeed that I honestly believed nobody else could possibly have matched. I thought the kids look great. I was excited about their potential. They were confident about themselves, very similar in fact to the team I played in when we got promotion in 1962. The team spirit was more than I dreamed of and they seemed anxious to prove themselves. I felt that they were strong and energetic and were definitely going to cause this league and the teams in it some serious problems. They were exactly where I had hopefully planned they would be at the start of this extremely important season for our Club. They were ready. They were ready to go and so was I.

My own demeanour through all this time and also through our first season perhaps I would describe as being very calm. Before games, during games, and after games, I don't remember ever raising my voice to any of my players. I preferred instead to continually encourage them. In my opinion, motivation doesn't include screaming at your players and criticizing them in front of their friends and colleagues. I was always grateful for the enormous efforts from all of my players. If I had things I had to say to any of my players, I would always attempt to be constructive, but never at any time would I embarrass them in front of their teammates, and if I did have occasion to be unhappy with any of them, I would speak to them privately and let them know exactly what was on my mind.

Several days before the season was about to start, Brian Mears visited me in my office at Stamford Bridge. There was a knock on my office door. He entered and I got up from behind my desk.

"Eddie, how are you?"

"Good morning, Mr Chairman, how are you?" I replied.

"I am just fine, thank you. May I sit down Eddie?"

"Of course, Mr Chairman."

"Well, it looks like we are getting ready to start the season, Eddie," he said. "I was wondering, Eddie, how you felt our season might go and perhaps how you felt also about our last season?"

I knew there was great pressure on him and the rest of the Board. They, of course, being the gentlemen our supporters and the media blamed for the position our Club was in financially (bankrupt).

"Were you pleased, Eddie, to finish where we did in the middle of the table?"

It was a loaded question and not one that surprised me. Most directors at our Club were far from being experts in the technicalities of our game and team tactics. Their main interest was winning, and losing just wasn't something they enjoyed.

"Mr. Chairman, with respect, it would be understandable to me if you and the Board of directors had doubts at this stage. But that I personally was more confident now than I ever was before that I would return our Club to the First Division as I said I would at the end of this season."

Regardless of what was to happen between us at the end of this season. I felt sympathy for him and our directors who I know were very influential in his attitude toward me at the end of the season. And briefly while we are on this subject, and I will elaborate on it later, but I want all of you who are reading this now to hear me good. I'm told my resignation has been a contentious subject for over 40-years at Chelsea. I'm grateful to all of the Chelsea supporters as their concerns over my feelings over what happened. But it is over. I am not mad at anyone, everyone makes decisions that we wish we hadn't made sometimes. I've lost count of how many wrong decisions I've made in my life. What about all of you? Have you made the right decision all of the time? Nevertheless, I felt he was asking these questions on behalf of our Board and himself of course, He didn't ask this question but I knew perhaps what they were thinking. How can we possibly end up in one of the top two positions in the league this season after only finishing in the middle of the table? It would only be the top two who'd gain promotion to the First Division.

My co-authors of this book have asked me questions as to why I resigned. It is not a subject I particularly want to go back to but it is my intention to answer them later in this book, and perhaps put this subject to rest once and for all.

Our second season was about to start. Our first game was away from home, but only across London where we would play Leyton Orient. We got off to a great start 1-0. Remember, this was a new team with eight youngsters in it. My defence was under some pressure at times, but I was pleased how they handled themselves and kept their composure and not conceding any goals. Our goalkeeper, Peter Bonetti, who I had played with for 10-years, looked very safe. In his prime he was one of the best goalkeepers in the world and I also knew he would set a great example for my young players. In midfield I was especially pleased with my two wide midfield layers, Ian Britton and Garry Stanley who were getting the width I needed for our system and were working overtime defensively and offensively. I wondered at times where they were getting their energy from. Everything was looking very promising early in the middle of our midfield was Ray 'Tank' Lewington. He was what I needed most in my midfield. Not many people were going to get past and if they did, they didn't go very far before they were slowing up tending to their bruises.

In the 'diamond' – which wasn't my word for our system but I have been told that other people named it that – we had Butch Wilkins. I particularly watched him with considerable interest as to how our system was working and how the opposition were attempting to deal with it. I thought they were having considerable problems trying to figure it out. I thought Butch was dropping back just a little too deep towards our midfield but I thought this might happen at the beginning, a tendency in him to want to defend. He was a very intelligent young man and I knew he would realise I didn't want him too far back there. I wanted him to wander wherever he wanted to go offensively and perhaps drag defenders into places they didn't feel comfortable with. They were confused by the places he was taking their defenders into and he was I believe finding spaces that forwards don't normally find up there. I also knew the more he played up there the more holes he would find in opposition defences.

Up front, Jock Finnieston and Kenny Swain were just what I was looking for. Jock was amazing in the opposition's penalty box and was a continual threat to their defenders who were having several problems trying to pick him up. He was constantly on the move. Kenny Swain was a very pleasant surprise for me. When I began to evaluate him a little more deeply, I discovered he was a lot faster than I had given him credit for and he also possessed great control of the ball at speeds and he would drag defenders from one side of the field to the other. Their tongues would be hanging out before he was finished with them and he would score goals, too. I also knew the both of them would give me the movement I needed up front in order that we might be able to benefit from Butch's vision and passing abilities. In the same style as these two, I had two other young gentlemen who I hadn't used a lot who I felt had I could use if there were injuries or even loss of form from either Jock or Kenny, I would have no hesitation in throwing these two in. Teddy Maybank and Tommy Langley who I believe was still only 18-years old. My back four defenders at this time were Gary Locke, Stevie Wicks, David Hay and Graham Wilkins.

Although it was a close game, it was also away from home, so I was delighted for my players. I felt even at this early stage, their potential was huge, but they would have to be brought along carefully and motivated the proper way and I believed I knew how to do that. As I have said, I was very pleased with our system. I knew they had to learn more about it and more games would surely enhance that and, to be honest with you, I was still learning about it myself. The team surely looked exciting at this early part of the season. They were so full of running and fast and that in itself was hurting our opposition.

It was the start I needed myself and the win gave me a little bit of breathing space to look at the other players in my squad and evaluate what I had in case I had injuries and perhaps loss of form. Our other goalkeeper, John Phillips, already had over 100 appearances to his name so he wouldn't let us down. We had another fullback John Sparrow who was only 17-years old, but I felt confident that if I needed him, he wouldn't let us down either. At centre-back, I was very strong I felt, with Ron Harris, Micky Droy, Stevie Wicks, David Hay and John Dempsey. I believe, unfortunately, John was one of the decisions I had to make which resulted in his leaving our Club. I could have tossed a coin with any of these players and would have been happy with any two of them.

To cover me in midfield and on the wide midfield roles, I had Brian Bason, Clive Walker and Charlie Cooke who would, at the end of our season, play a very important part in our success, and lastly our two young centre-forwards, who I have already mentioned, Tommy Langley and Teddy Maybank. I surely hope I haven't left anyone out.

I thought Butch was perfect for this new position I had found for him. But if it hadn't been for my two wide midfield players in Garry Stanley and Ian Britton, I'm not sure if it would have worked so well. Ian Britton was tireless and Gary was powerful, and both of them gave us the wide crossing service we surely needed. I thought Butch was outstanding in that position and his composure and maturity never failed to impress me. His confidence in making himself available to receive passes from his team-mates was admirable and courageous. I was always confident he would be a great success for us in that position and he was.

When I first appointed Butch as captain, I think most people thought that the pressure was getting to me and I was perhaps losing it. He was so young at 18-years old. But I knew exactly what I was doing, but I also knew the pressure on him was going to be huge. Not only from the media, but from our supporters as well. I remember when he was in my office when I told him, and he said, "Me, captain? Do you think I can do it Boss?"

"I know you can," I said, "when you are playing in front of an audience, their reaction to you is very important to your confidence, if you are not doing well they'll sure let you know."

We had a game at Stamford Bridge and although the Chelsea supporters had been fairly kind to him, I'm not sure if they fully understood why I would make such a bold move with someone so young. Anyway, I believe it was in the second half he picked up a pass and was about 30-yards out from our opponent's goal. He controlled the ball and hit a shot towards their goal and I don't think their goalkeeper moved until it hit the net behind him. He nailed it. What a great goal. The crowd suddenly went wild with applause. Again, it is so long ago, but I believe not long after that he scored another one and the crowd rose to him giving him a thunderous applause. I was sitting on the bench and I turned to my trainer Norman Medhurst. There was still about 15-minutes left in the game. "Go get Butch off! I told him. He looked at me with wide open eyes as if to say "What?" "Go get Butch off," I repeated.

"Yes, sir!" As Butch was walking off, obviously very surprised at my decision, the crowd rose to him again, applauding him all the way off the pitch.

After the game, there was a knock on my office door. "Come in," I said. It was Butch.

"Sit down... what do you want?" I asked.

"Boss, I was wondering why you brought me off?"

"You don't know?"

"No, not really Boss."

"Did you hear the crowd," I asked him.

He looked puzzled at my words. Then the penny dropped.

"Oh..."

"I brought you off to show you how much the supporters appreciate you."

I had put enormous pressure on him and I understood that, and it was my way of helping him to build up his confidence. I personally believed he was going to prove himself without my help anyway, but I thought my decision certainly wouldn't hurt. The Chelsea supporters helped me in many ways in my endeavour to succeed for the Club and I believe that was one of them. Thank you.

After our first win, I wondered what might be ahead of us. Failure to achieve what I had promised wasn't even in my thoughts, but I wondered if I had prepared my team properly. It was imperative to me that I had covered everything that they might need if indeed Chelsea were to return to the First Division. My part would be small compared to what was ahead for my players. It was going to be a long punishing season for 42 games, home and away. I started my own career in this league if you remember and there was huge pressure on all of us to return our Club back to where it belonged. But I truly believe that never in the history of our Club had so much ever been asked of Chelsea players. Do you think perhaps they didn't know that if they failed what might happen to their Club? My young players were in a fight and they knew it. They gave me an early indication of what it meant to them, winning eight of their first ten games in all competitions, drawing one and only losing one. Very early and very quickly they were surely making me look good.

I thought they looked powerful at times. It impressed even me how fast they were in springing from a defensive situation to a counter-attack. They were quick strong, exciting, adventurous. Their work rate was huge and their support for each other was a bonus I didn't expect so early. They knew what was expected of them and, I believe, they were telling all of us early, "We are on our way."

The season was very competitive and if I am correct, there were about six or seven teams pushing hard and playing well to capture the top two places in the league that would earn promotion. We were in a fight as I knew we would be and from where I was, we were winning. We weren't home yet, but I was absolutely delighted with my players, their promise and potential future looked very exciting and along the way and because of them, we had picked up an 'army' of supporters. Yes "Eddie McCreadie's Blue and White Army." They were fantastic and followed us everywhere, continually encouraging our young team. I will forever be grateful to all of them. My players knew the supporters were behind them and so did I. My players had so much on their shoulders, but those following the side surely told us, "We will carry this load with you."

We were picking up points here and there and that was keeping us up there in the top three or four, but I was watching our players very carefully and I could see some of them tiring in recent games. But I knew for sure there was no giving up in any of them. Then, all of a sudden, it seemed like a nightmare coming over me. What I had feared in the first season. That if I had played too many of my young players too early, they might take couple of bad beatings and it could crush their confidence in themselves. We had only six games left and we were up there competing hard for one of the two top places. We played away from home against Charlton Athletic, another London club and they beat us 4-0. The result was bad enough for us, but it was what I saw that concerned me the most. Two or three of my players had literally burnt themselves out. They were still running, but I felt they had lost their sharpness and because of that, their effectiveness. I went home that night and I kept saying to myself, "Not now, please, not now..."

We were so close and I had a serious problem and I didn't know how to fix it. I racked my brain trying to figure it out for two days. The conclusion I came to was that in some way I had to slow us down somehow. Their style was to do everything at 100-miles an hour it seemed. And they were so good playing that way. They were young and wanted to get at our opponents and I honestly believed that was the reason we were in such a great position in the league was because of their style. So many of our wins came because they wouldn't stop running at our opponents and would eventually wear them down. But I decided I had to find control again on the field which I felt we had lost and I needed someone in my midfield to slow us down. Butch was doing his job and doing it well, but I needed someone as Americans would describe as a 'quarterback' and to slow the game down.

I was in my office at Stamford Bridge. It was, I believe, a Monday morning and we had just finished some light training. Our next game was the Saturday at home to Nottingham Forest who were, at the time, in the top three. It was a game we needed to win at all costs. I knew I had to make a couple of changes in the team to turn this around for us. I had already decided that, with only six games left I had to get us back on track and quickly.

I sent one of my staff to our dressing rooms, telling him, "Find Charlie Cooke and ask him to come and see me in my office." Charlie had played less than ten games in the season. I had brought him in earlier in the season when we suffered some injuries. He had been playing in my reserve team. It was a difficult time for him at the Club. He was, I guess 34-years old at this time. I had released some of his team-mates who were also seniors. But I decided to keep Charlie. In his prime, he was perhaps one of the best players in the world and we both had the honour of representing our country, Scotland. He was a player who was very gifted on the ball with exceptional composure and would most importantly control the pace of any game by himself. He could make the game fast if he had a mind to or he could slow it up to a walking pace if he desired. In effect, I felt he could control my racehorses and slow them down a bit. He arrived in my office and I invited him to have a seat. "I've been told that you wanted to see me?"

I told him that was correct. I asked him how he was. He said that he felt fine.

"How is your fitness?" I asked him and also asked him if he had any injuries. "No, I feel good." he responded.

I told him I was bringing him back into the team on Saturday against Nottingham Forest. He seemed a little surprised at first. I told him I needed him and explained to him why I needed him. I told him we had five games left and I felt we were losing our way a little and said that I was going to put him in midfield and I needed him to control the pace of the game for us.

"Do you have any problem with that?" I asked him.

"No problem!" he said.

I told you before that my part was small compared to what my players were up against. It is my sincere opinion that my decision to bring Charlie Cooke back into the team at this difficult time for us may have been the difference in what we would eventually achieve. He played against Nottingham Forest. We beat them 2-1. He took control of the game and performed exactly as I had asked him to do. We were back in the 'driving seat'.

In all I had made two changes for the game against Forest. When I brought in Charlie, he replaced Garry Stanley. The other change I made was replacing Kenny Swain for Tommy Langley, our young centre-forward.

Here, I'd like to address the following few words to Garry Stanley and Kenny Swain. I have never forgotten how difficult and disappointing it must have been for you both when I decided to leave you out of the team with only five games left, especially after you had played that whole punishing season for me. If it were to be any consolation to you, I'd like you to know gentlemen that I thought you were both outstanding players for our team. Please never forget that I will never forget how much you gave of yourselves for our Club at this time in our history. I just felt that because you gave so much you had lost your sharpness slightly. I hope you might understand that I had a more important priority on my mind and it wasn't you, and it certainly wasn't me.

I would also at this time direct my words to Clive Walker. You were, if I remember, the only member of my squad that I didn't play. If I were to consider playing you in our team at the time it would have been as one of my wide midfield players. I believe that role may have suited you. But I wasn't about to make any changes in these positions. The gentlemen occupying them I'm sure you will agree were doing such a wonderful job for our team and our system there. I feel sure you were perhaps disappointed Mr Walker – my apologies, sir.

Getting back to our season and check this out for tension and pressure and a finish! We only had two games left and, in one of them, we had to play Wolverhampton Wanderers away from home. They were at the top of the league. Our last game of this exhausting season was against Hull City at home. All my players needed to take us back to the First Division and save Chelsea Football Club. From either one of these last two games (at a time when it was two points for a win and one for a draw) Chelsea only needed one to go up.

We were on our coach driving to Molineux, the Wolverhampton Wanderers stadium. I was sitting in the front seat by myself as usual. This is where I preferred to sit. It gave me the opportunity to be alone and to think my thoughts. I thought about my players all of them, I knew they must be tired. They had all given so much of themselves these two seasons. And although I knew the pressure that was on them, I thought also what a wonderful, exciting adventure they were all going through. Most of them were so young and I had insisted on them becoming men quickly to save our Club. As I am writing this, I'm remembering my own career and how it started.

As I was sitting there I began to think about our tactics. Should I play defensively and get everyone behind the ball when the opposition had it and play for the draw? And then I thought of how I had always encouraged them to play attacking football. They had got us here with that. But I kept telling myself, I can't let them go at them with all guns blazing. The other thing that was on my mind also was that if we failed here we would still have another opportunity to get that point we so desperately needed against Hull City. But that thought didn't last too long. We need to do it now. I told myself. Our style and our system had not let us down yet. I decided to play to our strengths. 'We're going at them,' was my decision. 'We can beat them.' I thought. They were young and inexperienced, but these two seasons had matured and hardened them. They had told all of us after our first ten games, "We're on our way." They had no fear of anyone. I personally believed they were the best team in the league by far. They were on the threshold of winning one of the toughest fights in the history of our Club and I wasn't prepared to hold them back. Our young forward Tommy Langley who I had just brought back into the side scored the goal that gave us the 1-1 draw we needed to save our Club and return it to the First Division. They, my players, had accomplished what I said they would. They had done it in style. We were back.

After the game in our dressing room my players were so excited. It was a wonderful feeling I was so happy and proud of them. They had achieved what many people thought might be near to impossible under our circumstances. They were wrong. I remember someone came to me and asked me if I would be available to the press anytime soon.

I walked out of the dressing room and was immediately surrounded by the media and all I said to them was this. "I am not going to take any questions at this time. The people you need to talk to are my players, not me. They are the ones that deserve the credit. You have my permission to enter our dressing room and I walked away. As I was walking down the tunnel, something rather ironic happened. Sir Richard Attenborough came running toward me and threw his arms around my neck. "Eddie, we did it! You did it!" were his words to me. Why do I tell you this? Because it's true. Richard Attenborough was a nice man and I liked him, but I just thought it was ironic when I think of how it all ended up for me.

We had one game left against Hull City at Stamford Bridge the following week. Oh, what a wonderful feeling that was for me. It didn't matter if we lost. It would be very difficult for me to explain to you what my players' achievement meant to me. I have loved my Club with a passion all my life and have always felt honoured to have been a small part of its wonderful history. To have been here when perhaps my Club needed me most was an honour and privilege I will never forget. We were also indeed most fortunate to have had these special and talented players there at perhaps the darkest hours in our history. Gentlemen, Chelsea owes all of you so much.

We had the most wonderful reception when we faced Hull. There was a huge crowd there at Stamford Bridge to welcome my players and I believe they surely let them know how proud they were of them. They showed their passion for the players by invading the field several times during the game in the thousands. Our young and exciting team decided to make no mistake that indeed they were back in the First Division and completely destroyed Hull, beating them 4-0. Unknown to me then, it was to be the last time I would see my players play at Stamford Bridge.

It was many years before the fact that a bar at Stamford Bridge had been named after me was brought to my attention. After I resigned from Chelsea, the ensuing years became very difficult for me. I had lost something that I had held so dearly to my heart for 16-years and the manner in which I lost it had hurt me deeply. I have always considered myself to be a kind of macho guy, but I must admit to you that I cried many times for many years. When you have loved something or even someone for so long and it, or they, are no longer there anymore, it can be dreadfully hurtful to all of us. I hope you might agree. I had completely turned myself off from what might be happening at Chelsea. It had become too painful for me to even think about them. It was about five years after I left that I heard that Chelsea had been relegated again to the Second Division after only two seasons. I was only recently that I heard that, some five years after that day Chelsea won promotion against Hull City that the Stamford Bridge supporters were singing for me to come back.

About a year or so after I had left Chelsea, I was still in London still trying to determine what my next move would be. I felt I had to decide on something soon as my drinking was getting worse. I was just trying to get through one day at a time it seemed. Anyway, several weeks later I was approached by a gentleman who told me he was representing the Memphis Rogues of the new North American Soccer League, whose new owner was apparently a very wealthy property dealer who resided in Miami called Harry Mangurian.

They offered me the head coaching job of what was then a brand new franchise. I thought it might be a change to start anew somewhere else and put Chelsea behind me. And it also didn't hurt that they were throwing a considerable amount of money at me. I worked pretty hard there and built another team in a very short time but my first season was to be my last. Harry Mangurian was a very powerful man and when he snapped his fingers he expected people to jump and most of them did.

The league was starting its second season which would also be my second season, too. The American players in the league decided they were going to start their own players union. Two of my American players who I was contemplating releasing happened to be the team's union representatives. Anyway, my general manger asked me if I would come into his office. I went in and sat down. He said, "Eddie, you have to get rid of the two players who are the union representatives." At this time I hadn't told anyone of my possible plans regarding the two players. He continued, "Harry Mangurian got all over me. He told me that, as general manager, I shouldn't have let this happen. That the American players were considering

going on strike all over the league and it wasn't going to happen at this club. You tell Coach McCreadie to fire both of them immediately or else."
I listened to him and when I asked him, "Or else what?" He replied, "He said he would fire you Eddie."

By this time my general manager was shaking in fear. I wasn't sure if he was shaking in fear because of the owner or what my reaction might be. I thought about it for a moment and then I said, "You tell Mr Mangurian that although I might agree with him that being a new league that the players shouldn't go on strike, it is my view that they are just young men and they are only doing what they think is right. And I would not be firing anyone. You tell him that."

When he fired me the next day, it wasn't very popular with the Memphis press, especially when they heard that two American players were involved and hadn't been given an opportunity to prove themselves on the field. I must also add that they were also very angry that he had fired me. In the short time I had been there, it would seem I had become very popular with the fans and the city in general. I like telling you these things because it is great for my ego. But at least Mangurian paid up my contract.

When you had only experienced playing in front of 2,000 people at East Stirling, walking out at Stamford Bridge in front of 40,000 or 50,000 was kind of scary. I grew to be very confident in my abilities, but I was still very nervous before games. It was important to get off to a good start. A good start for me was to be successful with my first couple of passes. If I could do that it would always settle me down. But if I had been, for instance, unsuccessful with these passes, two things would surely happen. One; your confidence would take a dive and two; you would immediately have your home crowd on your back. They expected a great deal from us and so they should. We are, after all, professional footballers. I always felt very fortunate playing at home in front of our own supporters. I felt they encouraged me nearly all of the time, and would especially get very loud when I would venture on an overlap at my top speed. Most of the time, they spurred me on. They were great and very loyal to our Club. I especially appreciated them when I became manager. In the second season, in particular, as you know we had a very young team and what was ahead of them as you already know was enormous. If indeed, they were going to be successful, they would need a great deal of motivation and encouragement from me. I felt I could take care of that responsibility on my side, but what I believed they really needed was there in abundance for them.

The Chelsea supporters were wonderful to my young team and I can't quite explain how much it meant to me and how important they were. I explained earlier that I needed my senior players and my young players to blend together and support each other and that we needed to be one. Anything less and we would surely fail. I really thought the supporters' contribution that final season was especially important to my young players. They were fantastic. There is absolutely no doubt in my mind the positive effect they had on my team. It was huge. I needed them, the supporters, to build them up because they were so inexperienced, I needed them to build their confidences individually and collectively. They consistently did both and I can say this right now; my players knew that in every game, the supporters were with them. The supporters have no idea how much they helped them. When I started this journey as the new Chelsea manager, I had looked around to see where I might find some help and there was no help. Well, that's not quite true. I found out very quickly that, because of the support both the team and I got, that I wasn't alone. It was difficult not to see your wonderful blue and white Chelsea scarves with the words "Eddie McCreadie's Blue and White Army," printed on them. How kind and thoughtful of them! I don't think I can quite explain how that helped my own confidence. I had believed I didn't need anyone to help push me forward to achieve our goals. I was wrong. Seeing what we meant to the supporters gave me so much more incentive to succeed. I will forever be grateful to all of them. I'll always be grateful.

People often ask me about my faith in Our Lord Jesus Christ. It's an interesting question to ask any Christian and I feel sure many Christians might answer it differently. I personally would say without any question that my faith is the most important thing in my life. Let me say that again – the most important thing in my life. I think perhaps the most curious question for most non-Christians like I was only 14-years ago was how non-Christians became Christians and why. And although I am a Christian now myself, I really don't believe I am quite qualified enough to answer that in any expert way. I feel sure there are many reasons my own situation might have been similar to perhaps what some others have gone through in their own lives. I think we all at times get to a place where life becomes more of a problem for us that we had ever encountered before and solving some of these problems becomes harder and harder for us. And when we find we can't solve them, we perhaps also find there is no one to turn to and we find ourselves alone, and even if there is someone there who really wants to help, there comes a time when even that is not enough.

I have been there on several occasions in my life.

The last time was only 20-years ago, but this time I found that I wasn't alone. It was the day I picked up the Bible for my first look at it ever. Previous to this I had several years before I slipped gradually into depression which is a place I had never known before. Never in my life had I ever felt so lost, alone and afraid and when it came upon me I knew I was to face perhaps the biggest fight of my life if I was going to survive. After many years I did survive, but it was to be at a considerable cost. I began drinking more than I had ever done. I had unwisely convinced myself that it was helping me with my past depression and it wasn't very long after that that I had to suffer the indignity of having to admit to myself that I had become an alcoholic.

I was coaching in Cleveland, Ohio. I had been there for five-years. I didn't particularly like it there and decided to leave. Several months before I left, I was advised by a friend that I needed to go and see a doctor because I had been losing so much weight. To be honest with you, I really didn't care much anymore. But I went anyway. The doctor asked me if I drank. I told him I did. He asked me how much. "All day if I'm able to…" I replied. "You need to stop now!" he told me. I thanked him and left. At this time I was drinking vodka. Anyway, if I were to leave Cleveland, where was I to go? I had two choices as I saw it. One was to go back home to London or go back to Memphis, Tennessee, where I had coached and also had made many friends. I decided there was no way I was going back to London, so I made the decision to return to Memphis and, it turned out perhaps to be the most wonderful and most important decision I had ever made in my whole life.

It was there that I met my wife Linda. She was a practicing lawyer and also a Christian and had been one all of her life. Anyway, one day, she told me she sang in the choir at her church and would I come and see her sing there. I told her I would but I knew this was going to be a new experience in my life. I had never been to church before. None of my family had ever attended church when I was younger. But I went anyway because I wanted to please Linda and certainly did not want to offend her. Perhaps for the same reasons some good folks who might not be Christians are going to read my words about my faith might know how I felt then too. But I'll take the time to explain my faith and hope all who read these words know that they're my own personal thoughts which are very important to me. I'm not a preacher or a minister, nor could I be, but I want to explain that two of the most important things I found when I read the Bible. I found that 'love and forgiveness' were waiting for me if I desired them. But the second thing that awaited me almost scared me to death!

I had told Linda that I had a drinking problem and that I was trying to overcome it. Several weeks later I went out to a bar with some friends to play pool and I ended up getting very drunk and attempted to drive home. I can't remember a thing but apparently I hit a parked car but, fortunately, there was nobody in it. I had been drinking for several months before my accident. I was trying, but I just couldn't stop. They took me to jail and I remember sitting with several other prisoners in a cell and I don't ever remember feeling so crushed, broken and ashamed of myself. I thought quietly, look at you, you are Eddie McCreadie and look how far you have fallen. Mentally I was on my knees and I believed I was just about ready to give up. The weight of my past depressions, alcoholism and my ever-returning thoughts about Chelsea seemed to be overwhelming me. I had often felt that I had never lost many battles before, but I was surely losing this one. Linda was coming to pick me up from the jail and as I was leaving one of the guards came by and said to me, "Have you ever read the Bible?" I looked at him and curtly said no. I had no idea why he would ask me that. As I left, Linda was waiting for me and, when I saw her, I just broke down and cried. I knew I had hit rock bottom and I had no idea how to move myself forward or upwards.

Several days later Linda and I were at home in our kitchen. She handed me a very large book. It was about 'Alcoholics Anonymous', and, in a very gentle but firm voice, she told me that she wanted me to read it. That I must try and help myself as she felt I might end up killing myself and that she couldn't possibly be around to see that. I thought about what she had said and told her I would not need the book. I would take care of it. She asked me what I had meant. I told her again, "Linda, I will take care of it." I had no idea at this time if I could really stop drinking. But, I knew I had to try harder than I had ever done before.

Perhaps it may have been a couple of weeks later that I remembered what the guard had asked me when he said, "Have you ever read the Bible?" I went into our living room and picked up Linda's Bible and opened it up for the first time ever in my life. It would be very difficult for me to try and explain all the wonderful things it told me over the ensuing years. That, even after all the dreadful things I had to endure in my life, that there really was a Heaven and when we got there, that God would wipe every tear from our eyes. There would be no more death, or mourning, or crying, or pain. There would be no more sickness, cancer or any other illnesses. To the thirsty, He will give water without cost, and those who are victorious will inherit all this and He will be their God and they will be His children and we would all live again, not for a 1000 years, but forever and ever, an eternity. Wow, they were for me the most wondrous and most beautiful words I had ever heard in all of my life.

I have a message now to all of good folk who are reading this now. I believe there are many of you who can relate to my faith and to you other good people, who perhaps are non-Christians. I never wanted to write my part in this book. I am doing this for all the Chelsea supporters, and I want all of them to know I am happy to do this now for them and that historical part in our wonderful Club's history, but I want to ask all of them now to do something for me. I am aware that perhaps many of them would prefer me to talk about football and Chelsea and I would hope that they all might agree that I have spent considerable time doing just that. But I want all who are reading this now to promise me something. That whatever I write about my faith now, you will finish reading it and go back even just once more and read it again and think about what I am saying. Will you do that much for me?

You know that I used to be a non-Christian. Remember? And I used to think perhaps the way some of you did. All these Christians want to do is spoil any fun we might be having. Right? 'Wrong'! That is the farthest thing from the truth that you can imagine about any Christian. I am a Christian and I know I am going to Heaven. My name is Eddie McCreadie and I want all of you to come to Heaven with me. That is how all Christians feel. They don't want to leave anyone behind. Let me try and explain something to you if you would allow me, that might help you to understand. Can you imagine your brother or your sister, mum or dad or even your closest friend, boyfriend, girlfriend, your wife or your husband, telling you that you were going to die because you had sinned so much in your life like I have, but that this person loved you so much that they were going to take your place and die for you. How would that make you feel?

That is exactly what Jesus did for us. I didn't know that until I read the Bible. He knew he was going to be crucified in order to save us. The Romans beat him badly, they spat on him, slapped him, kicked him, pushed sharp thorns down on his head until his blood was running down his face, they made him carry this huge heavy cross that they were going to crucify him on and made him carry it to the top of a hill, they then put the cross down on the ground and laid his body on it. They stretched both his arms out across it and with huge nails, nailed his hands to the cross. Then they overlapped his feet at the bottom and nailed them to the cross. They then lifted the cross upright and left him hanging there. It is impossible for us to even imagine the excruciating pain he must have suffered before he would eventually die. I wanted to make sure that I got the following two verses correct, so I asked my good friend, David Clark, our minister, to guide me.

John 3:16: For God so loved the world, that he gave his one and only son, that whoever believed in Him shall not perish but have eternal life.
Corinthians 5:21: God made him who had no sin to be sin for us, so that in him we might become the righteousness of God.

The Bible tells us that, after dying, Jesus rose from the grave three days later. Christians believe that without any question it is called 'faith'. How do people get faith? I am not really qualified perhaps to answer that properly. But what I say is how I got it. I feel sure there must be different ways. I found it by picking up the Bible and reading it and I would suggest you might do the same thing. I will promise all of you good folk one thing. I promise you if you honestly look for Jesus, you will 'find' Him. He is waiting for you. He wants everyone to go to Heaven with him. It has changed my life because of my faith in God. My whole personality has changed dramatically. I stopped drinking the night Linda handed me the book. I no longer suffer from depression. I smile most of the time and my friends even tell me I'm fun to be around. I attend Boones Creek Christian Church every week without fail. The most important part of the Bible which inspired me most was what I could look forward to when I get to Heaven. I mentioned the two things that first got my attention. The first was about the place that Heaven is but the second thing and the opposite most definitely got my undivided attention. I'll be honest with you. I found it terribly frightening to read. It explained to me about Hell and which ones of us would end up there. God tells us all about Hell because He doesn't want anyone to go there. It told me that the people who would end up in Hell would be the cowardly, the vile, murderers, the unbelieving, the sexually immoral and liars and they would be thrown into a fiery lake of burning sulphur and they would be tormented day and night without any relief for all eternity and there would be no water for them.

I wasn't guilty of all of these sins. But I was surely on that list. The other things people need to know also is something I never forget. We can't hide from God no matter how many doors we close or how many lights we turn off. He is ever-present with every person in the world. How can that be? That's impossible some might say but not if you are a Christian. The Bible also tells us that God knows the exact number of hairs on every human's head. He also knows what we are thinking and knows what we are going to say before we even say it. When we think we are alone in a room, we are not. He is there with us. And, finally, he also told us that if we 'believed' that Jesus rose from the grave after three days, we would be saved.

I am going to leave you now on this hugely important message with these words. I am a Christian and Heaven sounds wonderful to me and when my life is over and that might not be too far away, I can't wait to get there, the alternative being Hell. I don't mean to be funny, but are you kidding me? I don't think so. Listen to me, if you are not a Christian that is okay. I have been there. But if any of what I have said to you has aroused any interest in you, I beg of you don't leave it too long. Any one of us could die tomorrow and it would be too late. You know we all have choices. Some of you I know are probably reading this and saying to yourselves, "Yeah right... I don't believe all this stuff he's throwing at us anyway!" Okay, so let me throw another one at you my friends. What happens if you are wrong? C'mon, you guys, pick up the Bible. I promise you if you come to Heaven with me, I'll show you personally how I stuck it to Billy Bremner and Johnny Giles.

In 1998, Linda and I moved from Memphis to Johnson City, Tennessee. Linda was born here and it is where we live now. She was born on the family farm. It is a working farm where they grow tobacco, they have greenhouses, where people come and buy plants, etc. They have cows and pigs. The farm has been in Linda's family for six generations and it is run now by Linda's brother Larry. The farm itself is about 400 acres and it is really quite beautiful. We built our home on a lovely hill which overlooks most of the acreage. We had two German Shepherds. Sadly, our 12-year old male named "Mac" died recently. Apart from Linda, he was my best friend. We will surely miss him. Our female German Shepherd is named "Chelsea" and is six-years old. Aren't these names a coincidence?

Our house is large enough to, on occasion, host 50 or 60 of our friends from Boones Creek Christian Church and believe it or not, I cook for them. Yes, I taught myself how to cook many years ago. Am I any good you ask? Well, to my knowledge, I haven't poisoned anyone yet. What do I cook for our guests? Well, different dishes for different occasions. If we have a large crowd I'll make for instance lasagne, shepherds pie, chicken pot pie, chicken divan, jambalaya and most Italian pasta dishes, etc. Our guests always bring salad and desserts for everyone. So we have a pretty active social itinerary. Over and above that, Linda runs her own business, Tennessee Quilts. In actual fact, she wouldn't tell you this because she is very modest, but my wife is a very talented lady. Not only did she build her business from scratch but she has also won many awards for her quilts and, as you already know, was a very competent lawyer, having recently retired. We frequently play golf together.

Lastly, I personally feel very blessed to have so many new wonderful friends in my life here in Johnson City. If someone had told me many years ago that, in my future, my best friend would be a preacher, I would have told them to have another drink. But it is actually very true. As you already know his name is David Clark and he is someone I admire very much, and for several years we would both go and play golf. He is a pretty good player and on occasion when he would get lucky, he would beat me. But most of the time I'd whip him good. David baptized me and I have never looked back since. My past life has gone completely. I feel alive, healthy and happier than I have ever been in my life and there are no more tears even on earth here. God has wiped every tear from my eyes, except perhaps the sad ones I have shed while writing these words.

When I'm asked about the 'highs' I had at Chelsea, I have to say that there so many that I could, perhaps, fill a whole book writing about them. That said, one of them would surely have to be when was asked to sign for Chelsea Football Club by Tommy Docherty. Considering my background coming from the lower leagues and being told that I wasn't good enough to be a Chelsea player was for sure a memory I shall not forget. I have always felt honoured and privileged to be a small part of Chelsea's wonderful history. I have loved the Club, perhaps more than I could possibly explain to all the good Chelsea supporters. Another high for me would be the thrill and excitement of being part of the 1962 team – my first season – to be accepted into the team by so many highly talented Chelsea players such as Bobby Tambling, Barry Bridges, Peter Bonetti, Terry Venables and the like. I will never forget that their friendships and their encouragement were just the incentives I needed to begin my Chelsea career. I am grateful to all of them. There is no substitute, absolutely none, that can compare when you are trying to build confidence in yourself to find it coming from your team-mates. What a rare compliment. I will never forget our time together gentlemen.

Another thing I would like to mention is that becoming a Chelsea player was huge in my life without question, but never in my life did I ever dream that one day I would become only the 8th manager in the history of Chelsea Football Club. Perhaps the greatest honour of my professional career.

So, perhaps, all the wonderful Chelsea supporters who seem so determined that I should never be forgotten but should always be remembered will forgive me if I mention it perhaps one last time. Eddie, who? From where? How fortunate I am to have such wonderful memories.

I believe the last high that I would care to mention and perhaps the most important for me and maybe even the most difficult to write, it would be impossible for me to ever forget my own players. But I surely couldn't blame them if perhaps they thought I had. I never got the opportunity, Gentlemen, to properly say goodbye to you or to really thank you for your outstanding achievement. The fact that I never accomplished that was one of the many reasons that would drag me down in my life after I resigned. We had together been through a very special time in our Club's history for it to end the way it did was not what I had envisioned. If you would allow me now, Gentlemen, it would help me greatly in my life, even now, if you would all individually please accept my sincere apology to you. I have carried with me all these years the feeling that I had let you down and left you when perhaps you needed me most. Your outstanding efforts those two seasons and, especially, the last one, is something you should all be proud of. It was a magnificent and historical achievement. I have seldom seen so many players give so much of themselves for our Club. All of you, whether your part was smaller than others is unimportant to me, this time was unquestionably the most alarming time in our Club's history.

You, the players, could have failed. You didn't. Yours is a wonderful success story in our great Club's history. A story perhaps never to be forgotten. They tell me I am a legend. If, indeed I am, I owe it all to you, my players. There is no way I could have accomplished such an honour if it hadn't been for your courageous and highly successful efforts. Thank you, Gentlemen.

One thing that is difficult for me to go back to however is when I left Chelsea Football Club. But I have decided to put this issue to rest once and for all. I believe I owe that to all who follow Chelsea and perhaps also to defend my own reputation.

After I left, I was told there were all kinds of statements and rumours coming from the Club that I had demanded a very expensive car plus this and that. Yes, a normal Club car was discussed and that was it. I never ever got an answer to that but that wasn't such an important issue to me.

Now I am going to tell you the truth. Are you ready?

I didn't ask for anything! Let me say it to you again. I didn't ask for anything!

Brian Mears came to my office a couple of days after the season ended and after we had gained promotion he offered me a certain amount of money which I assumed was an offer from him and the board for me to continue as manager of Chelsea Football Club. I thanked him and told him that after I had a chance to look at it that I would be happy to sit down and discuss it with him. He was very abrupt and told me there would be "no discussion." I wondered to myself why I was being treated this way. This wasn't the Brian Mears I knew. I realised very quickly that this was the board speaking, not him. I didn't but perhaps I should have reminded him that he and the Board had not long ago asked me if I would sit down individually with every one of my players and discuss their contracts with them which I did successfully.

I asked him, "Mr. Chairman, are you seriously telling me I will not be allowed to discuss my own circumstances with you and the offer you have made to me?"
"Yes, that is correct." he replied.

He opened my office door and left. His attitude toward me hurt me deeply. It was so out of character for him. I had actually felt we were becoming closer friends. He would always ask me if he could sit beside me at the front of the coach when we would be travelling to away games and coming home. I got the impression other managers hadn't spent much time with him when perhaps he wanted to talk about their tactics before and after games. I would always take the time to explain to him my tactics before games and I always remember how grateful he was to me that I would take the time to do that. I thought he was a very nice man and regardless of what happened between us and I still do.

Not long after the season finished we were getting ready to fly to the United States for a three-game tour. So I decided to let things sit for a while hoping we might get the opportunity to talk about my situation. While we were on tour, I approached him on a couple of occasions while we were there and although he was very polite to me, he told me again he couldn't discuss it with me. This was the most difficult time for me and I really didn't know which way to turn. All I wanted to do was to discuss my situation with him.

When we arrived back in London, I thought about things for a few days and convinced myself that I really didn't have any other choice but to resign my position and I wrote a letter to that effect to the Board. Several days later, Brian Mears entered my office and, very guiltily I thought, told me that the Board had received my letter and had decided to accept my resignation and immediately left my office.

I threw a few things into a couple of boxes and left my office for the last time and the Club I have loved all my life. That was in 1977. Now, at this time, I feel sure all you good folks are perhaps scratching your heads right now and saying to yourselves, "How could this have been allowed to happen? It doesn't make any sense!" No, and it didn't to me either and it was to exact its toll on me for many years. Perhaps you can imagine how

EDDIE MCCREADIE'S BLUE AND WHITE ARMY

many times I have gone back to this nightmare in my head trying to figure out why all this happened to me. It took me many years, but I believe I have. Nothing makes any sense to you right? And nothing made any sense to me either, right?

I believe it was about five or six-years after I left Chelsea and I was coaching in Cleveland Ohio. I was at home one evening and my telephone rang. I picked it up.

"Hello, Eddie, this is Brian Mears. Eddie, could I speak to you for a minute?"

I feel sure you can all imagine my surprise.

"Yes, of course," I said.

"Eddie, I am in London right now, but I wondered if I could ask something of you?"

"What would that be?" I asked.

"Eddie, I would like to fly to Ohio in the next couple of days to see you if you would allow me…"

"I don't see what that might accomplish for either one of us, Mr. Chairman," I said, "What do you want to see me about?"

"Eddie, I would prefer not to discuss it on the telephone; it is too important for me to do that. I need to be with you. I have something I need to tell you. Would you let me do that Eddie? I can't tell you just how very important it is to me."

"I guess you had better come over then…" I told him

A couple of days later he arrived at my home in Cleveland.

"How nice it is to see you again Eddie!"

"You too, Mr Chairman, please come in."

We exchanged some pleasantries and then I asked him, "Why are you here Mr Chairman?"

He seemed very nervous.

"Eddie, I have something I have to say to you and I wanted to tell you personally and to your face."

"What would that be Mr. Chairman?"

"Eddie, we treated you so terribly at Chelsea and I am so ashamed of myself. I am so sorry Eddie, can you ever forgive me?" I looked at him and wanted to say to him have you any idea of the pain and suffering you have caused me in my life. But I didn't. What I saw was the man who I once thought was becoming my friend a long time ago. He was visibly upset and looking at me waiting for my response.

"That's not a problem Mr Chairman, of course I forgive you."

It is perhaps logical for me to assume that the much-needed success that I and my players brought to our Club was indeed going to be my downfall. I had successfully brought them back to the First Division. Our match attendances would surely double at least, and monies would be coming into the Club from many different directions. They would soon be able to get rid of Martin Spencer, their controller. The directors, in effect, were now back in control and it's my opinion that, when they initially sent Brian Mears to my office with their original offer, he was told that under no circumstances was he to discuss anything with me and that I had to agree, without discussion, to accept their offer. I believe they wanted people to know very quickly that they were now back in charge to a large degree and everyone now would play to their rules, especially me. I truly believe that by having handed in my letter of resignation I had given them the perfect opportunity to put themselves back in the headlines.

Now let me ask you this. If their first priority was the Club, which is what they wanted everyone to believe, why would they weaken it by letting a successful manager leave and in doing so automatically weaken the team? And why would Brian Mears travel half way round the world to ask for my forgiveness? I'll tell you why. Because he was full of guilt and ashamed and couldn't live with himself. As far as I know they never came up with any reasons for why they accepted my resignation, except for what I heard years later that I am supposed to have asked them for an expensive car. That is completely untrue and if that is what they told the press and you the supporters, even as a Christian I have to say it – they lied to you! It's quite apparent to me now that they used this Club car for cover and exaggerated stories about it.

I am going to add one last thing for you and then all of you can make up your own minds because, as I have said before, I really don't care anymore. About a year after I left Chelsea, I came back to London from the States to sign David Stride on loan to the Memphis Rogues. As I was in Christine Mathews' office, I looked out of her window and saw a very nice looking car parked there. I asked her whose car it was. She lifted her head up from her desk very slowly and told me it was a Club car and it belonged to Ken Shellito, one of my coaches who the directors had replaced me with.

Interesting? It was obvious to most people that they weren't exactly experts in their knowledge of the game. That surely must have been a fact. Again forgive me if I bring attention to myself. Do you think that they really thought that because I was a new and inexperienced manager and that they now had a successful team that they could replace me with anyone? That if I could accomplish what I did, anyone could do it. I don't believe they ever considered for one moment that I may have had some special talents. An example might be just for a start, inventing my own playing system. The "diamond" which I believe is still being used 40 years later even to this day by coaches in the Premier League and perhaps in many parts of the world. So what were their priorities? Was it the "Club" as they would have us all believe or was it, as I have already suggested, 'themselves' and I was going to be their sacrificial lamb.

In reference to my resignation, when I wrote my letter, did I mean it? Yes, absolutely. Did I perhaps think it might bring them to the table to talk to me? Yes, I did. Do I regret my decision to hand in my resignation? Absolutely not! No matter the cost to my life, I did what I thought I had to do, but I do regret the many tears I have shed in my life because of their decision. Chelsea meant everything to me. I loved our Club as I still do even now.

EDDIE MAC EDDIE MAC

As far as the directors who were there at that time in our history are concerned I have absolutely no ill feelings against any of them and I forgive all of them. If I have led you to believe they were bad people, then you have read me completely wrong. As I have said before, we have all made decisions in our lives that perhaps we regret and are ashamed of. I believe all these directors were basically good people. I have so many things in my life I truly regret doing and nobody is perfect. Only Jesus was perfect.

Now listen to me if you would, all of you. I want to ask you to do something for me, especially if you are not a Christian. I know I can't hear you but promise me you will think seriously of doing this for me, if not now, then soon in your lives. What I am going to ask you to do may well be the most important thing you have ever done. I have forgiven my directors for treating me the way they did as I surely did with Brian Mears. God tells us in the Bible that we must forgive each other and if we don't, he will not forgive us. And you know what that means. You might want to forgive a relative or friend who may have hurt you. If you haven't one, let me suggest this. Go into your bedroom or anywhere it doesn't matter, just be alone for a few minutes and get on your knees and pray to God for the very first time perhaps in your life. He is waiting for you. He wants to hear from you. I told you He doesn't want anyone to go to Hell, He wants everyone to go to Heaven and to be with Him and I am even going to tell you what to say to Him for the first time if you don't have anything you could just start by saying "'Father" over the years I have been very angry with (you supply the name) for the way they treated me. Father, I wanted to ask if you would forgive me and to tell you that I sincerely forgive them and that's it. You have spoken to God, perhaps for the first time ever and He heard you. It is that easy. But I have to warn you that whatever reason you might give in asking for God's forgiveness you must be sincere. He knows when we are telling the truth or trying to deceive Him, so if you need to take a few minutes to think about it before you say it, that's okay. But I beg of you to do it. Every Christian is a sinner. I am a sinner, only Jesus was without sin. But He tells us in the Bible that if we regret our sins and ask forgiveness from Him, He will never remember our sins ever again. C'mon do it! Do it now. You may want to confess another sin that may have been troubling you. He will take it away from you instantly. He's waiting to do that for you. I promise you, I feel wonderful for the first time in my life. I'm not really afraid of dying any more, apprehensive perhaps a little, but I believe in my heart I am going to Heaven.

The alternative is unthinkable to me. If you do what I am asking you, the next thing you will want to do is to pick up the Bible. It is God's own words. Read it, even if it's only two or three pages a day. God will know you are reading about Him and how wonderfully pleased and proud He will be of you to know that you have decided to come to Him and be saved. I make no apologies to any one of you in trying to encourage you to read the Bible. God has told us that we have a responsibility to save as many people as we can. To be honest with you I don't believe I have ever saved anyone. It is quite possible that I have, because I have spoken to several groups over here in the USA about my faith. But I really don't know if I have. I know my wife Linda has. I am saved because of her influence over me through her own faith.

I hope all of you have enjoyed reading these words and the rest of this book as much as I have enjoyed writing my part in it for you. But I must tell you this about me. It would absolutely thrill and content me if I could believe that, with God's help, I might have reached some of you before I will surely die and if perhaps not some of you which I truly pray for then I would humbly settle for one, knowing and believing in my heart that my Lord Jesus Christ did not die in vain and for Him to know that we were still coming to Him.

Do I look for Chelsea results? If it is at all possible, I watch every game over here in the USA. We have wonderful coverage over here on several TV stations and I insist that all of you in the future refer to me as Chelsea's 'Number One Fan' in these United States. I am absolutely thrilled at the success our Club has managed to achieve over the years. What wonderful accomplishments. I am so very proud of our Club. I believe we have established ourselves as one of the finest Clubs in the world.

I know one thing for sure – a simple 'thank you' to you good folks would hardly be sufficient for me to say to you. I'm not quite sure I really do know what to say to you. I can tell you this however. These will be my last words in writing my part in this book and I am glad they are addressed to you because as far as I am concerned, you, the Chelsea supporters should be the most important part of this book. You are also the people I will never ever forget. It is because of you that I finally decided to write part of this book. I wonder if any of you are aware what this has really meant to me, to think that after all the years that have passed, it would seem that you have never forgotten me. I can't ever remember in all of my life ever having been paid such a wonderful compliment from so many thoughtful people.

I've never ever told anyone this. But I've never ever had an army before. "Eddie McCreadie's Blue and White Army." Wow, I remember again seeing it printed on our banners and scarves, thousands of them. I think the next time my wife Linda suggests anything about my ego, I'm going to for sure blame it on you guys. I have already told you how much all of your support meant to my players and me during that difficult time for our Club. I am also especially grateful to you for keeping that time alive again for my players. I have thought of them often. Writing this book I have complimented you the supporters; you have complimented me by remembering me; and I would like to once again, if I may one last time, compliment my players.

We all played a part; those who followed the team by way of their outstanding support at that time, and I played mine. But the true heroes of this magnificent achievement were my players, not me. To have carried on your young shoulders the weight of this great Club at such a devastating time was a great accomplishment in the history of our Club. The fact that our supporters have pushed hard to make sure this important part of our history should never be forgotten by producing this book is a great compliment from them to you. Please never forget that Gentlemen. This is where I will say goodbye to all of you. Man… here come these tears again. I send to all of you my love and best wishes. None of you will ever be forgotten by me. If indeed some of your intentions were to perhaps take away some of the pain and sadness I have carried with me all these years, you most certainly have accomplished that in abundance. When I think of my Club again, and I will often, it will never be in sadness anymore. How kind of you to remember me.

Reflecting on my time at Chelsea Football Club has brought to mind two people who were the greatest of assistance to me while I was there.

I would like to therefore, if I may, say a "Hello," to Chris Mathews who was always helpful to me and a special "Hello" to my secretary Jackie.

And lastly, I would like to acknowledge my grown up children who live in Scotland, namely Paul, Sean and Ann Marie.

SMITH AND THE KID

The summer of 1976 had been one of the best on record. Despite there being a drought, people generally enjoyed the long spell of fine weather and the power strikes that had blighted the country earlier in the decade were now a long and distant memory. The kid – a 13-year old in secondary school was hoping that the summer to come – that of 1977 – would be even better. Chelsea, the side he'd supported since he was 6-years old, had been promoted and the team – made up mostly of home-grown players – had the potential to take the First Division by storm.

However, dreams of a second consecutive fantastic summer were shattered when Chelsea FC announced that manager Eddie McCreadie's contract would not be renewed and, unfortuntately for the Chelsea supporters who loved him, the Scot and Chelsea Football Club had parted company. For the kid, the world was now a very different place… it was a world that had begun in 1975.

The early 1970s had been somewhat of a golden period for Chelsea supporters. Manager Dave Sexton – building on the foundations laid by Tommy Docherty – had moulded a side that had won both the FA Cup and the European Cup Winners Cup in successive years and had also reached the League Cup Final in 1972. However, by 1974, infighting and disquiet within the Chelsea squad, coupled with the failed attempt to rebuild and complete a new stadium at Stamford Bridge had left the club in crisis.

Dave Sexton was sacked in 1974 and was replaced by Ron Suart but, in season 1974/1975 with three matches left of what had become a disastrous campaign, former Chelsea and Scotland defender Eddie McCreadie was appointed manager.

With Chelsea all but relegated, the Scot's first game in charge was an away league fixture against Tottenham Hotspur at White Hart Lane, a game Chelsea lost 2-0.

In those days, at Stamford Bridge, the 'vocal' support for Chelsea came from The Shed. There was also what might be described as a 'breakaway' faction who occupied the North Stand terrace hoping to not only intimidate visiting fans but also to engage in combat. However, at away matches, the two groups stood together on the terraces in order to protect themselves from attack as well as attempt to 'take' the home end of the ground they were visiting. In 1975 when Chelsea travelled to White Hart Lane, the game was nothing less than a relegation dogfight with the losing side almost certainly destined for the drop to Division Two. The two previous visits had seen the Chelsea support come away from north London relatively unscathed but, in 1975, with an estimated 10,000 Blues locked outside, the Chelsea supporters inside the stadium came off badly with the kick-off delayed by some five-minutes due to sections of the crowd encroaching onto the pitch, the aim of the Spurs supporters being to defeat their opposite numbers.

Once referee Jack Taylor eventually started the game, Chelsea were unlucky in the fact that Charlie Cooke had a goal disallowed after some 15 minutes of play, the effort being ruled out for the apparent use of his arm to control the ball. In the second period, after Perryman had given Spurs the lead, Chelsea's Micky Droy also had a goal ruled out, this time the official deciding that a home player had been pushed unfairly in the lead-up to the ball crossing the line. Shortly after that, with Chelsea looking for the equaliser, a ball was pumped into Spurs' keeper Pat Jennings' area and Teddy Maybank managed to chest the ball into the path of Ray Wilkins who, despite being well placed, could only direct the ball past the wrong side of the post. A second for Spurs scored by Scot Alfie Conn gave the home side the victory and the two vital points that ensured their top-flight status.

The crowd violence at the game was frightening but, far from discouraging the kid from standing with those who were fighting, it encouraged him – and hundreds of similarly aged youngsters – to stand with those who were most likely to be able to defend them to ensure a safe but, nevertheless, an eventful return down Tottenham High Rd and the Seven Sisters Road to Seven Sisters tube station and a tube to the relative tranquillity of West or South London.

Chelsea's two remaining fixtures that season were at Stamford Bridge but, unable to pick themselves up from the defeat at Spurs, a 1-1 draw against Sheffield United at Stamford Bridge, the Chelsea goal scorer being Teddy Maybank and a similar result against Everton, also at Stamford Bridge, a game in which Ray Wilkins scored for The Blues, were not enough to secure survival.

The following season began with a match against Sunderland at Roker Park. In those days, trips to the north-east were gloomy affairs, those from London almost dreading the long trip to an area they regarded as populated by Neanderthals.

For The Kid, a trip to Sunderland to watch Chelsea in their first game of the 75/76 campaign left him with mixed feelings. The excitement he was feeling at the thought of making what would be the longest journey he'd ever undertaken was tempered by the worrying stories he'd heard about the inhabitants of the 'strange land' that was north-eastern England.

The older kids at his school and indeed, the Smith brothers with whom he made friends, had regaled The Kid with tales of previous visits to places like Newcastle and Sunderland that had fired his furtive imagination and, within his mind's eye, he had visions of giant men sporting unkempt sideburns who, at best, were sub-normal and wore hand-me-down, poor quality clothes.

On the other hand, The Kid's compatriots from London and the surrounding areas were sophisticated, worldly-wise fashion leaders who were, without doubt, a cut above those from the northern regions of London.

Fortunately, brothers Smith and The Kid had negotiated the grim looking area in which Roker Park – Sunderland's stadium – was situated without meeting any unfriendly local inhabitants and, although somewhat perturbed by the score, they returned to the normality and sanctuary that was southern England without incident. A goal from Bill Garner had given Chelsea the lead but, after conceding two, the Londoners were defeated 2-1. It was a match in which Eddie McCreadie had given 21-year old Garry Stanley his debut.

The Wednesday following had been preceded the previous day by countless conversations between employers and employees concerning arrangements to see either a doctor or a dentist. Somewhat fortuitously, these appointments had also coincided with an evening kick-off away at West Bromwich Albion that would mean that those travelling from London to follow Chelsea would have to leave in the afternoon to make it to The Hawthorns in time for the kick-off. The elder of the Smith brothers had generously offered to drive both his younger sibling and The Kid to the game in his Austin 1100.

The journey was punctuated by many pit-stops as a result of a fourth travelling companion who was feeling the effects of a dodgy curry consumed the previous evening.

The service stations were full of Chelsea supporters many in Ford Transit vans sporting the names of the different hire companies and of businesses whose drivers had coincidently happened to have pre-arranged planned trips to a dentist or a doctor.

Arriving at the ground, those who'd made the journey were pleased to find they were amongst a Chelsea following of probably three to four thousand finding their voices among the crowd of just over 18,000.

As the kick-off approached, attention was drawn to a mob of a few hundred youths entering the away end from the left hand side and a 'rumble' looked likely until it became evident that the late arrivals were 'Chelsea Midlands' and they were welcomed into the throng of Londoners as acceptable allies.

West Brom, a team who, like Chelsea, had enjoyed better times in the top-flight and were amongst the bookies favourites to be promoted back to the big time.

Chelsea found their feet quickly in the game and looked the more threatening side and their cause was made even better when the Baggies midfielder Len Cantello was dismissed for kicking Bill Garner in retaliation after a reckless challenge was sustained. Bill offered his apologies and Cantello departed after the pair shake hands!

Despite having the man advantage and attacking for the entire second-half, a breakthrough was not possible and the game finished goalless. Garry Stanley had a fine match and was unlucky not to find the net on a couple of occasions with efforts from some 25-yards. Micky Droy and John Dempsey also performed commendably at the back restricting veteran World Cup hero Geoff Hurst to one effort on target in the game.

With little sign of any disorder in or around the ground, the four head back down the M6 – George was still feeling unwell and didn't intend to go to work the next day but would make an honest visit to the quacks! A phone-call the following evening confirmed suspected food poisoning but he expected to be fit for Carlisle's visit to the Bridge on Saturday.

Following his return from the Midlands and the rollicking he received from his anxious father for staying out until 11.40pm when Smith Snr had dropped him home, The Kid was relieved that Chelsea's next match was at Stamford Bridge meaning he'd be home well in time to beat the 8.00pm curfew that his parents had imposed.

Meeting the Smith brothers and the now fully recovered George outside The Swan pub at Fulham Broadway at 2.30pm, The Kid and his friends were in their usual position in The Shed in plenty of time to see the game against Carlisle United kick-off at 3.00pm. Teddy Maybank headed a brace netted with the third in Chelsea's 3-1 victory being a blistering 25-yard strike via the crossbar from Brian Bason, his effort eventually winning ITV's 'The Big Match' Goal of the Month.

A Wednesday evening fixture at Stamford Bridge followed, Chelsea mirroring their previous score with Ray Wilkins notching two and Kenny Swain netting for The Blues in a comfortable victory against Oxford United.

Having attended the game with his father, The Kid was more than pleased that he'd been given permission to travel to Chelsea's next game – away to Luton Town – but only on the proviso that he was accompanied by his travelling companions with whom he'd made the journey to West Brom.
The young Chelsea side were now beginning to capture the imagination of their long suffering supporters and notably the attendance of 19,165 for Carlisle on the Saturday was bettered in mid-week with a crowd of nearly 23,000.

With the apparent upturn in fortune, Chelsea descended upon Luton in their thousands the following Saturday, buoyed in the belief that the team were now to establish themselves as promotion candidates. Sadly a poor performance saw Luton record a 3-0 victory but the game paled into insignificance by events involving hooliganism upon the terraces.

In the corresponding fixture the previous January, a train carrying Chelsea supporters back to St Pancras had been set ablaze although, fortunately for all onboard, there were no fatalities.

As in the previous fixture, there were outbreaks of fighting at the home end prior to kick-off with many youths sporting Chelsea colours being ejected from the ground or moved to the away terrace. Upon the award of a penalty to the home side on the hour which secured a 2-0 lead, a concerted effort began from the away end to invade the pitch with the intention to disrupt the game and cause an abandonment. Play was indeed held up for several minutes on two occasions and, despite the fact that the Luton Town goalkeeper was physically assaulted, the referee saw the game out.

Outside shop windows were broken and motor vehicles damaged, some overturned. This display of thuggery was some of the worst experienced to date and the media were quick in their condemnation of Chelsea Football Club.

The papers carried their stories on throughout the week with the usual cries for imprisonment, national service and far worse for the perpetrators of the violence that has ensued.

They also waited with bated breath as Chelsea's next home fixture saw Nottingham Forest, another team with a sizeable following and hooligan element, visiting the Bridge.

It was widely reported that Forest would run a supporters excursion via train for some 500 followers and that they would be escorted from Kings Cross by the Metropolitan Police to Stamford Bridge to avoid any confrontations.

Indeed, this military style manoeuvre was well executed, and whilst a few skirmishes occured when the visitors were departing Stanford Bridge, all was fairly quiet compared to the previous week at Kenilworth Road.

The assembled Chelsea aggressors outside the North Stand gate bellowed to the strains of Land of Hope and Glory "We hate Nottingham Forest..." to which the red hordes bellowed back "And Nottingham Forest hates you!" Against the backdrop of the Luton riot and impending actions against the club and supporters, the side's form plummeted over the next few weeks with defeats at Oldham, Ray Wilkins scoring for Chelsea in a 2-1 defeat, a 1-0 League Cup loss at Gresty Road to Crewe Alexandra and a 0-0 home draw with York City, the game notable for the fact that Ray Wilkins missed a penalty.

Many of the teams that Chelsea were facing in Division Two were previously unknown to the Chelsea supporters who, only a few years previously, had travelled to Athens to see the club lift a major European trophy. Indeed, it was reported that after the disastrous start to the season, a number of high profile longstanding supporters had sought out Chairman Brian Mears after the York debacle and demanded that Eddie McCreadie be removed as team manager.

There were also sporadic outbreaks of violence at the away game at Portsmouth, a midweek 1-1 draw, a header from Bill Garner via the crossbar rescuing a point for Chelsea. A visit to Fulham saw McCreadie's youngsters endure a 2-0 defeat, the Chelsea supporters exhibiting their ire with another pitch invasion and a 4-1 reverse at The Dell to a Southampton side that included Chelsea legend Peter Osgood with Ray Wilkins' name again going down as The Blues' goal scorer. The game featured on that

Saturday's edition of Match of the Day, with the commentator mentioning the accompanying strains of barking police dogs at the Chelsea end!

Despite the poor run of results, there was some good news on the playing side with the return of Peter Bonetti for the home game against Blackpool in late October. Steve Sherwood, who later would find some success at Watford, had not experienced very good form in his dozen appearances between the sticks since the start of the season. With Bonetti between the sticks, Chelsea raised their game and goals from Ray Wilkins – a 78th minute penalty and a last minute strike from Tommy Langley gave Chelsea a 2-0 victory over Blackpool and a much better run of form up to Christmas.

British Rail announced that it would suspend the operation of it's football specials for those who followed Chelsea. However, flyers were handed out at home games for alternative excursions organised by CAT and Camkin Sports. 'CAT' was an acronym for 'Chelsea Away Travel' hosted by Chelsea stalwart Michael Greenaway.

Another club almost foreign to Chelsea, Plymouth Argyle, visited the Bridge on November 1st and, despite the game taking place in a deluge, saw an improved crowd of just over 20,000. Argyle's support on the day numbered nearly 2,000 and there were several outbreaks of fighting on the North Stand terrace throughout the game with many arrests.

On the field, Ray Wilkins gave Chelsea a 2-0 lead, a bullet diving header at the Shed End from a left-wing cross supplied by Bill Garner only for the visitors to grab a point with two late goals. However, with the score at 1-0 Bonetti had made a save as good as any in his career when pedalling backwards and clawing out a header from Paul Mariner.

Chelsea won all four of their remaining November fixtures, three away at Hull City (2-1; Hutchinson, Britton), Blackpool (2-0; Droy, Maybank) and Bristol Rovers (2-1; Maybank, Hutchinson) and Notts County at the Bridge,

Garner and a penalty from Ray Wilkins securing a 2-0 win. The game at Bristol Rovers saw Teddy Maybank net after a run from the half-way line and Bill Garner dismissed for brawling before he endeavoured to re-enter play during descending fog!

Promotion seeking Bolton Wanderers were next to visit the Bridge in early December and another crowd of over 20,000 witnessed a 1-0 victory for the visitors their team including Peter Reid and Sam Allardyce. Regrettably Ray Wilkins saw a possible equalising penalty saved by Barry Siddall. Following that miss from the spot, Wilkins later told of being verbally abused and spat at when leaving the pitch at full-time by "a fan"!

Another defeat was suffered the following Saturday at Carlisle when Wilkins found the net early on but could not prevent a 2-1 reverse. A train carrying travelling fans back to London was met by the Metropolitan Police at Euston after staff manning the buffet car reported that passenger doors had been opened at speeds of up to 100-miles per hour.

Second Division leaders Sunderland visited the Bridge on 20 December and their side included Jim Montgomery, Dick Malone, Bobby Moncur, Bobby Kerr, Vic Halom and future Blues manager Ian Porterfield who had all received FA Cup Winners medals in their 1973 success over Leeds Utd. Chelsea turned in a fine performance, winning by the only goal of the game courtesy of an Ian Britton strike from a knock down from Ian Hutchinson at the Shed End.

This was the first time that the brothers Smith, along with their late father and friend George, had watched a match at the Bridge from the East Stand Upper Tier. The Smith's father's visits to Chelsea were however, only occasional at the time as he despised the hooliganism which had become prevalent in the game as well as what he saw as the lack of sportsmanship on the field.

When Chelsea were eliminated upon the away goals ruling by Swedish part-timers Atvidaberg in 1971 he offered warm applause to their players at the end of the game from their position adjacent to the Shed by the Bovril entrance, much to the dismay of those around them.

On the occasion of the match with Sunderland, some visiting Maccams offered the Smith attendees cigars and tots of whisky prior to kick-off but by the end were screaming obscenities at our players and supporters. The Smiths' father wished them compliments of the season... and invited them to go forward and multiply!

The Kid however, not wanting to 'miss' the atmosphere that was generated by those standing under the corrugated tin roof that covered The Shed, moved from his now usual place that was by the Bovril Gate and found a new position to watch the games that, in future, he'd call 'his place'. Recognising a soon to be engaged couple near the front in the middle of The Shed proper, he decided he'd stand with them and, like thousands of others who'd met new people at Stamford Bridge, a new friendship was formed.

The place he'd chosen was to the left of the aisle that was closest to the police observation platform from where members of Sergeant Bilko's Black & White Army would regularly choose victims who were then unceremoniously hauled out, the ritual usually taking place after the traditional "Knees Up Mother Brown" had been sung.

This involved the person who started the song off being joined by all around him in both singing the words and at the same time bouncing up and down and pushing the person in front forward. Adapting the lyric from the chart hit "The Mighty Quinn", the Chelsea words were, "You go in on your feet, come out on your head, You ain't seen nothing like the mighty Shed!"

Boxing Day witnessed the first Orient versus Chelsea league fixture since 1929. Unfortunately, the form shown in the previous game was not taken forward into this one and a 3-1 defeat was suffered. The legendary Laurie Cunningham was Chelsea's chief tormentor scoring one and having an assist with another.

Bobby Fisher, Orient's young right-back had been a classmate of one of Smith Junior's pals who was attending the game with him and had predicted that they would beat Chelsea. However, it had been Fisher's poor back pass that enabled Teddy Maybank to chip in an equaliser with only some 12 minutes remaining but there was still time for a capitulation by The Blues. The bulk of Chelsea's vocal support was housed upon the side terrace opposite the main stand and at kick-off came under threat from itinerant followers of both West Ham and Tottenham.

Whilst Spurs had played at home earlier in the day, the Irons were at Villa Park. Tottenham regaled the Chelsea supporters in chants of "We put you in Division 2", referring to the defeat at White Hart Lane the previous year which largely contributed to The Blues' relegation. Meanwhile, Chelsea baited West Ham with chants referring to them not travelling to support their own team. All in all, it was a strange afternoon which ended with another pitch invasion which was included in the referee's report.

The following day, Chelsea suffered another defeat, this time at home to Charlton, losing 3-2. Trailing 0-2 at half-time a comeback looked on the cards when Kenny Swain and Ian Britton scored within two-minutes of each other only for a John Dempsey error to let in Derek Hales for the winner. Eddie McCreadie commented after the game that the performance, and that of the previous day at Orient, had been good and the outcome very unfair upon the balance of play.

Chelsea, wallowing in mid-table mediocrity, now turned their attention to the FA Cup with a Third Round home-tie against Bristol Rovers. It had been well reported that, as a club, Chelsea were in debt to the tune of some £3m. In order to secure increased income from the cup-tie, Chelsea requested that they stage the match on New Year's Day instead of the scheduled date of Saturday 3 January.

Astonishingly, the request was sanctioned and attracted a crowd of in excess of 35,000 (10,000 up from the local derby with Charlton a few days earlier). In true Chelsea fashion however, a goal from Garner meant the game ended in a 1-1 draw and Chelsea had to head back down the M4 for a replay at Eastville on the Saturday. The game saw a large Chelsea following attend and celebrate a 1-0 victory courtesy of a late winner from Swain.

The attendance at Eastville was not as big as it might have been due to the fact that several Bristol Rovers fans decided to view proceedings from their vehicles above the away terrace on the elevated hard shoulder of the M32. They had enjoyed some banter with the massed ranks of Chelsea supporters and their enforced departure following the arrival of the motorway police was greeted with raucous applause.

The following Saturday saw an ignominious 0-3 home defeat to relegation threatened Oldham Athletic. In true Chelsea tradition, The Blues then travelled to the City Ground, the home of Nottingham Forest and produced perhaps their best performance of the season so far enjoying a 3-1 victory after conceding early on.

Whilst the goals came from Garner, Ray Wilkins and Hutchinson, with injuries ruling out both regular centre backs Dempsey and Droy, a new partnership of Steve Wicks and David Hay was tried out and worked sufficiently well to remain in place for the rest of the season – surely a case of 'serendipity'! Garner's equaliser was notably celebrated by Chelsea infiltrators in the notorious Trent End.

The following match saw Chelsea in FA Cup fourth roundaction which meant a visit to York City, the first time that the two sides had ever met at Bootham Crescent. Chelsea's following accounted for half of the attendance of 9,591.

Together with three other die-hards, brothers Smith and The Kid travelled up in a cramped Ford Cortina 1600 which had hastily been hired from Keeler rent-a-car that morning. This, after everybody in that party had decided that none of their own vehicles were trusted to get them there and back!

Arriving adjacent to the Bootham Crescent Ground, the six parked in a nearby hotel and were enjoying the normal pre-match fare when their genial host announced that the game had been postponed for some reason - perhaps a power failure.

Driving up there had seen mild snowfall and looking out from the hostelry, the intrepid traveller had noticed a light settling but nothing too concerning. One of the number, Frank, a rapidly approaching octogenarian expressed outrage to this news and demanded that all present finish their drinks and head over to the ground and offer to clear any precipitation from the pitch. He then departed alone whilst other Chelsea supporters who had travelled up the night before and were resident announced that they were going to debark to Leeds to see their tie with Palace.

Whilst pondering their situation over another ale or two, those who'd travelled in the hired car then learned that the game was 'back on' and a power problem had been resolved. Frank had obviously sorted the matter out.

A fairly easy 2-0 victory thanks to goals courtesy of Garner and Hutchinson was recorded and they would soon learn that the Fifth Round draw had pitted Chelsea at home to Third Division Crystal Palace who had beaten Leeds United by the only goal of the game. It's still shrouded in the mists of time whether those who'd decided to travel to Elland Road ever made it back to Bootham Crescent.

With the FA Cup tie with Palace approaching the next two league games saw a home defeat to promotion chasing West Bromwich Albion and a draw at Oxford United. Although the friends arrived at The Shed entrance some 60 minutes before the Palace tie, it was soon evident that the match had attracted all and sundry and that the gates were soon to close with a full house – something rarely witnessed since the visits of Manchester United and George Best in the 1960s. Indeed, a massive crowd of 54,407 was recorded.

The guys managed to take up their normal viewing point between the Bovril Gate and the West Stand. However, their entrance was suitably delayed after they had to disentangle Frank from a programme seller who had announced that, just as he tendered the correct coinage, the last copy had been sold. Frank was heard to utter to me that this was poor and that whenever there was a big game the club failed to print enough programmes.

"Just like the other season against the Dynamo!" he exclaimed. This was, in fact, a reference to a friendly played at the Bridge against Moscow Dynamo after the Second World War in 1945.

The game was well documented and remembered for Malcolm Allison's pre-match gesticulations to the Shed End, Chelsea's remarkable comeback from two goals down at half-time, Peter Taylor's free kick winner and kung-fu fighting upon the North Stand Terrace.

Unfortunately, BBC TV's 'Match of the Day' that evening and the television news channels chose largely to show the terrace brawling and the appearance of nine mounted police horses. Some of the miscreants are still visitors to the Bridge to this day.

Back in the league, Chelsea endured a run of indifferent form, as ever. The only good news sees the introduction of free scoring Steve Finnieston being promoted from the reserves and going on to net in five of the remaining dozen fixtures.

After an encouraging 3-0 win at Plymouth Argyle, where an Ian Britton goal rivalled that early season effort from Bason against Carlisle, Chelsea entertained a strong Southampton team including Peter Osgood. This was Ossie's first return to the Bridge since leaving in acrimonious circumstances. In The Shed, some opinions differed as to the reception that should be afforded to Peter.

The older of the Smith brothers declared that he was a traitor and cost Dave Sexton his job, whereas others insisted that he was still a hero in their eyes. The mood changed soon after kick-off and two supporters were seen to disagree most vehemently, with one urging Ossie to score against Chelsea. A bloody nose was sustained and the bickering ceased.

A Mick Channon opener was cancelled out by super-Jock Finnieston – accompanied to the strains of, "Super Jock, He scores goals, Twice as good as Stanley Bowles" – and a poor game passes without any notable contribution from Osgood – only a booking for a foul on his one-time team mate Peter Bonetti.

The Blues were destined for a mid-table finish the only notable remaining games being a 2-1 defeat at Bolton where, after Britton gives Chelsea the lead, both David Hay and Graham Wilkins net for the opposition and a lively 2-2 draw at promotion bound Bristol City where Kenny Swain and Garry Stanley scored fine goals.

Before the last home game of the season against Orient, the then Chairman Brian Mears addressed the crowd of 17,679 from the centre-circle and promises that, despite the dire financial position that the club found themselves in, none of the promising youngsters would be sold in the summer.

True to form, Orient then went onto win 2-0, with Laurie Cunningham scoring a remarkable solo effort at the Shed End – a goal suitably acknowledged and applauded by all sides of the Bridge.

The last game of the season took Chelsea back to York but this time courtesy of CAT. A 2-2 draw capped a season of glorious unpredictability. The Chelsea followers made various presentations to Micky Greenaway upon the return trip in thanks for all his sterling efforts to ensure that as many supporters as possible could attend away matches following the withdrawal of British Rail's cattle truck 'specials'.

At Kings Cross, the friends bade their farewells to each other for the summer and prayed for better times, hopefully, ahead.

*****

Despite finishing in 11th position the previous season, after suffering relegation the season before, there had been signs of promise for Chelsea supporters going into the new campaign.

Ray Wilkins had been capped by England, and a 4-4-2 formation had begun to take shape with Peter Bonetti ever dependable and the Wicks and Hay centre-back partnership beginning to blossom. To add to that, youngsters Ian Britton, Garry Stanley and Ray Lewington were ably assisting captain Ray Wilkins with Steve Finnieston and Kenny Swain also striking up a good understanding.

It was also reported that the players had offered to waive their expenses in order for a pre-season tour to Sweden to go ahead when the club had looked to postpone the trip due to the parlous financial position it found itself in.

Some 20 hardy souls followed the team to Sweden and witnessed a defeat to Halmstad but enjoyed victories against Orgyte and GAIS of Gothenburg.

In August, Chelsea played three fixtures in the Anglo-Scottish Cup against Fulham, Norwich and Orient! Ominously, after a goalless game with Fulham and a 1-1 draw with Norwich (Finnieston), both games at home, Chelsea suffered a 2-1 (Droy) defeat at the hands of Orient seven days before they would begin the campaign at the same Brisbane Road venue.

So the season began with the only changes in personnel from the previous Saturday being Bonetti for John Phillips, Steve Wicks returning from injury replacing goal-scorer Micky Droy and Kenny Swain in place of Teddy Maybank.

The opening day attendance was, contrary to the previous week's Anglo-Scottish cup-tie, some 5,000 up with nearly 11,500 assembled, with an estimated 7,000 sporting Chelsea colours. Thankfully, unlike the 75/76 encounters, there were no apparent agitators from other London clubs.
Some three-minutes from time, Jock Finnieston shrugged off a couple of challenges and rifled home the only goal of the game. Cue mayhem upon the terraces.

At the final whistle, jubilant youths invading the pitch to salute the victory brought down the perimeter wall opposite the main stand and a large bang, sounding like a cannon being fired, resounded around the ground.

Amazingly, Orient's Chairman Brian Winston was reported to have banned Eddie McCreadie from attending the Directors Lounge after the match due to the fact that he didn't like tactics used by The Blues in suppressing the talents of Laurie Cunningham, Chelsea's chief tormentor the previous season.

A midweek crowd of over 17,000 then witnessed a 1-1 home draw with Notts County with Ian Britton netting a second-half headed equaliser at The Shed End.

This would be the first of the diminutive Scotsman's headed efforts over the course of the season with Britton, at five-foot five-inches, drawing comparisons with the legendary Chelsea adversary and Leeds United and Scotland captain Billy Bremner.

At the time, it was noticeable that the press were continuingly commenting on the club's £3m debt and the need for attendances to increase if there was to be any chance of financial survival. Carlisle paid their now customary early season visit to the Bridge upon the following Saturday when goals from Swain and Finnieston secured a 2-1 win in an entertaining game. Chelsea were top of the league upon the first compilation of division tables.

Following this victory, the Sunday papers reported that Chelsea supporters were hoping to hand a cheque for £100,000 to the Board at the end of the season in an attempt to stave off the financial pressure. As well as that, Chelsea received income from a series of sponsorship deals, the price of the said advertising dependent on whether their games were televised.

The following week, Saturday 4 September, Chelsea supporters took a daunting visit down the Old Kent Road to visit Millwall, a side whom they hadn't played since 1960 when Ted Drake's side recorded a 7-1 League Cup victory. Upon the production of the fixtures pre-season the press had earmarked this encounter as a potential bloodbath on the terraces as both clubs had their hooligan factions. However, although the Millwall fans had, over many years, acquired a reputation for violence, they had become particularly fearsome with the rise of hooliganism that began in the late 1960s.

Hailing from leafy Buckinghamshire and having little geographical knowledge of East London, the Smith brothers had decided upon a 'dummy run' on a Saturday afternoon in what was an extremely hot summer to acquaint themselves with the area and perhaps obtain seats for the fixture. Alighting at New Cross Gate and venturing towards the ground, it was noticeable that adjacent to painted slogans proclaiming that East End villain "George Davis was innocent" were new offerings warning "Turn back Chelsea – you are dead". The scene was already set for the game some six weeks before the fixture was scheduled to take place.

Stand seats were duly obtained via a colleague who worked in the area and it was decided not to risk the Underground but drive through London to the game. Their worst fears were confirmed when, after parking, they witnessed a young father and son sporting Chelsea colours being assaulted in the street next to Cold Blow Lane. Their seats were in the very front row and they scanned the ground wondering where any of the Chelsea contingent may emerge. There were sporadic outbursts of violence chiefly in the Cold Blow Lane End but also in the two other terrace areas.

When the game got underway Millwall tore into Chelsea and scored three times in just over 30-minutes. Unfortunately, Jock Finnieston was injured early in the game and was replaced by the veteran defender Ron Harris. Strangely it was later reported that Harris had already played for our reserve side earlier in the day!

Meanwhile, The Kid, this time travelling with some school friends, had caught a train from Victoria but, with the area being unfamiliar, had alighted at New Cross. Unbeknown to them, they would have saved the time it took them to go back 'up the line' and catch a connecting train to New Cross Gate if they had left the station and walked to Cold Blow Lane and the frightening prospect that was The Den, the home of Millwall FC.

It was 3.05pm by the time they neared the stadium but, worryingly, they encountered several Chelsea supporters making their way from the ground and back to the railway station. Asking them why they were not staying to watch the game, the youngsters were told that those departing had 'had enough'.

Naively ignorant of anything to do with Millwall, The Kid was under the impression that The Lions wore a strip similar to that of Blackpool and, upon entering the ground, was surprised to see that the vast majority of those who'd made their way through the turnstiles were wearing blue. "It's all Chelsea!" he joyously exclaimed to his friend but, as soon as he'd uttered the word, he realised his mistake as the people within earshot who'd heard him turned and gave him and his companions the most evil of stares.

Immediately, concerned for their safety, the young Chelsea supporters made their way quickly away from the scene of The Kid's faux pas and found themselves standing close to a bar that was situated on one side of the ground. Surrounded by men who looked in their mid to late 30s and early 40s, the young Chelsea supporters felt somewhat safer than they had done when they'd endured the threatening looks from youngsters of their own age a few minutes earlier. However, with the Chelsea supporters who'd been standing under the covered section of one end of the ground surrounded by home fans, the cry of, "Come and join us, come and join us, come and join us over here!" went up and the men whose company The Kid and his friend had sought for 'safety', disconcertingly knocked back their pints and began to make their way around to where the fighting was taking place to answer the request of their compatriots. With some 20-minutes of the game remaining and Chelsea losing, The Kid and his friends somewhat wisely decided to call it a day and, to use a phrase reserved for those whom others had decided had 'bottled it', they 'melted' and were on a train back to Victoria before the final whistle.

Despite trailing by three goals, midway through the second-half a chant of "Chelsea, Chelsea, top of the league!" rang out from the middle section of the Cold Blow Lane end. The Smiths spotted, among others, Daniel Harkins and Babs leading this chant.

The Smiths were more than pleased to return to Buckinghamshire, unscathed but obviously disappointed that Chelsea's great start to the season had received quite a blow. Eddie McCreadie was fairly upbeat however, and complimented his young team for attempting a spirited comeback in the second period.

The next fixture took Chelsea back down to Plymouth Argyle and it was heartening that after the defeat at Millwall, two football specials carrying some 800 Blues supporters departed from Paddington.

After a non-descript goalless first-half, the game burst into life in the final 20-minutes. First, Britton netted a penalty after a foul on Lewington and then Swain scored a fine solo effort to give Chelsea a 2-0 lead. However, within five minutes Argyle had levelled through Brian Hall and Paul Mariner. With only a few minutes remaining Ray Wilkins picked out Swain at the far post who rose magnificently to head across the six-yard line where Finnieston bundled the ball home and ended up entangled in the net with the goalkeeper and two defenders.

The trip from Home Park – Argyle's ground – to the railway station was quite eventful as it involved crossing playing fields where a number of rugby matches were still in progress. Rival factions clashed upon the pitches whilst the local constabulary, accompanied by Alsatians dogs endeavoured to keep order. In the ensuing melee, a German Shepherd became aware of a Cornish pasty in Smith minor's carrier bag and sank his teeth into it!

Bolton were the next visitors to the Bridge and again were fancied for promotion. However Chelsea erased the memories of that drubbing at Millwall by putting on a first class performance running out as 2-1 winners. David Hay scored just before the break with a header after a sprint from the halfway line and Garry Stanley rifled home a free kick from some 25-yards early in the second-half. Bolton replied in injury time but, for them, the goal was a mere consolation.

There then followed a trip to Blackpool, another team amongst the early front-runners. Abandoning their cars in favour of a train journey courtesy of a Chelsea 'special', all onboard were dismayed when it arrived at the destination some time after the game had kicked off due to some mindless vandalism to a train carriage. This resulted in an unscheduled stop at Preston where transport police were called upon. Alighting at Blackpool, there was a mass sprint to Bloomfield Road, with those running hoping to catch at least part of the first-half.

Upon entering the ground, the late-comers were made aware that Super Jock Finnieston had given Chelsea an early lead and another rear guard action with Bonetti performing excellently in the second-half saw Chelsea finish the game victorious thanks to the solitary goal. On the return journey, those on the special train were witness to Daniel Harkins – universally accepted 'leader' of The Shed – administering an enquiry to find out who were the perpetrators of the vandalism on the outward trip and arranged a collection, handing over some £150 to British Rail back at Euston. Two youths were unofficially banned by a kangaroo court.

Despite torrential rain and blustery conditions a crowd of some 28,500 assembled at the Bridge the following Saturday to witness top of the table Chelsea beat Cardiff City 2-1 in another excellent display of attacking football. Swain gave The Blues an early lead and Ray Lewington added a second with a supreme half volley on the hour. Cardiff's reply was an injury time penalty.

The wet conditions seemed to dampen the hooligans' spirit with only a few arrests in the Fulham Road prior to the game with Cardiff having a following of some two-thousand.

With Ray Wilkins being selected for international duty, Bristol Rovers requested that their fixture against Chelsea that was due to be played the following Saturday be brought forward to Tuesday as a Blues team with the future England captain would guarantee them a bigger attendance. Chelsea agreed and 13,000 witnessed Rovers run out as 2-1 winners.

Prior to the game, a hooligan element from Chelsea infiltrated the home Tote End and in the ensuing violence missiles thrown from adjacent waste ground shattered windows in the home dressing room. Tannoy announcements early in the game requested that apprentices of Bristol Rovers were required to leave their seats and clear up the glass before the teams returned at half-time. However Chelsea – with Wilkins – conceded an early goal and, despite a headed equaliser from Finnieston, were beaten with the winning goal coming some two-minutes from the end. Smith senior's Austin 1100 chugged back into Buckinghamshire at around 2am with a broken alternator requiring garage attention the following morning.

Following the international break, Chelsea were buoyed by another home crowd of nearly 26,000 for the visit of Oldham. Another exciting encounter saw The Blues score early on from Swain and Wilkins only to be pegged back to 2-2 by the half hour. However, before the break, two further efforts from Finnieston and Wicks restored the two-goal margin.

Oldham offered a spirited comeback scoring the only goal in the second-half but The Blues hung on to remain in pole position in the Second Division.

Despite the damage sustained to the British Rail rolling stock on the previous visit to Blackpool, two football specials ran to Blackburn's Ewood Park the following Saturday. The second, carrying The Kid and Smith's group, experienced mechanical problems and arrived at the local Mill Hill station at around 2.45pm.

With Ewood Park being a mile or so away, those onboard alighted and, in scenes similar to those seen at Blackpool, ran to the ground. Having given the police escort the slip, The Kid et al managed to obtain good stand seats away from the Chelsea contingent behind the goal. Jock Finnieston again delivered scoring once in each half, the second being a penalty after Garry Stanley had been upended after a solo run into the Blackburn penalty area. Being housed in the main stand, the Smith's celebrations were not shared by the local support and they decided to leave early and ensure a good seat on the train home.

Nearing Mill Hill, a young local constable enquired if they were Chelsea supporters and, after replying positively, he warned them that an ambush by disgruntled Blackburn hooligans along the route was a possibility. After initially advising that they wait until the bulk of Chelsea's support caught them up, he decided that he would provide an escort. Indeed, a few hundred-yards later, some would be aggressors in wait were espied. Amazingly, the young police officer quickened his step, drew his truncheon and gave chase dispersing the awaiting mob. At Mill Hill, the Chelsea supporters offered their thanks. "No problem, he replied. "I'm Burnley and hate Blackburn!"

Travelling back to Euston, the jubilant Chelsea throng joined in the singing of many anthems including; "Que sera sera, Whatever will be, will be, We're going to Wembley via Highbury!"

All the talk was of Chelsea's impending visit to Arsenal on the following Wednesday for a League Cup tie, and that every Chelsea supporter should endeavour to view proceedings from the home North Bank terrace. "We're gonna take the North Bank Highbury (again!)"

When the game took place, Arsenal's Highbury stadium saw a lock-out crowd, London's biggest of the season at 52,305, with those inside witness to a classic cup-tie. There were Chelsea supporters in every part of the ground with The Kid being one of those in the home North Bank end from where the strains of one the favourites of the Chelsea supporters' repertoire in "Eddie McCreadie's Blue and White Army!" could be heard ringing around the ground. Learning the art of 'bunking' – trains, tubes and buses at an early age, The Kid had skipped into Highbury twice before when he'd seen his side play Arsenal in the 1st Division fixtures in 1973 – the 0-0 draw and the Boxing Day 2-1 victory in 1974 when Chris Garland notched a brace – and this occasion was no exception. However, it was the first time he'd ventured into the home end, his previous two visits having been to the official 'away' Clock End.

The game was marred by a badly broken leg sustained by Brian Bason in a tackle with Northern Ireland International Sammy Nelson with the game scoreless. Chelsea eventually went down 2-1, this after David Hay had cancelled out an early second half strike by Trevor Ross, Frank Stapleton headed the winner. Jock Finnieston was unlucky not to land The Blues with a lucrative replay when a last minute effort flew just wide. Although Chelsea lost the game, for The Kid and his friends who'd gone to the game with him, any fear of potential 'trouble' with Arsenal fans had, after their entry to their home end, been dispelled right there and then, and it was a feeling that stayed with them for life.

Although disappointed at going out to a London rival, most Chelsea supporters knew that the real focus of the season was the drive to return to the top flight so, when Southampton visited Stamford Bridge the following Saturday, there was no 'hangover' from the League Cup exit and, in fact, there was a real buzz about the place, the Chelsea team receiving many plaudits from the press following the gutsy performance at Highbury. Despite the fact that the visiting side were minus the still much loved Peter Osgood due to him suffering a minor injury, there was a big crowd with many jostling for seats and access to the Shed End in chaotic scenes not witnessed since the Crystal Palace FA Cup tie the previous season.

Although the Smiths had purchased a pair of East Stand Upper Tier season-tickets at a reduced rate, this fixture – along with the Fulham Boxing Day fixture were not included. However, entry to the game was secured from the Portacabin box office for the East Lower among some visiting fans.

The game stands up to the occasion and, whilst the first-half ended goalless, there was much to admire, with Chelsea passing the ball quite superbly and carving out a few half-chances. A Saints' follower located next to Smith minor remarked at the break that Chelsea's first-half performance was the best he could recall for sometime but added the caveat, "Don't be surprised if we nick a goal and the game though!"

His words rang true when with, some 15-minutes remaining, the journeyman Ted MacDougall found the net in a rare visiting attack. A few minutes later John Phillips, deputising for the injured Bonetti, saved bravely at the feet of England International, Mick Channon, when a second goal looked ominous. However, Kenny Swain netted at the Shed End with a neat near post header from a Wilkins corner and a draw looked the likely result.

The Bridge then erupted when Steve Finnieston added a second and then, with time running out, Phillips launches a long throw out to Swain in the left wing position and after a brilliant run his cunning cross is met at the far post by Wilkins who scored a third for Chelsea.

Smith was quick to remind the Saints fan that he was quite right about them snatching a goal but not the result but he smiled, offered his hand and wished both Smith and Chelsea well in the race for promotion.

The next game saw Chelsea travel to Hereford, unchartered territory for Blues followers, the home team having enjoyed giant killing status since defeating Newcastle in the FA Cup as a non-league side in 1972 and then securing successive promotions.

Parking in the adjacent cattle market, the Smiths made their way to the Edgar Street ground and began enquiring as to the availability of stand seats. A friendly local had informed them that they were all sold but they did not offer a good view as they faced the pitch! This was, of course, a joke as Hereford were occupying bottom position at that time. Upon approaching the visitors' terrace, the Smiths noted some felt-tip jottings above the admission gates which read, "Icky says go up other end – Tunbridge Wells Mental Squad".

Somewhat unsurprisingly, just prior to kick-off, those within the ground witnessed a few skirmishes in the home terrace. Almost comically, the matchday announcer broke off from reading out the teams over the Tannoy and urged the home fans to defend "their Meadow End!"

As the local constabulary led some of the invaders to the away terrace, the teams entered the field of play whereupon the miscreants joined the Chelsea players in the pre-match kick-about before being again reprehended and placed back on the terraces. Despite their lowly position, Hereford twice equalised two strikes from Jock Finnieston in what ended in an entertaining 2-2 draw.

Charlton Athletic were Chelsea's next opponents and another massive crowd of just under 39,000 attending Stamford Bridge witnessed Garry Stanley score an unstoppable 30-yard strike at the Shed End to secure victory in the second-half. Kenny Swain had provided Chelsea with the lead after a fine move involving five teammates before Giles headed an equaliser upon the hour-mark.

With the Blues riding high, a trip to Nottingham Forest was viewed as probably the sternest test to date for McCreadie's young team. Arriving early and after driving to the game, the Smith brothers met up with The Kid who'd travelled courtesy of British Rail and together they took a short tour around the city and then visited the box office to obtain stand seats. Whilst surveying the perimeter of the ground at around 1pm, they noticed hordes of Chelsea supporters queuing at the home Trent End.

Taking up their seats at around 2.45pm, it was clear that some 7,000 Chelsea supporters had made their way to the City Ground and would witness a very good performance that was captured by the BBC 'Match of the Day' cameras.

Prior to the game kicking off, it became evident that the entire Trent End was now occupied by the Blue masses. Forest fans who had previously been in their 'home' end were now located in the East Stand paddock below where the Smiths and The Kid were sitting, the locals having been removed and placed there during disturbances.

Shortly before kick-off, Shed 'leader' Daniel Harkins and his entourage made their way from the Trent End and completed a circuit of the playing area. However, when approaching the Forest contingent, the police became wary of their intentions and ushered them back to where they had come from. During this time and with play only just having commenced, the referee decided to take the teams off for some five-minutes before restarting the game.

The game was a credit to the Second Division – a close encounter with honours equal. After Martin O'Neill had put the home side in front after half-an-hour, Chelsea equalised through an Ian Britton headed goal that was gifted to him by an errant future England International Viv Anderson. When a great number of Chelsea supporters celebrated Britton's goal, they were showered with coins and missiles from the paddock in front of them. Both sets of supporters taunted each other with the chant of, "You're going in the Trent!" A month earlier a visiting Wolves fan had indeed suffered such misfortune.

Leaving at the end and making their way across a car park, the Smith brothers witnessed a Forest hooligan whirling a chain around his head and several cars with smashed windscreens. Somehow or other, The Kid had become separated from the Smiths and found himself upon the shore of the River Trent. There, he was set upon by several Forest fans who started to drag him towards the water. Fortunately however, some Chelsea supporters had noticed the skirmish and 'rode to the rescue' of the Chelsea youngster, releasing him from the grip of the home fans and allowing him to run away to safety. However, he was now on his own and, after getting lost and having to seek safety from a marauding gang of disaffected Forest fans in a tobacconist's shop, he eventually found his way back to Nottingham station and sanctuary amongst the many other Chelsea supporters who were waiting for the first train heading back to London.

The following Saturday witnessed a routine win over Burnley at the Bridge with yet another headed goal from Ian Britton and a Steve Finnieston penalty in a 2-1 victory.

*****

A letter in the Chelsea programme from the Burnley match read as follows:

THE HAT THAT MEANS SO MUCH

Can anyone answer this plea from Southampton fan J. Alfred, of 280 Shirley Road, Southampton, SO1 3HL?

He wrote to Eddie McCreadie to say he had his 1976 Cup Final blue and yellow bowler hat snatched from his head in the West Stand by overjoyed Chelsea supporters when "Butch" Wilkins scored against Saints here on October 30th.

"While I accept it was done without real malice," says Mr. Alfred, "it means so much to me to get the bowler back. Perhaps I am asking the impossible, but a mention in your

programme might prick someone's conscience."

We hope it does, and that "someone" will get in touch with Mr. Alfred – phone number Southampton 774772.

*****

Chelsea then travelled to Sheffield United for a Friday evening fixture and went down 1-0, the winning goal being a penalty taken by Ian "Chico" Hamilton who ironically was the youngest player ever to play for Chelsea at 16-years 4-months back in 1967. A frozen surface was not conducive to Chelsea's passing game and chances were far and few between.

The following Tuesday saw Chelsea visit the Dell where their striker Ted MacDougall again gave the Saints an early lead on a mud-bath of a pitch which was only deemed playable by the referee some 20-minutes before kick-off.

Thankfully for the travelling supporters, Finnieston scrambled an equaliser in the second-half and a draw was an acceptable result. Unfortunately, the elder of the Smith's unreliable Austin 1100 had broken down on the M3 prior to the game but a group of fellow Chelsea supporters had pulled over onto the hard shoulder and offered them a lift in their Ford Transit van.

Three of the passengers who'd previously been travelling in the now broken down car, gratefully climbed aboard the van, leaving the owner of the 1100 calling for assistance at a roadside AA phone box. Needs must! The rescuers however, were insistent that there new acquaintances accompanied them into the home Milton Road terrace as part of the deal. Sheepishly, they let them queue at the turnstile in front of them and then beat a hasty retreat around to the visitors end in Archers Road! The younger of the Smiths arrived home shortly after midnight to find that his brother had only just got back himself, courtesy of the AA, the problem with his car being a faulty alternator!

High-flying Wolves were next up at Stamford Bridge with ITV's 'The Big Match' cameras witnessing a classic 3-3 draw in front of over 36,000. Whilst Butch Wilkins had cancelled out an early John Richards opener which sent the team in level at the interval, Chelsea found themselves trailing 1-3 with only some 15-minutes remaining. Cue another header from Britton and a last minute equaliser from Jock Finnieston to bring the house down.

Following the game, those at Fulham Broadway Underground station were witness to a Wolves hooligan element numbering some 50 persons who were obviously disgruntled by the result bearing their teeth and insulting all around them. The tube trains were then subsequently held up and it wasn't too long before the visiting fans met their match with a similar Chelsea North Stand mob, the Wolves fans – unfortunately for them – not escaping as their team had done with honours even.

There then came a pre-Christmas visit to lowly Hull City at Boothferry Park. British Rail laid on a 'football special' and, although those who partook enjoyed possibly the best fish and chips ever prior to kick-off – mainly due to the fact that the fish, as it should have been, was as fresh as fresh could be – somewhat disappointingly Chelsea only returned with a point. This after a last minute Ian Britton goal, after a long surging run from deep by David Hay, secured a draw.

Local hero, Jeff Hemmerman, had given the home side an interval lead but when Britton's equaliser had hit the net, the younger of the Smith brothers and a friend broke ranks from the Chelsea supporters situated in the main stand and ventured forward nearer the pitch. However, they were then reprimanded as they had unknowingly entered the Directors' box. Discussions then ensued with the local constabulary as to their punishment and they were then escorted to the front of the queue at the adjacent railway station and told to get out of town!

Boxing Day saw local rivals Fulham travel the short distance to Stamford Bridge with George Best and Bobby Moore in their side but lacking the injured Rodney Marsh. Over 55,000 saw Chelsea run out 2-0 winners, the goals courtesy of Micky Droy – deputising for Steve Wicks – who scored with a towering header at the Shed End with only 15-minutes remaining before Kenny Swain added a second in injury time.

Two days later however, Chelsea suffered a 0-4 reverse at Luton upon a snow-covered pitch. As in previous years, the town centre felt the brunt of the result with many shop windows smashed.

Memories of the defeat in Bedfordshire were soon forgotten in the next fixture, played on New Year's Day, when bottom of the table Hereford United were beaten 5-1 at Stamford Bridge. The highlight of the game was an audacious 30-yard chip from Ray Wilkins, the other scorers for Chelsea being Garry Stanley, Kenny Swain, Steve Finnieston and a last minute own-goal inadvertently put across his own line by Galley. Former England International Terry Paine had replied for the visitors but, when he netted, there was little sign of any 'Meadow Enders' in attendance.

The following Saturday, Chelsea returned to The Dell for a Third Round FA Cup tie against the holders Southampton. Right back, Gary Locke, netted his only strike of the season to give Chelsea a half-time lead but former Blues legend Peter Osgood assisted an equaliser for England international Mike Channon to make the final score 1-1.

Back at the Bridge for the replay on the following Wednesday, Saints ran out 3-0 winners with all the goals coming in extra time upon an almost unplayable pitch. Making their way to the game prior to kick-off, a car full of Saints fans pulled up in Parsons Green and enquired as to the location of the ground. Unfortunately for them, Rob, a colleague of the younger Smith, proceeded to send them in the general direction of Putney.

After a break of 21-days, it was back to league matters and another disappointing home draw on a bog of a pitch with lowly Orient, the game ending 1-1 after Garry Stanley produced another belter after the East-Londoners had taken the lead. Whilst Kenny Swain netted a late winner, the only goal of the game, at Carlisle the following week, there was bad news. Chelsea's top scorer, Steve Finnieston suffered a broken jaw and, as a result, missed the next few matches.

The next game saw Millwall visit Stamford Bridge where a crowd of nearly 35,000 had gathered. Somewhat unsurprisingly, Millwall's hard-core hooligan element chose to occupy an area low in the Shed End below the Bovril gate and were suitably repelled prior to kick-off. Again, Chelsea were grateful to Garry Stanley for rescuing a point in a 1-1 draw after the Lions had taken the lead through Terry Brisley.

Four days later, a Tuesday evening fixture took Chelsea to Meadow Lane where an ever-improving Notts County defeated the Blues 2-1, Ray Wilkins netting another long-range effort after the Blues shipped two early goals. Chelsea's form and the state of the pitch coupled with Finnieston absence through injury were causing concern to those with Chelsea dear to their heart.

The next weekend, honours were even after a 2-2 draw at Stamford Bridge with Plymouth Argyle. This, after Chelsea lead twice through an Ian Britton penalty and a goal from Kenny Swain.

Next came a top-of-the-table clash against Bolton Wanderers at Burnden Park, a game for which three special trains carrying a total of some 2,500 Chelsea supporters made their way to darkest Lancashire. As at Nottingham Forest, prior to kick-off, it became evident that the home terrace had succumbed to a groundswell of visiting supporters with London accents causing the home fans to beat a retreat down the middle of the pitch to the Railway End.

As the game progressed, it was clear that Bolton were the better team in the first-half and went in at the break deservedly leading 2-0. However, luck was with Chelsea in the second when first, the returning Jock Finnieston latched onto a wayward back pass to reduce the deficit and then Kenny Swain dispossessed an unfortunate defender to fire home the equaliser.

On the way back to the railway station, the Smith brothers and those with them managed to drop into an off-licence before getting back onto one of the specials for the long haul home. However the journey back was a joyous one after Chelsea's fine comeback. 'Mad' Tony decided that everyone in the Smith's carriage must stand up and deliver a song before the train arrived at Euston and that the best performers will be rewarded with more ale in the Tumbledown bar in Paddington before the midnight express back to Hayes and Slough.

The winners were a duo – Steve and Nobby – with their rendition of 'More Than a Feeling', a song that was in the charts and performed by Boston. Unfortunately for the younger of the Smiths, his rendition of the 'Muppet Show' theme was voted the worst.

Blackpool were Eddie McCreadie's youngsters next opponents, taking a point from their visit to Stamford Bridge after twice coming from behind in a 2-2 draw, with Kenny Swain and Steve Wicks netting for Chelsea. The match was covered by ITV's 'The Big Match' and commentator, Brian Moore, voiced his concern for Chelsea when two pitch invaders attempt to confront a Blackpool defender after a crude challenge upon Ian Britton. Thankfully, they were headed off by a couple of stewards and returned to the Shed terrace.

A trip to Ninian Park was next for Chelsea where they'd face Cardiff City and, at long last, they returned to London victorious for the first time since New Year's Day. Goals from Britton, Swain and Stanley produce a 3-1 win whilst, at the other end, Peter Bonetti produced a world class save with Chelsea only a goal in front midway through the second-half.

Walking back to the station to catch their train back to London, the Smiths and The Kid witness a series of ructions in the adjacent park. An elderly Welsh gentleman, looking on at the rampaging youths, turned to the younger Smith and remarked that the perpetrators should be sprayed with an indelible green dye so that they couldn't escape punishment. Then, when the fighting spilled over in front of him, he drew his walking cane and delivered a lash to a grounded lout.

When the Londoners joined the train which had been in the sidings at the station for the duration of the game, it was evident that it had been vandalised from the outside, leaving the embarking passengers the task of removing broken glass from seats before setting off. The daily papers however, reported that it was the Chelsea supporters who caused the damage returning to Paddington – talk about giving a dog a bad name!

There then followed a couple of routine home wins over Bristol Rovers 2-0 (Wicks and an own-goal) and Blackburn Rovers 3-1, with Jock Finnieston scoring twice and another from Steve Wicks. With Easter approaching, Chelsea looked set for a return to the First division.

A Good Friday 3-1defeat at Fulham, where the home side are buoyed by a goal-scoring George Best and Ray Wilkins netted a late consolation, appeared to be a minor setback when promotion contenders Luton Town were beaten 2-0 at the Bridge the next day. Steve Finnieston gave Chelsea an early lead before left-back John Sparrow scored with a 25 yard strike, his only goal of the campaign. The following morning, the sports pages of the newspapers press were quick to acclaim Sparrow's remarkable strike with 'Sparrow's Arrow' being amongst the red-top headlines the next day.

Nonetheless, an Easter Monday visit to South London and The Valley proved disastrous with Charlton Athletic hammering a shell-shocked Chelsea side 4-0, with local hero Mike Flanagan claiming a hat-trick. The game was over-shadowed by events off the field, with windows being broken in the Charlton social club and fires lit at the end housing the bulk of the visiting support.

However, The Kid – attempting to change ends at half-time in order to watch Chelsea attack – grew impatient as people queued to walk through an access gate. Clambering over the adjoining fence, he was set upon by stewards and thrown out of the ground. Walking out of the alleyway that formed the walkway to the turnstiles, he was accosted by a group of seven or eight youths.

"Are you Chelsea then?" asked one of them, eagerly eyeing the silk scarf the youngster was wearing.

"Of course…" The Kid replied, answering with the only reply he could have made.

"Well we're Millwall!" said one of the group who spoke like he was their leader, "Give us your scarf!"

Outnumbered, the Chelsea youngster timidly untied the 'prize' and offered it to the youth who'd asked for it but, before he could hand it over, another of the youths said, "Leave him, he's on his own, let him go…"

Hardly believing his good fortune, The Kid hastily made his way along the street in the direction of Charlton railway station but, he'd hardly gone 20-yards when a young boy aged about 10-years old ran up to him and curtly demanded, "Give us your scarf!"

For a split second, The Kid thought about simply telling the boy 'where to go' but, looking past him, he could see the gang of older youths he'd just encountered gleefully, expectantly but also somewhat menacingly looking on. Good sense got the better of The Kid and, reluctantly, he gave the youngster his scarf. Turning back triumphantly, the boy ran back to the rest of the group, laughing and holding his 'trophy' aloft.

The following morning, the daily newspapers were again full of reports about the hooligan element that followed Chelsea with many of the journalists recommending that the club's supporters should be banned from their remaining away fixtures.

Chelsea's next fixture was, in the grand scheme of things, massive! Promotion rivals Nottingham Forest were the visitors to Stamford Bridge where another big crowd of over 36,000 eagerly awaited the start of the game.

As at Forest's City Ground the previous November, Martin O'Neill again gave the Brian Clough's side a half-time lead but, after Ian Britton netted an equaliser, Jock Finnieston sent the home support into delirium with a late winner, with 'Match of the Day' capturing the booming Shed End and a jubilant pitch invasion at the final whistle.

The outspoken Forest manager – obviously upset by the result – complained about the 'lousy facilities' available to his side and also muttered something about the winning goal being offside.

*****

A letter in the programme for the Nottingham Forest game read as follows:

GROUND-SHARING: OUR REPLY

It pained me greatly to read in the Evening Standard last week of a suggested merger between Chelsea and Queen's Park Rangers. I noticed there was not a single comment from anyone connected with Chelsea, so I have been trying to convince myself that this scandalous suggestion is a figment of someone's overworked imagination. Please could you confirm this, as the thought of sharing our great ground with Queen's Park Rangers is causing me to lose sleep.

Yours (worried),
Ross Fraser, John Clements,
Ealing

Chelsea Chairman Brian Mears replied:

"There was no suggestion in last week's Press report of a merger between the Chelsea and Q.P.R. clubs but speculation about a possible sharing of Stamford Bridge. We cannot prevent such speculation, neither can we prevent other clubs admiring our facilities and, perhaps, wanting to share them. Related to the Club's best interests, everything has to be considered, and ground-sharing has been discussed from time to time. While it is still not beyond the bounds of possibility, I would say the prospect is receding. Chelsea F.C. will never lose its identity. Chelsea will be Chelsea for always – and at Stamford Bridge."

*****

There then followed a midweek jaunt to Oldham Athletic and British Rail announced that no alcohol would be allowed on their excursions to both this game and Burnley the following Saturday. Chelsea escaped from Oldham with a scoreless draw, with goalkeeper Peter Bonetti again in superb form and denying local hero Alan Groves on a number of occasions. Chelsea introduced young winger Clive Walker to the game as a late substitute after suitably impressing in the reserve side.

Returning to work the next day, Smith was interrogated by his boss as to his absence with a mysterious virus the previous day. Apparently, he'd noticed Smith's "Up Chelsea" car sticker and was somewhat suspicious.

The game against Burnley saw Chelsea encounter more problems 'on the road' and suffering a 1-0 defeat at Turf Moor where Bonetti was unable to keep out a late strike from the Claret's Billy Ingham. Following on the back of the alcohol ban, it was also announced that Chelsea would not receive an allocation of tickets for the final away game at Champions elect Wolverhampton Wanderers.

On the train journey back to London, the Smith brothers were approached by Danny Harkins who informed them that a delegation of Chelsea supporters were making a journey to Wolverhampton the following Sunday to obtain as many tickets as possible. Exchanging phone numbers, the Chelsea supporters leader promised to let them know how they got on.

Sheffield United were then put to the sword in Chelsea's penultimate home fixture. Another Ray Wilkins volley from some 25 yards was the pick of the goals in a 4-0 rout, with Tommy Langley, Ray Lewington and Finnieston also finding the net.

Prior to kick-off, in the Fulham Road tickets for the Wolves game were being touted. Upon enquiry, those interested were advised that South Bank terrace tickets were available at £2, the face value being £0.80. The Smiths snapped up as many as possible and after the game discussed travel itinerary. The Kid however, was not with the Smiths at point of purchase but, later in The Shed, he paid £3 for a ticket for himself. Danny phoned Smith that evening and learned that he and his friends were 'sorted'. He also said it wasn't a problem as there had been no shortage of takers.

Whilst there were rumours of special excursions running to Walsall and then linking buses, the Smiths decided to hire a Ford Granada and along with four other Chelsea supporters they crammed into the reputedly reliable motor.

Arriving in Wolverhampton, they took up residence in a hotel bar close to

Molineux and caught sight of comedy duo Mike and Bernie Winters. Making their acquaintance Bernie declares a lifetime romance with Chelsea but revealed that brother Mike supported Arsenal!

The Kid meanwhile had travelled to Euston where, to his and the other Chelsea supporters amazement, they found that British Rail had – somewhat wisely – decided to lay on special trains to not only transport the travelling army to Wolverhampton but also keep them away from the 'ordinary' train travellers who were not football fans.

Walking along the platform to board one of the trains, The Kid was accosted by Joan Thirkettle and an ITV News camera crew who were reporting on the thousands of Chelsea supporters who were ignoring the ban and travelling to the game to cheer their side on to promotion. Asked if he was going to Molineux without a ticket, he reached into the inside pocket of his Harrington jacket and pulled out his ticket before proudly holding it up before the camera and explaining how it had come into his possession.

The planned invasion by the soldiers of Eddie McCreadie's Blue and White Army had been the 'talk' of the newspapers the week preceding the game with a story carried by The Sun and The London Evening Standard amongst others about a group of Chelsea supporters led by somebody called Emu who were intent on going to the game and mugging Wolves fans for their tickets in order to gain entry to the ground.

After a journey on a train full of expectant and boisterous Chelsea supporters, the train The Kid was travelling on slowed to a halt just outside Wolverhampton station. The Londoners leaning out of the carriage windows drew the attention of the residents of the houses that backed onto the railway line. Aware that the 'so-called' banned supporters had ignored the instruction and had indeed arrived, the shocked and worried looks on their faces told their own story.

Tommy Langley fired Chelsea in front and an equaliser from John Richards arrived with some ten-minutes remaining. A draw suited both teams as Wolves were crowned champions and Chelsea promoted.

The Smiths – along with thousands of supporters of both teams encroached onto the pitch at the final whistle to salute the team and whilst the younger of the Smith brothers and four of his friends made it, the elder Smith was rugby-tackled by a constable and thrown back into the celebrating throng. Those on the pitch yelled to him to return to the motor and get the engine running.

Although initially wary of each other, jubilant Chelsea and Wolves supporters met and shook hands with each other on the halfway line and joined together in singing, "We all agree, Chelsea and Wolves are magic!" while the players made their way to the Directors' Box in the West Stand.

At the front, Smith caught sight of Charlie Cooke and beckoned for him to throw him his shirt. Whilst he duly obliged it sailed over Smith's head and became a priceless souvenir for another true Blue.

Departing the pitch and making their way to their transport, Smith and his companions saw a riot taking place in a nearby underpass. The police and media later reported that attempts to ban Chelsea followers from the game was a failure and that some 8,000 in a crowd of 33,465 had beaten the ban. Of 125 arrested, most had southern addresses.

A comfort break on the southbound M6 provided the Smiths with a chance meeting with the team. They smothered all the players and manager Eddie McCreadie with boisterous enthusiasm. Once Eddie was able to free himself he loudly enquired, "Are you happy lads?" Venturing outside, they found Ray Wilkins still in his playing kit and joined in with the assembled staff on the team coach singing, "On Mother Kelly's Doorstep!"

The Smiths et al journeyed back down the M6 knowing that the team coach was only a short distance behind them and, as they would have to leave at Watford, they pull over onto the hard shoulder with a fleet of other vehicles. A few minutes later, the team passed acknowledged by the accompanying sound of car horns heralding the promotion. The scene was set for the last game of the season at Stamford Bridge and a massive celebration.

The Kid, unaccustomed to drinking, awoke late on the Saturday after a few too many the previous evening. Arriving late to Stamford Bridge, he was denied access to The Shed due to the numbers already in that end of the ground. Frantically, fearing he'd miss the game altogether, he rushed to the North Stand turnstiles and, although concerned he wasn't in his usual place to watch his side celebrate their return to Division One, he was more than happy that he wasn't locked out all together.

Hull were humbled 4-0 as Steve Finnieston bagged a hat-trick, the last a penalty and Ian Britton netted his tenth of the season. Eddie McCreadie had to plead with the supporters to refrain from invading the pitch each time a goal was scored and the game ended in chaos when the massed ranks engulfed the playing area. Although the attendance is officially recorded at 43,718, many observers are certain it was over 50,000.

The Kid was one of those who encroached onto the playing area and, once the game had finished, he managed to dig up a piece of the turf from near the players' tunnel, the sod being later transferred to one of his Nan's fruit bowls and placed on her window ledge.

The Chelsea supporters partied into the small hours in the Kings Road and many new friendships were made that remain to this very day some 40 years on. The most popular song of that particular evening referred to the Sports Minister's failed attempts to ban Chelsea supporters from away games, the lyrics being, "Dennis Howell kiss my arse, Division One we're back at last, woah, woah, woah!"

A few days later, The Kid travelled to Fulham Broadway and, exiting the underground station, he spotted a familiar figure. Eddie McCreadie was there, in the flesh. Wearing his now trademark dark glasses and dressed immaculately, the Scot looked cool and somehow mysterious. Too shy to approach him, the youngster smiled awkwardly at the Chelsea manager who responded likewise. Had he known then what he knows today, The Kid would have spoken to Eddie McCreadie and most likely thanked him for everything he did for Chelsea FC. As it was however, the only words that came into his mind were those sung enthusiastically (to the melody of Keith West's 1967 chart hit *Excerpt From A Teenage Opera*) by The Shed, *"Eddie Mac, Eddie Mac, Is it true we're going back to... Division One?"*

CASH FOR CHELSEA
Julie Carr

It seems fitting that in the summer of 1976, when it was disclosed that my beloved Chelsea football club were in financial crisis, that "You To Me Are Everything" by The Real Thing were topping the charts. Chelsea had given me so much joy over the previous 9 years that it was now my turn to do something for them.

My Chelsea story had begun on the 16 December, 1967. I had travelled up from Kent with my Dad and I can distinctly remember walking down Carnaby Street and then the King's Road on our way to the ground. The Beatles were number 1 with "Hello, Goodbye" and London had a buzz. It was vibrant and exciting. I can recollect going through the turnstiles of 'The Shed' and us taking our place in the middle of the East Side.

Was it the atmosphere of 'The Shed', or the falling in love with Peter Bonetti and Peter Osgood that clinched it? Despite the fact that we lost 3-0 that day, I remember looking up at my Dad and announcing " I will support Chelsea for ever more. This is my team." I knew that this is where I belonged, my spiritual home, and this feeling has never gone away. The left back that day was a young player called Eddie McCreadie, who was our manager at the start of the 1976 season, to which I will return.

To help my club financially I decided to buy a season ticket for the princely sum of £62.50p. It was with great pride and excitement that I took my seat in the new East Stand – middle tier – Inner Wing – Row C, seat 175.

During the game against Notts County (in which we drew 1-1 courtesy of an Ian Britton goal) an article had caught my eye in the match day programme. It was calling for volunteers to give up an hour or two on match days to assist in the promotion of a 'Cash for Chelsea' campaign. The campaign had been devised by season ticket holder Ted Baillie and 4 others, in which they were asking supporters to sponsor Chelsea for as little as 5p for every point the players gained on the pitch.

I just knew I had to do more for Chelsea than purchase a season ticket. We had been given 12 months to show the creditors the club could pay its way. There was a real risk that if we could not, there would be no Chelsea Football Club to support by the end of the season. Therefore, after the game, I found the office the Club had given the campaigners to use as a base and simply stated "I want to help. What can I do?".

From then on I would leave my Birmingham home slightly earlier in order to arrive at the ground 2 hours before kick-off. Along with the other volunteers we collected sponsorship forms from eager supporters, counted the money handed in, and (outside our office) rattled buckets, into which fellow Chelsea fans would throw in any spare change. Young supporters threw in their pocket money. Everyone stopped for a chat enquiring how we were getting on. There was a unique atmosphere at The Bridge that season. It was one in which the club, players and supporters were all working together with one aim: the survival of Chelsea Football Club.

The campaign certainly seemed to catch everyone's imagination. The stars would call in. A frequent visitor to our office was Lance Percival, and Cathy McGowan would give a wave as she walked past. The players called in too, and we even persuaded some of them to shake the buckets. The campaign was gaining momentum. By the start of October we had 1,500 sponsors, passing our first target of £10,000. I knew that personally I could, and wanted to, do more.

On the 9 October at 6am I set off from my home in Birmingham on a sponsored walk to Worcester and back. The legacy of that walk remains with me today. I have never again been able to wear high-heeled shoes. I walked until dusk, when a concerned Dad came to find me. I had not quite completed the walk, but nobody cared; they handed over all their sponsorship money willingly. At the next home match against Oldham I was able to hand over £63 for the 'Cash for Chelsea' campaign.

I thought no more of it until my aunt handed me a letter from Eddie McCreadie. Unbeknown to me, she had written to the Club to let them know what her niece had done. He sent such a lovely letter describing me as 'one of Chelsea's greatest ever supporters'. I regret that over the years, that letter has been lost but perhaps Eddie will write me another one someday!

This was however not an end to my surprises. Following the walk, I was contacted by the Club to say that they wanted to do an article about me for inclusion in a programme. At the home game against Southampton on 30 October , the Chelsea official photographer whisked me away from the campaign office to take me onto the hallowed pitch for a photo shoot. I had to pose in the goalmouth half an hour before kick-off, in front of an already full Shed End. Thank goodness my fellow Chelsea supporters were kind to me and the wolf whistles were gratefully received.

The article duly appeared in the programme for the match against Charlton on the 10 November. Of course I was excited that day but I did not realise that there was yet another unexpected event to come. I was busy counting money in the campaign office when an official from the club walked in and said "Julie, the players have seen the article and would very much like to meet you. Would you be able to join them after the match in the player's lounge?" You might have thought that I said 'yes' straight away. However, I hesitated, and asked the only other female volunteer, Betty, "What should I do?" My contributions to the Campaign were not with a view to meeting the players. It was much deeper than that. It was for Chelsea Football Club as a whole. I decided to go.

After the match I was collected from the office to be introduced to the players although I felt a little guilty about leaving my voluntary duties early. The first player I met was John Phillips, as someone had commented that I had a passing resemblance to his wife. I was so lucky to meet them all, including our captain Ray Wilkins, Tommy Langley, and Garry Stanley. Tommy Langley and I (bizarrely) ended up having a chat about school, and O levels achieved. He nearly exploded when I told him how many I had. Garry Stanley and I shared a common bond - the Midlands (he was from Burton-on-Trent). A few of the players were intending to go to 'The Rising Sun', the pub opposite the ground, and they asked me to join them. This included some of the youth team and I met a young player called Michael Nutton who subsequently became a good friend of mine.

I would like to think that meeting the players, and describing to them what we were doing for the club, raised their awareness of the 'Cash for Chelsea' campaign. We certainly seemed to have more of them coming in to see us. Garry Stanley became a frequent visitor on match days. He would very patiently take time to sign autographs for many of my female friends at college, who adored him.

Ian Britton would also pop in and would often leave tickets for me for the away games. I accepted this kind gesture as I did not consider that this was taking any money out of the Chelsea coffers. Even though I had a season ticket I frequently sat with the Youth team behind the Chelsea dug-out. They included Mike, Gary Chivers and John Bumstead, who all went on to play for the first team. The great spirit at Chelsea that season had been passed down to the Youth Team, and plenty of banter and mickey-taking went on during the match. When one of the first team fluffed a tackle, or mis-kicked a chance on goal, it left them all in fits of laughter – I didn't join in of course.

They also loved to tell stories about the senior players, however I cannot reveal them all!! I remember one about Steve Wicks, who was our handsome centre back and took great pride in his appearance. A young member of the Youth Team took great delight in running into the dressing room during training to say "Steve, your hairdresser has just phoned. She can fit you in now to do your highlights"! Poor Steve received such a ribbing. He never quite lived that one down.

However they were all brought down to earth with a bump when they would have to clean the senior players' boots, and the terraces, at the end of the match. Many an evening after match day I would while away my time drinking tea in a café on the Fulham Road, waiting for Mike to arrive after completing his duties.

At one home match I was asked to go on the pitch to draw a raffle at half time. I had an interesting encounter with our players in the tunnel, coming out for the second half; I had to avert my eyes! At the Milwall home match on 12 February , myself and three other volunteers went round the pitch at half time in a 'Chelsea blue' beach buggy. It was owned by one of the 'Cash for Chelsea' campaign founders, and we used it as a way to say 'thank you' for all the support from the fans. As we waved to the crowd we approached the Milwall fans in the North Stand with some trepidation. They began to hurl things at us but we had the last laugh, as what they were throwing was money. I am not sure they realised that all they had achieved was to contribute towards saving their rivals from extinction. A Garry Stanley goal earned us a draw that day, and we remained top of the league. Needless to say, on the occasions I went on the pitch at half time I then sat safely in my own seat. In that way I could avoid being teased by the Youth Team.

Despite being a big part of the 'Cash for Chelsea' campaign, at the end of the day, I was first and foremost just a supporter like everybody else. That season I attended nearly all the away matches too. It provided another opportunity to raise more funds for the campaign. At every away game buckets were passed around the trains and a lot of money was collected that way.

The season was drawing to a close. I secured a much sought after ticket for the away game against Wolves on the 7 May, 1977. Wolves had 54 points and we had 52. A Tommy Langley goal that day earned us a 1-1 draw, and that meant that both teams gained promotion. At the final whistle there was an outpouring of emotion. For the first and only time as a Chelsea supporter I ran onto the pitch and supporters and players from both sides were hugging each other.

The 53 points we had achieved up until the last game against Hull City meant that the sponsor pledges total was near to £32,000. We had already handed over £25,000 to the Club. In the programme on the final match against Hull City there was one last plea for everyone to keep sending in their money. There was a great big 'thank you' to those supporters who were keeping their promise to pay double if we won promotion; the money kept rolling in.

On the last day the Chelsea supporters had wanted to start the party a little earlier than planned. The referee had to ask Eddie McCreadie to address the 'Shed End' via the public address system, and ask them not to invade the pitch again otherwise there was a risk he would abandon the match. A 4-0 win (with Steve Finnieston 3 goals, Ian Britton 1 goal) meant we gained 2 more points, came second in the league and were back in Division 1. The rest, as they say, is history.

So there it is. 'Free' by Deniece Williams was now top of the charts and my beloved Chelsea were free from the stranglehold of debt. We had survived.

There was no longer the need to continue the 'Cash for Chelsea' campaign. But that season will never be forgotten by me. When it was suggested to me that perhaps, as I sat with the Youth Team, there was no need to renew my season ticket for 1977/78 my response was an emphatic 'no' – Chelsea need my money. That feeling has never really left me and in April 2016 I was reminded of it at the Aston Villa away match. I was admiring a cashmere Chelsea scarf but noticed that it was not official merchandise. When I commented that I would like to buy one, but if I did, Chelsea would not make any money, everyone laughed. They said, "Julie, Chelsea do not need your money any more".

This was a stark reminder of the difference between the Chelsea of 1976/77 and modern Chelsea, but I say they are inexorably linked. We had started the 1976/77 season with one objective: to survive. We did this by management, players, staff and supporters all working together. There would never be another season like it in the history of the Club because of the unique atmosphere, the camaraderie, the feeling we were all equal and all playing our part to ensure there would always be a Chelsea Football Club. Without this spirit there would not be the wonderful success we have today. I am proud to have played a small part in that.

EDDIE'S PLAYERS
IN THEIR OWN WORDS

IAN BRITTON

CHARLIE COOKE

JOHN DEMPSEY

MICKY DROY

STEVE FINNIESTON

RON HARRIS

DAVID HAY

TOMMY LANGLEY

RAY LEWINGTON

GARY LOCKE

TEDDY MAYBANK

JOHN PHILLIPS

STEVE SHERWOOD

JOHN SPARROW

GARRY STANLEY

KENNY SWAIN

CLIVE WALKER

STEVE WICKS

GRAHAM WILKINS

RAY WILKINS

EDDIE MCCREADIE'S BLUE AND WHITE ARMY

BRIAN BASON*

PETER BONETTI*

BILL GARNER*

IAN HUTCHINSON*

(*biographical article)

IAN BRITTON

I joined Chelsea as an apprentice when I was 17-years old. Initially, I played with the youth-team which was great and five of our group were signed as professionals which was an achievement in itself. Chelsea were and still are a big club and I loved every moment of it and I made some great friends and we're still friends. I got on well with Gary Locke as we were in digs together and signed pro at the same time along with Garry Stanley and Ray Wilkins. I think we were all characters in our own way.

Playing with the likes of Peter Bonetti, Ron Harris, Eddie McCreadie, Alan Hudson, John Hollins, Charlie Cooke, Peter Osgood and many others at the age I was then was fantastic. I found out I was making my debut on the Friday before a game on the Saturday with Derby County as the opponents (30 December 1972; Chelsea 1-1 Derby County, Osgood). I was 17-years old.

I played alongside Eddie McCreadie many times. He was a very hard tackler, a left-back who was very quick and was a Scottish International. He was a good organiser on and off the field. He was very quiet in the dressing room but, out on the pitch, he was very different. He never stopped talking from start to finish in an effort to try to get the best out of the team.

It was a real pleasure to play for him and I'm sure all the lads that played for him wouldn't have a bad word to say about him. Everything he did at the time was for the players. Eddie was always positive on and off the field. We had a good laugh during training, but when it came to the games his motivation and team spirit were excellent.

I scored a few goals for Chelsea but my most memorable ones were the one I got at The Kop end against Liverpool (1 March 1975; Liverpool 2-2 Chelsea, Britton, Finnieston), the two penalties at home against Charlton

(17 November 1979; Chelsea 3-1 Charlton Athletic, Fillery, Britton 2 (2P)), an equaliser against Wolves at Stamford Bridge in the '77 promotion season (11 December 1976; Chelsea 3-3 Wolverhampton Wanderers, Britton, Finnieston, Wilkins) and a header against Nottingham Forest (20 November 1976; Nottingham Forest 1-1 Chelsea, Britton).

Eddie had the foresight to give Ray Wilkins the captain's armband in the game Chelsea played against Spurs in the game in which we were more or less relegated (19 April 1975; Tottenham Hotspur 2-0 Chelsea).

I can't remember much about the match itself but I feel sure that, in Eddie's mind, it was a building process and his thinking was solely about the future. Relegation is something that's very hard to take and it's certainly not a nice feeling but then, when you look forward to the next season, you try and put things right.

As the rebuilding of the side began, players like Ray Wilkins, Gary Locke, Ray Lewington, Graham Wilkins, Steve Wicks, Steve Finnieston, Tommy Langley, Clive Walker, Garry Stanley, John Sparrow, Clive Walker, Mickey Droy and Kenny Swain all came through. We were a young side and we finished 11th at the end of the season.

The following season, we had great support home and away all season and, for me at least, the Wolves game (7 May 1977; Wolverhampton Wanderers 1-1 Chelsea, Langley) had to be one of the best as, when the ref blew the final whistle, both sides were promoted and the Chelsea supporters who'd travelled erupted.

Another of my highlights was scoring in the last game at home and the 3 goals scored by Steve Finnieston (14 May 1977; Chelsea 4-0 Hull City, Finnieston (3), Britton). A great season was had by all.

I was home in Scotland at the time and, hearing the news that Eddie had left Chelsea left me feeling numb. We'd just gained promotion and to lose the manager after all the hard work was a big blow to me.

I think Eddie would have done well in the First Division as the players were all for him and each other, both on and off the field, but there again, in truth, we'll never know.

I still see Garry Stanley, Gary Chivers, Colin Pates, Paul Canoville, Graham Wilkins, Ray Wilkins, Steve Finnieston and met with Gary Locke when he was over from New Zealand.

I had 12 great years at Chelsea. There were lows of course, the biggest being relegated and the highs being promoted. Also, playing against some of the best players in the world such as George Best, Bobby Charlton, Bobby Moore and Peter Shilton.

I have to be honest and say I miss the lads, the banter and the rapport as we had a good time when we were together and I also miss the atmosphere at the big grounds.

The Chelsea supporters were absolutely tremendous home and away, especially when they sang your name during games which is something I'll never forget.

After leaving Chelsea, I went to Dundee United and was a part of the team that won the Scottish First Division for the first time in the club's history (1982/83). Then, in 1983, I left to go to Blackpool where we gained promotion (2nd, 4th Division, 1984/85). They were three good years. I then went to Burnley where we nearly got relegated out of the Football League, but I scored the goal that kept us up (Burnley 2-1 Orient, 1986/1987) and then I played at Wembley the following year (Sherpa Van Trophy, 1988, Wolverhampton Wanderers 2-0 Burnley 0) in front of 83,000 fans.

Once I'd finished playing football as a professional, I became a manager of a leisure trust and did the job for 23-years until I was forced to retire due to ill-health.

*****

Our interview with Ian took place in March 2015. Although he had already been diagnosed with prostate cancer, when we spoke to him about this book he was only too happy to provide an interview. Despite the fact his condition left him permanently tired, he kindly provided us with a contribution in his own words which we always remember him for doing. Since carrying out this interview, Ian Britton sadly passed away on 31 March 2016 at Pendleside Hospice.

CHARLIE COOKE

I started my professional career at Renfrew. It was a junior football team I joined when I was 16. Back then, the players didn't get paid but did get their expenses. I was paid two and sixpence back then and, in those days, that was pretty good going!

It was semi-professional football and I was playing with guys my own age but I also played with guys who had come down from pro teams and they were coming towards the end of their career.

Although there was a lot of talk about me going to Celtic or Rangers, I took the first offer of a club that came along and that was from Aberdeen. The Chief Scout at Aberdeen was a guy called Bobby Calder who came down to watch me and my pal Jim Geddes play. He spoke to us after a game and he wanted us to sign for Aberdeen and he said he wanted to speak to our parents.

I used to think when I was a kid that your word was your bond. I didn't tell lies and I gave my word to Bobby Calder that I would sign for Aberdeen and he said that he'd come down to speak to my parents the following Tuesday. The trouble was I missed out on a chance to join Rangers.

I was in the Renfrew dressing room, still a 16-year old schoolboy – the only one on the field. I was putting my shirt on and getting dressed and getting ready to leave when Donald McNeill, the Renfrew manager, walked into the dressing room with a smartly dressed guy wearing a trilby hat called Jim Smith who, it turned out was the Head Scout at Rangers. Speaking to me, he said, "I'd like you to come to Rangers next week." I replied, "Sorry, I've given my word to Bobby Calder that I am going to Aberdeen." If I was a seasoned pro, I would have said, "Sure I would go to Rangers and I will sort it out with Bobby Calder later. Of course I'll come to Rangers with you."

To be fair to Jim Smith and Rangers, they didn't try to persuade me or to put the knife in Bobby Calder or Aberdeen for that matter. I imagine that, if it happened today, there'd be agents who would be sniffing around hoping that maybe I would change my mind. Back then, there was no one to advise me and say, "Hey Charlie, think about this for a couple of days."

I was at Aberdeen for nearly four years and I was so pleased to be voted their Player of the Year in 1964. The following season, I joined Dundee. One of the things I would pat myself on the back for is that I was voted Player of the Year at all the clubs I played for. At Aberdeen, Dundee and, while I was there, I was voted Player of the Year three times at Chelsea.

I wasn't a natural goal-scorer and I didn't score enough. The goal-scorers who get goals are the ones who win the awards but to be voted Player of the Year at every club and to win it 3 times at Chelsea is something I am very proud of, partly because of the fact that it's the supporters who vote for whom they think should get the award.

The wheels for my move to Chelsea were set in motion after I'd won my first cap for Scotland. Jock Stein, the Scotland manager, gave me my debut against Wales just before we played Italy in a World Cup Qualifier in Italy. Jock played me at sweeper and I could not believe how easy it was! I could see everything on the pitch. I could see the runners who ran where, what through ball was played and I just stepped in and intercepted each ball. It was the easiest game I have ever played and I enjoyed it immensely.

Three weeks later, we played Italy in a World Cup qualifier and Jock took Willie Henderson with him although he knew he was not fit enough to play. Back then, players had to contend with such things, squads having lots of injuries or people saying that the opponents were too good.

Jock was the master of all that and he liked to keep the opposition guessing. He even lined up Ron Yeats as centre-forward again just to trick the Italians. Sadly, it didn't work and we lost the game and were knocked out. However, a lot of people reported that I'd played well and I received a lot of praise for my performance including some from Tommy Docherty who told the press.

I was getting attention from the newspapers even though I didn't have any relationship with any of the press boys. Some of the guys at Dundee knew all the newspaper guys and made a point of getting to know them but I didn't. I didn't have the connections some of my teammates had but I did hear through the grapevine that Chelsea had expressed an interest. One of the newspapers also wrote that Manchester United, Celtic and Rangers were interested in signing me.

My departure from Dundee was strange. I had been at Dundee for a year and got the Player of the Year Award for the 1965/66 season. I had to go and receive the trophy and say, "Thank you – it's been a great season and I'm looking forward to next season," but I knew I was going to Edinburgh the next morning to sign for Chelsea. To me, that was bizarre!

I met Tommy Docherty at the Caledonian Hotel in Edinburgh and I agreed to join Chelsea. I signed the forms with the Assistant Club Secretary Alan Bennett and he then rushed back to London to get them registered with the Football Association so I could play in the 1st leg of the Fairs Cup semi-final against Barcelona. Despite the urgency, I couldn't play in the first-leg (27 April 1966; Barcelona 2-0 Chelsea) because I had a bad ankle and wasn't fit so I made my debut in the second-leg at Stamford Bridge a couple of weeks later.

I flew down to London with Tommy Docherty and we joined up with the first-team squad on the way to Barcelona for the first game against Barcelona but, when I met up with the rest of the players, it became clear that not everyone in the team got on with Tommy Doc. This was after he'd sent some home previously from Blackpool. I walked up to Terry Venables and said, "Hi, how's it going?" and I was standing there thinking I would be playing with these guys, that they would be my teammates. Little did I know that everyone else knew that I was being bought in not to play with Venables but to replace him as that was his last game for Chelsea. I didn't know what was happening – I didn't have a clue but, as things went on, I saw what happened take shape and it was only afterwards that I realised how naïve I'd been.

I made my debut for Chelsea in the return leg against Barcelona (11 May 1966; Chelsea 2-0 Barcelona, O.G, 2). I can't really remember much about the game but I was disappointed with both my own and the rest of the team's performance against the Catalan side. Chelsea scored twice against them courtesy of two own goals but we didn't get the result we wanted.

In those days, there wasn't extra-time and there would be a one-match play-off with the venue – either home or away – being decided by a toss of a coin. We were all sitting there in the dressing room wondering how it went. We lost the toss which was another disappointment as that meant we had to go back to Barcelona for the play-off game and sadly we got stuffed (25

May 1966; Barcelona 5-0 Chelsea).

Before I joined the club, I didn't really know much about Eddie McCreadie. That might seem strange in today's media driven world and with the television saturation of football but, in those days, people only knew about football matters if they picked up the local newspaper. I did however know about Tommy Docherty and that the press had labelled his side 'Docherty's Diamonds'. I was attracted to Chelsea because of his reputation.

When I first saw Eddie play, I thought he was a very good full-back and it was only when I found out later that he played as a forward in his early playing days that I realised why he was such a good defender.

I scored my first goal for Chelsea at Upton Park (20 August 1966; West Ham United 1-2 Chelsea, Hollins, Cooke). It was the first game of the season and it came after England had won the World Cup.

If one goes to a Premier League or, in my day, a First Division game there is nothing better than the opening game in August when the sun is shining – it's fantastic! The pubs are full, the streets are packed with supporters, everyone is having a drink and a good time, the sun is out, everyone is in short sleeves and, that August day in 1966 it was just like that. It was so busy around Upton Park that the Chelsea team needed a police escort through the crowds to get to the ground. Everyone was excited after England's World Cup win.

We were sitting in the dressing room when we heard that Geoff Hurst, Bobby Moore and Martin Peters are walking round the pitch before the game with the World Cup. We couldn't believe it – one doesn't want fellow professionals doing that before a game and then, just as we're about to go onto the pitch, a West Ham official with a clipboard came in and said, "Mr Docherty, would it be okay if the Chelsea players made a guard of honour for our West Ham players who won the World Cup?"

We thought Tommy Docherty was going to explode and to his credit he agreed to do it. We did do it and we applauded Bobby Moore, Geoff Hurst and Martin Peters on to the pitch. Can you imagine clapping them on? We played the game – it was local derby with all that that entails and I got the ball inside their half, ran past Bobby Moore and, as I did, I said, "See you Bobby…" I got to the edge of the box and hit the ball with my left foot and it flew past Jim Standing in the West Ham goal. It was the winning goal and we were up and running for the season.

My best friend at Chelsea was Tommy Baldwin. We went out and socialised together. Even if I didn't go out drinking with some of the others in the dressing room I had so much respect for those guys. I always respected Johnny Hollins. He had a good work ethic and he was a very good energetic player and a good guy. On the pitch he scored some great long range goals and he was a good person to have around the dressing room.

The guy everyone respected in the dressing room was Peter Bonetti. A fantastic pro, he was someone who took training very seriously. Try as hard as I might, I couldn't get near him on cross country runs. I always felt for him being a goalkeeper at that time as he had to compete with Gordon Banks and then he had Peter Shilton and Ray Clemence to contend with and never really got his chance with England which I think he deserved. I also think he was also unfairly blamed for what happened in Mexico. England, leading 2-0 against West Germany in the 1970 World Cup quarter-final, were eventually beaten 3-2.

I had so much respect for Peter Osgood – what a player he was! He played so much of his game with his back to goal but scored some amazing goals for Chelsea. People often talk about how current players such as Ronaldo and Messi compare to players from days gone by and ask whether players from my day would star in today's game. I would say that Ossie would.

I know some folk have said that he was not the same player after he had his leg broken and he came back a little bit heavier and was not as quick. He still had a great career in my view and was a key part of our success and I'm sure he'd be successful if he was playing today.

A lot of people ask me about the 1970 FA Cup Final replay and the pass I provided for Ossie to score the equaliser (29 April 1970; Chelsea 2-1 Leeds Utd (AET); Osgood, Webb). I have to be honest and say that it was something that we tried in training a thousand times but it didn't always come off.

When I took the ball off Ian Hutchinson, I knew there wasn't long to go and we were in the late stages of the game and Chelsea were a goal down. We knew how good Leeds were and we knew they knew how to kill a game so we had to do something. The game was getting away from us and it was a heavy pitch. Out of the corner of my eye I could see Ossie and Big Jack (Charlton) in the box. If it had been 30 or 40-minutes into the game I probably would never have tried it and I would have kept possession, kept the ball and tried to create a real chance patiently.

However, that night, I saw Ossie and I thought we need to get a goal. I didn't know if he'd get it but as I watched that ball in those split seconds, I thought that he had a chance. I was aiming for Ossie and he connected with it and scored a fantastic header. The nice thing about that goal is every time they show something about Chelsea's history, that goal is usually included and I am tickled to death about that because, as I said, I didn't score that many goals myself and I probably wouldn't feature much for other things I did so that moment really means a lot to me.

I remember the changing rooms after the game and hearing that Jack Charlton went straight into the Leeds dressing room, got changed and stormed out. By the time we got back to the hotel, we were already drinking like fish and the party was in full swing. I remember staying up till about 1am and then coming back on the train to Euston the next day and the bus to Stamford Bridge. By the time we got back to the ground, the streets were packed with thousands of people.

When Eddie became the Chelsea manager, there were no obvious signs leading up to him being appointed that the club would give him the position. As a player, he was very easy going. A kind, thoughtful guy, he was not a shouter or a screamer in the dressing room. I don't think any of us at the time – including Eddie – were thinking about coaching. That said, I'll give myself a pat on the back if a conversation I had with him helped him become a manager.

The team was in decline and Eddie and I were talking about the speculation in the newspapers on who would become the next Chelsea manager. I said to him, "Look at these guys who are being linked with the club in the press. Eddie... you're better than them." I told him he knew everyone at the club, he knew everything that was going on and he knew the strengths and weaknesses of all the players. I had no ambition to be a coach back then, but I think he was out of the side through injury or had retired and he was doing some coaching in the reserves. I have no idea if Eddie up until then had been interested in the job as he kept things to himself but I'm glad he took on the job.

He was a terrific manager and, what with all the turmoil that had been going on in the club, everybody wanted him to succeed. He took a gamble on appointing Ray Wilkins as the captain at such an early age and I waited to see how it worked out but, credit to them both, it did. It was a brave decision by Eddie and Butch was brilliant, both on and off the field.

Had he stayed as Chelsea manager, I think he would have gone from strength to strength. That's no reflection on Ken Shellito. I think with Eddie's confidence, we would have gone places with him in charge. He was a nervous guy though and he took losing badly and he had his moments when he worried a lot. Overall, I think Eddie would have done well in the

First Division. He is a good guy, a super guy.

Having been transferred to Crystal Palace on 29 September 1972 for £85,000, I re-signed for Chelsea on 17 January 1974 for £17,000 and was shocked at how far the Blues had fallen since I'd been away. The following season, we were relegated but I wasn't really surprised.

Nowadays, when one sees teams relegated from the Premier League, one also sees how upset the players are. Back then though, I don't remember feeling distraught at relegation. I thought it had been coming and for some time at that. I didn't think we had the talent in the team to stay up. We had no money and things were going wrong on and off the pitch. It was inevitable. We were all aware of what was going on financially and the fact that Chelsea was in debt just added to the general demise of the club.

That first season in Division Two was a period of consolidation but towards the end of the campaign Jock Finnieston got into the side and started to bang in the goals. I knew he was quick and lively in the area but I didn't think it would turn out the way it did. I'd watched him play for the reserves and knew he could come in and do a job for the first-team and score goals but he was absolutely sensational!

We'd been struggling to score that season until he came in and then, the following season, he started where he'd left off and carried on and finished it with a total of 24 league goals to his name. It's rare to see a player come in as Jock did and make such an impact.

We knew how important it was to go up with the club's financial position but, in the same way I saw the relegation coming and didn't get too caught up in that hysteria, I saw the promotion as well as the next step. We were a good side under Eddie and deserved to go up.

The draw at Wolves (7 May 1977; Wolverhampton Wanderers 1-1 Chelsea,

Langley) was a great day. The draw took Chelsea back into the First Division and I'll always remember the celebration immediately after the final whistle with both sets of supporters on the Molineux pitch.

I don't remember where I was when I heard the news about Eddie having left the club but I remember being dumfounded at the time at the absolute stupidity of letting him go.

I really regret not trying to contact him when I was told what had happened but I never believed for one minute the story about the car. Maybe it was true – and there were other stories doing the rounds at the time – but I don't believe one make decisions around a football club that centre over the use of a company car. I think the Chelsea Board messed up badly by getting rid of Eddie. After I'd left Chelsea for the second time in 1978, I went to the USA to play for Los Angeles Aztecs and I ran into Eddie when he was managing Memphis Rogues.

It was a strange time back then. The North American Soccer League was trying to establish itself but the funny thing was, a lot of people can't remember that far back and the days of Major League Soccer. Chelsea played against the New York Cosmos in 1978 at Stamford Bridge (26 September 1978; Chelsea 1-1, New York Cosmos, Wilkins R) and they had Dutchmen Johan Neeskens and Johan Cruyff alongside West German international Franz Beckenbauer in their team.

While I was playing in the States, I came up against the Cosmos on 4 July (American Independence Day). It was a celebration and there were 78,000 people in the stadium! I also played in the Coliseum in Los Angeles which could hold 100,000 but, for that game, the crowd was only 5,000. There was no TV revenue like today. While I was there, Memphis bought some TV time and sold space to local businesses to get some exposure. Now in the USA, every stadium is full and they get good crowds and the state of the game in the US today is fantastic. The NASL wasn't the terrible thing that some people portrayed it as and, it was far from rubbish as far as I was concerned.

I finished my playing career with an indoor side called California Surf. I played the indoor game for two years with Gordon Jago (former QPR manager). The outside game suffered badly when Warner Brothers pulled the plug on the sponsorship of players such as Brazilian international Pele and Giorgio Chingalia who played for Italy.

The NASL collapsed without the money that Warner Brothers had previously put in. You are, as they say, only as strong as your weakest link. It was almost bizarre that, with all those clubs getting those crowds, when Warner pulled out the game folded almost immediately. Everything was gone. In the States, many clubs are franchises and Memphis Rogues were eventually sold and moved to Calgary, Alberta and played under the name of Calgary Boomers as an indoor team.

When I stopped playing I became a coach and, since 1984, I've been working with Coerver® Coaching. It is a company founded by Will Coerver who has set up training camps, schools and academies all over the world. We train thousands of kids. Our raison d'etre is to focus on an individual player's ability and we specifically focus upon developing particularly skilful players. We've had a lot of support from high profile players and coaches in the game and on one occasion we were lucky to do a session with Geoff Hurst, Gordon Banks and Sir Stanley Matthews.

He was speaking to the kids and asked them, "Who is the most important player on the field?" One kid said, "The midfield players," to which Stan replied, "No!" Another kid said the goalkeeper and yet another said the goal-scorers. Again, Stan said, "No," but went on to say, "The important player on the field is the man off the ball."

However, that is the exact opposite of what we teach the kids at Coerver®

Coaching. I'm not suggesting that a man off the ball is not important but, for us, the most important player is the man with the ball. Look at the 1953 Cup Final – they didn't call it the Nat Lofthouse or Stan Mortensen Final even though they got the goals. They called it the Matthews' Final. Why? Because everyone remembers the skilful things he did with the ball. He crossed that ball time and time again. He was dragging, pushing, dragging and pushing and he kept beating his man and sending crosses in that led to four goals. These are the players that get supporters off their seats – the innovators, the creators.

I used to go with my father to watch Morton at Cappielow Park and, when some of the players tried to do something with the ball which didn't come off, half the crowd would moan but my dad would say, "Yes, but the idea was a good one…" That was ingrained in me – it was always the skilful part of the game that caught my eye.

We were brought up as kids with a certain mentality that dictated that if a guy was big and strong and a bruiser, he'd be a defender. If a guy was small, he'd be a forward. We at Coerver® Coaching say that it doesn't have to be that way. We train both the big guy and the little guy to be skilful players. When the kids I teach find out I played for Chelsea, they make a really big deal out of it. All the Chelsea games are on the TV and the club has a big following in the States.

When the kids come up to me and shake my hand, I ask them what position they play and almost 9 out of 10 say they play midfield. My next question to them is, "Do you score goals?" At Coerver® Coaching, we're in the business of youth player development. Some coaches make the decision to concentrate on just one aspect of a player's game but we do things differently. For instance, if one makes a young player a good defensive midfield player but nothing else, I think he's being short-changed. We believe in encouraging any young midfield player to reach his full potential and that includes scoring goals from midfield. If we get a young player who regularly scores half a dozen or more goals from midfield each year, we think we'll have a viable player. If a midfield player can guarantee goals from midfield, that player will be in demand.

Once, when I was at a convention centre doing a coaching event with kids for the Special Olympics, I saw Eddie. We did stuff for fun with the kids and all the folks were sitting around watching and I looked up and saw him there and even though it had been a few years, I recognised him instantly. "Hey Eddie, it's really good to see you – what are you doing here?" I asked, and we started talking about what he was up to and he told me he was coaching a team there. He also said he'd got married and was living out in the country and, do you know what? He looked great! I had to go down and do my coaching thing with Coerver® Coaching and said I would speak to him later but by the time I had finished and everyone who wanted to speak to me had done so, I went back to where he was sitting but he had left by then. That was the last time I saw him but it was good to see him.

As far as my time at Chelsea is concerned, the best period for me was when we won the FA Cup and that replay was the highlight for me. It was a memorable and emotional time for everybody – the players and supporters. Not only had Chelsea won something, we'd won it for the supporters who'd waited long enough to see us win the FA Cup. We did well in cups and we were always up there near the top of the league but we could have been so much better. We should have been up there challenging for the league but we often fell short.

Foolishly, it was often against the lower teams that we dropped silly points. We always gave the likes of Leeds, Liverpool and Manchester United a game. I also look back on those Player of the Year awards and winning it three times at Chelsea make me really proud. If the FA Cup and Athens (European Cup Winners Cup Final and replay (19 May 1971; Chelsea 1-1 Real Madrid (AET), Osgood) & (21 May1971; Chelsea 2-1 Real Madrid 1 (AET), Dempsey, Osgood) and winning those Player of the Year awards

(1968 & 1975) were the highs. I'd have to say that going to Crystal Palace was not a good experience for me. If you read my book (The Bonnie Prince: Charlie Cooke – My Football Life, by Charlie Cooke with Martin Knight, ISBN: 9781845962272), you'll see I have tried to set out how difficult it was for me there.

I worked really hard there in training and on the field on a match day. People could see what I was doing week-in, week-out but it was not great to be honest. Although I was able to chip in with a few goals, the team was struggling and we got relegated (1972-1973). I think if I was able to score a few more during that season it would have been gold-dust to them. I was there for about 14-months and nobody treated me badly and the fans were great to me – it just didn't work out. Don't get me wrong – I gave 110% while I was there, I worked hard every day but it all came to nothing.

As far as the Chelsea supporters were concerned, I feel that we the players had a good relationship with them. There was always a good atmosphere when we used to travel away on the same trains and recognised the commitment these people gave to following Chelsea and how they felt about the club. We, as players realised that and we wanted desperately to reward that somehow. I thought the supporters were fantastic.

When I came over a few years ago to do a book signing in the Chelsea Megastore, I couldn't get over how many came along to buy a copy. I was shocked. I couldn't believe the queue and how far it went back. People were bringing their children who were called Charlie – boys and girls – and it was great to see that.

One of the things I really miss about not being involved with a team these days is maintaining a fitness regime but I play squash to try to maintain a certain level. I also miss the conditioning, something I didn't really appreciate when I was playing football.

I'm not too good at keeping in touch with my former team-mates but when I do see them, we have a good time reminiscing. One person who I don't see enough of is John Dempsey. The effect that guy had on the dressing room was enormous. He was a very funny guy. He was a very simple player and he played the game with no frills and fancy stuff. If he was under pressure in defence, he would kick it out for a throw. He was never a 'look at me, ain't I good' player, but rather he was a cool dude on and off the pitch and just a fantastic guy to have around the dressing room.

I always look for the Chelsea results as they are my team and I manage to make it back to the UK once or twice a year and usually get to Stamford Bridge for a game. When I do come, although I don't like a fuss, Neil Barnett he always somehow manages to drag me out onto the pitch. I could strangle Neil every time he does that but I really appreciate the support I get from the Chelsea crowd.

JOHN DEMPSEY

My professional football career started at Fulham when I signed for them in 1964. I had five good years with them before Dave Sexton paid £70,000 to sign me for Chelsea in January 1969. I made my Chelsea debut in the same game as Alan Hudson made his. We suffered a bad defeat (1 February 1969; Southampton 5-0 Chelsea) and, the next time I played, we also lost (15 February 1969; Leeds Utd 1-0 Chelsea) but, when I made my home debut, I was relieved when the final whistle was blown and I walked off the pitch at Stamford Bridge as a winner (22 February 1969; Chelsea 5-1 Sunderland, Birchenall, Tambling 4) in a game in which Bobby Tambling scored four in just 18-minutes!

Although I'd been alongside some very good players at Craven Cottage, I was delighted to have the chance to play alongside the likes of Peter Osgood, Charlie Cooke, Eddie McCreadie and the rest. Eddie was very fast as a player and, when I was at Fulham, one of the first games I played was against Chelsea. They had Ron Harris, John Hollins, Peter Bonetti and the usual suspects plus Eddie at full-back. The first thing I noticed about him was how quick he was to the tackle and he was quick on the overlap down the wings.

In those days, players were able to tackle a lot harder than these days and Eddie was good at diving in and winning the ball cleanly. He was great going down the wing and whipping in crosses with his left foot for the likes of Osgood and Ian Hutchinson.

Eddie was a hard-working player who, if he lost the ball, would run back into position or win back possession – unlike some players these days who seem to amble back when they lose it. Eddie was always chasing back. He was a very fit player. Training and playing with him regularly, one couldn't have asked for a better left-back. I can't remember many wingers getting the better of him.

In those days, there weren't many left-backs around. There was Ray Wilson of Everton who'd been a member of the 1966 World Cup winning side but there weren't that many top-class ones. Arsenal had Bob McNab but, for me at least, there was none better than Eddie. He was rarely beaten and, week-in week-out, not too many people had the beating of him. Even Manchester United's George Best who, as part of his game, liked to float around over the 90-minutes but, when he played out on the wing and whenever he came up against us, Eddie could handle him.

Eddie was a brilliant teammate. He was very jolly and he liked a laugh, liked a smoke and he also liked a drink. Although he got on well with everyone, his best mate was probably Charlie Cooke. He was a very friendly guy. In those days, we only had 16 players in the squad unlike today and there was a great team spirit. It was a great dressing room with real characters like Ossie, David Webb and John Hollins – we all got on well and Eddie was part of that group.

Whilst I admired him as a player, I would never have foreseen him becoming the manager. There were people in the dressing room who I thought might have become a manager like John Hollins. He was always looking to learn more but not Eddie – he didn't seem the type. The likes of Ken Shellito were already doing some coaching with the youth team but Eddie taking over as manager came over as bit of shock.

He started bringing in the younger players the Wilkins brothers, Tommy Langley, Clive Walker etc and started getting results. At first, he started with the older players but gradually more of the younger players came through and there were fewer places for the seniors. It really took off in the 1976/77 season when we were in the Second Division and got promoted that season. It felt that we were at the beginning of a new era and I often wonder what would have happened if he'd stayed on.

I think it might have been difficult for him if he'd stayed on and led the side into the First Division but it would have been interesting to see how he'd have got on that first season back. He did a good job at Chelsea getting them promoted and it's a shame he didn't get a chance to show what he could do the following season.

He wasn't afraid to try new things but I must say that, it came as a bit of a surprise to say the least when he made Ray Wilkins the captain at such a young age. Ray is a really nice guy – one of the nicest in football – but nobody could have predicted that. It turned out okay though didn't it! Eddie took a big risk. Ray probably thought to himself, 'Why am I being made captain ahead of the more senior players' but Eddie was brave enough to make that call and it paid off.

It was a bit of a shock for Ron Harris who was still there when it happened but, in end, it worked out well for the club, and for Ray himself but he proved what a good captain he was at Chelsea. Eddie's faith in him paid off and that set him up to have a successful football career.

I played regularly for Eddie alongside Marvin Hinton and Micky Droy in that first season we were in the Second Division but then I picked up an injury and, by the time I got back to full fitness the following year, I couldn't get back into the side. Steve Wicks and David Hay were playing regularly in the team. When I was fit, I was playing regularly for the reserves. Dario Gradi was in charge which was tough as he was very much for the younger players. He pushed for the younger players to be in the first-team and it seemed like he'd no time for the older players in the squad. It was difficult to cope with but I had to accept it.

Eddie's style of management was to motivate people. He rarely lost his cool and none of us ever received the infamous 'hair-dryer' treatment from him. He did have his moments when he let people know what he thought and he gave them 'what for' but, overall, he was a very cool manager. He would explain things methodically to players. He was very calm and he was very good at getting players 'up for' the games. He was great at telling players how good they were. It worked tremendously well especially some of the younger ones. He did a great job as manager for Chelsea.

I didn't know that he'd left Chelsea until a couple of days after it had happened. There were different rumours going round at the time as to why he left. Some said he didn't have a contract and wanted one and some said he asked for a car and left when the Board refused but, in truth, no-one really knew why he left. It came as a complete surprise to us all. Everyone thought even after he'd gone, he would come back. I think he came back and they said no. It was a real shock for those of us in the dressing room, especially the younger players like Ray Wilkins, Ken Swain and Tommy Langley.

I didn't have any contact with him when he left although he asked me to come and play for him when he was manager at Memphis Rogues. That was in 1978 but I had already made a decision to play for Philadelphia Fury with Peter Osgood. At the time Eddie and I did speak about a possible move but

I had made up my mind and to had to turn him down. I only saw him once and that was when Philadelphia played against Memphis. I understand that he spoke to some of the younger players after he parted company with Chelsea but my only contact was the Memphis gig.

Eddie apart, I still see some of my old Chelsea team-mates quite regularly as I go to the Annual Lunch (Pitch Owners) each year where I hook up with the likes of Paddy Mulligan, Marvin Hinton, Tommy Baldwin, Charlie Cooke and John Hollins. We chat about the old days and, almost inevitably Eddie's name crops up. That said, I'm not sure any of the other guys have seen him or spoken to him. I know he's afraid of flying but, despite that, he went to America and decided to stay there and make a new life for himself.

He was very nervous about flying but, when Chelsea played in Europe, he had no choice. He didn't enjoy the experience and being on the aircraft when it took off and landed were the worst parts for him, although once in the air, he was fine. I remember one occasion when we were flying back from a game when we had to fly through thunder and lightning. Everyone was scared but Eddie was extra scared! That flight probably did not help his anxiety about flying. I'm sure that he probably could have support or treatment to help him with his fear. In my view, it would be nice if, after 40-years, he came back to England and Chelsea did something special to recognise his contribution to the club both as a player and a manager.

Eddie's nickname was Clarence and he was called that because he had poor eyesight. There was a TV show called "Daktari" which featured a lion called Clarence who was cross-eyed. When he wasn't playing football, he wore glasses but, on the pitch and especially under floodlights, his eyesight was a bit iffy.

There was an incident in the 1970 FA Cup Final replay (29 April 1970, Chelsea 2-1 Leeds United (AET), Osgood, Webb) where he literally flew through the air feet first and nearly took off Billy Bremner's head. I know what people said about that tackle but I know he didn't mean to do it. He couldn't see properly because of the lights. At the time I thought, 'Woah Eddie' but Eric Jennings, the referee for the replay just shouted, "Play on, play on!" so we did! It was no wonder he didn't connect with Bremner's head.

If a game was under floodlights, Eddie would rarely head the ball – he could not see it for starters!! Whilst I have only seen Eddie fleetingly in the time since he left Chelsea, I still keep in contact with people like John Hollins, David Webb and Micky Droy. Micky and I were good friends outside of the game even though I am ten-years older than him. He lives in Florida now for much of the year even though he owns an electrical wholesaler on the Harrow Road.

I left Chelsea in 1978 and moved to Philadelphia Fury and stayed there a couple of years before I moved to Ireland to play for and manage Dundalk. While I was in America, I was voted the North American Soccer League's 'Defender of the Year' ahead of Germany's Franz Beckenbauer who finished second which is something I'm really proud of.

I've been retired for a couple of years now but I used to work at a centre with people with learning disabilities, such as Down's syndrome and autism. I like my garden, my wife and I go for long walks and we have grandchildren to keep us busy. I did the job at the centre for 25 years and I got as much enjoyment out of it as I did from my playing days.

When I was playing, I never thought about reaching 60 or 70-years old but it comes to us all. That said, I am happy and enjoy my life. I get down to Stamford Bridge sometimes but, to be honest, the thing that puts me off going is the atmosphere. It seems although the ground is dead for some games. It seems even worse when I watch the game on TV. Other grounds seem to have a better atmosphere although I do understand many supporters can't afford to go all the time.

Perhaps, if they had a larger stadium and a 60,000 crowd, the atmosphere might be better. It might also be because the area local to Stamford Bridge has changed a lot from my playing days. There aren't as many 'local' supporters living near to the ground as there were in my day. It's really sad. Even in my day, we had the greyhound track and the supporters were further away from the pitch but the crowd seemed to be noisier back then. I notice when I go to games the Matthew Harding is the vocal part of the ground that gets the rest of the ground going along with part of The Shed but everywhere else is quiet which is sad.

MICKY DROY

I was born in Highbury in 1951 and I still live there today. My first club was Hoddesdon Town in Hertfordshire and, after playing for them, I was asked to join Slough Town. I didn't want to move there initially as I was living in North London but part of the deal I was offered included a car which would make it easy for me to get to the twice weekly training sessions and to the games on a match day. They were playing in the Isthmian League in those days and they were managed by Tommy Lawrence. I made my debut for Slough against Southall but I was only there for five months and I signed for Chelsea in October 1970.

I came straight from amateur football and a few of the guys at Chelsea were internationals – Peter Osgood, Peter Bonetti, Charlie Cooke and Eddie McCreadie. They were really good to me, what with me being an 'outsider'. But I got into the first team very quickly and I was soon training regularly with the first-team. They were nice people, very friendly and made me feel welcome.

I don't remember all the games I have played in but I do know I made my debut against Wolves away and we lost 1-0. (13 February 1971 Wolves 1 Chelsea 0). I was marking Derek Dougan that day and I thought I had a good debut and got praise from Dave Sexton after. It was a good transition from amateur football to the first team. I enjoyed it.

I remember when we played Manchester City in the Cup Winners Cup semi-final in 1971. It was a two-legged game and I played in the first leg tie at the Bridge as Ron Harris was injured and David Webb played up front as Osgood and Hutchinson were injured. We won 1-0. (14 April 1971: Chelsea 1 Manchester City 0 Smethurst). I was marking Francis Lee that night and Derek Smethurst got the winning goal.

The guys who were out injured for that game returned to the side for the remainder of the successful European campaign so I didn't play in the return-leg at Maine Road, nor the final against Real Madrid in Athens.

Most of the early games I played in defence were beside Eddie McCreadie. He was a very good player. He was very quick and a very strong tackler. He was a good guy, a no nonsense player. He won the ball and gave it to the people in the team who could play. He gave it to the players who could make things happen.

It was a strong group of players that I joined. They were all friends and they were like a little family. There was a squad of about 15-16 players at the time who played regularly and then there were the others who would come in the team and go back out again after the odd appearance.

I remember doing a sparring session and photo shoot with professional boxer Joe Bugner. The people who organised it wanted a footballer his size so they asked me. I still have the photo somewhere at home. It was great. I also did another photo session with Charlie Magri who was also a boxer and there was another occasion where they did a photo session with me and Ian Britton and I think I had to carry him in a sack!

Unfortunately, things went wrong off the pitch. The club was in trouble because of the idiots upstairs in the boardroom. Peter Osgood and Alan

Hudson had both left after disagreements with Dave Sexton and then he left too.

By then, I was playing regularly in the first-team. I broke into the first team during the 1973/74 season and even managed to get myself on the score sheet. I scored my first goal at White Hart Lane when we beat Spurs (3 April 1974; Spurs 1 Chelsea 2, Droy, Harris). My only worry was that the referee might abandon the game as the floodlights were failing.

We were struggling for money and, in 1975, we were relegated to the Second Division. By then, Eddie had been appointed manager. I never thought he would be a manager. There were others taking their badges back then but Eddie wasn't one of them.

I thought it was a good idea to give him the job. It was someone from the playing side who knew the club inside out and exactly how the club should be run. He was such a good guy and we got on well. Although when he became manager, I didn't play all the time but we used to talk all the time. He made me Club captain and he would ask for my advice. I was now one of the senior players. We used to talk about different stuff. He was not the type of bloke who thought he knew it all. He wanted to learn. He was a good listener. He wanted the best for the club. He kept the club going. He had to play the kids. He didn't have the money to sign any players and had to let some of the older players go as well. He would ask my advice on things like player bonuses and their pay before speaking to the players themselves. Rather than be directed by the idiots upstairs, he sought my view which I appreciated.

In football, there is a big difference between managing and coaching. There are people who have not actively played at a high level and are probably very good coaches but I think they can't understand what goes on with players if they have never played the game. Unless you have been a player you won't know but Eddie knew what it was all about. He knew what it was like to be injured, he knew what it was like not to be picked or be left out of the side and how all those things can effect players.

In that first season in the Second Division, I started the season as first choice and played regularly until I got injured in a home defeat to Oldham Athletic. That sidelined me for the rest of the season and while I was injured David Hay and Steve Wicks formed a strong partnership.

Eddie knew he had to get a balance between the players who played every week and the players who didn't and keep them onside. He managed that so well. I think he is one of the best managers Chelsea has ever had. How they were able to get rid of him I will never know. Someone told me it was over a car or a bonus. It was joke letting him go. I remember Christine Matthews ringing to tell me but, at the time, I thought she was joking.

Although, I have heard the story about the Bolton game, I didn't pick the team. I had a lot of time for John Neal. He was a lovely fella. I told him who should play to give us a chance of getting a result. It was important to us that we did and it turned out alright. Whether or not John took my advice I don't know and who knows whether he would have picked the same players that I said he should. It was a very important game as Chelsea in the Third Division was unthinkable.

I wanted to stay at Chelsea and I didn't want to play for anyone else. If I was playing for Chelsea I was happy. Middlesbrough and Jack Charlton came in for me but I wouldn't have gone to live there!! A few clubs came in for me including Arsenal and my mum and dad were season ticket holders there. When I first signed for Chelsea my dad didn't speak to me for ages!

I never wanted to leave Chelsea but I was having a difficult time with Ken Bates. I had a contract with a couple of years to run and I always was a union man and made sure I got my view across. I was the Club captain so we had to discuss and agree pay increases and I also helped the other players with their negotiations with Bates, something he didn't like.

It was a stupid situation and in the end he let me go to Crystal Palace. I knew Steve Coppell well and they trained at our old Mitcham ground so I thought I might as well go there. I liked Palace and should never have left them. They were a good little club. I should never have gone to Brentford. Frank McClintock was manager and was a mate and he persuaded Steve Perryman and I to go there. I didn't like the set up or the football so I didn't stay there long.

I always said when I packed up playing I would return to non-league football so I played for Dulwich Hamlet and Kingstonian at the end of my career, and then got the chance to manage Kingstonian. I was interested in management but there were jobs I could have gone for but they were all out of London and my wife didn't want to move out of London. I did apply for the Millwall job. I knew George Graham and he said I had a great chance of getting it. I was 35-years old and it proved to be a bad experience. When I went for the interview, the guys running Millwall talked about everything apart from football. I knew some of the players and thought I could do a job but I said to them why are you talking to me about the non-playing side? I was only interested in the football and coaching side and I didn't want to know about tickets, sponsorship and the like but that was all they talked about.

Then the job came up at Kingstonian. I thought I would give it a try. I really enjoyed it. I did all the coaching myself. Their Kingsmeadow home was a nice ground and they are a nice club. I did that for a few years but when the politics began to become more important than the football so I thought 'stuff it' and quit.

The supporters at Chelsea for some reason really took to me and were always good to me. A lot of them looked at me and saw a bloke from the street just like themselves. In all the years I was there they were great to me.

I was as happy as Larry when I was playing for Chelsea. I still have my 1978 Player of the Year trophy which takes pride of place at home and I still have got a Wilkinson Sword Man of the Match award which was a giant sword which my granddaughter loves playing with.

While I was at Chelsea, I was always reminding the players that there was a life after football and they would not survive on what they earn in football when they retired. I was a working man before I joined Chelsea so I knew what the outside world was like compared to football. Some of the guys they did not have a clue. I had to remind them to prepare for when they finished playing. You're never going to earn enough money not to work. You have to think long term.

Unfortunately, some of the guys would rather play snooker, go down the pub or go to the bookies. I used to tell them all the time but it is difficult to tell people something they don't want to hear.

I set up my firm – Westminster Electricals – about 30 years ago. I have a few branches and the head office in Welywn Garden City. My son now runs the business for me as I have been retired now for a few years. When I am over in England I still though go up on the train and help him rather than sit indoors.

I have retired to Florida a few years ago. I know the area well now as well as I know Highbury where I live when I am over here. Florida is huge it would fill the whole of this country five times over. I have a great life. When I'm there you'll never see me without a smile on my face. I have one love which is racing. It's not a hobby, it is almost a business. That is my one guilty pleasure. I spend hours looking at the form and I have done well on the horses.

I'm an ordinary bloke who loves his family, I love my life, I love Florida and I like going everywhere with my wife Lorraine. We are best friends, and that is more important to me than anything. She goes out in her car and does her own thing and then we'll meet up for lunch or dinner. It's a great life I have. My only worry is that I am not getting any younger!

I spend six-months now in the USA and six-months here in London. I am usually back in Florida by the time the clocks change in October but I stayed longer in 2016. I went to the Chelsea Annual Lunch and they were all surprised to see me. I saw the old faces and it was good to see the guys especially John Dempsey who used to live near me in Camberley. He was a very good player and was very under-rated. He got too many injuries like me which was a shame.

I have a mobile phone but I probably use it less than anyone and I am not the type to arrange things and keep in touch with the guys. The last time I saw them was when I attended a fund raiser for the late Ian Britton.

Although I came from an Arsenal family, I'm a Chelsea supporter. I don't go to games. I don't like crowds. They keep asking me to go to Chelsea and I say no. I live near Highbury right beside the Emirates and Pat Rice is always asking me to go to watch Arsenal but I always say no. I have never got on with big crowds. It's not my thing.

We get all the games on TV in America so I keep in touch with Chelsea that way. Football is more of business these days. People moan about what players earn but I would say good luck to them. My only concern is that it is hard for kids today to come through and play in the first-team as opposed to the way Eddie did things by regularly playing the kids.

STEVE FINNIESTON

I made my debut against Leicester City in 1975 (1 February 1975; Leicester 1-1, Kember). I thought I should have got my chance earlier but I remember the Daily Express phoned me up the night before the game and asked me was I excited to be making my debut. I was little bit cocky back in those days and the week before Leicester had played Leatherhead in the FA Cup, and I said I was going to do a Chris Kelly on them and score. I had a bad game and we drew 1-1 and I think Steve Kember got our goal.

Ron Suart was manager when I made my debut. I had scored a lot of goals in the youth team and in the reserves and I thought I might have got a chance in the last days of Dave Sexton's reign. I never did, so I thought that Dave did not rate me.

Then I heard he had put in a good word to Jimmy Andrews at Cardiff City and I went on loan to Cardiff for a couple of months. I actually made my league debut for Cardiff City before making my debut for Chelsea.

I had a great time at Cardiff. All I wanted to do was play football and I got my chance at Ninian Park. I enjoyed my two months there and I scored some goals and also had some great team-mates there. I've been lucky throughout my playing career with the players I have played with. I've always enjoyed the social side of football and have always had good mates who, whatever the result, always would be up for a beer following the game. Don't get me wrong – I wanted to win every game I played in, but win, lose or draw, we always went out for beer wherever I played.

I can't understand people who say 'if we don't win this game, or win the league, or win the cup it is the end of the world' and end up having a miserable evening. There are only a small number of trophies to win each year and a lot of teams so, if you live like that, there are going to be lots of occasions when you are miserable. I loved playing football but I enjoyed the social side as well.

Ray Lewington, Kenny Swain, Tommy Langley and I were very close. When I made my debut for Cardiff on a Tuesday night against York City (27 August 1975; York City 1-0 Cardiff City), Ray, Teddy Maybank and

Derek Richardson who was our reserve team goalie all drove down to Cardiff to lend their support to me. They stayed down and slept on the floor of the hotel room Cardiff had arranged for me to stay in while I was playing for them.

It was never work. It was fun. We all knew each other and got along really well. What better job than kicking a ball around every morning and then a game on a Saturday? Also, once training had finished, it was off to the snooker hall or to the bookies or we went racing or played a bit of golf. Actually, I still do most of that now if I can get away with it!!

As I've said, it wasn't work. I did what I enjoyed with my friends – playing football. Teddy and I were good mates even though we were both competing for the number 9 shirt. Even though he was a couple of years younger than me – he'd made his debut aged seventeen-years old – he was a good footballer and Eddie loved him but I always scored more goals than him. We always had a rivalry even when we were in the reserves – I scored more than Ted though and he will be first to admit that! We were good mates and I still see him at the odd golf event and nothing changes between us. He's still the same as he always was. I see Graham Wilkins nearly every week. We play golf regularly. I used to see Clive Walker a lot before he moved to Oxfordshire. I see Tommy Langley and Garry Stanley– we all keep in touch with each other – and I also see Ron Harris, Ray Lewington and a couple of the others quite regularly as well as Ray Wilkins. I also got to know the old 'young' boys through playing for the Chelsea Old Boys.

My ambition though had always been to play in the first team for Chelsea. Even one game would have done for me. If, when I was 13 or 14-years old, someone had shown me a piece of paper saying I would get to play for Chelsea just once, I would have taken that paper and signed it!!

My first goal for Chelsea was against Newcastle United at home not long after I made my debut. We won (22 February 1975; Chelsea 3-2 Newcastle

United, Hollins (P), Finnieston, Cooke) and I scored a disputed goal. The ball hit the crossbar and I headed it and Ian McFaul the Newcastle keeper saved it just a little bit behind the line. There was no goal-line technology then. The referee gave the goal and Malcolm McDonald missed a penalty late on in the last couple of minutes.

We were relegated at the end of the season and, for the first part of that first season in the Second Division, I spent my time in the reserves. Eddie didn't fancy me at first. I don't know why. He loved Teddy Maybank who was a really good footballer. I was always a goal-scorer but I have to say that Ted was the better footballer so he started in the first team.

As was the case with Dave Sexton, I thought I might have got my chance earlier. I was scoring goals in the reserves regularly but I didn't come into the first team until after we had been knocked out of the FA Cup by Crystal Palace (14 February 1976; Chelsea 2-3 Crystal Palace, Wilkins R, Wicks). I got my chance at Hull City (18 February 1976; Chelsea 0-0 Hull City) a few days later, a game in which the crowd was a touch over 10,000.

I then played the last 12 or so games and I scored five goals in the run in so I had a great end to the season. Eddie must have thought, 'He can score goals' and from then on I could do no wrong. I started in the first team the following season and got the winning goal in that first game at Orient (21 August 1976; Orient 0-1 Chelsea) I got away with murder with Eddie after that! I'd just got married and if I wanted a day off Eddie was great. He'd let me have a day off. He was really good to me.

According to some, I scored a few key goals for Chelsea with many of them proving to be winning goals against sides such as Orient (21 August 1976; Orient 0-1 Chelsea, Finnieston), Blackpool (25 September 1976; Blackpool 0-1, Finnieston) and Nottingham Forest (16 April 1977; 2-1, Britton, Finnieston).

In particular, I loved that goal against Nottingham Forest. That was important. I think it was a cross that came over, Steve Wicks headed it down, and Tommy (Langley) was up front with me that day and I think I probably pushed him out of the way to get that! My favourite goal was against Liverpool – not the cup game – but the year I made my debut when we drew at Anfield (1 March 1975; Liverpool 2-2 Chelsea, Britton, Finnieston). It wasn't a televised game and I scored a 30-yarder from outside the area.

From 1976/77 of course I remember the last game of the season when we beat Hull City (14 May 1977; Britton, Finnieston 3). I scored a hat-trick which was probably the worst ever... sorry the most simple of hat-tricks – two tap-ins and a penalty!

Since the arrival of Mr Abramovich to Chelsea, there is a box at Stamford Bridge that ex-players get invited to. I was in there once at the same time as the Spanish journalist Guillem Balagué. He thinks he knows everything and he was talking about José Mourinho and saying what a great manager he is and how great he is with players. I told him that, in my playing days, Eddie McCreadie was a great man manager as well. He looked at me as if say, "Why?" I told him how Eddie was with the players. He got the best out of us. He would tell us on Saturday before a game, "Guys, if you win today I'll give you Monday and Tuesday off." Now some of us still probably went in and trained when he gave us the day off but his telling us you do well for me and you can have time off on a Monday or Tuesday or both meant a lot. Once I'd proved myself to Eddie I could do no wrong in his eyes. Even if I had a couple of bad games he was still on my side. He'd say, "You're my centre forward..." and that meant a lot.

He did however upset me when he first took over as manager but it also showed to me how good he was at management. I got married in 1976 and I had a conversation with Eddie at the time. I played from February and I was getting married the following July. I think I was on £30 something – it might have been £50 a week. I remember having to call from a phone box in West Byfleet and saying to Eddie, "I have a year left on my contract but I'm getting married in the summer." I think I asked a £5 a week pay-rise. Eddie said, "Jock, you're on £30 per week and if I have my way you will be on the same wages for the next ten years!" Players didn't have agents in those days so managers decided your wages and he had me in tears!

But, by the start of the season when I scored the winner at Orient, things had got better and I was on £70 per week and then, at the end of the season, Eddie did a very good bit of management. He called in all the players one by one to agree contracts.

I remember even in Dave Sexton's day sitting outside his office with Gary Locke and Steve Sherwood. Back then we were paid £15 per week. We were all sitting outside Dave Sexton's office and saying "I'm not signing for less than £25 per week!" Dave Sexton called me in and said "Jock, I think you are doing well so I would like to offer you £15." I replied, "I want £25!" Dave replied, "Sorry Jock, Peter Osgood only got £25!" That however, was what he'd been paid about five-years previously!

I went in to see Eddie, and I was wondering what he was going to offer me. I was on £70 per week by then and he said to me, "How much do you want Jock?" I hadn't really thought about it but I said, "£140 per week." Eddie said, "That's fine!" I can remember thinking at the time, 'Wow I've doubled my wages!' I was very pleased with that and Steve Wicks followed after me and Eddie asked him how much he wanted. Steve asked for £200 a week but Eddie told him he had no chance and offered him £180! So Steve Wicks got £180 and I got £140. I have to say that was good management!

Eddie was great. He had a great sense of humour and he was easy to get on with but he didn't do much on the coaching side. Ken Shellito has to take a lot of credit for work he did with the youth-team and the seven or eight of us who had grown up playing together. One of the people who probably

EDDIE MCCREADIE'S BLUE AND WHITE ARMY

didn't get enough credit was Dario Gradi. We used to train in the morning but when he was reserve-team manager, he'd have anyone back in the afternoon who was interested in improving their game and wanted to become better players.

As far as my career's concerned, I can say he's the only coach that ever improved me as a player. He helped me on my technique and my reading of the game. I used to be good in the air and I used to win a lot of headers and flick them on but then Dario said to me, "It's alright flicking it on, but who is behind you? Think about who and what is around you and always be looking to see where other players are."

Dario loved coaching! Dave Sexton was a real nice guy but I always felt when he was coaching he'd practice things far too long. When I was in the reserves, we'd make up the numbers at set pieces in training and practice a corner for over half an hour at a time and players rapidly lost interest after about 10-minutes especially Ossie and Huddy who knew everything or thought they did... Dave's decision to bring in Dario might have led to the fall out with Ossie. Dario was a great coach and he'd played non-league football to quite a decent standard but, at the end of the day, he was a school teacher by trade. Some of the senior players didn't take to Dario some thought, 'He's just a school teacher, what does he know? What can he teach us?' Dario never had a chance with the first-team but he stepped down to the reserves and did a good job.

We could play a bit and, with Eddie in charge, I'm sure we would have done well in the First Division. Then Ken Shellito took over. I know we knew Ken well as we'd worked with him in the youth team but I don't think he wanted the job in the first place. The club wanted him but Ken wasn't sure but they persuaded him to take it. He was good in the youth-team with the kids but I don't think he was a good manager for the first-team.

The one thing one couldn't escape from during my time at Stamford Bridge was the debt that the club was in. Lot of people were collecting loose change from the supporters in the 'Cash For Chelsea' buckets and around that time the players all agreed to take a pay-cut. Mr Abramovich has done a great job for Chelsea and it's completely different from our day. It is all about the money now. Even if he ever decided to pull out, something that other teams' fans keep saying will happen, there'd be one hundred billionaires who would be interested in taking over Chelsea. It's a big club.

It annoys me when people say Chelsea have only become a big club in the last few years – they're wrong. They were a big team in the 1960s and the 1970s both playing wise and crowd wise. Chelsea has always been a big club. We got big crowds in our day with crowds of 40,000 plus. The away support we had following us was fantastic. The day we were promoted was brilliant. It was a really good atmosphere. Wolverhampton Wanderers were already up and we needed a point to join them. Tommy Langley scored early on for us but they equalised and the game ended 1-1 (14 May 1977).

I remember the Chelsea supporters on the pitch after the game celebrating and then the Wolves fans came on but the police got it badly wrong. Everybody was on the pitch and was happy. The Wolves fans were happy they had won the title and the Chelsea supporters were happy – there was no need for the police to get involved and start whacking people. They were pushing people around and I thought this is not right. Chelsea supporters did nothing wrong. They were just happy. I know they were not supposed to be there and they had a bit of a reputation but they were good as gold that day. After the game, we headed back to London and went to a pub near Stamford Bridge. I remember there was a famous actor in there named Tony Britton who was probably in there having some food and a quiet drink. I think we probably ruined his evening. We'd all had too much to drink and I think we were giving him a bit of stick. I remember putting a sandwich on Brian Mears' head! I had a lot of time for Brian, I liked him. He was a nice guy. I know he got a bit of stick in later years but I liked him a lot. I still keep in touch and see his son Chris who goes to Chelsea.

After the promotion, came the parting of the ways between Eddie and Chelsea Football Club. I don't know why he left…was it a car? Was it a contract? I don't know. Did he try to call the Board's bluff? I do know Brian Mears was on Eddie's side. There were a couple of Board members and other directors who weren't keen on him so, if he said something like, "I want this or I'll resign!" and perhaps thought someone would come back to him and say, "Come on Eddie…" because there was some middle ground, it looks like he was mistaken.

To be honest, in all my football days – and I was at Chelsea from 12-years of age – I played for a lot of different managers. Dave Sexton was manager and left, then Ron Suart came in and he left, Eddie left and Ken Shellito came in and, to a lot of players, it becomes an occupational hazard. The attitude was 'Eddie's gone, but Ken is a good guy.' We thought he knows us all so nothing would really change. I'm a good mate of Tommy Langley and it was him who told me that Neil Barnett had flown out to America to interview Eddie. I actually subscribed to Chelsea TV for six-months just so I could watch Neil Barnett's interview with him. The interview was good.

One thing I can say is that the supporters were great. If I knew then what I know now, I think I would have done things differently. I would have celebrated more of my goals with them. They chanted the names of the players and their support was great and I know it might sound stupid but we didn't celebrate goals with the crowd like they do today. We would shake hands, pat each other on the back and head back to the halfway line or celebrate on the pitch. It might sound stupid but we were closer to the crowd than players are now but, when players score a goal now, they're on top of the fans every time, celebrating with and in front of them. That said, nowadays they don't interact with the supporters after the games. We were closer to the Chelsea supporters off the pitch but we didn't show it on the pitch as much. If I was playing now and scored, I would be high-fiving and shaking hands with all the supporters behind the goal every time I scored!

I became friends with a couple of supporters called Elaine and Jeff who lived near me in West Byfleet who ended up running the Players' Bar at Stamford Bridge. That was how it was back then. If you knew one of the players it wasn't uncommon for you to come up to the Players Bar and have a drink with them. You can't do that now, it just doesn't happen. When we trained at Mitcham, supporters used to come and watch and, if they had a bit of cheek about them, they would nip into the canteen and have a coffee and a chat with Ossie – and many did! Supporters could stand behind the goal and we used to let some of the kids be ball boys. It was good for us players as well to be mixing with the supporters.

It was just a dream come true to play for Chelsea. There was nothing to beat that and it's the dressing room I miss – being with your mates at work every day. It's not like work though. A football dressing room is something else and that one was a special. As a group, we worked hard and we played hard and everyone got on. We all grew up together, played in the first team together and had a laugh together. If anyone walked in wearing a dodgy shirt or a dodgy jumper, everyone else would slaughter them.

After I left Chelsea, I joined Sheffield Utd but suffered a bad injury. The club were good at looking after and insuring their players. There was a group of people who were responsible for underwriting footballers and the chairman of the group was Brian Mears, so he might have helped me out. I struggled for about a year and had had an operation on my groin. I went to Harley Street regularly and I was desperate to get fit and keep playing but it wasn't getting better. I played a few reserves games but I was still having problems so I went back to Harley Street and saw a specialist. He was very honest with me and told me that as much as I wanted to carry on playing it was not going to get better. I went back to Sheffield United and they agreed a compensation deal with me. Chelsea sold me for £100.000 and I think Sheffield United got their money back through their insurance.

I never wanted to leave Chelsea. At no time while I was at the club did anyone say, "So and so had come in for you with a bid." I was happy at Chelsea but suddenly, at the end of the 1977/78 season, Ken Shellito said to me, "Millwall have been in for you and Orient and Sheffield United. You have been here a long time so maybe it is time for you to move on."

To be honest, Sheffield United were my last option but it was clear that Chelsea wanted to get rid of me. I'd been injured for a large part of that season and maybe the First Division might have been too fast for me but I always did well against Liverpool who were probably one of the best teams in the world back then. I scored in both games I played against them including two in the league game when we won 3-1 (4 March 1977; Chelsea 3-1 Liverpool 1, Finnieston (2), Langley) and I also scored up in Anfield in my first season (1 March 1975; Liverpool 2-2 Chelsea, Britton, Finnieston). The funny thing about Liverpool for me was that, even at Sheffield United we played against them in the League Cup. They were all over us that night but we won. I played against Liverpool six times in my career at a time when they were European Champions and I was only on the losing side once.

Harry Haslam was the manager at Sheffield United but he used to manage Luton Town and I always seemed to play well against Luton and scored against them (9 April 1977; Chelsea 2-0 Luton Town, Sparrow, Finnieston). So, because of that, Harry probably thought I was brilliant. I remember Ken telling me I could talk to all of the clubs and I remember speaking to Jimmy Bloomfield at Orient and Gordon Jago at Millwall but, to be fair, Harry Haslam made a great effort to sign me.

He said to me to come up to Sheffield and take a look around, so I took my wife up there for the weekend. They put us up in this nice hotel and then they rang me the next week but I still didn't want to move up there. Then they said, "Come up again this weekend," and this time, they put us up in this hotel out in the country and they showed us the countryside but I still didn't want to sign. So Harry rang me on the Monday and told me that the

Club Secretary Ken Walker was on his way down to London with a contract for me to sign. It was bizarre how keen they were. Somehow, he also managed to get my wife's work number to get her to speak to me, which she said at the time was the probably the worst mistake he will ever make and it proved to be. It probably sounds stupid now but because Harry was so persistent – I signed for him. If Gordon Jago from Millwall had followed up with an offer I would have jumped at the chance to play for him and stay in London. I admired Harry's persistence and so I joined Sheffield United.

After I retired on medical grounds, I played to a decent standard in non-league football. I played for Hartley Witney and Atherstone and Weybridge. I was playing in the Southern League and I was top goal-scorer for two or three seasons. I played Sunday football as well until my mid-fifties. I miss the football on the playing side but I miss the social side more. I loved playing football for Chelsea Old Boys as well but I ruptured my Cruciate.

My son John also played non-league football and I used to follow him around everywhere he played. He played with Darren Barnard at Camberley and he played with Gareth Hall. We both actually scored hat-tricks in the FA Cup so I can't imagine there are many father and sons who have done that. He also played for Chelsea Old Boys with me so we have travelled around Europe and played in places like Barcelona and Germany together.

My son and I played for Chelsea Old Boys in a charity match against Chelsea supporters at Carshalton after Matthew Harding died. He was a great guy. When my son was 12 or 13-years old, I took him and his friend for a whole season when Glenn Hoddle was the manager. They played Newcastle in the FA Cup (7 January 1996; Chelsea 1-1 Newcastle Utd, Hughes) and I just remember that there was a great atmosphere at the game – probably one of the best I can remember. We were sitting in the Family Section in the East Stand below the Directors Box.

I had just been on a programme on ITV called 'There's Only One Brian Moore'. They'd done a show that featured the last game of the '77 season when we beat Hull City (14 May 1977; Finnieston 3 (1P), Britton). I was on the show with Butch and Matthew Harding and I'd brought my son John along. We met Matthew afterwards. The following week it was the Newcastle cup game and, when it ended, we were waiting for the crowd to go. Matthew, who used to sit above us in the Directors Box, looked down and he shouted, "John! How are you?" That was a nice touch for my boy and it meant a lot.

Not long after that when Glenn Hoddle was England manager, he organised a golf day at Mill White near where I live in Royal Berkshire. My son and his cousin went down there because all the England squad were going to be there. He turned up and was watching the people going into the changing rooms, when Matthew Harding came up to him and said, "Its John isn't it, Jock's boy? I haven't got a caddie today. Fancy being my caddie today?" He gave my son £50 that day. As I said, Matthew was a nice guy.

When I stopped playing football, my love of gambling kept me going. One thing that might be a claim to fame is that I found an angle on a bet called 'The Tote Place' and I made a living out of it! I'm self-employed now and I'm a brick specialist now, but for nine years I was lucky to make money from gambling.

Nowadays, I try to get to Stamford Bridge for about ten games a season. As an ex-Chelsea player, I often get invited to attend games and I really love it but, I have to say, I enjoy meeting the old players more. Sometimes, I can take or leave the game – Chelsea v Burnley doesn't do a lot for me – but I've been to some brilliant games in recent years, where the atmosphere has been amazing and the support has been brilliant. The Napoli game in 2012 (14 March 2012; Chelsea 4-1 Napoli 1, Drogba, Terry, Lampard (P), Ivanovic) was fantastic. The crowd were amazing that night.

My daughter has a good job and one of her clients at work has tickets in the Centenary Lounge. I've been to games with him a few times and it's very nice. They provide lunch and he's a proper diehard Chelsea supporter but, when you look at half the people who are there, some of them just seem to be there so they can say, "I was at Chelsea on Saturday." They are not the same as the proper supporters. One guy who sits nearby reads a book for most of the game. I've been in the East Stand about half-a-dozen times in the past few years and there's often an empty seat beside him as well. They both might be his or his company's seats but I don't get that.

I must admit Stamford Bridge is lot different these days but the one constant is the die-hard supporters. There are a lot of new supporters following Chelsea now but the ones who have been going for years – the fanatical ones – are still there. Players come and go, chairmen come and go but the one constant is the support.

RON HARRIS

I made my debut in the 1961/62 season. It was against Sheffield Wednesday at Stamford Bridge in February (24 February 1962; Chelsea 1-0 Sheffield Wednesday, Harrison) and Micky Harrison scored the winning goal for us. I marked a lad called John Fantham and they had Peter Springett, Bronco Lane, Tony Kay and Peter Swan playing for them.

I didn't score many in my career but I beat one of the finest keepers in the country, actually one of the best goalkeepers in the world in Gordon Banks. That was my first goal against Leicester City at Stamford Bridge (6 April 1964; Chelsea 1-0 Leicester City).

I played with Eddie for quite some time – he was a tremendous player. He was a great lad and a great character to have in the dressing room. He was the only one who'd have a drink before getting onboard an aircraft as he was so scared of flying. He was allowed to have a few glasses of Bacardi and

Coke. Dave Sexton was good to him. He used to let him have a few drinks and some tablets to calm him down before he got on the plane.

Eddie was a very funny man in the dressing room and a top-class player. He played over 400 games for Chelsea, and when someone plays that many, it's obvious he's not a two-bob player. He'd have to be a bit special and he was. He was one of the characters when we all used to go out together. When he became manager, he couldn't be 'one of the lads' any more – he had to change and he did that well.

When Eddie took over, everyone knew that the club was having money problems. I remember Brian Mears coming in one day because our wages hadn't been paid on time and he came to explain what was happening. To be fair, it was resolved quite quickly.

Eddie did a good job getting Chelsea out of the Second Division back into the First Division. He tried to say that his side would be as good as the old side of the 1970s. In my opinion, I don't think many of the players from Eddie's time as manager would have got into the 1970s side.

Even with the players who got Chelsea out of the Second Division, I don't think that Eddie would have survived the First Division. I think he'd have had to buy some stronger players. If one looks back at my time, Chelsea had one or two truly exceptional players with the likes of Charlie Cooke, Alan Hudson and Peter Osgood. I can't remember any of those players from Eddie's era that would've licked their boots in my opinion.

I'd like to think I was a good influence in the dressing room during that season, bearing in mind there were a lot of younger players and, for instance, if anyone of them had any sort of problem I tried to offer them good advice.

Eddie was very superstitious and in those days there was one substitute and

I was on the bench for about 30 games in a row as I was Eddie's lucky mascot. One game I played for Eddie really stands out – Millwall away. I wasn't in the first-team at the time and on that Saturday I expected to play in the reserves in the morning and he told me to try and keep myself fit as he might need me at Millwall in the afternoon.

I played in the reserves in the morning and a car came and picked me up and took me over to The Den for the Millwall game (4 September 1976; Millwall 3-0 Chelsea). I was on the subs bench but Jock Finnieston got injured and I came on and played 45 minutes in the second-half. I don't think one would see a player playing two games in one day these days.

I was in the side when Chelsea played at Molineux to get promoted (07 May 1977; Wolverhampton Wanderers 1-1, Langley). Eddie brought me back into the side before the end of the season as results had not been going well. I was regularly on the bench but I came in for the last 12 games. We drew 1-1 with Wolves and I was marking Bobby Gould that day. They needed a draw to win the league and we needed a draw to get promotion. We took the lead but Wolves equalized before half-time. I think with 20-minutes to go, both sides were happy with a point and I don't remember a single tackle of worth being made after they scored. After the game, everyone was on a high as we'd got the club back in to the First Division. It was good to get Chelsea club back into the top flight.

I had mixed feelings about that season. I was obviously pleased that we'd gone up but I was disappointed that I didn't really feature in the side until the last third of the campaign. I trained as hard as anyone at the club at the time but I didn't get much of a look in. It was good to come back towards the end of the season and be part of winning promotion but it was disappointing to only come on with only ten or 15-minutes to go.

I don't remember where I was when I heard that Eddie had left the club. He left because he asked for a car but the club said, "No!" because of the financial position. I think he later changed his mind but the directors had already accepted his resignation. Eddie came back soon after when he changed his mind but it was too late then.

I didn't see him before he left for America but some years later I took my family on holiday to Tampa in Florida. We walked into our hotel and Eddie was sitting in the bar! I couldn't believe he was there – it was great to see him.

I still see some my old team-mates regularly at Stamford Bridge when I am working for the Hospitality department on home match days. Bobby Tambling and John Hollins are the two I see the most.

The supporters were great to me throughout my 21-year career at Chelsea and I think that they're terrific. I've been involved in hospitality at Stamford Bridge for a number of years now and I enjoy meeting the supporters before the game, having my photo taken and signing autographs – I love every part of it and I'm thankful I'm still involved with the club. I've been lucky enough to have been invited by the club to travel on some of the European trips with the players! I get on very well with Bruce Buck and all the other people at the club. If there are things to do at Chelsea, they'll invite along and I'm always happy to go there for them.

Some people ask me if I'm envious of what today's players earn. When I played, I earned good wages compared to what my parents earned but I suppose I would love to be earning a six-figure sum every week.

I left Chelsea because my contract came to an end. Danny Blanchflower took over as manager and I was coming to the end of my tether. David Hay and I were helping out running the youth side and I was really enjoying that working with the kids. Then Geoff Hurst took over with Bobby Gould as his number-two. I wasn't a great fan of either of them and I was offered the opportunity to go to Brentford as a player-coach so I decided to go there.

Once I finished my career, I bought a golf club in Swindon and ran that for about eight or nine years. I then bought a little holiday complex down in Warminster near to where we lived. Nowadays, my main income is public speaking.

I did stay away from Chelsea for a number of years because of a certain fellow who sued for a comment I made in a newspaper. However, soon after Mr Abramovich bought Chelsea, I received a telephone call from Neil Barnett who asked me if I'd like to appear on Chelsea TV. I was reluctant to do so at first but they twisted my arm. I did the interview and then I was asked to go into a room and it was there that I was introduced to Roman Abramovich.

We sat and talked for an hour and he asked me various things about Chelsea. At the end of the meeting he got up thanked me and said that he would like me to come back to Chelsea Football Club and I have been here ever since.

What used to disappoint me was Peter Bonetti, John Hollins and I have spent a lifetime here and it is only since Roman Abramovich arrived here that you now have the Bonetti suite, the Hollins suite and the Harris suite players who are a big part of the club's history.

No disrespect – I am just being truthful – but there's the 'Nigel Spackman' entrance and how long did he play for the club – a couple of seasons? It's all changed since Mr Abramovich has been at Chelsea. I have no axe to grind with Nigel, I see him here often and he is good lad but, during the time the current owner has been in charge, the club has started to remember its history.

I once went up to Leeds a few seasons back to speak at dinner when Chelsea played at Elland Rd in the League Cup (19 December 2013; Leeds United 0-5 Chelsea, Mata, Ivanovic, Moses, Hazard, Torres) when a certain ex-Chelsea chairman was in charge.

Before I got up to speak, a fellow came up to me and said, "There are 40,000 supporters here tonight, 35,000 of them Leeds fans and 5,000 Chelsea and, out of those Leeds fans, 34,999 hate a certain bloke up here. I won't tell you who it is but I think you know who I mean…"

Everybody knew in football that Glenn Hoddle was coming to Chelsea at the time when David Webb was manager and who succeeded in keeping Chelsea up. I used to write a column in 'The Sun' newspaper and I wrote that I thought Webby had been duped as he took over when the team was down near the bottom of the table, he saved the club from relegation and kept them up. Soon after I got a letter from a certain individual's solicitors saying the article I'd written had caused distress and I was subsequently sued. Thanks however to The Sun newspaper who agreed to pay the damages and the costs that I incurred.

DAVID HAY

Although I signed for Chelsea in 1974, I nearly joined them when I was a boy. It was in the days before academies and I was training with Celtic twice a week. I must have been 15 or 16-years old and, at the time, I was playing for a boys' club.

Along with my dad, I went to meet Tommy Docherty and John Boyle at a hotel in Edinburgh. I remember the Doc saying that he knew I was with Celtic and asking me I wanted to play for – Celtic or Chelsea? I said Celtic and that was that. They were my team as a boy. He never pursued it further. I know he was a Celtic man himself. It was Tommy Docherty who gave me the nickname 'The Quiet Assassin' when I played for him for Scotland. 10-years later I arrived at Chelsea.

I was in the last year of my contract at Celtic. Unlike today, back then, the clubs had complete power over players. The previous season I had had a contract dispute at Celtic and I had almost signed for Tottenham when Bill Nicholson was there and Tommy Docherty was also interested in bringing me to Manchester United when he was managing them.

I actually went out on strike for a couple of weeks at the time at Celtic. Looking back now, it was stupid of me but I went back after I got a call from a press man who I trusted who said to me I should go back and play again for Celtic.

I played for Scotland in the 1974 World Cup and had a good tournament. I won 27 caps for Scotland and if things had not been against me I might have won some more. I really enjoyed the World Cup in 1974. We played Yugoslavia, Zaire and Brazil. We beat Zaire 2-0 with goals from Peter Lorimer and Joe Jordan (14 June 1974) and then we had that amazing game with Brazil when Billy Bremner nearly scored for us (18 June 1974; Brazil 0-0 Scotland). Yugoslavia had beaten Zaire 9-0 so we had to beat them in the final game to qualify. We drew 1-1 (22 June 1974 and Brazil had to beat Zaire 3-0 to get through and we heard that Brazil had managed a 3-0 win. If only we had scored more in that first game.

However, I still enjoyed the experience. I got to play with a hero of mine in Denis Law and I also have got Rivelino's shirt from the Brazil game. I loved playing for Scotland. I also played at Wembley too. Little did I know that I would never play for Scotland again after the World Cup! I was selected for a squad in 1975 and I had to pull out because my mother died suddenly. If anyone had said to me that I'd never play for Scotland again after the World Cup I would have been surprised.

Following the World Cup, I decided I was going to stay at Celtic and sort out a new contract on my return, whatever terms they decided to offer me but on my first day back at Parkhead after the tournament I met Jock Stein. He said, "We've had an offer for you from Chelsea and I think you should go."

That took me back a bit but in the space of 48-hours I had signed for Chelsea. I went down and met Dave Sexton, Brian Mears and Lord Chelsea and they put me up in Claridges. That was the way that Chelsea treated me from day one. They really looked after me. I remember the last words of my wife Catherine before I left for London which were, "Don't sign anything until you get back home so we can discuss it."

What did I do? I signed straight away! Despite all the injury problems I had, I have no regrets at signing for Chelsea. I would liked to have been more successful not just for myself but for Chelsea and the Chelsea supporters. They were always good to me. From day one I liked Brian Mears the chairman, I liked the players and it was a great dressing room to be in. But, before I joined up with Chelsea, I nearly didn't get there at all! After the World Cup, I took my wife Catherine and my daughter Allison to Cyprus. We were there when Turkey invaded the island. We were staying in Famagusta and the Turkish Air Force was bombing the town. We were evacuated out of Cyprus in an RAF Tornado. I saw the aircraft on their bombing raids. It was a scary moment. There were bombs going off all around us. It was almost if fate was against me from that Cyprus trip going forward. Things started to go down hill for me from there.

Unfortunately for me, when the season started, I wasn't playing well. I had my cataracts in that first season and my vision wasn't correct. I tried to persevere but at the end of the season I had an operation on my eyes. By the time I came back to Chelsea, Eddie was the manager and I believe that he wasn't sure of me to begin with. He'd probably have known me from our Scotland days but in that relegation season he wouldn't have seen me at my best.

I am now blind in my right eye and back then, I wasn't performing the way I knew I could. I managed to play in defence but I struggled in midfield with two eyes, never mind with one. If a player has an injury, they're sometimes able to come back, but with the problems I had with my eye in that first season, I didn't perform as well as I know I could have done.

That day we lost to Spurs at White Hart Lane (19 April 1976; Tottenham Hotspur 2-0 Chelsea) – the match that effectively relegated us in 1975 – I was playing wide on the right. I didn't play well but it wasn't the only game that season that I was having constant problems due to my cataracts. It was a period in which my vision was just not right and it wasn't just that game against Spurs game in which I played poorly.

It wasn't until I had an operation to remove the cataracts that I realised myself that something wasn't quite right. I wore contact lenses but I never told anyone. I used to put them on in the toilets before the game. Nowadays, loads of players have contacts but back then it was not heard of so I kept quiet. I had a soft lens in one eye and a hard lens in the other eye after I had the operation.

Making Ray Wilkins the captain for the game against Spurs was a good choice and a brave decision by Eddie. When I first arrived at Chelsea, he was working with the reserves. There was no perception then amongst the players that Eddie would be the obvious choice after Dave Sexton and Ron Suart. But he made it an easy transition. He was Chelsea – he brought continuity and it made sense.

He also had Dario Gradi helping him as well. Dario was helping with the first team and the reserves. I played under Dario when I was coming back from injury and he was first-class. The foundations were there for Eddie. Because of the World Cup in 1974 and my visit to Cyprus, I missed part of my first season at Chelsea as I was in Cyprus and had just played in the World Cup. The following season, I missed some of my second year because of my operation.

The 1975/1976 pre-season was the first I had with Eddie in charge and it was hard and enjoyable. Apart from my first season at Chelsea when my confidence was low, I always looked forward to going into training. Picking up Ron Harris in Ewell and then heading up to Mitcham was memorable. Eddie was disciplined in his training sessions but we would have some light hearted moments.

The season after Chelsea went down was all about adapting to life in the Second Division. Chelsea were a big club and down in the Second Division there were teams waiting to scalp the 'Billy big-timers' who'd been just down from the First Division. The promotion season was different. We had that experience of one year in the Second Division.

As for me, I wasn't happy but accepted the situation, rolled my sleeves up and tried my best whenever I could to play my part in getting Chelsea back into the First Division. The season we got promotion I was much happier. I was back playing as I thought I should be and I think I played most of the games that season. That year, I played regularly with Stevie Wicks and we did well together.

I remember playing against Fulham on Boxing Day and there were 55,000 at Stamford Bridge and many were locked out that day. They had Bobby Moore, Rodney Marsh and George Best but we beat them (27 December 1976; Chelsea 2-0 Fulham, Droy, Swain). It was like a big match, a really big match – like a First Division match even though it was in the Second Division. The stands were full and that was the sort of occasion in which Eddie made the difference. He lived for those occasions and I'm sure he would have made a difference in the First Division had he stayed.

I missed the last few games of the season as I had the detached retina so I missed the promotion games. I was in hospital at the time and at the end of the season the club went on tour to America to play in Vancouver and Los Angeles. To Eddie's credit he took me over there even though I was not able to play.

I had a really good relationship with Eddie and enjoyed working with him. I would have preferred Eddie to have stayed longer. If he hadn't left, I'm sure he would have gone on to bigger things with Chelsea. I'm not saying it would have happened but who finished third in the Second Division behind Chelsea that season? Nottingham Forest. What did they do the following season when they got promoted? They won the league and the following year the European Cup. I can't say that Eddie would have done that, but we were a better side than Forest and if Eddie had stayed we would have done well.

Ken Shellito was really well liked by the players. The results didn't go for him though. I don't know why. I wouldn't criticise Ken but, for some reason or other, it just didn't work out. I think the difference was that Eddie had the 'Midas touch' with that particular group of players he was working with. He got the balance between youth and experience spot on and he gave you a sense of belief. We had total belief in ourselves as players because he instilled so much confidence in us. We all went onto the pitch knowing exactly what was required of us.

He had Ron Harris there a former team-mate and he made Butch Wilkins captain instead at 18-years of age. He also let some of the older players go at the same time. We were a young team and he was not afraid to make the tough decisions. But I wasn't aware how bad things were. Personally, I didn't get the sense that the club was in a bad way financially – nobody said we couldn't buy boot polish. We knew that we couldn't sign any players and there were no large or long contracts given but I think that Eddie kept as much of that from us as he could. I don't think it affected what was happening out on the pitch.

I have to say though, if you think about that the East Stand is still there today. It's clearly had a lick of paint since my day but it looks like a modern stand to me. In truth, one has to give Chelsea credit for the vision they had.

I can't remember how I found out that Eddie had left. I know on the American tour I heard that there might have been a problem with his contract. There were undertones something was not right. Eddie though would never discuss those sorts of issues with anyone. He was very private. He would never show his hand. We weren't in training so it was close season when he went. I would really like to have seen him stay on. For Eddie's sake, for Chelsea's sake and for that team's sake but sadly history tells otherwise.

I bumped into him a couple of times when I was in America when he was manager of Memphis Rogues. I would love to see him again. Maybe one day I will get the chance to go to Tennessee and see him.

The Bolton game when we won 4-3 (14 October 1978; Langley, Swain, Walker, (OG)) is one I'll always remember. We came back from 3-0 down. It was my final game for Chelsea so a good way to go out. My depth of vision had gone and to get back playing for me was an achievement. I enjoyed my time at Chelsea and under different circumstances without the injuries I had I would have liked it to have been better.

I remember all the guys in the Chelsea dressing room with fondness but I became friendly with Ron Harris from the start. Ron didn't drive so I used to pick him up on the way to training and we used to be room-mates on away trips. Ron and I were very similar on and off the pitch. I liked Ron a lot. We never got sent off when we played together and we were hardly ever booked. We could both tackle but tackle fairly – we were hard but fair.

I stayed with Ron when I first moved to Chelsea. He put me up in his house while I was sorting out my own place to live. I moved to Epsom and we would regularly go out for a Chinese meal in Ewell and we'd pop into the Green Man pub for the odd pint. I have happy memories of my time

EDDIE MAC EDDIE MAC

spent with Ron. I speak regularly to him and I'm sure you'll see us together me at a Chelsea game at Stamford Bridge soon!

I saw Ray Lewington when Scotland played England (18 November 2014; Scotland 1-3 England) game. I used to see Butch often when he was playing for Glasgow Rangers. I've also run into Tommy Langley at Celtic Park when he was involved in bringing Amido Baldé from Waasland-Beveren to Celtic. Tommy's doing well as an agent. When I saw him, he said, "How are you Jim?" He used to call me Jim in our playing days after the Russ Abbott character 'See you Jimmy!'

I really enjoyed my time at Chelsea and I have nothing but fond memories. They looked after me superbly from the very first day in more ways than just contract wise and financially.

I'm glad to hear how all the guys are doing from my playing days and one day I will come down to Chelsea and meet up with them all. I have fond, fond memories of Chelsea.

For different reasons, things might have worked out better for me at Chelsea but the supporters were always good to me and I really appreciated their support. They would come into the players lounge after the game and would always be appreciative as to what we did on the pitch. Although I didn't perform as well at times as I would like to have done, it was never held against me by the supporters. They were always great to me and it's something I'll always appreciate. I miss playing and hated being forced to stop playing. I would have loved to extend my time at Chelsea. I was 30-years old when I had to quit. I did some coaching when Danny Blanchflower was in charge after he asked me to do some work with the Chelsea youth teams.

When Geoff Hurst came, he told me I'd have to get my coaching badges. I said, "Fair enough." However, then there was some pettiness on my part and I over reacted to something he said to me so I told him where to stick his job. I should have bitten my tongue but, as one gets older, one learns to do that. It was impulsive on my part and moment of rashness. At the end of the day, I was wrong to act like that.

When I left Chelsea, I landed a coaching job with Motherwell where I was an assistant to Ally McLeod but I went to the USA for a job that did not materialise. When I came back, I got the Celtic manager's job and we won the league for first time in 9-years while I was there. This was when the Souness revolution was going on at Glasgow Rangers.

I went on to manage Livingstone and we went on to win the Scottish League Cup. I then went to Norway and won the Championship there with Lillestrom but they've never won it since. I brought four of the six teams I managed trophies.

Nowadays, I spend a lot of time with my grandchildren and I'm working with a college in Lanarkshire and I also have a regular column in the Glasgow Evening Times. I go to the Celtic games and one of my grandkids is a goalkeeper playing at the Celtic Academy. That said, we got him a Chelsea goalkeepers' kit. His favourite player is Thibaut Courtois.

I still look out for Chelsea's results but, in truth, although I'm a Chelsea supporter, Celtic were and will always be my first love. There is no bond from a supporters' point of view between the two clubs. It is Chelsea and Rangers now and when I say to people I played for Chelsea they look at me as if to say are you sure? I have to say Chelsea are good to me still. Chelsea send me a Christmas hamper every December and they keep asking me down to the Chelsea Pitch Owners Lunch every year. I've not made it yet but one day I will definitely come down. I will probably do it with my grandson. I watch them every time they are on TV. I think Mr Abramovich has been great for Chelsea. I admire what he has done for the club.

I have definitely got divided loyalties but I have such fond memories of my time at Chelsea. I would love to Chelsea draw Celtic in the Champions League but there's not much chance of that happening at present. Put it this way... if Celtic are not in the Champions League, I would always want Chelsea to win it!

TOMMY LANGLEY

I made my debut for Chelsea at home to Leicester City when I was 16 (9 November 1974). We drew 0-0 at home and I was the third youngest debutant in Chelsea history. It was featured on ITV's 'Big Match' the next day. By then, Dave Sexton had gone and Eddie was working with Ron Suart with the first-team and it was Eddie who gave me my chance. We met at the hotel opposite Earls Court Arena for a pre-match meal of steak and rice pudding which was an unbelievable menu. How we were ever able to play after that, goodness only knows!

Then Eddie took me to the ground in his car because, at the time, I didn't drive. When we got to Stamford Bridge, Eddie got me out of the car and past the TV crew and quickly took me into the safety of the dressing room. I had a couple of shots but I have to say I didn't do particularly well. Although I was training regularly with the first-team, I was out of the side for the next game as whoever I replaced got fit. I then picked up an injury and had to wait until February for my next chance. I can remember the date. Eddie came up to me the day before the game and said, "Are you alright son?" I said, "I'm fine," and he replied, "I'm going to put you on the bench tomorrow."

We were at home to Birmingham City on 8 February 1975, my birthday, and I came off the bench to score the winning goal with 15 minutes to go. We won 2-1 and Ray Wilkins scored his first goal for Chelsea that day. It was unbelievable for me! To play for the team that I supported was just an amazing feeling.

I'm from Kennington near Elephant and Castle so it was either Chelsea or Millwall but my family chose Chelsea. The reason why they went to Chelsea was because they were all gamblers. In the old days, they used to have greyhound racing at Stamford Bridge so they went for the dogs and the football.

I went to the three consecutive FA Cup semi-finals in the 1960s (27 March 1965; Chelsea 0-2 Liverpool), (23 April 1964; Chelsea 0-2 Sheffield Wednesday) and (29 April 1967; Chelsea 1-0 Leeds Utd). When Tony Hateley scored the goal that took us to Wembley to face Spurs. My dad, my uncle and granddad were all Chelsea season-ticket holders and we all went together. I missed the Final (20 May 1967; Chelsea 1-2 Tottenham Hotspur, Tambling) as I was just 9-years old then and because of the cost of the tickets. We were a working-class family and couldn't afford them.

In 1970, I was 12-years old and, by then, I was on the books at Chelsea as a schoolboy. A member of the backroom team had tickets for the replay at Old Trafford (29 April 1970; Chelsea 2-1 Leeds Utd, Osgood, Webb), and I got two tickets for the game. I wanted to go but it was a school night so I wasn't allowed to go.

I remember David Webb scoring the winner, and my brother who is 10-years younger than me was in bed. My mum had just managed to get him to sleep. Hutch throws the ball in and Webby heads it in and I just screamed at the top of my voice with joy. Trouble was, my mother could not get him back to sleep because I frightened the life out of him with my screaming. My brother is an Everton fan and hates Chelsea – I suspect it all stems back to that night!

I ended up playing with Tommy Baldwin, Demps, Ossie, Catty, Ron Harris, Johnny Hollins, Hutch, Alan Hudson and Charlie Cooke and they were my idols. One minute I was watching these guys from the stands, then I got to meet them, then I got to train with them and then I got to play on the same pitch as them. And finally they then became my mates! I still get excited at functions when I am with these guys. Bobby Tambling was my granddad's idol when he watched Chelsea and I love him and love meeting up with him and also the likes of Bert Murray and Barry Bridges all of whom I now can call my friends.

When I used to go with my dad, Ossie was my idol and when he came back the second time I got the chance to play with him for about a dozen games. Better still, I became Ossie's mate and we used to go racing together. Hutch also became a mate and for a supporter growing up to have these guys as my friends you can imagine, I was like a kid in a sweet shop! I am playing football with my idols for the team that I have followed all my life. It does not get any better than that! I was 10-years old when I joined Chelsea and I loved being there. When I was older, during the summer holidays, I used to go into the office and help out around the place. I just loved being at the football club. I would do any work they asked, put letters in envelopes, put them through the franking machine and things like that.

Contrary to what you hear about them, the likes of Ossie, Hutch, Charlie Cooke and the rest were a very disciplined group. They wouldn't stand for any nonsense from any young kid coming into the first-team, especially from a 16-year old like I was. If a player went in with an attitude, it was soon knocked out of him!

When we were eating, Ron Harris took great delight in ripping into the young kids and the older pros would be there laughing. All the kids would be thinking, 'I hope it's not my turn today'. I remember Ron looking across at me when we were sitting down at dinner and shouting, "Oi! You Langley! It is Mr Harris to you sir!" Even to this day whenever I see Ron I say 'Mr Harris' to him.

I was really upset not to play in the side against Tottenham (19 April 1975; Tottenham Hotspur 2-0 Chelsea). I'd just got into the side when Ron Suart

274

was in charge but Eddie, who'd been helping him run the club, officially took over from that game. I knew the importance of that game to the supporters. I wanted to fight with the boys especially against Spurs to stop us getting relegated but Eddie decided to go with Teddy Maybank that day ahead of me. That hurt, I wanted to play. Ted's a good lad and was a good player but we still lost and that as good as put us down.

The following season, although I got a few games in the first half of the season, I didn't play too many times in the second half of it. I played in the Fulham game at Craven Cottage (27 September 1975; Fulham 2-0 Chelsea) and I started the game on the right. Les Strong was playing left-back for Fulham. He became a mate of mine in later years since when we played together at Crystal Palace. On this occasion, I knocked the ball past him and made him look a bit silly. As he next came past me he turned to me and said, "You do that again and I'll break your legs! The next chance I got, I still took him on and went past him!

A lot of supporters tell me that they remember the interview I did with Brian Moore on ITV's 'Big Match'. It was the home game against Sheffield United (30 April 1977; Chelsea 4-0 Sheffield Utd, Langley, Lewington, Wilkins R, Finnieston) and I scored an unbelievable goal. I had my back to goal and I watched the ball bounce in the six-yard box and I swivelled and I smashed it on the volley. That was the first time they allowed the cameras into the dressing room. Brian Moore talked to all the players and said to me, "You're the new kid on the block, you've replaced Kenny Swain – is there pressure on you to score today?" I said that I needed to score as Kenny had done such a great job in the team. They showed the game on the Sunday. We really smashed Sheffield United that day. We then had a week off and went up to Wolves and got promotion.

Eddie McCreadie was fantastic and a major help to me a player. It was Eddie and Ron Suart that gave me my debut. Eddie was a major part in me playing in that side and me getting my chance at Chelsea. I did play a few games for him in that first season in the Second Division before he left me out of the side but as a 16, 17, 18-year old, I was still very much in my infancy – I was still learning.

Sometimes my legs would go but Eddie recognised that I was still learning but gave me lots of encouragement and support. He was great for my Chelsea career. When I was 15, I used to go up to the training ground at Mitcham to play where the first-team were training and sometimes they used to play the rest. They dragged me into the side to play against the first-team. Once, I was playing wide right and I was up against Eddie McCreadie. I went down the wing and he's came flying in and I got past him. I looked up to cross the ball and next thing I know he has come in and whack! He's tackled me. He'd got up and recovered quickly just when I thought I was clear. He was that quick in the tackle and players needed a good half-yard plus to be clear of Eddie in training – no, rather a whole yard!

As a manager, he had a big impact on what I did. He used to gee me up in the dressing room before the game and come up to me and tell me I was the best striker in Europe. I knew I wasn't, but at just 17 and 18-years old he was saying this to me! Wow! He was one of my idols when I was watching Chelsea as a supporter and he thinks I am one of the best strikers in Europe! I'd walk out down the tunnel feeling ten-feet tall with the self-belief he instilled in me. Football is as much about belief as it is about skill and ability. How many players have there been who had great ability but did not believe they were good enough? Then, how many players who may not have had the same level of ability made a career driven by a high level of self belief? Eddie was just brilliant. He nurtured these boys – Garry Stanley, John Sparrow, Butch, Ray Lewington, Jock Finnieston, Clive Walker, and also me of course.

It helped that he knew us all well from when he was involved with the reserves. Eddie and Ron Suart were in charge of them when Dario Gradi and Dave Sexton were looking after the first-team. Dave got the sack and then Dario was moved to the reserves. Just before Dave was sacked, I'd been brought back to train with the first-team just before we played Manchester City. I was told I'd be involved in the game but then, instead, I played for the reserves at Tottenham and scored twice in a 2-2 draw. Dave lost his job after that game – I hope it wasn't him not selecting me for the first-team that was the cause of it.

As a result of the decision to try to build a new stadium, Chelsea were in financial difficulties and I was aware of the situation. We heard about it as players because we had to take a 20% pay-cut. I don't know about the other lads, but I was a Chelsea supporter. For me, I was doing the best job in the world. I would have probably played for nothing. We took a cut in our wages on the basis that the Board would then try and deal with it at the end of the season. Hand on heart, I cannot remember if we got the money back at the end of the season but it didn't matter to me as we were back in Division One.

Following the first season that he was in charge, Eddie made a few changes and brought Jock in, the goals followed and we won promotion. I didn't get my chance until that Sheffield United game (30 April 1977; Chelsea 4-0 Sheffield United, Wilkins, Finnieston, Lewington, Langley) but I then played in the run-in and got that goal at Wolves (7 May 1977; Wolverhampton Wanderers 1-1 Chelsea, Langley).

Before the game, we knew that the 'boys' had been banned and that there was not meant to be any Chelsea supporters there. We weren't really expecting many, if any at all, to be there. On our way to the game, we stopped at the hotel near West Bromwich Albion's ground for lunch before we made our way to Molineux. We headed off early as we didn't want to hit lots of traffic. We got to the ground and stepped out on to the pitch.

In those days, when the players walked down the tunnel and onto the Molineux pitch, they'd just see the stand opposite and, at that stage there were few people there. But as we came into sight of the pitch, we heard an enormous roar from the terraces to our right and all we could see was this massive sea of blue. It was the boys – they'd beaten the ban, so we went over and had some banter and found out that the police wisely thought it was safer to have them all in the ground, rather than running around the streets of Wolverhampton.

All the players knew the supporters had been banned but, from that moment I swear to you, we knew we wouldn't lose that game. It was impossible after seeing all the Chelsea supporters there. There was no way we were going to get beaten! As it happened, we took the lead when I scored and then John Richards equalised for Wolves. Halfway through the second-half, the Wolves captain said to Ray Wilkins, "Are you happy with a point? We're happy with a point…" Ray gathered the players and said to us, "They need a point to win the title, we need a point for promotion and the reality is we don't want to go into the Hull City game still needing a win for promotion…" We would have probably beaten Hull if we had to but we wanted to avoid having that problem. Ray had a quiet chat with the boys, and if you watch the last 20 minutes of that game, there wasn't a tackle made or a shot in anger. Yes, it would have been great if we had won that game and we might have won the league as there were no runners-up medals but it was more important getting Chelsea promoted back to the First Division.

We loved the supporters. Clive Walker was my room-mate for six years. He was continually in Eddie's squad but he didn't get many chances until the following season. We then got the opportunities to play together regularly and there were many games when we were under the cosh and, if you look back at some of those seasons, the results were not good. One game I do remember when Clive and I played up front was against West Ham and I remember it was a match when their fans tried to take The Shed. Both Clive and I were slow reacting to a ball out of defence as we were both watching what was happening on the terraces! We had a great affinity with the supporters.

We were of similar age in Eddie's side – Clive, Butch, Ray Lew, Garry Stanley, Jock and I, and the supporters were not much younger or older than us. There was a rapport between us and the supporters as we were the same age group and some of us knew a few of the people on the terraces. If one thinks abut it, when there was no real success for Chelsea between the 1970s and until Glenn Hoddle arrived but I do believe the foundations of Chelsea's travelling support were built during that era when Eddie was manager. We took thousands to every away game and our following has evolved from there. Nowadays, you see the same guys are still coming down the Bridge and are bringing their children or their grandchildren with them.

I don't know how Eddie would have fared as Chelsea manager if he'd have stayed. Chelsea were relegated again two-years after the promotion in 1977. The club was still in financial turmoil after Eddie had gone. No slight on Ken Shellito, but there was something about Eddie's manner. We used to do sprints on a Friday, and a cough or grunt from Eddie was the cue to start and that would a fun debating point. Did he cough? No it was a grunt. Was it a start or not? You'd have a laugh in training. On Fridays, we used to play five-a-side behind the goal in front of The Shed. We went into games on a Saturday relaxed and that was down to Eddie. I think he would have been the same in the First Division.

We had this great camaraderie which I don't think the current squad will have in years to come and we all got on really well together. I'll never forget that when Lee Frost got in the side while I was out injured. He came in when we played West Ham at home. I came off the pitch at Hereford playing in the reserves and heard that Frostie had scored the winning goal. Now, believe it or not, I was pleased for him as I was his mate, but there was also a part of me that also thought, 'Oh great... I'm going to be in the reserves again now for another week...' But I was pleased at the same time for my mate. Jock is still a big mate and we see each other every week. We often chat why we were such a close knit group. We were a great bunch of guys and it helped that we had all grown up together and came through the youth and reserves together.

A few of us keep in touch. I look after Ray Lewington's son as his agent. Ray Lewington trusts me. His son Dean is at Milton Keynes and is club-captain and is a fantastic professional as was his dad. Because the trust and loyalty is there, I was at his dad's wedding to Angie. That group was a great group. We meet up regularly still and have a good craic when we get together. We also have the likes of Colin Pates, Gary Chivers and some of the lads that followed on after who have become part of our group. I have to say that I do miss the banter and the energy in the dressing room and the idiots in the dressing room like Teddy Maybank who kept us all entertained. He's another who I play golf with. We're also fortunate in that we still get asked by the club to go to a lot of functions such as the Chelsea Pitch Owners events and the Annual Lunch and suchlike. I also miss playing.

I used to stay with Ron Harris on a Friday night. We used to go to the dogs at Wimbledon and he used me as his chauffeur on match days which was something I was very happy to do. We'd go to the dogs on Friday, have a bite to eat and I would take him to the game on a Saturday. I used to look forward to that every week.

People often ask if I wish I was playing today, rather than back when I was and I can truthfully reply that I'm happy to have played when I did. I'm of the opinion that nobody owes us anything! We had the pleasure of playing for a great football club. I had a career because Chelsea brought us through the youth system and taught us the right way. Guys like Ken Shellito and Eddie McCreadie taught us good habits. I count myself lucky to have played for Chelsea when I did and I would not swap it for anything. They were a fantastic group of guys I was lucky enough to play with and be friends with.

Nowadays, things have moved on so far from where they were back in the 1970s and 1980s. The training ground at Cobham has pitches that are like carpets and the players have everything they want. We had to train at Mitcham and, if it rained, the pitches got flooded. The facilities there are great but I wouldn't swap my time again.

Looking at the game, now it is a non-contact sport and players can't tackle and, more often than not, the player goes to ground and the one who's made that tackle runs the risk of getting booked. I remember playing in the reserves against Southampton's John McGrath and he had Vaseline all round his legs and he'd growl at you before you even got anywhere near the ball. That was what the reserves was like every week. Playing in the reserves was part and parcel of your development at Chelsea. They don't have that now. That said, we wouldn't get in the reserves today, never mind the first team. It was a different time for football. I wouldn't change one minute of my time at Chelsea for the present day. I'm privileged to have played for Chelsea and still be involved with the club to this day.

I left Chelsea for crazy reasons. I was very much in a state of mental turmoil at the time. I was in love with the club, I'd been following Chelsea for years, I knew the history of the club and I'd been a season-ticket holder. Then my mum died and that took a lot out of me that I didn't really appreciate it at the time. That's why I have so much admiration for Frank Lampard when he took that penalty against Liverpool just after his mum died. I was desperate for him not to take that penalty as I didn't want him to miss it. Imagine if he had have missed – how would that have left him? I couldn't imagine what was going through his head with 40,000 people looking at him but he smashed it in. That was so emotional. Credit and massive respect to him and that is why he is a legend. A total gentleman!

Steve Wicks was at QPR when my mum died, He told me it was a great club and really well run, better run than Chelsea. At that time, I had a year left on my contract at Stamford Bridge. Geoff Hurst and Bobby Gould were in charge and I didn't get on with them at the time although I get on with them fine now. There was a lot going on in my mind. I wasn't enjoying playing for Geoff and Bobby when Wicksy asked me if I'd come and join QPR.

Tommy Docherty was manager and Ken Shellito was his assistant and we spoke over the telephone. At that time West Ham were also interested in me, but then, instead, they signed Paul Goddard from QPR. A week before the season started, QPR came to me and said they were keen for me to sign and wanted to meet me on the day before the season started. We trained that Friday at Stamford Bridge and I told Geoff Hurst and Bobby Gould that I was going to speak to QPR. They told me not to but, if I did, I was to make sure I spoke to them before I signed anything. Anyway, Tommy Docherty picked me up and we both went to meet Jim Gregory the chairman. I was 22-years old I was promised a pay rise but, if I didn't sign for QPR there and then, I wouldn't get it. Even to this day, I feel the knots I had in my stomach when I signed for QPR. I mentally and physically felt the pressure on me by Jim Gregory to sign. I have to say that was a really, really bad decision.

I joined QPR for all the wrong reasons, the main one being money! I went out and a bought a racehorse, a car and two new fur coats for the missus with the extra money I got from signing that deal and there I was a QPR player. Their training ground was terrible! Chelsea were at Harlington then and I had gone from Stamford Bridge where, on a good day, we'd had pulled in 40,000+ crowds to Loftus Road.

I scored against Chelsea at Stamford Bridge (30 September 1980; Chelsea 1-1 Queens Park Rangers, Chivers) and I also got the winner in the return at Loftus Rd (17 January 1981, QPR 1-0 Chelsea). It was strange as my family were there supporting Chelsea and I scored against them. Can you imagine it? They didn't know whether to laugh or cry! That was the path I had chosen and I had to live with it. Not long after I joined QPR, Tommy

Docherty got the sack and Terry Venables came in as manager. I liked Venners and got on really well with him on a personal level and scored three in three games for him but I was in and out of the team. "It doesn't matter how well you do, you will never be one of my players," he said to me.

He saw me as a Tommy Docherty player. Little did I know that there was previous history between them and I believe that my exclusion was a political decision rather than one made for footballing reasons. Don't get me wrong, I wasn't playing out of my boots but I wasn't playing too badly either. QPR wasn't a good time for me. I hated it and I should never have left Chelsea.

I left QPR and joined Crystal Palace but, after one-year, I went to Greece to play for AEK Athens in Greece before having a year at Coventry City, Wolverhampton Wanderers and Aldershot. I then went to Hong Kong and signed for South China. By then, football for me was just about earning a living and my work had taken me there. I have to say however that living in Hong Kong was brilliant. It's a very special place but it was the 'outback' as far as football was concerned.

There were just two good teams then, one being Seiko and the other was South China. Tony Morley, Gordon McQueen were out there playing for Seiko and Derek Parlane and I played for South China. We won the league the year I was there. Soon after, they introduced a rule where teams could only have Chinese players so I had to come home. I was on £600 per week at the time and they gave me a 3 bedroom apartment in Causeway Bay to live in. The down side was it was on the 32nd floor and there were no bars on the window and, one day, I found my son playing with the window!

I returned to England and met a friend of mine called Gordon Cox who'd played for Aldershot, but, as well as being a footballer, he also had a job as a photo-copier salesman. He told me he could get me some work. My first cheque was £192.53 a week but I was also earning £400 for playing for Slough Town. I did the photo copying for about 7-years and I played for Slough, St Albans, Basingstoke, Staines, Wokingham and that was it. I stopped playing when I was aged 35.

At that stage of my career, it wasn't just about football – it was about still playing and enjoying playing the game and having the banter. There are plenty of ex-professionals still playing non-league football simply because they enjoy it.

Nowadays, I have my work at Chelsea TV so I'm still involved at Chelsea but I'm also a football agent. Although people who do what I do now often come in for criticism but I'm at the lower end of the food chain. There are good agents and there are bad agents. There's a Division Three agent and then there's a Premier League agent. Those who do work as agents have to understand where they are and where the club they are working with is and everything works from there. If I think of my own situation with QPR and when I went in to meet Jim Gregory, if that was now I would have probably had a couple of days to consider the offer and I would still probably be a Chelsea player. Geoff Hurst would have gone to Brian Mears and said QPR have offered Tommy this and it could have been resolved via my agent or another third party. Back then, when an owner got a 22-year old footballer in a room on his own with no representation and put a financial offer in front of him as in my case, it was a hard call. I defy anyone back then to look at what was £100 per week wage increase and not have had their head turned. I was on £400 per week and I was being offered £500 per week and that was hard for someone like me to say no to. Now, an agent representing a player can barter with the home club and the player might end up staying.

In the modern game now, there is a definite place for agents so long as they represent themselves in the right way. Look at the current young prospects at Chelsea... When we were kids, we looked after ourselves. Modern day agents should make sure they look after their players. They have a good structure at Chelsea. There are good people such as Neil Bath working with the youngsters and the young players have the best food, the best pitches and their playing structure mirrors the first-team. The first-team pros are adults and can look after themselves but the agents have a responsibility to look after their players.

When we were young, we had each other so we discussed things with our mates in the dressing room. Christine Matthews was also great. She was a confidant. She was the Mrs Fixit. She looked after the young players and made sure they stayed on the straight and narrow. She is lovely, a big part of the club in her day and she was someone we could go to if we needed help or advice.

As a Chelsea supporter, to have played back in that era was fantastic. On the flip-side, that era was a funny time to play for Chelsea. We were good enough to beat the likes of Liverpool (7 January 1978; Chelsea 4-2 Liverpool, Langley, Walker (2), Finnieston) in the FA Cup but then get knocked out by Orient (27 February 1978; Chelsea 1-2 Orient, O.G.).

When we played at their place, I had a shot at goal about 30 seconds into the game and the wall came down behind the goal where the Chelsea supporters were. They all came onto the pitch and the game was stopped for several minutes. Fortunately, nobody was hurt and everyone was alright. We did a job and got a draw (19 February 1978; Orient 0-0) and got them back to The Bridge for a replay. We even took the lead in the replay through an own goal but then Peter Kitchen scored two goals. Orient got to the FA Cup semi-final that year, a game that was played at Stamford Bridge and they were beaten by Arsenal who went on to the win the cup at Wembley. We had every chance that year, and we were truly disappointed that we got knocked out by Orient. I seriously think we thought we had got the job done at Brisbane Road by getting them back to Stamford Bridge for the replay. If we'd have got past Orient, I think we could have gone on to

Wembley. That was probably my biggest disappointment at Chelsea. We really thought we had a good chance that year of winning the FA Cup.

RAY LEWINGTON

I joined Chelsea as a boy aged 10-years old but I signed professional forms with Chelsea in 1975 and I was at the back end of the group who broke into the first team. At that time, the youth-team of a couple of years earlier had become the first-team. Ray Wilkins was the same age as me and had already made his first-team debut but he was still eligible to play in the FA Youth Cup.

I was one of the last to break into the first-team and I did begin to wonder if I would ever get my chance but I got into the side at the end of the 1975/76 season. It was easier for me to make my debut as I was not going into the first-team on my own amongst a group of senior players. I went into a first-eleven that had my reserve-team team-mates and my youth-team team-mates. My debut was against Notts County, a game Chelsea lost (21 February 1976; Notts County 3-2 Chelsea, Stanley, Finnieston).

I found out I would make my first start for the club when Eddie gave me a heads up. He'd already had me on the bench for a number of games that season and he told me I'd get my chance before the season was out. It wasn't a total surprise when he gave me the nod – he told me the day before I would start. I fitted in quickly and I stayed in the side until the end of the season. Although I was pleased to play in the first-team I didn't go into the next season thinking I would be in every week.

In those days, most top clubs played a non-league or lower league team and then there were a couple of games abroad in Europe. With Chelsea we usually went to Scandinavia – Sweden or Norway. Pre-season was far harder then than it is now. Players don't come back now and get walloped with long distance running or cross country. Looking back, I'm amazed at the amount of running we did. Nowadays, sports scientists would claim that all that cross-country running we did back then was worthless. All that pain we went through in pre-season running around Richmond Park or up and down Epsom Downs in 80 degree heat was a waste of time!

In 1976, we went to Sweden for a pre-season tour and, although I played in the majority of the games there, I still didn't think I would be in the side for the first league game against Orient (21 August 1976; Orient 0-1, Finnieston) but I was. We got off to a flying start and it just went from there. I went through the whole season and played every game along with Ray Wilkins and Gary Locke.

Eddie had taken over as the manager in 1975, and because some of the older players in the squad like Gary Locke and Ian Britton had played with him and knew him well he was very relaxed and easy to be around. We called him Ed, not boss or gaffer. He was very outgoing – but his instructions were very simple – just play your game. We enjoyed playing for Ed because he was one of us. He was a player's coach. We played a different system at the time to other teams. It wasn't 4-4-2 like most clubs played at the time. In 2015, the England team changed to playing in a diamond formation and much has been said about that, but we were playing a diamond formation in our promotion year in 1977! Even though Eddie was about you playing your game and keeping it simple, it wasn't a case of Eddie putting us out on the pitch and letting us play – he set us up well and he had a system.

I don't think any of us truly believed we would go up that year. We finished mid-table the season before and went into that second season thinking about consolidating our position and building upon it the following season. In fact, we hit the ground running and were in the top four early on and we stayed there for the rest of the season and we topped the table for most of the time as well. The crowds started to get bigger and, even by today's standards, we played in front of some big crowds. I remember playing

Southampton 30 October 1976 (Chelsea 3-1 Southampton, Wilkins, Finnieston, Swain) and we got 42,000 and Fulham on Boxing Day (27 December 1976; Chelsea 2-0 Fulham, Droy, Swain) we had 55,000 in the ground.

They were incredible crowds who really got behind us and I think that rubbed off on all the players and we started to believe as well. Eddie was perfect for that as he was a very positive man, an attribute he didn't hide and he'd encourage us by telling us we were at the top and that we should 'go for it'. Very early on we just hoped we would do 'okay' but, after about six or so games when we went to the top of the league, we thought 'maybe we have a chance here' and it just went from there.

I think Dave Sexton was the first Englishman to coach in a style that would be acceptable in today's modern game. Then, most coaches/managers kept the team happy and training would be 5-a-sides, some running and every team played a 4-4-2 formation. Dave was different and Eddie was different from everyone else. There was none of the usual man-to-man marking, the 'this is your man, that's your man' mantra. Ed's philosophy was the nearest man closes the man with the ball down. If he goes to the other side of the pitch you leave him and whoever is nearest will close him down. We didn't play 4-4-2 and didn't have four in midfield. We used three with Ray playing in front of the midfielders.

I didn't score many goals for Chelsea and I remember them all. Omid Djalili, the comedian, is a big Chelsea supporter. I was at a Chelsea game just before Christmas and he came up to me and introduced himself and said, "I remember your first goal for Chelsea." And I said, "Cardiff at home" (7 October 1976; Chelsea 2-1 Cardiff City, Lewington, Swain) and he said, "Yes and I can describe how you scored it". He did say, "Well I'm cheating a bit as it was my first ever Chelsea game." The goal came after a throw-in and we were kicking towards the North Stand. I got a flick on from the throw and chested it and volleyed it left footed into the net. My second goal was a flukey one. It was against Sheffield United (30 April 1977; Chelsea 4-0 Sheffield Utd, Langley, Lewington, Wilkins, Finnieston) and I half-hit it and it also got a deflection to go in.

When I was with Chelsea, the club was hamstrung financially and was in a bad way. I've been through similar situations since then with other clubs. At Watford, we had the same thing happen where the players took a wage cut and the very next game we went to Sheffield United. They were riding high at the time and we won 2-1 and the togetherness of the squad was unbelievable. I hadn't thought about the Chelsea days for a while but that event with Watford took me right back. I remember 'Cash for Chelsea' and the blankets and boxes going round and people throwing money into them at every game. I remember Teddy Maybank and I going to a pub in Streatham near where both of us lived and found out they'd raised £2500 for the cause by playing darts. Ted and I went along and picked up the money on behalf of Chelsea.

In those days, the players were far closer to the supporters back then than players are today. A lot of the time, after a home game, we would go into the Rising Sun (now called The Butcher's Hook) for a drink and the supporters would come over and say hello. It was no big deal to us and the supporters didn't think it was either. It was what players and fans did together back then. Everyone seemed to be of the same mindset on and off the pitch, especially when the players agreed to take a wage cut. I think the fact the players agreed to it had an enormous effect on the supporters. The players weren't money grabbers and they were doing something positive for the sake of their club and, as far as the supporters are concerned, it is their club. Players and managers come and go but supporters don't and to see a bunch of players taking a wage cut for their club was massive and showed we were all pulling together for the club.

There were several highlights for me in the season we won promotion and playing Fulham in the Boxing Day fixture was one of them (27 December

1976, Chelsea 2-0 Fulham, Droy, Swain). There was a computer at Chelsea that showed the number of people going through the turnstiles at each gate and how many were in the ground at any time. The players went onto the pitch before the game and then the lads had a look in the computer room and the crowd was unbelievable. We went into the room and at 2.30pm it was showing there was already a crowd of 36,000. We knew it was going to be a special gate and we got 55,000 on the day and we went on to win the game. The Southampton game (30 October 1976; Chelsea 3-1 Southampton, Wilkins R, Finnieston, Swain) was another memorable game for me, not just because there was a big crowd but also because of the fact that Chelsea came from behind to win the game.

The game against Wolves at Stamford Bridge was another game I remember well because we came back from 3-1 down to draw 3-3 with two late goals (11 December 1976; Chelsea 3-3 Wolverhampton Wanderers, Britton, Wilkins, Finnieston). The game up at Wolves (7 May 1977; Wolverhampton Wanderers 1-1 Chelsea, Langley) was a memorable day. It was a strange sort of game. The draw suited both of us and it was almost like we had a truce in midfield in the second-half. It was a fantastic season and, game after game, it was brilliant from the very first one at Orient (21 August 1976; Orient 0-1 Chelsea, Finnieston) to the last one at home to Hull (14 May 1977; Chelsea 4-0 Hull City, Britton, Finnieston 3)

On our way to Molineux for the game in which we won promotion, the players were all talking about the ban that had been imposed on the Chelsea supporters. We were expecting there to be no supporters there but when we walked out on to the pitch before the game and we saw all the Chelsea fans there it was brilliant but, in truth, I don't think we were surprised to see them. We were always well supported that season and there wasn't one away game that we played where we couldn't hear the Chelsea supporters getting behind us and there was a good following at every game. They were incredible.

Steve Finnieston broke his nose in the game at Molineux and I kept pulling his nose afterwards so he was in agony all night. We headed straight back to London after the game and there were plenty of cans of beer on the coach and we were drinking all the way back. Some of us decided to get the driver to drop us off at a pub but not to go back to Stamford Bridge. We went to a quiet backstreet pub somewhere off the Kings Road and we were there until about ten o'clock that night and, by then, our families started arriving to pick us up.

I gave the number 10 shirt I wore in the Hull City game to the Chelsea museum. Another souvenir I have from the time is a photo of the old East Stand with me standing next to Ray Wilkins. John Sparrow is there as is my brother Chris who played for Chelsea at the time, Tommy Langley and Clive Walker.

A short time after we'd won promotion, Micky Droy Chelsea's club captain, phoned us all to say that he'd heard that Eddie was having contract talks. We were oblivious to be honest as it was none of our business but obviously Micky knew people within the club and had been tipped off that Eddie was on the verge of walking out after he'd fallen out with the Board. He called us all together and we made our feelings known to the powers that be that we didn't want him to leave but, by then, it was too late. It had gone too far and Eddie decided that he'd leave. He was going to stick to his guns and quit. It was very sad really. We'd done so much together and so quickly and then, suddenly, it was gone. That was very disappointing.

Had he stayed on and led us in the First Division, I think he'd have 'gone for it' as he had done the season before. Ken Shellito came in but I think he was too conservative and I think he thought we weren't ready for the First Division. His approach might have been proved right as we stayed up the first year whereas Eddie's approach to games might have not worked out. That said, I think Eddie would have stuck with the youngsters and he would have said we'd sink or swim together. Ken knew us all as he had been our youth-team manager but I don't think he completely trusted the younger players in the top flight. We were fine in the Second Division, but Ken thought we needed more experienced players to try and compete in what is now the Premier League. It was a struggle the following year. We had a couple of nice wins over Liverpool in the FA Cup and in the league and we had a couple of other big scalps that year but it was a hard season after Eddie left.

Ray Wilkins was my best mate. We both joined Chelsea on the same day when we were 10-years old. We came from similar backgrounds. We were both one of a family of six, not very wealthy, we didn't have much money and we lived in council houses. We stuck together, probably because we were a couple of years younger that most of the lads. Teddy Maybank was another. I sat next to him at school for five-years when we were between 11 and 16-years old as alphabetically L and M follow each other and we were put in the same class. That was an experience in itself! Ted was scatty, crazy one might say, but crazy in a nice way. He was a character and he hasn't changed since. He was the dressing room clown. He would do bizarre things and we always expected Ted to do the unexpected and he never let us down.

We were all in the youth-team together and we all got on really well. We were all friends. The proof of the pudding is that the same group of players still play veteran matches together with the nucleus of the old boys being Clive Walker, Tommy Langley, Ian Britton when he was alive and Steve Finnieston. They've all kept in touch over the years. I've not been able to play but I have gone along and watched. John Sparrow comes along as well. I don't know of any other group of players who have stayed together like this group. I have been to and played for other teams but I don't think I keep in touch with any players from any of my other clubs, the odd Christmas card apart but to keep in contact and to continue to have a social life with the Chelsea players after all these years is a bit special. John Sparrow and I speak regularly, I talk to Ray Wilkins to a certain extent but he has always got something or other going on to keep him busy.

I'm in touch with Garry Stanley and Ken Swain but John Sparrow and I go back a long way. John played for East London and I played for South London and we always seemed to be playing against each other. I would stay at his house and he would stay at mine. In those days, we weren't allowed to play for Chelsea at under-16 level so most clubs also had a Sunday league side to get around this rule.

We all played for Senrab, a team that once featured John Terry, which was basically a Chelsea side which included Tommy Langley, Ray Wilkins, Steve Wicks, John Sparrow and me. I last saw David Hay when England played Scotland in May 2015. I haven't seen Davie since the early 1980s. I went out on to the pitch before the game and I got a tap on my shoulder and a voice with a strong Scottish accent said, "What the heck are you doing up here?" I turned round and it was Dave. He looked really well. I liked Dave. He was a quiet lad. He came in from the World Cup as the big star from Scotland but he settled in really well.

Nowadays, although I'm on 'the other side' as it were, I miss the banter of the dressing room – I don't expect to walk into a dressing room now and be part of the jokes. Back then though, we all knew each other and we all could take the Mickey out of each other. There was no holding back – if you did something wrong you were told about it straight away. It was a great place to be each day. A lot of the time and when it went quiet we could always rely on Ted to pipe up and make us all laugh.

I didn't have any intention of leaving Chelsea but, after Danny Blanchflower had taken charge, he called some of us into his office. Garry Stanley, Steve Wicks and I went in and he said, "No offence, but I've had a look at the squad and decided that I want to move a few out and move a few in." I was a little bit surprised to be honest. Everybody knew that if people weren't in the team that this might happen sooner or later but I had been at Chelsea so long that it came as a shock that they wanted to let me go.

Norwich came in for me and Danny Blanchflower came to see me and told me that they'd made an acceptable offer for me but I didn't want to go to there so I turned them down. Tony Waters, the manager of the North American Soccer league side Vancouver Whitecaps, rang me and said, "Don't put the phone down – listen to what I have to say." It was the year after the 1978 World Cup and Johann Cruyff was going to be playing there, Franz Beckenbauer was already there and a lot of the Brazilian World Cup squad playing for New York Cosmos.

Vancouver was a very British city. The weather was very British and a lot of ex-pats lived there and they wanted to get some English players in to play for them. They offered the incentive that, if one stayed for 3-years, one would qualify for Canadian citizenship. I was told they would embrace me if I did that and I'd become a big star. I must admit I was tempted and, although the season ran from February to September, I agreed to sign for a year to see if I liked it. They had to buy me from Chelsea but agreed that, if it didn't work out, they'd sell me back to a British club for the same fee. I thoroughly enjoyed myself there and we won the Soccer Bowl at the end of the season. Vancouver was a beautiful city and, in my opinion, it's one of the top cities in the world, it's in a lovely location and had a real British 'feel' about it so I didn't feel out of place.

I had a really good year there but my wife Anne and I felt we didn't want to leave England so I came home and signed for Fulham. I did have a brief spell at Wimbledon while it was close-season in America.

It then transpired that Fulham had money troubles and had to sell all their main players. I was sold to Sheffield United but I wasn't there long when I got a call from Ray Harford telling me he was leaving Fulham to take a job at Luton. Ray was my mentor and taught me much of what I know now.

He said, "Fulham have a new chairman and are looking for a player-manager and I have put your name forward. If you really want it, the job is yours." That was start of my coaching/management career. I was only 28-years old at the time and it wasn't the greatest job in the world but it got me on the managerial ladder.

I didn't pay much attention to contracts in those days and I thought I'd signed one to be player-manager. However, two years later, Jimmy Hill came to see me and, although we got on fairly well, he said, "I don't like player managers!" It turned out that my contract was a player first and a manager second and he didn't want me as a manager. He demoted me and said, "I want you to concentrate on playing – you can't do both jobs." At the time, I thought he was wrong and I argued my case with him and we fell out over it for a long time afterwards. However, he was right. One can't do both jobs properly. I was one of the better players in the side but with the weight of the world constantly on my shoulders, I became one of the also-rans in the team. What all managers eventually do is drop themselves and that is what I did and Jimmy was not happy. He told me he wanted me out on the pitch playing so he demoted me to coach and brought in Alan Dicks as manager. I became first team-coach which, to be honest, suited me better.

I eventually left Fulham and went to Crystal Palace as reserve-team manager and, a year later, became first-team coach when Ron Noades was chairman. I actually enjoyed working with Noadesy but he could be hard work. I did a number of jobs at Palace including assistant to Alan Smith but then Ron wanted to buy Brentford and sold Crystal Palace to Mark Goldberg. Ron's next project was Brentford and he wanted to be manager. He did say he was only going to be manager if I was his number-two so I went to Griffin Park with him. There, I was in charge from Monday to Friday which was down to me but Ron picked the team on Saturdays and decided on transfers and who came to the club. Everything else was down to me including team talks in the dressing room. To be honest, I was not sure about doing the job but Ron put me on a four-year contract and on more money than I was on at Palace.

It was great – we got promoted in the first season and it was all going really well but then Ron being Ron decided to resign as manager. The trouble was, he wanted me to resign as well. I stayed on as manager but Ron and I fell out and he was making things really tough for me.

I'd been telling Ray Wilkins that I was being driven crazy by Ron and then, one day, Ray called to say, "Keep this secret but Luca Vialli has got the Watford job and I'm going there as his assistant and there is a job there for you as reserve-team manger if you want it." I was desperate to get out of Brentford and get away from Ron so I said, "I'll have it and, if you can guarantee it, I will resign today!" I did resign and eventually I took over from Luca when he left Watford.

Elton John had previously disassociated himself from Watford but he had got himself involved again when Luca was there and they created this big feel-good factor at the club. Luca was given a big transfer budget to spend on players. He'd won trophies at Chelsea and Watford hyped it up with a huge fanfare. I guess the Watford fans bought into it and thought we would get automatic promotion. After six-months, we were mid-table with no chance of promotion and the fans quickly turned on us and Luca suffered as a result.

That was tough on Luca and they sacked him at the end of the season. At the time, Ray thought that we'd all be out. It was very Chelsea orientated – Ray was there, Kevin Hitchcock was there and so was Terry Byrne who was another Chelsea man. In the end they only sacked Luca and Ray which was a shame. Luca is a lovely, lovely man, a charmer. I don't think I have ever met anyone in football as nice as Luca. I think he suffered a lot at Watford. He took a lot of things to heart over what happened.

The Championship and Premier League are two very different leagues – they are worlds apart. To manage in the Championship is not like managing a Premier League club. It was a tough time for Luca.

Ray Harford had once given me some very sound advice and said, "Listen, if you stay loyal, the only thing you'll guarantee is the sack. When it's time to move on, move on – don't wait around to be sacked." Ray also told me to be prepared to do anything, not to pigeon hole myself to only coaching or management. So, as a consequence, I've done lots of jobs at different clubs. Having said that, I got sacked at Watford and I can say I didn't see that coming!

We weren't in trouble, we'd got to the semi-final of the League Cup that year and the FA Cup semi-final the year before. I got a phone call at 11.30pm from a local newspaper reporter who I trusted who said, "I hope I am wrong but I have heard a whisper that you are being sacked in the morning..." Lo and behold, at 7am next morning, I got the phone call from the chairman and that was the only time I spent out of work – those three months after leaving Watford.

At the time, Chris Coleman was manager at Fulham. I knew Chris as he'd played for me at Crystal Palace. I always got on well with him and he said to me, "I need someone to help me – I have Steve Kean as the first-team coach and Billy McKinlay with the reserves but it's his first job in football. I don't want you do a specific job but I want you to keep an eye on things and look at our academy set up." I had a roving role with Chris – one day he would say, "Can you help out with the first-team?" and then, on another, he'd ask me to work with Billy with the reserves or work with the youth-team. Chris left the club and Roy Hodgson came in and I became first-team coach.

When Roy Hodgson left Fulham for Liverpool, he wasn't allowed to take any of his staff with him except for Mick Kelly. Roy told me, "I can't take you with me but keep in touch." We kept in touch and, when he moved to West Bromwich Albion, I nearly joined him there but there were a few problems between Fulham and West Bromwich Albion at the time and the deal didn't happen.

I then got another call from Roy about three months later so I thought all the fuss had died down and the deal was back on for me to go to West Brom but he said, "You can't tell anyone but I have got the England job." I thought he meant he was going for an interview but he said, "No, I've got the job and I want you to be my assistant!" We met that night in Battersea and we talked it over and I was sworn to secrecy. That is how football works it's all about associations. Roy and I get on well – he believes in me – and the job I have now is fantastic. I don't have the day to day business as I would have at club level so when the team has played the last game, be it a friendly or World Cup qualifier, you don't see the players again for a couple of months.

Outside of that, the FA keep me busy. I have a lot of PR commitments and, of course, I get to watch a lot of games. Roy and I will, between us, cover games on Saturday, Sunday and midweek too if there are Champions League games being played. Sometimes we can watch two games on a Saturday and on a Sunday. We keep a list of all the top English players hoping someone will catch our eye and we've been lucky with some of the young players who have broken through more recently. Then there's something like the World Cup where the world goes mad for about ten days before the tournament. Then, one has all the chaos and mayhem to cope with while one lives an absolute mad existence for a few weeks while the tournament is on.

There is all the media interest which Roy handles and I'm quite happy not having to deal with them. Gary Neville is a little different as he's part of the media but also part of the management team for England. I have to say he manages the role very well.

It's a fine balancing act and when he is doing his Sky Sports role, he might criticise some of the players who are in the squad. But, if they're in the squad when he is there, he deals with it well. He'll speak to them and explain straight away or he rings them beforehand and will explain that anything he says is constructive criticism. He's very good at speaking with players and he conducts himself well. I enjoy what I do but I don't envy Roy. He has wall-to-wall media saturation all the time but he copes well. I can go down to my local pub and there are a few people that know me there and know what I do but most of them don't, but Roy can't do that.

The best part of my job is working with the players. I might have fallen into a trap where I'd be dealing with a lot of egos but it's not been like that. The egos in football are the wannabees – those players who have not yet made it but think they are better than they actually are. At Fulham, we had a couple of players who weren't as good as they thought they were. The top players we had at the club were Mark Schwarzer and Danny Murphy and they were great. They had nothing to prove but some of the younger players were not as good as they thought they were.

The same applies to the England squad. They are in the squad because they are at the top of their game and they are the best players in the country. They don't have to prove themselves and so they are the easiest group of players to work with. They train hard, work hard and Roy does not mind coaches from other clubs coming down to watch England train and everyone who has come down has been impressed with the intensity of the players training and how hard they work. We haven't got them for long but when they are with us they work hard.

I'm pleased to say that my work often takes me to Chelsea to watch games. Although there are not many English players in the Chelsea side, teams like Liverpool, Everton and Manchester City make up a lot of the England squad so you will find me at Stamford Bridge when they're playing. It's a great excuse for me to go to Chelsea.

Chelsea have got a hardcore of very passionate supporters. They were there in Chelsea's hour of need and I don't think we really knew how bad it was at the time in terms of the debt, but the more one reads about that time, it seems we were lucky that the club survived. We were a well supported club when we went down but, in Division Two everyone got behind us and it made you feel so humble when we saw the supporters throwing money into those bins and blankets. They were great. They travelled in huge numbers, and they were good to us and I had a lovely few years there. I can safely say that in all my football career, this was easily my most favourable time.

GARY LOCKE

I grew up in Willesden, north-west London and, like any youngster, I always dreamed of playing professional football. I was a Chelsea supporter as a boy and, when my dreams became a reality and I joined the team and players I supported and idolised, it was very special – words can't describe it.

I signed professional forms in 1971 and I initially tasted first-team football in testimonial matches against Celtic and Fulham. My league debut was later at Coventry away in 1972 (30 September 1972; Coventry City 1-3 Chelsea, Garner, (O.G.), Houseman). Paddy Mulligan was the regular right-back at the time but he had a hamstring injury. I remember going over to the notice board after training on a Friday where the team was pinned up. My name was next to the number 2.

I scored my first Chelsea goal against Coventry City (24 August 1974; Coventry City 1-3 Chelsea, Locke, Cooke, Garner) and, as on my debut, the game was at Highfield Road but, in truth, I can't remember that much about it.

I played alongside Eddie and he was a footballer I really admired. As a defender, he was very agile and stylish on the ball. His greatest asset for me was his tackling – he was ruthless. As a team-mate and as a manager, he was very vocal and had a wealth of knowledge of the game and he was very positive in his encouragement of me.

Eddie was a determined and confident character. When he took over the reigns at Chelsea, it was a very difficult time for him due to the development of the new East Stand. The cost of building it escalated out of control. That drained the resources for buying and introducing new faces to the playing squad.

Because of the problems on the pitch, Eddie's alternative was to rely on Chelsea's youth set-up from which there was an abundance of young talented players coming through. His first major decision was to appoint Ray Wilkins captain in a crucial relegation match at Spurs. This was the beginning of Eddie's short but successful managerial career. Even though the result went against us and we were later relegated, he stayed true to his beliefs, selling the experienced players and introducing the home-grown talent such as players like Ian Britton, Garry Stanley, Ray Lewington, Steve Finnieston, Steve Wicks, Tommy Langley, John Sparrow and Graham Wilkins. The blend of youth and experience with the likes Charlie Cooke, Ron Harris, Micky Droy, Bill Garner and Peter Bonetti was the right combination.

The one abiding memory I do have of the relegation defeat at Spurs was not the fighting between the supporters, but it was the shot I hit from 30 yards. Pat Jennings, their goalkeeper, didn't move but he just stuck out a hand and tipped it over the bar, just like squatting a fly.

I played every game in the season we won promotion and I enjoyed it all. I scored against Southampton at The Dell in the third roundof the FA Cup (8 January 1977; Southampton 1-1 Chelsea, Locke).

I only found out that Eddie had left Chelsea when I received a phone call from a newspaper reporter asking me what I thought about the situation. It came as a great shock and it was the first I'd heard of his departure.

Leaving Chelsea was a wrench after so many great years there but I felt I needed a new focus. I joined Crystal Palace where I stayed for 4-years before moving to Sweden and signing for Halmstads BK. From there, in 1987, I went to New Zealand to play for Napier Rovers, a move which came thanks to Ray Lewington who recommended me to them. In 1989, I won a league winners medal with them. I then went to Waikato United and I still live in New Zealand today and I'm now an accounts manager at the local newspaper.

After I'd joined Crystal Palace, I returned to Stamford Bridge to play for them against Chelsea and I scored a goal. It was like a dream. I remember the ball dropping to me 35-yards out from the Chelsea goal and I struck it on the volley and it flew into the top corner of the net. It was unstoppable! It could have easy ended up in Fulham Broadway Station. The reception I received from the Palace and Chelsea supporters was unbelievable.

In 1987 I moved to Napier in New Zealand and played for Napier City Rovers for the next 5 seasons and we won the National League in 1989.
I played over 300 games for Chelsea and I really enjoyed my time at Stamford Bridge and I didn't want to leave. Winning Player of the Year in 1974, captaining Chelsea and playing against the likes of Franz Beckenbauer and Johann Cruyff were fantastic for me and the only low-point of my spell with the club was suffering relegation.

I remember very early on in my career going up to Old Trafford to play Manchester United (3 November 1973, Manchester United 2-2 Chelsea, Osgood, Baldwin). I walked out on the pitch before the game with Peter Osgood to warm-up and the Manchester United players were also warming-up. George Best was one of them. Ossie turned to me and said, "Gary, Bestie's here. He's going to run rings around you today. He's going to crucify you!" It was Ossie's way of encouraging me in his own sort of way.

He knew I'd be nervous as my job that day was to mark George Best. Although I got booked two minutes in for a foul on him, I played well, we drew and George didn't score.

The Chelsea supporters were always very good to me and I'll always be grateful to them for the time they voted for me to become their Player of the Year.

TEDDY MAYBANK

I signed professional forms with Dave Sexton in the 1974/75 season, the year we were relegated so it wasn't the best of starts for me. My debut was the Tottenham away game (19 April 1975; Tottenham Hotspur 2-0 Chelsea) where the loser went down so I didn't exactly have a great initiation to the first-team.

My mum and dad were there to watch me play my first game and I was really nervous. The game had been delayed because the two sets of supporters were fighting and that added to the sense of panic I was feeling. I have a couple of memories from the game that are unprintable but what I will say was you wouldn't believe what was said to me by one of Tottenham's most experienced and well-known players. It didn't bother me. It was part and parcel of the game. It still goes on today but that part of the game will always be there.

The following week, I scored my first goal for Chelsea (23 April 1975; Chelsea 1-1 Sheffield United, Maybank) against Sheffield United. I'd had a bet with Ray Wilkins for £50 even though I was only earning £40 a week. Ray said, "I bet you £50 that if you score, we'll not be able to catch you." I remember a throw came in that was flicked on by Micky Droy and it hit my left knee and went in. I stood there completely still for a couple of seconds with my arm raised, looked at Ray Wilkins and was off running around the pitch and they couldn't catch me. I did manage to stay still for a moment – I had to pay Ray £50. I said I'd just put my hand up and take the applause of the crowd and salutes but I did that for all of 5-seconds.

When I got into the first team, I played the remaining games at the end of the season and then started the following season as the centre-forward. Then Jock came along and he took my place towards the end of the season. I was an all-round player. I wasn't an out and out goal-scorer but if one looks at my playing record, I did score goals. The point is, if one has a couple of games without scoring, the confidence goes down and then ones game suffers and someone will come in and takes ones place.

I can say though that playing in the reserves did help at the time. I don't understand why they disbanded what was the Football Combination. It was a good way to get players fit, keep them fit and also keep them happy because they were playing football. I'm not saying players were happy playing in the reserves – everyone wanted to be in the first-team but I think it helped that when they played away, the reserves played at The Bridge. We used to get decent crowds and it helped the players because it made us match ready.

I don't know what the current Chelsea players do who aren't in the first-team on match days. It's the same with the youth-team players. There is still the equivalent of the South East Counties League but as soon as they get a youngster who can play in the U21 side or joins the first-team squad, they're not allowed to play for the youth-team anymore. Some of the players don't get a chance to play football regularly on match days.

Out of that South East Counties side that I played in, we probably had about eight players who all made the first team together. John Sparrow, Steve Wicks, Ray Wilkins, Ray Lewington, Jock Finnieston, Tommy Langley and Clive Walker. I got in the first team squad when I was 18 and I went from being part of the youngsters to being part of the first-team and it is different.

But then, all the lads started joining me in the first-team and suddenly we were all there together. It was one of those dressing rooms where all those picked for teams would be put on the notice board on a Friday after training. The first-team, the reserves and youth-team would all be listed and displayed together. We would shower and change and then our first port of call was the notice board to see who was playing. We used to mess with each other, telling players they were in the reserves to wind them up. It was all taken in good heart. It was that kind of dressing room.

Ray Lewington was a friend of mine whom I'd known since I was at junior school when we were in the same class together. We played in the same school team, the same Sunday side, we played for South London together for a few years and, by then, we were training on Tuesdays and Thursdays at Stamford Bridge. We're life-long buddies but, as well as being best friends with Lew, I feel that I got on with everybody in the squad.

The camaraderie with the lads was fantastic. We grew up with Chelsea, we trained hard and we worked hard and we spent all day together – we grew up together, we went from getting the bus to training together, to all getting our own cars. Graham Wilkins was first to get a car – an Escort Mexico. My first motor was a Rover 100. Derek Richardson went out and bought a Mach 1 Mustang. I then bought the same car as Eddie McCreadie. He had a TR6 so I bought myself one. The car cost me £1050 and the insurance cost me £1100!

My earliest memory of Eddie McCreadie being in charge was when we went on pre-season tour. He'd finished playing and he was helping out with the reserves. Dario Gradi had come in the year before under Dave Sexton and he was put in charge of the reserves. Dave Sexton was manager and we went away to Dawlish in Devon for pre-season training and Dario set a curfew. He was very meticulous and everybody had to be in by 9pm. The following year, Eddie had taken over the reserves from Dario and we went back to Dawlish for pre season.

On the first night there, Eddie told everyone they had to be in by 9. We all looked at Eddie and then someone said, "Come on Eddie, you know setting a 9 o'clock curfew is stupid". Eddie turned to us and said, "if any of you miss breakfast in the morning there will be a ruck with me!" Eddie was talking about 9 o'clock in the morning and Dario was talking about 9 o'clock at night! We loved Eddie for that. He was as good as gold.

Eddie was great to play for. He wasn't the best coach in the world, but he was probably the most enthusiastic. He would put his life on the line for you and would expect you to do the same. He put his heart and soul into his team – yes, his team. That's how he saw it. We were his team. We knew that and it gave us an inner strength every time we walked out on to the pitch. Eddie wasn't the greatest coach in my opinion but he had Ken Shellito assisting him.

Ken was absolutely brilliant and all the lads liked him. He brought us all through together from the youth-team. His contribution to the club's history producing all those players should not be forgotten. He was also a great player in his day but a knee injury ended his career. I'm the only one who has got a worse knee than he has now!

Both Eddie and Peter Bonetti were as fit as butcher's dogs. When we used to run around Epsom Downs in training, half the other lads used to hide behind one of the bushes at the bottom of the hill and join in on the run in on the way back. I am talking about Huddy, Ossie and Micky Droy etc. Not Eddie McCreadie though – he led from the front.

Jock (Finnieston) always used to tell people that I was the better footballer and he was the better goal scorer. Initially, I got in the side before Jock but then, once he was picked, he was incredible. I know it's an old adage but he was scoring goals for fun. Jock was one of those players who was gifted in the penalty area. For me, he was like Jimmy Greaves. He was that sort of player. He didn't come alive until he was in the penalty area and the ball was played into his feet. His ability to turn and finish was special. He didn't always get the cleanest hits in the world but they went in. That used to bug me when we were vying for the same position. I would always be the one who struck one cleanly and the goalie gets up and tips it over the bar and makes a great save whilst Jock would get one that hit his shin and goes in for a goal. That said, he wasn't 'lucky' – great goal scorers are always in the right place and at the right time, time and time again. It is an art and a gift I didn't have but Jock was always in the right place.

Because Jock was doing so well, I asked Eddie if I could go out on-loan. I went to Fulham and I did pretty well there. Fulham played Chelsea during my loan period but I wasn't allowed to play. They had a lot of good players then, including the likes of Bobby Moore, George Best and Rodney Marsh. It was a great time for me, I scored four goals in five games but when the loan spell ended, I went back to Chelsea. I took my football very seriously. I had one day of my loan left before I returned to Chelsea and I asked to play in the reserves for Fulham.

I came back to Chelsea but Jock was still scoring goals for fun and making it look easy. I went to see Eddie and told him I didn't want to play in the reserves. He said, "Ted, you're not leaving, you're staying and your time will come. Be patient!" So I did and I hung around and I played three or four games when Jock was injured. But then Jock came back so I said to Eddie, "I think my time has come to go." I don't think it was mistake to go to Fulham. Jock scored 24 goals that year and finished the season as the top scorer in the league. I had no chance. I had to leave. But I have to say I did miss the lads when I left.

I loved playing football, as did the rest of the lads in the dressing room. We would have played for Chelsea for nothing – well with the money problems the club had at the time, we almost played for nothing! That love we had for the game really stood out for me. We loved the game. We loved playing for Chelsea. I honestly think it was the best time of all our lives. We've all moved on and have done our own thing since but for me it was a great period in my life.

When I heard that Eddie had left, I thought 'really?' That was a sad thing to happen. He didn't achieve everything he set out to – he was let go by Chelsea far too soon and we all know the story. I think leaving Chelsea had a big effect on him. He'd got the lads up to the First Division and I think he deserved a contract. He needed security for his family and I don't think he was asking for too much from the club. I'm not sure if it was only a one-year contract he was offered but it was obvious that something was going on in the background for him to leave.

As a group, we were young and some of the older players had to move on but I think the squad still needed two or three years together with the same manager and same coaching staff. Ron Harris, Charlie Cooke and Peter Bonetti were needed as well. They played their part. It wasn't completely out with the old and in with the new.

After I went to Craven Cottage on a permanent basis, I probably only played about 30 games for Fulham before they sold me. At the time, Bobby Campbell was their manager and asked me to have a chat with him. He told me there was a good chance he'd be going to Chelsea as manager and Brighton had come in with an offer for me and I should consider it. Fulham had bought me from Chelsea for £65k and Brighton had bid £240k for me. I think Bobby was given me a strong hint to go as that was a hefty profit for Fulham.

They were bottom of the Second Division and Brighton were pushing for promotion, so I went and spoke to Alan Mullery (their manager) and signed for them. We finished third, third again and then won promotion to the First Division. Unfortunately, I got injured in my third game and I wasn't really told the truth about the extent of my injury. I was pumped regularly full of steroids and cortisone to play every week. I could only train twice a week and it got to the stage where I couldn't play anymore. I kept falling over like Bambi so I had a knee operation. They opened the knee up and I was told I was lucky that I'd be able to play again. My knee was ripped to shreds. I can't see that happening today. The medical staff take greater care of players these days. I left Brighton and returned to Fulham who paid £150k for me.

I only played a few games for them when PSV Eindhoven came in and offered Fulham £250k for me. Fulham did alright out of me. They sold me twice and paid off all the debts they had on The Riverside Stand with my transfer money. They should rename it the Teddy Maybank Stand!

Once I moved to Holland, I only played 6 games for PSV Eindhoven when I got injured again. I went to hospital where the surgeon opened my knee and it was shot to bits. They gave me no option. They told me I either retire or I'll never play in the first-team again and that I'd be played in the reserves and youth-team. That was a pretty hard decision to make and take.

I was 24-years old when I had to retire. It was complete carnage for a while. I did not know what I was going to do with the rest of my life. I didn't expect to stop playing. The next five-years were horrible for me. I was a mess. I was going out all the time, I was drinking non-stop. What could I do? I didn't know what I was going to do with the rest of my life. Clubs look after players better these days. Kids get that education at clubs nowadays. We didn't have agents or mentors or anyone to help us through a difficult period like I had then.

After I stopped playing, I discovered squash and it's something I love. I actually got to county standard. It was amazing that I could even play with my knee. The thing about squash is that it's played on a springy floor and you also don't have anyone running round trying to kick you! The thing I am most proud of is that I have two great kids.

Jack played rugby, hockey and cricket and all to county level. He went to university and made the rugby first-team but he got a horrible injury and that finished his rugby career aspirations. My daughter Charley has the wanderlust. She has been travelling all over the world and now works as a travel agent so she still has the wanderlust. Both of them are great and I have to say that being their dad has made me the proudest I have been since I finished playing football.

I've also been on a few TV shows. I was on the Weakest Link and I was also the first ever bloke they picked for Blind Date. I did the first pilot show that was made before Cilla Black became the host. A comedian called Duncan Norvelle – whose catch-phrase was "Chase me!" presented the pilot that I was on. I don't think he could handle doing the show – he seemed more nervous than the contestants! The next thing I heard is that Cilla Black took over. They must have liked me because they called me to do the show with Cilla. The trouble was I got stitched up and it appeared on the front page of the Daily Mail that I was living with a woman when I appeared on the show. The front page of the Daily Mail had a picture of me with Cilla and a headline reading, "TV Romeo Fools Cilla!" I got £300 to appear on the show – I wouldn't have done it otherwise. I only went up there in the beginning as a reserve and I didn't expect to get picked. Maybe they chose me because I like a laugh and a giggle. I was also on a programme presented by Rob Jones called The Pyramid Game. I was on it three weeks in a row and appeared on it with Wendy Richards and Rob Buckman. My brother Martin was on Game for Laugh and my brother-in-law also was on Catchphrase. My family's definitely not shy about going on TV!

I still go to Stamford Bridge to watch Chelsea when I can. The ex-players get to go into a box specially provided for them by Mr Abramovich. It's a really nice thing he has done. If any of us want to go to a game, we call the club and if there are places, we can have a ticket. Obviously, if Chelsea are playing a side like Manchester United there would be a big demand and we wouldn't all be able to go but it works well between the old boys.

One never knows who is going to be in the box on the day but Tommy Langley, Garry Stanley, John Dempsey, Jock Finnieston have all been there on days I've been invited. Since Mr Abramovich bought Chelsea, the club has set a good example and really tried to look after the old boys and that's something that other clubs could and should try to replicate.

It's not like that for me at Brighton. They hate me down there! When I started there I got my share of goals but, after I got injured, I really struggled. In one game I was playing, the crowd started moaning at me, I bared my butt cheeks at them! Alan Mullery wasn't happy and said, "Ted, that won't win any fans over!" but I don't think people should boo when they don't know what's going on. I could barely stand up without injections but one couldn't tell everyone I had a bad knee as I'd be wacked by every defender I'd have to play against.

I liked Brighton, loved the players but some of the crowd weren't good to me. I still get a good welcome down at Fulham though. I see Les Strong, Tony Gale and even Gary Chivers sometimes.

I loved my whole time at Chelsea. I joined as a youngster and, as an apprentice, some of my duties included cleaning Peter Osgood's boots. For me, coming through the ranks with all the lads was fantastic. We had the best of times. It was like being in the armed forces. We spent so much together and the squad was one in which everybody, as individuals, stuck together – we lost together and we won together – but we had a group of players who would live and fight for each other.

I hit a really low point in my life when I stopped playing football. I felt had a whole life ahead of me and I have to say I felt a bit vulnerable. At 24-years old, I had a lot less football playing time than I had planned for so that was tough. Looking back though I've had a great life and I have to say I am in a

311

good place now!

JOHN PHILLIPS

Eddie McCreadie was very competitive with no quarter asked and none given. I liked and respected him as he was a good trainer and teammate and I always looked upon him as a senior player and a good professional. He was one of those guys who just got on with the job but, back then when we played together, the thought of him becoming a manager never crossed my mind.

When he did take charge, I wasn't personally aware that he was inspiring or anything out of the ordinary but I know the young players enjoyed playing for him. He enthused them and got them to believe in themselves. But they were a group of players who were much too good to play in the Second Division but would probably have found life very difficult in Division One. Chelsea was a very sick club when Eddie took charge. It needed a complete overhaul and that involved getting rid of the older players. I don't think any money was available to buy new players, so the club's only hope was in the youngsters. It was inevitable that that we were going down when they gave Eddie the job, we were not good enough and confidence was at an all time low. We got what we deserved. It hurt to see Chelsea hit rock-bottom.

To this day I always look out for Chelsea's results. It was a dream come true for me to join Chelsea in 1970 and the first three years of my time there was great. Top players who I'd only ever read about were now my colleagues. John Hollins nicknamed me 'Sticks' because he said that the ball always used to stick to my hands.

At the start of Eddie's first season we were overseas on tour. Playing very badly and having some poor results. It is common on these trips that players spend a lot of time together in hotel rooms, lobbies, etc. talking and chatting. It was through these conversations that I knew what everyone thought as they were quick to express their opinions. Eddie called a team meeting to try and put things right. I was always one of the more outspoken individuals but I decided I'd say nothing and give others a chance to voice their views. As usual nothing of any real substance was aired.

Frustrated, I told Eddie that I believed nobody knew what they were supposed to be doing in relation to their team mates. Eddie went ballistic, obviously saying that I was wrong, asking others if this was the case and everyone said no! The meeting ended but the next day Eddie had all the players in his room explaining what he wanted and expected. He'd obviously slept on it and given me the benefit of the doubt in that I may have been right. He gained my respect that day whilst I never forgave my teammates.

I didn't believe we would ever win a championship because we lacked the discipline, but we'd always finish in the top 6 and could win cups. But then, a succession of dreadful managerial appointments changed the club. I watched was happening and was a part of something I cared very deeply about that was being destroyed by bad decisions after more bad decisions. It wasn't a happy time. It affected the relationship I had with the supporters too. They vented their displeasure at individuals without any understanding of the cancer that was present in the club.

STEVE SHERWOOD

When I joined Chelsea, I was a quite a shy country boy coming down to the big city, and at times I needed an arm around my shoulder. It would be unfair of me if I didn't thank two people who helped me during the early years of my development as a goalkeeper – Ken Shellito and Dario Gradi. As an apprentice in the early days, Ken was brilliant for me. I made plenty of mistakes as a young lad and he gave me the confidence I needed. I remember the turning point for me was a youth tournament in Cannes where I won 'Goalkeeper of the Tournament'.

Later, as I progressed, Dario was the first to give me specialist goalkeeping work. I remember thinking at the time what a good coach he was. There were four goalkeepers in front of me in the pecking order after I signed as a professional – Peter Bonetti, John Phillips, Tommy Hughes and Alan Dovey. This was a major problem for me in my early days as I was getting very few reserve team games.

Going on-loan to Brentford later was to prove the turning point in my career giving me the confidence in my own ability. When I finally made my Chelsea debut, I was third in the pecking order behind Peter and John. I was allowed to go home at Christmas as they were both in front of me. Peter got a stomach injury the week before the Boxing Day match (27 December 1971; Chelsea 2-0 Ipswich Town, Garland, Kember) but he was expected to recover and as John was okay, I went home to my family's house in Selby, North Yorkshire.

Peter failed a fitness test on the Friday before the game and John woke up with a bad back on the morning of the game and I received a phone-call around 10am on the morning of the game. No problem you might think but unfortunately, my dad had never driven and I didn't drive at the time. A scout from Halifax – Jack Noble – was beckoned to pick me up and drive me down to the game. We set off and there was thick fog on the motorway and, even with a police escort, we only arrived at Stamford Bridge at 2.50pm. Bobby Robson who was manager of Ipswich at the time gave me until 2.45pm to arrive so unfortunately, I had to watch the game from the stands. David Webb played in goal and had one shot to save during the game.

Luckily enough for me, neither Peter or John was fit the following week and I made my debut on New Years Day at Brian Clough's Derby County (1 January 1972; Derby County 1-0 Chelsea), a team that went on to win the league. We lost thanks to an own goal with around 10 minutes to go by, who else but David Webb!! I had a good game though and have fond memories of one particular save in the game. I then went on-loan to Brentford during the 1974/75 season, a move that was the making of my football career.

Mike Everitt, Brentford's manager, spent time on the training ground with me and I quickly became a favourite with the fans. It may seem strange, but during the time I was at Griffin Park, I never heard anything from Chelsea and I was enjoying my football so much and felt very much part of the dressing room, something I had never had before, so Eddie becoming Chelsea manager had little effect on me at the time.

Eddie was a no nonsense left-back, a good professional and someone you could rely on. He came into training, gave his best and went home – he was, I imagine, a mangers dream! Both Eddie and Johnny Hollins were always willing to pass on any advice and made me feel comfortable whilst I was at Chelsea. I often wondered then whether Eddie might make the grade as a manager.

Most of the guys liked the good life and it was easy to get distracted at a club like Chelsea but Eddie was meticulous. If we won, we used to watch the game back and Eddie used to pick parts out and praise the players involved. He was very strong on confidence building. He was the first manger to praise me for the length and accuracy on my drop kicks. He put the hours in and I liked him and fully respected him.

I only played 10 or so games under him but he was a great motivator and I really thought he'd be successful and the Chelsea's manager for many a year. Whilst I was at Brentford, I'd been voted their Player of the Year and John Docherty – who'd become their manager during my second spell there – told me he'd offered Chelsea £30,000 for me which they had accepted but, before he signed me, he wanted a chat with me.

Chelsea sent him to my old digs but I had moved to Mitcham and he didn't know how to find me. I had a good pre-season at Chelsea and they then wanted to keep me. I started the season with the keeper's shirt and I was enjoying my football and until one bad game at Southampton (11 October 1976; Southampton 4-1 Chelsea 1, Wilkins R), I was really full of confidence. I lost my place to Peter and once I was out of the team, I thought that was it and I lost the confidence I had found.

I was happy being at Chelsea and was going to give it 6-months but then Mike Keen came in for me and I signed for Watford for around £5,000. It turned out to be a massive move for me as I went to Vicarage Road at about the same time as Elton John and just before Graham Taylor and the club rose from the 4th Division to 1st Division and got to the FA Cup Final (19 May 1984; Everton 2-0 Watford) and into Europe.

Before Graham arrived, there were big differences between Watford and Chelsea. There was a dog-track around the pitch and we had to finish training early on the days when the dog racing was on! We often trained up on a hill exposed to the weather elements, we washed our own kit it and cleaned our own boots after training and matches – it wasn't glamorous! There were also one or two bad apples in the dressing room but once Graham arrived, he got rid of the bad apples and the dog-track and things started to improve. I was battling for the number-one spot with another good goalkeeper Andy Rankin. Luckily for me, Andy's kicking legs were going (otherwise he was very consistent) and Graham saw that he could utilise one of my strengths which was my kicking.

When I had the ball in my hands, we played with four forwards, Graham's philosophy being to pin the opposing team in their own half and only play neat clever football against them. The rest is fairytale stuff. Don't get me wrong, it was hard work. We often trained until 4pm and it was very physical. I was lucky enough to be the only player who went from the Fourth to the First Division where we finished second to Liverpool, play in Europe and play at Wembley in a cup final. I still pinch myself to make sure that it really happened!!

Graham Taylor was fantastic and if a player worked hard and gave 100% he would support him. He had a group of players that would do just that. Elton John was also great and, apart from his music being brilliant, he would open the doors to his grounds and mansion each pre-season to ensure the team spirit was there from day-one. We played 5-a-side football, met other celebrities and even had races in Sinclair C5s! I have some great memories of my time there.

When I left Watford, I joined Grimsby Town where we were promoted twice under Alan Buckley. I then played a few games for Lincoln City, had a rewarding spell at Gateshead in the Conference and ended my career with Gainsborough Trinity where a knee injury ended my career at 41.

While paying part-time with Gainsborough, I met John Stiles and Rod Belfitt – two ex- Leeds Utd players who were financial advisers. After speaking to them about what they did, I took the time to do the training to become a financial advisor myself and it's something I've done, in various forms, since I stopped playing football.

Nowadays, I get invited to the occasional Watford game as part of their 'Legends Suite' package. They have a question and answer session with supporters and I also go to a function or two now and again. In my spare-time, I have several hobbies. I love the outdoors, walking my dog and I also like cricket. I watch Yorkshire regularly and also like horseracing. My step-daughter was a good show jumper and I love horses.

I'm lucky to have a good bunch of ex-schoolmates and we meet up 4 or 5 times a year for various trips out etc. I never earned the money footballers earn today, but as I've got older, I've realised that the best things in life don't cost much and I feel I was truly lucky and blessed to be at the clubs I played for during my playing career.

As far Chelsea is concerned, I loved being a part of the club. At the time I joined, there were special characters there and, if I was honest, I was a bit overawed. I feel quite good to think I played 14 games for Chelsea and have very fond memories of the times there. Although I needed to leave the club to fulfill my ambitions and further my career, I have very few regrets but I suppose the low-point of my time at Stamford Bridge was getting dropped from the first-team.

One thing I must say about Chelsea is that the supporters were fantastic to me. I was by no stretch of the imagination a first-team regular but I was treated like I was somebody 'special'. Towards the end of my time there though, I thought it was sad that there was crowd trouble at the games.

JOHN SPARROW

I made my debut against Burnley as a 16-year-old in 1974 (13 March 1974; Chelsea 3-0 Burnley, Kember, Houseman, Hutchinson) and the game was played on a Wednesday afternoon because of the Miner's strike. The country was experiencing power cuts and to save energy, games played under floodlights were not allowed.

I scored my first goal for Chelsea at Stamford Bridge against Middlesbrough the year when we got relegated. (22 March 1975; Chelsea 1-2 Middlesbrough, Sparrow). I scored with a header from a corner. Although I joined Chelsea in 1972, I never got the chance to play in the same team as Eddie as he finished his playing career in 1973.

He didn't do a great amount of coaching but he was a fantastic man manager. He was a character too! One day, he came out onto the training ground wearing his suit and he just dived into a puddle of water in front of us all.

At the start of the following season and what with us knowing each other so well and playing together so long, we got off to a good start and it just built confidence from there. We went out thinking we were going to win every game.

I wasn't involved until the second-half of the season because the team was doing well. I'd go in and see Eddie and I say, "I'm doing well in the reserves, why aren't I playing?" He'd ask me to sit down and he'd say to me, "You are my 'baby'. I love you and you are going to make it. You're a really good player" etc, etc and I'd walk out of his office half an hour later after a long chat and say to myself, "I'm still not playing in the first-team but I feel a lot better! "

That was his management style. He kept the unity of the squad including the players who weren't in the first-team. Nobody who wasn't playing was sitting around sulking, and when you were called into the team you were ready. I think that, if he'd stayed at Chelsea, it would have made a great difference in the first season back in the Division One.

Ken Shellito was quieter than Eddie and he was a coach, whereas Eddie just had an enormous belief in us that when we played, he was convinced we'd get a result. It didn't matter if you were playing against an international player.

The players had a great belief in Eddie when he was there and I think it is safe to say that the atmosphere at the club changed when he left. I don't think that was anything to do with Ken. If Eddie had stayed I think we would have carried that self-belief into the First Division.

Eddie had such faith in the youngsters that he was brave enough to make Ray Wilkins the captain for the game against Spurs that we lost 2-0 which effectively sent us down. (19 April 1975; Chelsea 0-2 Tottenham Hotspur) but I think Eddie then was already planning for the future.

There was a massive fight on the pitch before the game. Jack Taylor, the referee, lined everybody up in the tunnel and he had the two teams ready to go out but the police told him he had to delay the kick off. He said, "I don't delay kick offs!" and he walked up the tunnel and marched us on to the pitch.

The supporters were still fighting on the pitch but then they saw the two teams walking out on to the pitch with Jack Taylor holding the ball out as he used to do. He was an imposing figure and they stopped fighting and ran off the pitch.

That first season we were down in 1975 was one of consolidation. Playing in the First Division is completely different to playing in the Second. We didn't think we'd go up automatically but we thought if we did well we might have a chance of promotion.

I think though, Eddie in that first season was planning for the future. Everybody was aware of the mess the club was in financially. We were all brought to Stamford Bridge with Brian Mears who was the Chairman and the players agreed to take a wage cut. It wasn't a lot of money to lose at the time but we weren't paid an awful lot of money at the time, especially compared to what players earn today.

With all that was going on, Eddie had his work cut out to manage the club but he did a good job and he was a great man manager. He could gee you up before a game and you'd go out believing you were better than the bloke you were playing against. We knew how to play. We had such a good upbringing with the likes of Dario Gradi and Ken Shellito.

When I broke into the side, I was playing well and I kept my place. I scored a great goal against Luton (9 April 1977; Chelsea 2-0 Luton Town, Sparrow, Finnieston) if I say it myself – I caught it well.

My mum used to keep a scrapbook and kept all the press cuttings. One of the headlines read, "Sparrow's Arrow"! Sadly, she's dead now but I've got the scrapbook at home somewhere.

There are a lot of cuttings about the game at Wolves when we were promoted which, to play in, was amazing! The Chelsea supporters weren't meant to be there but there must have been 10,000 inside the ground. Tommy Langley opened the scoring for us and Wolves equalised and the referee may as well have blown the final whistle there and then. We weren't going to do anything to throw that away and neither were Wolves.

We were both promoted so we played out a rather dull second-half with no one taking any chances and we had the unusual situation of both sets of supporters deliriously celebrating at the end. We were so up for that game. We were so happy after to have got Chelsea back into the First Division we had a big party on the coach back to London and by the time we got back I was exhausted. My dad in those days used to come and collect me after games and I was just relieved to get home. We had done what we'd set out to do and I was just glad to be back home. We had achieved our goal.

I was so pleased about getting into the team for the end of season run that culminated celebrating promotion in front of our supporters at Stamford Bridge against Hull. It was lovely to end the season with our own supporters, even with those one or two pitch invasions. Some of the crowd ran onto the pitch but look it was all good natured. It was a celebration – it was a lovely day.

The supporters were fantastic, especially if the liked you but, If they didn't like you, it was different story. On the whole though, I think they were fantastic especially away from home where we always had a big following. It helped us having thousands of supporters behind us when we turned up in some of those large towns and you had thousands of fans there to see you and I have got nothing but good memories of the Chelsea supporters. They were always very good to me.

I remember one year when we played at Anfield (1 March 1975; Liverpool 2-2 Chelsea 2, Britton, Finnieston). Our coach broke down on the way home and we got a lift home on the Supporters' Club coach on the way back. They stopped to pick us up. They loved having the team on their coach. There were bottles of every spirit imaginable available on the coach and they were passing them round to the players saying, "Go on! Get that down you!" The Supporters' Club used to put on discos at Stamford Bridge and I loved going to them. The supporters would have a drink and a chat to the players and it was always a good evening.

Life as a footballer back then was different to what it is now. We used to run around Richmond Park or cross country on Epsom Downs. When I was an apprentice I used to paint the training ground at Mitcham. Apprentices only got three weeks off whereas when I was a pro I got eight weeks off. We did pre-season tours and, one year, we went to Germany to a place called Hennef where the facilities were so far ahead of anything we had In England back then.

After getting promoted, we went to the USA and played in Seattle and San Jose and were out there for 3 weeks. Pre-season tours nowadays are at the start of the season and they go to countries to sell the shirts and improve the fan-base. Teams travel half-way around the world to play football and then people then say the players are tired.

We used to play 42 league games and we also played on Good Friday, Easter Saturday and Easter Monday. If you did that now – three games in four days – they'd think you were mad.

I read about Eddie leaving in the newspaper. It was a shame that it happened but I think it was coming as Eddie had had battles with the Board during the season and once we got up, I suspect the board probably thought we are back in Division One, job done, lets get rid of this pain in our side. They probably thought that they had a ready made replacement in Ken Shellito. But as Ken Shellito would tell you – managing the first team is nothing like managing the youth team and developing young players and bringing them through. It is very, very different.

It was just a dream come true to play for Chelsea. There is nothing to beat that. I miss being with my mates at work every day. It wasn't like work though. A football dressing room is something else and that one was a special. As a group, we worked hard and we played hard and everyone got on. We all grew up together and played in the first-team together.

I got on well with Ray Lewington and Ray Wilkins. We'd known each other for years as we played together, along with Teddy Maybank, for Senrab FC. They have got a fantastic reputation for producing footballers for the professional game. I still speak to Ray Lew on a regular basis. We have kept in touch all these years. The others I get to see usually every year at the Chelsea Lunch.

It was a laugh all the time back then, with people like Teddy playing-up all the time. Ted was mad and he still is!

There were a few quiet ones but even they chipped in from time to time. Swainy was up there with the best with his Liverpool humour. Everyone held their-own in that dressing room, and then there was Ron Harris who was liked by everyone.

John Dempsey was another who liked a laugh. Norman Medhurst was trainer at the time and John used to drive him mad! When he was recovering from an injury he would ring Norman at all hours just to tell him that he was okay. Once, when he was going to play badminton, someone said there was no court so John ran off to the shop and came back with a loaf of bread and marked out a badminton court with slices of bread!

Micky Droy was great. He liked a laugh though, saying that, if Micky Droy laughed at a joke, you all laughed too if you know what I mean… he was so funny. If he told a joke you laughed! The last do I went to at Chelsea Micky was there and I was planning on going home after and Micky put his arm round me and said, "We're going to the pub!" I looked up at him and I nodded, "Looks like I am going to the pub then…" I blame Micky for me getting home drunk that night!

I left Chelsea in 1979 after Geoff Hurst became the manager. Danny Blanchflower had taken charge of Chelsea when Ken Shellito left. Danny was as mad as a box of frogs – he didn't even realise that I was a first-team player! I thought that some of ideas about training were just crazy and I put on a lot of weight when he was there and then Geoff Hurst took over.

I didn't get on with him and he didn't fancy me as a player. That said, myself and David Stride did extra training and I got back into the side under him.

I thought I was doing a reasonable job but clearly Geoff thought differently as he went out and bought Dennis Rofe. That was the end for me.

When I went to see Geoff to ask him why I wasn't playing in the first-team, all he said was, "You'll never play for me again." That was it and I left in January.

Hindsight is a wonderful thing. I left in January and Geoff was sacked in March so maybe if I had hung on, who knows?

I had to go though because I needed to play. I'd been in the reserves for too long. I started in the reserves when I was 15 and was fine in the early part of my career but I didn't want to be in the reserves for ever. It didn't matter how well I was playing in the Chelsea reserves, there was no light at the end of the tunnel. I couldn't see myself getting a first-team game so I had to move on.

I joined Millwall and the history books show I got relegated with two different clubs in the same season. Chelsea went down in 1979 and so did Millwall. The old Den was a fantastic place to play. It was such an intimidating place for away teams to come to. It was a scary place!

I finished my playing career at Exeter. I had a bad knee. It all started around the time when Chelsea beat Liverpool in the FA Cup in 1978 (7 January 1978; Chelsea 4-2 Liverpool, Walker (2), Finnieston, Langley). We played Coventry the following week where we were spanked (14 January 1978; Coventry 5-1 Chelsea, Wilkins R) and the next day in training I had problems with my knee.

In those days, players only received a quick diagnosis and treatment. I was getting my knee treated, coming back to play football and only lasting 10-minutes in the reserves and then needing treatment again.

This went on and on and I had to have a cartilage operation in the July at the end of the season, six months on but I continued to have problems in later years. I stopped playing and took a pub in Hanworth near Twickenham. It was called The Oxford Arms and it was right under the flyover underneath the A316. Then I split up with my wife and went back to live with my mum. I needed a job and I heard about a milkman who'd just resigned. I rang the dairy, asked them if they had any vacancies and got the job. I was a milkman for 18 months and I hated every minute of it! I then got a job with BT and I've been with them ever since.

I also do a bit of scouting and have worked for Brentford, Crystal Palace, Watford and Fulham and I've sometimes watched players I've been asked to look at playing against Chelsea at Stamford Bridge.

When Ray Lewington was manager at Watford, I scouted for him for 3-years. I did 3-years scouting at Fulham, and 5-years at Coventry and then Bristol City. It's kept me involved in the game over the years.

When it comes to Chelsea now, I always look out for their results and I really enjoy seeing them play – they're a joy to watch.

GARRY STANLEY

I signed my professional contract with Chelsea in 1971 and had been at the club through its youth-team and reserves with Dario Gradi, Ken Shellito and Frank Upton. We were based down at Mitcham but when I first came to Chelsea we used to be based up in Hendon. There was a lake there where we played (The Welsh Harp) and I played there in the youth-team for a year before Chelsea moved us down to Mitcham.

I made my debut up at Sunderland in 1975 at Roker Park. We were beaten 2-1 (16 August 1975; Sunderland 2-1 Chelsea, Garner) I was chuffed when, at the end of the game, Ron Harris complimented me on how I played.

Gary Locke and Ian Britton had already made their debuts and were playing regularly and I was the last of our group to make my debut – I was aged 21 – there were times when I thought it would never happen. I thought my debut went well and after that I got a run in the side.

I was fortunate in as much as I had a fabulous group of players to train with and play with. Ossie, Huddy, Ron Harris, Eddie and Ian Hutchinson – they all made me feel welcome. Ian was from my part of the world in Derbyshire so he was very good to me. Sadly, some of those guys in the dressing room died far too young – Ossie, Hutch and Keith Weller. Very sad.

The best bit about being a professional footballer is that you go to work every day and play the game that you love. I miss the lads and I miss the craic and the banter. You still get all of that in any work environment with your work-mates but there's something unique about a football dressing room.

I signed when Dave Sexton was manager and, although he must have had me on the bench about a dozen times, never once did I get a sniff of getting on the pitch so I am grateful to Eddie for giving me my chance but, when he was a player, I would never have thought of Eddie as a manager. If I'd been asked at the time whether I could have seen anybody becoming a manager I would have said John Hollins. He was a natural and it was no surprise to me that he went into football coaching and management.

Credit to Eddie though, when the opportunity came up at Chelsea at what was a difficult time he had enough in him to go for it. He'd taken over after Dave Sexton had left and Ron Suart had been in charge for a short time. It was like a conveyor belt to begin with. Eddie moved a lot of the senior players on and brought in players from the youth-team. Although most of the lads in the first-team had come through the youth-team and reserves together with a few exceptions, it still took a while for us all to really gel as a team but we were all good mates and that's what made that side so special. Eddie had a lot of belief in me. He encouraged me to shoot and he used to regularly say to me the way I struck the ball reminded him of Bobby Charlton. He said some nice things to you as a player. As a manager he gave me confidence. He just said to me to concentrate, concentrate, concentrate! Eddie was good to me. He would say to me, "I want you to practice hitting that target as often as you can. If you hit the target you score." He liked the way I played and was always encouraging me.

I scored my first goal for Chelsea at Meadow Lane against Notts County (21 February 1976; Notts County 3-2 Chelsea, Stanley, Finnieston) and I was so pleased that my parents and my brother were there to see it. I scored the opening goal – it was a 30-yarder and the keeper did not move – not a bad start!

I scored a few cracking goals that year. I would say one of my best goals would have to be against Charlton (10 October 1976; Chelsea 2-1 Charlton Athletic, Stanley, Swain). The goal against Millwall (12 February 1977;

Chelsea 1-1 Millwall, Stanley) was a bit special. We had a great side. We had a lot of lads chomping at the bit at the same time to play but the only downside for me was I missed the last few games of the campaign.

That season, everybody in the dressing room and at the club gave Eddie 100% and personally, I didn't want to let him down.

I must admit that when I heard that Eddie had left, it came as a huge shock. It was disappointing for Eddie that, having got us up, he didn't have the chance to try his luck out in the top flight at least for a season. I don't think it would have made a difference if Eddie had stayed instead of Ken taking over. They were both inexperienced managers and only had a couple of seasons in charge behind them. I don't think Eddie would have been different. We were still immature, still learning and we needed more experience but there was no money at the club at the time. You don't as a rule come up from the Second Division and start taking the First Division by storm.

We knew about the problems the club had due to the building of the East Stand. We obviously lost a lot of our top players around that time but we were left with senior players like Ron Harris, John Dempsey, Bill Garner and Micky Droy.

I remember going to Old Trafford and beating Manchester United (17 September 1977; Manchester Utd 0-1 Chelsea, Garner) and, on our day, we pulled off some good results but we were still very naïve

That first season in Division One was difficult especially for me. I missed a lot of 1977 due to pelvis and groin problems. There are ligaments across the pelvis that hold it in place and mine was inflamed. The thing was, I could rest for two or three games and then train, feel alright and then it would go again. I think I only played about half-a-dozen games that year. The supporters were brilliant and so was the Shed End. I remember the violence on the terraces in those days. When I was playing, it was a distraction. Nobody wants to see anyone getting battered but that was the culture back then on the terraces.

The game that stands out for me was when we went to Millwall. A message was sent to us in the dressing room saying that the supporters were chasing each other across the terraces. There must have been about a 100 Chelsea supporters in the Millwall end and they couldn't get them out. The Millwall fans started chasing the Chelsea supporters onto the pitch so the referee brought us back to the dressing room.

In 1979 and after we'd been relegated, Clive Walker and I went over to play for Fort Lauderdale Strikers. I think the club were happy for us as it got us off the wage bill! We played in same side as George Best and, in general, enjoyed living there. Clive took his wife with him and I was single at the time so I had a better time than Clive.

When I got back to England, Danny Blanchflower rang me. I got on like a house on fire with him but he said, "I don't want you to go son… but sadly it is not down to me. The club is in deep debt." Almost before I knew it, I was transferred to Everton for £300,000.

I guess someone thought it we a good idea to try to get some money in to the club by selling us. I was told by a load of Everton lads that I was going to Everton before it even happened but I didn't want to leave Chelsea. All around me, my team mates had slowly been leaving. Kenny (Swain) was one of the first to go to Aston Villa, Steve Wicks went to Derby and Ray of course went to Manchester United.

I didn't want to go. I had been at Chelsea all my life but if it helped the club get out of debt, then that's what had to happen. Kenny had gone and he was one of my best pals so it was time to move on.

I didn't really get on at Goodison Park and left Everton to play for John

329

Toshack who paid £150,000 for me to play for him at Swansea. In 1984, I joined Portsmouth.

The Swansea move I had a lot to thank Bill Shankly for. When Bob Paisley took over at Liverpool, Shanks was moved upstairs. I think he was a bit put out so used to come down to our training-ground as he was a good friend of Jim McGregor the physio. Shanks had loads of football stories to tell and he liked a tot of whisky with Jim McGregor.

Bill Shankly died in 1981 while I was at Swansea and we went up to Anfield to play them. There was a minute silence and, after it was over, Tosh, who'd been like a son to Shankly when he played for Liverpool, took off his tracksuit top and he had his old Liverpool number ten shirt on in memory of Shanks. I don't think the Swansea fans were happy with him but he had played for Shanks for years so I didn't see a problem. We were 2-0 up at Anfield but typically, the Kop sucked in two penalties at their end and we only drew 2-2.

On the Monday after the game, Tosh called me in to his office. He said, "Can I be honest with you? I bought you on Bill's recommendation. He used to watch you play and train at Everton and liked your attitude and he told me to buy you as he thought you were a top player!"

In 1988, I went out to America with Charlie Cooke and played indoor football for a team called Winchita Wings. It was an amazing experience. We used to have sell out crowds each week, Charlie looked after himself well and played regularly. Back in the day, he had been fond of a drink but he was off it by then and keeping himself in shape. My time in the States was interesting. We flew to every game we played away so I saw a lot of different places.

I came back from America, played a few times for Bristol City before I ended up playing for Waterlooville who are now Havant and Waterlooville.

I was also doing coaching at Pompey's Centre of Excellence. I played till I was 40-years old.

Then I got offered a job with 9x Cable Communications and that was the best money I have ever earned. Even as a player, the most I used to earn was between £500 and £600 a week with a win bonus on top. 9x offered me £700 a week as a start. They were one of the very early cable companies so I packed up the Centre of Excellence at Pompey.

After that, I spent 12-years in the pharmaceutical industry. I was working in West London but my patch covered everything south of the M4 down to Kent and over to Devon and Cornwall. Eventually I got made redundant – we were supposed to merging with another company but ended getting taken over. I then worked in the tax industry.

I still see or keep in touch with the lads I knocked around with then to this day such as Ian Britton, Kenny Swain, Ray Lew and Gary Locke – who was one of my best mates – although I don't see so much of him now because he lives in New Zealand.

Chelsea are my team and always will be, and I'm pleased to say that I get to Stamford Bridge a few times every season and watch the games from the box provided for the ex-players by Mr Abramovich.

KENNY SWAIN

I joined Chelsea in 1973 from Wycombe Wanderers. As I didn't have a long-term contract with Wycombe, Chelsea only paid £500 for me. I got into the side at the end of the season and played the last half a dozen or so games. I made my debut in March 1974 against Newcastle (16 March 1974; Chelsea 1-0 Newcastle Utd, Hutchinson) and I scored my first goal against Arsenal (13 April 1974; Chelsea 1-3 Arsenal, Swain) a couple of weeks later. I played 7 times that season.

I didn't play with Eddie because he had a few injuries and by the end of the season he was helping out either the reserves or youth team with Dario Gradi.

The following season, when Chelsea were relegated, I didn't play at all. We didn't get off to the best of starts, losing to Carlisle United (17 August 1974; Chelsea 0-2 Carlisle) on the opening day and it didn't get much better. I never got a look-in that season and I was a substitute on only one occasion which was away to Everton.

It was a complete surprise when Eddie was appointed as manager to be honest. Dave Sexton was in charge when I joined but he got sacked the following season in the October. Then Ron Suart took over but that didn't work out and towards the end of the season Eddie got the job. I was in the stands for the last home game that Dave was in charge. I was sitting in the same section as his wife and he was getting dogs abuse from the supporters in the main stand.

We were in a state of flux for a while but they gave the job to Eddie. They must have seen something in him as he got the job ahead of Dario. I have to thank Dario as he told me he'd spoken to Eddie when he took over and had convinced him to offer me a one-year contract. I was pleased but, by then, Dave Sexton had taken over at QPR in and he was keen for me to go to Loftus Road.

I looked at the QPR team at the time – Stan Bowles was striker, Dave Thomas was a flying winger who was playing for England and they also had Don Givens up front. I thought I'd no chance of getting into that team and I looked at what we had at Chelsea and I thought if I don't make here, I might as well pack it in!

I've worked for many managers – and Eddie was not what I'd call 'business like', like some managers. He was a footballers' manager. He spoke like the ex-player that he was. In terms of coaching, it would be safe to say that Eddie didn't do much. He was a very confident manager. There was always an aura about Eddie. There was something 'Hollywood' about Eddie - he was calm, he was confident but he was cool!

Eddie's first full season as manager saw us finding our feet. I played most of that first season. We had some good results because we had so many talented players complemented with the likes of Ron Harris who was a stalwart for Chelsea, especially during those seasons. Even players like Gary Locke and Ian Britton who'd been there before us had blossomed into terrific players. Then there was Ray Wilkins who was a class act. Steve Finnieston also came into the side in 1976 and started banging in the goals so, at the end of that first season in the Second Division, I thought we could challenge the following year.

I played 36 games in the promotion season but it went a bit sour for me as I missed the last half-dozen or so games. I was left out with Garry Stanley. I vividly remember the day we went to Wolverhampton and got a point to be promoted. Where was I? Walking round Sainsbury's in Wimbledon and listening in to the radio to check the score.

I remember thinking that I should have been at Wolves that day celebrating with my teammates and the supporters. I do believe that just because you don't win a trophy at the end of the season doesn't mean it wasn't successful. After all there is only the league and two cups.

I wasn't at Molineux because, unlike today when clubs bring the whole squad to games, it was only the 12 that were named on the team-sheet that travelled. When I look back, I can say we were not successful on one day, it was a season long thing. We didn't just get promoted at Wolves that day. Not being at Molineux did leave a momentary sour taste but we got promoted over the whole season and I am proud of that achievement.

We were all looking forward to life in the First Division. It was a great opportunity and we were confident we could do well. Then we heard Eddie had gone. Eddie was bit stubborn and we'd got feedback that all was not well between him and the Board. Brian Mears was the chairman at the time. We all knew that something was just not quite right.

Some said it was a contract negotiation that didn't work out, while others said he had a row about a car but I think Eddie – or whoever was advising him at the time – thought the club was still negotiating and would come back with a revised offer and that they'd find some common ground.

The club though saw it as an opportunity to cut ties with Eddie instead. They had their replacement in Ken Shellito lined-up to step in straight away.

I think he might have had the same problems that Ken Shellito had. Ken Shellito had an advantage over Eddie in that he was proper coach. He had been doing the job for years and he knew all these players as he'd been coaching them for years all the way from the youth team.
What Ken and Eddie if he had stayed didn't have was the years of experience to deal with a squad of players which included international players, egotistical players plus the never ending financial crisis Chelsea had at the time.

When I was a younger player, I just wanted to play football and I left the politics of the football club to the senior pros who would normally take an interest in and report back.

I do recall all of us agreeing a percentage reduction in our salaries at the start of the season. I can't remember if we signed something or agreed to it as a group but we all took a 5% cut in wages to help the club. The players who weren't picked for the first-team on a Saturday walked around Stamford Bridge with the Cash for Chelsea buckets for people to throw money into them.

Neither Eddie nor Ken had any money to spend on players so could not do much to change the team and even for an experienced manager it takes some extremely good management skills to make that work. The budget was non-existent so I think it would have been tough for Eddie if he stayed.

Like most of the lads, I haven't seen Eddie for years. But once, when Neil Barnett was interviewing me for the Chelsea programme, he received a call. He passed me the 'phone and the voice at the other end said, "Its Eddie..." and we had a ten-minute chat. It was good to speak to him. It was the first time I've spoken to him since he left Chelsea as our paths never crossed since.

I still see a few of the lads I played with at Chelsea. Steve 'Polly Perkins' Perkins, who was an apprentice while I was at Stamford Bridge, celebrated his 60th birthday and all the 'old-boys' were there. It was a great day.

Together with Colin Walsh, a team-mate of mine who played with me at Nottingham Forest, I was in the side that faced Celtic in the UEFA Cup. At the time, David Hay was the Celtic manager. Colin was a massive Celtic fan and, before the game, David Hay came into our dressing room looking for me. It left Colin feeling completely star struck as David Hay was one of his idols. He asked me how I knew him and when I said that I'd played with him at Chelsea, he was 'knocked-out'!

I take a lot of pride in the three promotions I won during my career at Chelsea, Crewe and Portsmouth. It gives me as much pride as winning the European Cup with Villa. As I've often said to the young players I've coached for England, there are only a small number of trophies.

I've had management spells at Wigan and Grimsby but I wouldn't go into it again. I was 'in-post' at Wigan for 14/15 months but I had no money, I was continually having to borrow or loan players, I was working long days, finishing late at night and ended up getting the sack. That's football.

I went to Grimsby as assistant coach to Brian Law who wanted to carry on playing and then took over after he left but lost my job there. I can't see Chelsea calling me any day soon to be manager!

I can't say I enjoy not working and I'm lucky that I've been able to work in football for 40 years and I'll look to carry on working in the game. I feel I still have lots to offer to the game.

That said, I've never made a plan in my life and I take life as it comes. I've been a very lucky man in that I've rarely been out of work for too long. I've never had to chase a job. I had to apply for one or two, but I thought beforehand that I was in with a chance. That's always been the case for me. I've got jobs just through word of mouth. People have put a good word in for me and I've been lucky and grateful for what the game has given me.

I coached the England U16s and U17s for a number of years and, during that time, Neil Bath – who's done a fantastic job for the Chelsea Academy provided me with some good, quality players who were a pleasure to work with.

A journalist called Brian Beard who'd followed my career and together with him, I wrote a book called 'A Game Of Two Halves'. He'd followed my career and our paths had crossed a few times. He thought my story was worth telling and worthy of a read. I think it is the type of book you could take with you on holiday and sit there by the pool reading it while you are having a beer. I would like to think the book portrays me like who I am.

There aren't many winners in football but you can achieve or under achieve it is up to you. There's only one FA Cup and one league winner, but getting Chelsea promoted was a major achievement. With the financial problems

Chelsea had getting them out of the Second Division is something I am very proud of. Yes for me a major achievement.

I had a bitter-sweet moment when, after I joined Aston Villa, I played for them against Chelsea at Villa Park towards the end of the season (17 April 1979; Aston Villa 2-1, Chelsea, Langley). Tommy Langley scored for Chelsea to give them the lead but, with 20-minutes remaining, Graham Wilkins scored an own-goal and a minute later, I scored the winner for Villa beating Peter Bonetti with a shot to the top corner.

Some of the goals I've scored for Chelsea will always stick in my mind and I vividly remember my first goal for them. It was at Stamford Bridge and we lost 3-1 at home to Arsenal. I took a cross on my chest and volleyed it in past the great Bob Wilson, the Arsenal 'keeper (13 April 1974, Chelsea 1-3 Arsenal, Swain). It was a nice goal to score but I'll always think of the dressing down I got from Dave Sexton after the game for not tackling Geordie Armstrong after chasing him for 60-yards and allowing him to cross for John Radford who scored.

The two goals I really remember were the two I got at White Hart Lane at the start of the 78/79 season (28 August 1978, Tottenham Hotspur 2-2 Chelsea, Swain (2)). It was a fantastic day. It was roasting hot and they had Ardilles and Villa and a tickertape reception for them. We played well that day – Chelsea always seemed to have good days at Tottenham.

Although I was a born and bred Evertonian, the day I signed for Chelsea I became a Chelsea supporter. In my day, when we were young, everyone always had a second team and mine was Chelsea. Like Everton, they played in blue and they had won the FA Cup and they had those quality players like Alan Hudson and Peter Osgood and Charlie Cooke. To sign for Chelsea and play in that blue shirt in front of those supporters was just fantastic.

I was always amazed at what die-hard supporters Chelsea had. It didn't matter where we played, we always had a large hardcore support who turned out. It amazes me to think of what Chelsea has grown into since I played for them and I think that those who followed us home and away in those days probably are too.

One of my great memories of my time at Chelsea was the London music scene. I loved going to gigs and there was always a band I liked playing somewhere or other. I used to pick up the New Musical Express each week and see who was playing where and I must admit that I bunked into a few venues here and there... London is the best city in the world in for live music.

I went to see The Who at Charlton and Little Feat were also on the bill. They're my favourite band. I loved the 'Southern Rock' sounds that bands like Lynyrd Skynyrd, ZZ Top, The Allmann Brothers and bands like that used to make. There's a photo in the Chelsea archives of me in my digs and, on the back of the wall behind me, was a huge Led Zeppelin poster. I'd just been to see them and I think that picture went in one of the match programmes. My favourite venue was The Rainbow in north London and I loved Hammersmith Odeon and Earls Court.

I occasionally get invited back to Stamford Bridge. I couldn't believe it when I was first asked. I thought to myself, "They're asking me whether I'd like to come as a guest to watch this wonderful team and come out on to the pitch at half-time? I would love to!"

I have to say just coming back and walking up to Stamford Bridge and seeing how it looks now from my playing days... it's unbelievable! I must admit I did lose touch with Chelsea. I don't think Ken Bates ever wanted to have the old players around. Doug Ellis was the same at Aston Villa. He didn't want to be reminded about the European Cup team as he wasn't chairman at the time.

It was great to be invited back to Chelsea for the first time since I'd played for them. What I really liked most was how long it took for me to walk through the ground to get to the stands.

It was a long time between me being at Stamford Bridge as a Chelsea player and returning. So many supporters stopped me to say hello, and some asked me to sign something or have a photo taken. It's not an ego thing but that was a nice surprise and it really, really touched me how so many Chelsea supporters remembered me. It meant a lot to me. It just shows how powerful football is and that it can leave a lasting impact that people can still remember you after so many years. Coming back to the Bridge and getting that reception meant a lot.

CLIVE WALKER

It all started for me when I was about 11-years old. I had been playing for Oxford Schoolboys and we played in English FA Schools FA Trophy Final at Wembley. Chelsea scouts were at the game and I was subsequently invited to Stamford Bridge. I'd been invited to Aston Villa and Manchester City and I think I came to their attention when I played for England Schoolboys. But, by then, I'd already decided on Chelsea.

I was a Manchester United fan as a boy, mainly because Oxford United weren't a team to support as they only got into the league when I was aged about 8-years old. That said, their ground was at the end of the same road as my school so I did go to watch them but, obviously, at school, with everybody else supporting big teams, it would have been hard to follow a smaller club.

Manchester United had players like George Best and Bobby Charlton and had just won the European Cup so they were an easy club to follow. I was an impressionable 11-year old and they were my team.

I signed for Chelsea as an apprentice when I was 16-years old but I'd been associated with the club for about 18-months before that. I was with players such as Ray Wilkins, Tommy Langley, John Sparrow, Ray Lewington, Steve Wicks, Teddy Maybank, Peter Bonetti, Charlie Cooke, Ron Harris and Peter Osgood and the like.

Ray Lewington and Steve Wicks had left school and joined Chelsea when they were 15-years old but, because my mum was a teacher, she insisted that I stayed on until I was 16 and had taken my exams. I finished my formal education and got some qualifications and in July 1973, I signed for Chelsea as an apprentice and was paid £7 per week which, after National Insurance deductions, left me £6.43. After I'd been there a year, it went up to £8 per week.

The club were paying my digs money and my travelling expenses so all the money I earned was my own. I was over the moon but, because of that extra year I'd stayed at school, I'd missed a year of educating myself about football and I felt although I was a year behind everybody else around me at Chelsea.

I was very starry eyed when I joined the club. Because I'd never really been out of the Oxford area, I didn't realise that my accent was quite strong and, when I came to London, it hindered me. Most of the people around me were from London and I have to admit that I felt quite intimidated.

Fortunately, I went into digs with Kenny Swain, a Scouser and, because he was also an 'outsider', we stuck together and got on really well. Sometimes in training, we used to have 'London' v the 'rest of the country' in 5-a-side games. It was tough and those of us in the 'rest of the country' teams had to represent our towns and cities. But, after I'd been with the first-team for about six months, I felt more comfortable. I'd integrated and I'd also managed to lose my country accent!

Ken Shellito used to take training although Dave Sexton also coached us for the odd session as did Dario Gradi and Ron Suart. Dave was brilliant. Every time he took a session, we all stood to 'attention'! Not because we were intimidated by his manner, but rather because of who he was. We had a lot a lot of respect for him as youngsters. We also felt the same way about Dario. No disrespect to Ken Shellito, but Dave and Dario were on another level coaching-wise and Dave went on to prove that in later years. But we loved Ken. We'd all grown up with him and he was our mate.

When I was 16 and trying to break into the first-team, I had players like Peter Houseman who was left-sided ahead of me and, if he didn't play there, Charlie Cooke would and then, in the reserves, there were a couple of good players so I knew it wasn't going to be easy.

I only started to play with the first-team players and after I'd signed a professional contract in March 1975, the same day as Tommy Langley. My wages then increased to £18 per week and I thought, "Wow! I had made it as a professional footballer with Chelsea Football Club!".

Although some of the senior players helped the younger ones, some seemed quite indifferent. There was a lot of banter given to the youngsters from the older players – I think they thought it might help toughen us up – but that was in training and not in a game. Once we were on the pitch and representing Chelsea, we all stuck together and helped each other out.

As far as I was concerned, at the time, I didn't like being geed up by some of them and although individually they thought they might have been helping us to develop in some way or other, I often felt although I was being belittled. Some of those were, in my opinion, giving us stick and trying to put us in our place because they thought that their places in the team might be lost to some of us. That said, I must admit that at the time I didn't really appreciate the professionalism that they had.

Nowadays, I hear about a lot of the first-team players doing lots to help the younger players out and I think that that can only be of a benefit to them. I think it's great that the senior players do that kind of thing. I'd like to think I always did my best to try to help the younger players.

When I left school as a 16-year old, all I wanted to do was play football. It was then that the real learning curve began. But, at that age, it's hard to take onboard every bit of information. I learned from my mistakes but I had the want and the need and the desire to make it as a professional footballer. Sometimes, I probably didn't do as much listening as I perhaps should have done but I changed in myself somewhere along the line and managed to make the grade.

We learned discipline, that we needed to get in for training on time, the basics of football and how to incorporate our natural talent into how we approached playing the game professionally. I used to love training, I loved the camaraderie, I loved being with the lads and I loved every aspect. Obviously I didn't like being shouted at – nobody does – and I didn't like being wacked by an opposing player but that was all part and parcel of the type of player that I was – I didn't kick but I got kicked but it was all something I had to get used to. All in all, there wasn't much I didn't like.

I'd come to London from rural Oxford and loved it! I soon discovered a lot of things outside of football that were, for me at least, fantastic. I love my music – just ask Kenny Swain! We liked a bit of heavy metal and, when we were in our digs in Wimbledon, there were many times you'd have caught him and me playing air-guitar to bands like Led Zeppelin, Genesis, Deep Purple and anything heavy but I liked all kinds of music.

We used to go to gigs and we saw bands like Genesis, Supertramp, Rod Stewart who was brilliant. Although we enjoyed going out for a few drinks and sometimes had a few too many and suffered the next day in training as a result, we didn't always go out with the likes of Peter Osgood, Alan

Hudson and the 'Kings Road boys'. We respected them for the fact that that was their 'manor' and we went out in places like Wimbledon and away from where the senior players went. When we did end up in the same pub or club, I used to think to myself, "What are they doing here? We're the young kids – it's our time!"

Even though I enjoyed my time outside of football, I was still playing well for both the Chelsea youth side and the reserve team. Before I became a winger, I was a centre-forward but although I switched positions, I always loved to score goals and I'm proud of my record to that regard. I always managed to get my name on the score-sheet.

At that time, we didn't have that much to do with Dave Sexton. He used to be with the first-team whilst we trained as youngsters and reserves. Occasionally however, if Chelsea had a big match coming up, we had to go and play against the first-team in the style of the team they'd be up against. That's the only real 'interaction' I had with him.

Ron Suart then took over but, even at that point, I wasn't ready to play in the first-team and I wasn't really affected by the change in manager. I was still looking at the players in front of me and I caught up with them during my time in the reserves. When Chelsea were relegated in 1975, I was still concentrating on trying to break through and, as an individual trying to achieve the goal I'd set myself, that was my main focus. By this time, I was earning £45 per week and I had a two-year contract with Chelsea so, within myself, I was totally at ease.

The relegation however, brought its own miseries. It was sad, it was heartbreaking and miserable but, never once did I regret signing for Chelsea Football Club and never, in my whole time there, did I think that. However, even in the midst of relegation, what with the older players leaving and the club having no money to spend on new players, it meant that Chelsea had no choice but to give the younger players a chance so I tried to put a positive spin on a negative situation. Those of us who realised this had the mindset of coming back the next season with a fresh determination to prove ourselves.

Looking back now, I think in us, Chelsea had a squad of young players that had the potential to produce in the same way as Sir Alex Ferguson's Manchester Utd side of the 1990s with the likes of Scholes, Beckham, and Giggs etc.

The trouble was, as a club, Chelsea was poorly managed. Brian Mears' vision for a new stadium and the building of the East Stand almost led to Chelsea becoming bankrupt, a situation that eventually saw a fantastic nucleus of talent broken up.

Eddie McCreadie came in as manager after he'd gone from being a first-team player to becoming a coach. He was great for us. At the old training ground at Mitcham, the first-team trained on a pitch next to the reserves and occasionally, he say, "You're with me today son!" and I'd train with the seniors. Now that was a buzz!

As a group, we needed someone with Eddie's mentality. Dario was a brilliant coach to us, Dave Sexton had been and Ken Shellito was learning to be one but Eddie wasn't a coach. Nevertheless, he was in charge and he was someone everybody looked up to. To me, it made sense. I'd learned a lot when I was being coached but Eddie was the man to put it all into place, to make it work. He was authoritative in the way he went about his business, he was in control – even though some people didn't think he was – he was slightly on the edge of 'barking', but in a nice way. We needed that! We were young kids that needed direction.

The reserves used to go to Dawlish every year for pre-season training – I went three years in a row – and Eddie had been there for one of them so I felt I knew him and, in my own mind, I thought it would help me.

By this time, some of the big name players had left and some of the barriers that had been in my way a couple of years previously had gone and I saw the opportunity to progress. I was first included in the first-team squad for a game a game at Stamford Bridge against Nottingham Forest (16 April 1977; Chelsea 2-1 Nottingham Forest, Britton, Finnieston) but although I was named as the substitute – there was only one in those days – I didn't come on.

Prior to that though, I'd had the odd 20-minutes here and there alongside the first-team players in testimonials for players like Peter Osgood and Ron Harris and the benefit game for Ian Hutchinson. I was up against the likes of Eusébio and George Best and, when I was a kid, I dreamed of playing on the same pitch as people like them.

Nevertheless, I made my debut the following Tuesday against Oldham (19 April 1977; Chelsea 0-0 Oldham Athletic), coming on as a substitute in place of Tommy Langley. Once I'd got into the first-team, I thought, "This is my time – I've got to make it now!" I was an unused sub for the next few games before I started for the first time at St James' Park the following season (22 October 1977; Newcastle Utd 1-0 Chelsea). Just going to a ground like that, with the stature and the noise coming from the Gallowgate End was something that, coming from reserve-team football, I hadn't experienced before. Although the game just passed me by I do remember coming out of the tunnel and the tightness of it and the feeling of claustrophobia that I had. It was cold, it was windy and, even though Chelsea lost, I thought I'd had a fairly good game but, saying that, I didn't play for the next few matches.

My next game was away at Molineux against Wolves (10 December 1977; Wolverhampton Wanderers 1-3 Chelsea, Langley, Walker 2), a game in which I scored my first goal for the club. Kenny Swain put the ball across from the right, it got deflected at the near post and looped over the keeper to the far post and I tapped it in from a yard – I never missed there! My second and Chelsea's third came after I'd picked up the ball on the halfway line, roasted their full-back Geoff Palmer a couple times on the way to the penalty box and smacked it into the bottom corner. After the game, I thought to myself, "Now leave me out" and, after that I got a run in the team, bar one or two games, until the end of the season.

I played in the third roundFA Cup tie at Stamford Bridge against Liverpool (7 January 1978; Chelsea 4-2 Liverpool, Walker 2, Finnieston, Langley) and it turned out to be the last game that Charlie Cooke played for Chelsea. It was being recorded and was to be shown on ITV's The Big Match on the Sunday so it was a massive game for us as players and the club too. I played against Joey Jones – who would later sign for Chelsea – and I must have had a good game against him because he never played again for Liverpool.

I also played in that game where Chelsea were losing 0-3 at half-time to Bolton Wanderers but came back to win the game 4-3 (14 October 1978; Chelsea 4-3 Bolton Wanderers, Langley, Swain, Walker, OG). I scored the equaliser a couple of minutes before full-time and Sam Allardyce put through his own net with almost the last touch of the game to give Chelsea the win.

Eddie had come in at a time when the club was falling down around us but as a group, we all realised that that was our chance. We all knew Eddie and he knew us and we could all stick together and get through together. It left a massive hole when he left. Then Ray Wilkins was sold.

Ray was our mentor and he was two-seasons ahead of everybody else. I'd played with him at England Schoolboy level and even then, he was way up above and beyond everyone else. He was captain at 18-years old. When he left we all missed the quality of his distribution, the way he could see a player and deliver a long ball to him and Ray could do it with both feet.

Had he stayed, I think Chelsea would have established themselves as one of the First Division's top teams and would hopefully have gone back to winning things. In my whole career, I think that Ray was the best player I have ever played alongside.

I was sitting next to Eddie on the bench at Molineux when we were promoted against Wolves (7 May 1977; Wolverhampton Wanderers 1-1 Chelsea, Langley) and he gave me his glasses because, when the final whistle blew, he ran on the pitch. I tried his glasses on and I couldn't see a thing a thing through them they where dark and that thick – it was no wonder he made the tackles he did!

We'd been promoted and it was party time! I thought that every season would be like that. All the players had been given eight-weeks off and I was away from London and didn't see anyone else from the club. Although I was always on the telephone talking to Tommy Langley, in those days, we found out what was going on via the newspapers and, when I read that Eddie had left, I was heartbroken but, my immediate thought – and I'm sure all the other players thought it too – was what was going on at Chelsea and who would take over.

It was another stage in the overall decline of the club. Again, it went back to the people who were running the club. Why couldn't they pay for the East Stand? Why couldn't they have kept Eddie? Why couldn't they avoid the sale of Ray Wilkins? These were the questions I was asking myself at the time.

As a player, I learned something from every club I was at where there was a change in managers. All players just learn to cope with a new manager coming in and just face the fact that they'll have to put the work in to impress whoever it is that comes in. However, Eddie gave me both the confidence I needed and the chance to play and for me, he was a great manager. He made me feel wanted.

As far as the supporters were concerned, the day we'd been promoted at Wolves, everybody was a friend. We used to win a few and lose some but it didn't matter – we were all friends. But then, the following season, the supporters were on and off the pitch fighting all the time, but that was the way that football was going then but I don't believe that it was purely down to the game. That's the way the whole country was going, not just football. On some occasions, the supporters looked after us.

By the time I'd reached the age of 27, the club offered me another contract but it was for less money that my previous one and, well… let's just say, that's another story.

A lot of people remember the goal I scored at Bolton in 1983 (7 May 1983; Bolton Wanderers 0-1 Chelsea, Walker) that gave Chelsea the win that kept them out of the old Third Division. I remember that, at the time, John Neal had been in charge for nearly two years and Chelsea were on the verge of relegation. Whilst the supporters saw him as a favourite, the club was in a mess at the time and I often wonder what they'd have thought of him if he'd taken Chelsea down. Sometimes, I think that the supporters often have tunnel vision when it comes to some things.

I hadn't played all season and the truth is that the manager didn't fancy me and I didn't really take to him. I'd hardly played all season and then with two games to go, all of a sudden he wanted to pick me.

I'd been told on the Friday by Micky Droy that I was playing and I expressed my thoughts about my sudden recall to the first-team. I said to Micky, "Now, right at the end of the season he wants me to play?" He replied, "I want you to play!" Micky picked the team that played against Bolton that day after John Neal had gone to him and said, "What do I do?" To be fair, the lads that Micky picked pulled out all the stops and everybody was trying to score. I was the last person to want to see Chelsea relegated – I loved the club – and I was grateful that during that game at Bolton, I was the one who got the goal that saved Chelsea from the drop. I was also pleased that I'd scored for the 3,500 Chelsea supporters who'd made the long, difficult trip to Bolton and who were soaking wet on the terraces.

I didn't really get on with John when he was the manager. I didn't really understand his philosophy at the time but I was the last one remaining of the guys I'd grown up with at Chelsea. I was struggling, I wasn't getting into the side and mentally, as far as Chelsea was concerned, my head was in a mess.

I was playing in the reserves and when I should have been in my prime but I had Ian McNeill – John Neal's assistant – telling me that my career was over. I proved him wrong in the end because I played until I was 42-years old so I must have been doing something right. Following that goal at Bolton and Chelsea subsequently staying in the division, I managed to stay with the club for another year.

The summer after Chelsea stayed up, I spent the time away from the club concentrating on getting fit. In my mind, even though I knew I was up against it with John and Ian in charge, I felt that I could still make my mark at Stamford Bridge and I was determined to try to change their minds.

That season – the year Chelsea won the Second Division title for the first time – I was picked for the first game of the season against Derby County (27 August 1983; Chelsea 5-0 Derby County, Hutchings, Walker, Spackman, Dixon 2) and played in the next 7 matches. But then I broke my jaw and people like Joe McLaughlin, Peter Rhodes-Brown, Paul Canoville and Pat Nevin – who'd missed the first month of the season because he was taking his Masters Degree – got their chance and, once I'd been off for a month, I never got back in the side. I was back in the reserves and although I was playing well and scoring goals, I knew in my heart that my time at Chelsea would soon be coming to an end.

In those days, players had to play a minimum of 11 or 12 matches to qualify for a medal. But with Neal and McNeill – who I'd totally fallen out with – not doing anything to help me, there was no way that I'd play enough games so, even though I was a part of the team that won the promotion and the title, I got no recognition for it.

At the time, I felt although my heart was being ripped out. Chelsea was my football club and I desperately wanted to stay but, what with being told that I wasn't wanted, I knew I had to get away. When the season finally ended and even though I did have the offer of a new contract, I felt it was the right time for me to leave Chelsea and look for a new club.

I left at the end of that season and joined Sunderland. My last Chelsea game had been at Stamford Bridge against Middlesbrough (24 September 1983; Chelsea 0-0 Middlesbrough) and the next time I played at Chelsea was in their first home game of the new season for my new club (27 August 1984; Chelsea 1-0 Sunderland, Canoville).

Later that season, Chelsea drew Sunderland in the League Cup semi-final. Sunderland had won the first-leg (13 February 1985; Sunderland 2-0 Chelsea) and, in the return, I scored a couple against Chelsea and helped Sunderland to win the game and get to Wembley (4 March 1985; Chelsea 2-3 Sunderland, Speedie, Nevin). As everybody knows, I got plenty of abuse in one form or another throughout the game but, as I said in the post match interview I did, I wish I'd been playing in a semi-final wearing blue and going to Wembley playing for a club that I really loved.

The truth is, although I wished that things had worked out better for me in regards to my time at Stamford Bridge, I went into the game against them feeling that I had a point to prove – especially to John Neal and Ian McNeill. I was just being professional about the way I went about playing football but, as far as the Chelsea supporters were concerned, I didn't want to upset them. They were always very good to me during my time at

Chelsea and I loved playing both for Chelsea and in front of the Chelsea supporters.

I always tried my best when I played for Chelsea and, even when I had a bad game and trust me – the supporters let me know if I did – I didn't mind. It just made me try even harder in the next game. But, if I did have a good game, they also let me know and they were brilliant to me.

The fact that I'm associated with Chelsea Football Club in the present day is fabulous for me – I couldn't have wished for anything better. I've been very lucky in that I had a good career at Chelsea. I judge myself on the number of goals I scored for Chelsea – I got 65 – and personally, I think that the return I gave by way of goals in the number of games I played is 'up there'. I'm proud of what I did for the club.

Following my time at Sunderland, I then went on to play for Fulham, QPR and Brighton & Hove Albion and then non-league for Woking and Cheltenham Town.

I've was kicked the whole of my career by people like Sam Allardyce and Joey Jones. They were 'cloggers' and that was a part of their game but I didn't mind. Although I had to put up with constant bruising and knee and ankle ligament damage, I didn't mind. The pain I suffered from the kicks was nothing to what I felt inside if I couldn't get past these players but, on the 'up side', the satisfaction I got when I beat them and perhaps put in a cross or a ball that led to a goal or even if I scored one myself made all the kicks and knocks I took from opposing defenders all worth the while.

The two players I hated playing against the most were Steve Perryman and Kenny Sansom but that was because they were very difficult opponents. They were quick, very clever and very good footballers. I always struggled against those two and they always had a good game against me. Don't forget, Kenny played 86 times for England so in a way it's not surprising that, when it came to me versus him, he came out on top more times than I did.

Since I stopped playing, I'm pleased that I was able to build another career in the media which I thoroughly enjoy. Working for Chelsea TV is great and, even though I occasionally get asked to do a bit for the BBC, most of the work I do now is for the club. I cover the first-team, the U18s, the U21s and the Chelsea Ladies side – all very interesting work.

Football has moved on since my day in the same way that it moved on from what it was like in the 1950s when the goalkeepers were allowed to be barged over the line for a goal. Nowadays, the players have better managers, better coaches, better facilities, better pitches, better medical treatment and advice. When I was playing, I was quick, had a good touch, I could kick with both feet and I could score goals so if I was around playing alongside the likes of Eden Hazard for a José Mourinho or a Carlo Ancelotti, I like to think they might have picked me. The worst thing I think I'd have to get used to is being dropped or, as they say in today's modern football, rotated. Mentally, I think I have had to get used to the 'modern way' but I like to think that, had I been a footballer today, I would have had enough inside me to have made the grade.

STEVE WICKS

I signed for Chelsea when I was 12-years old. I made my debut against Ipswich Town in 1975 (31 March 1975; Chelsea 0-0 Ipswich Town). Ron Suart was in charge at the time and I think Eddie McCreadie was his assistant if I remember correctly. I got the call at Mitcham. I was training there and all of a sudden I was pulled out of a training session and told I had to get to Stamford Bridge.

A car came and picked me up and when I got to the Bridge I found out I was playing. It was good to be thrown in at the deep end with no notice as against having days to worry about it and getting myself worked up and getting uptight about it. I thought I played well. Ipswich Town were title contenders in those days and had Trevor Whymark and David Johnson up front. They were quite a handful but I thought it went well for me.

Back then, they would pick the first-team and pin a sheet up on the notice board on a Friday and those who weren't playing would either train at Mitcham or play in the reserves instead. I didn't expect to play but I got the call as Micky Droy had pulled a hamstring.

Eddie was in charge of the reserves and gave me the sense that he had so much belief in me and that I would make the first-team. I was lucky and I'm also thankful to Ken Shellito. He was the youth-team manager who converted me from a centre-forward to a centre-half.

The Chelsea youth side back then were as good as any youth side back then. Four of us were in the England U18 side who won the European Championships. It said a lot about Ken and Eddie that so many players made the first-team.

I played with Eddie in the reserves a few times. He was Chelsea through and through. At the time he became reserve-team manager, his favourite person in the world was the TV detective Kojak who was played by Telly Savalas. He used to call us his babies and he used to walk around saying to people, "Who loves ya baby?" which was the catchphrase used by Kojak.

Talking about television, I also remember Raquel Welch coming down to the dressing room before a game (which was very distracting) and Eddie also bringing down actors Paul Michael Glaser and David Soul (American TV detectives Starsky and Hutch) into the dressing room at another game.

Having played with most of us in the reserves and then managed us in the reserves, Eddie put great faith in us by promoting so many to the first-team.

I have a photograph at home of about 7 or 8 Chelsea players from the Chelsea U14s team who all went on to play together in the first team under Eddie. The whole experience with that group of players and Eddie was a special time which I don't think will ever happen again in Chelsea's history.

Eddie had the utmost respect of everyone at the club for what he had achieved as a player and he was what Chelsea needed at the time. They needed someone who knew the players, who knew the potential of the players and someone who could 'get' what Chelsea was. He sold himself as the man who could take that group of players and work with them and take them to the next level.

From day-one, he made it clear he was playing the younger players. When Eddie took over, just before Tottenham game, he dropped a lot of the older players, put a few in from the youth side and made Ray Wilkins captain. When the bus pulled up at White Hart Lane, some of the Chelsea supporters who were there to cheer the players off the coach asked, "Who's that?" as they walked into the players' entrance. Even though we lost that day, I thought we outplayed them and were unlucky to lose to two late goals from Alfie Conn. In some ways it needed to happen. .

Chelsea had been struggling for a while and if those young players had been in the First Division, they could've been on a hiding to nothing at the wrong end of the table. However, in the Second Division, experience was built, we learned a lot and we played a lot of good football.

That first season down was a bit 'in and out'. We learned a lot but the one constant was a belief built into us by Eddie that next year was going to be the year. Every player believed that once we'd found our feet in the Second Division, we'd get promotion. It was a very physical league and I remember one game we played against Notts County (15 November 1975; Chelsea 2-0 Notts County, Wilkins R, (p), Garner) and all they did for the whole game was try to kick us off the pitch but we though kept on playing football and totally outplayed them to win.

I scored my first goal for Chelsea against Crystal Palace (14 February 1976; Chelsea 2-3 Crystal Palace, Wilkins R, Wicks) later that season in the FA Cup. Chelsea were losing 2-0 but we came back to level with me getting the equaliser but to then lose the game so late on was absolutely heartbreaking. Unfortunately, we lost Micky Droy at half-time to injury but we regrouped and showed some real character in that second-half. We often had games like that when we were losing but we never gave up.

I remember when we were 3-0 down to Bolton (14 October 1978; Chelsea 4-3, Swain, Langley, Walker, og) at home with 18-minutes to go and won the game 4-3!

Back then the club was £3m in debt. In those days, that was a huge amount of money. We knew what was going on. Once, the players had a whip-round to ensure the coach went to a game and we were all asked to give £25 a week wages back to the club which we all did.

Most of the players were on about £250 to £275 per week back then so the outgoings on wages were a lot less than most big clubs with senior pros on the wage bill. It was heartbreaking for everyone when the likes of Peter Osgood and Alan Hudson and other senior pros left. When Eddie took over the ones that remained were so important to the club. Ron Harris, David Hay, John Dempsey, Micky Droy, Bill Garner and Peter Bonetti who was a magnificent person to us all. In those bleak times, these were the people who kept everyone going. I learnt so much and got so much help from David Hay.

He was a fantastic player to play with. Ian Hutchinson was still there and although he was having major injury problems he was fantastic in and around the club. They were great to be around and without them it would have been a lot harder at Chelsea with the money problems there at the time.

There were things going on behind the scenes which did not go down well. The stopping of lunches for the players, the milk disappearing due to the lack of money and all expenditure having to be approved by the accountants. That was bleak but I have to say that throughout all this, the Chairman Brian Mears was one of the loveliest men one would ever meet. If he offered a contract, he'd honour it – there was no need for signed papers and suchlike. He was a man of his word, I think he went to every game on the bus, every tour, every friendly, everyone respected him but, when it got to the stage that Martin Spencer and the accountants were running the club, that's when it became a nightmare.

Despite the financial problems Chelsea faced, Eddie was great throughout. He used to tell the newspapers reporters that Ray Lewington was the new Billy Bremner and Ray Wilkins would one day captain England. He promoted us at every opportunity he got. If he believed it, he showed it with a passion so others believed it too. If anyone was having a hard time, he'd put his arm around them and reassure them. As far as I was concerned, I can only tell you how I felt playing for him. I thought he was absolutely fantastic.

It was a tribute to Eddie that Chelsea were promoted in 1977. At one stage we were way ahead but then we had a bit of a wobble. We played against Southampton (30 October 1976; Chelsea 3-1 Southampton, Wilkins R, Finnieston, Swain) and we couldn't get near the ground because of the crowd. We won that day after going a goal down and I think from then the Chelsea supporters began to believe. In some games, we started to get crowds in excess of 30, 40 and once, against Fulham (27 December 1976; Chelsea 2-0 Fulham, Droy, Swain) there were 55,000 inside Stamford Bridge.

Unfortunately, we drew successive games at home to the likes of Plymouth,

Orient Blackpool and Millwall which was, I think at least, down to the state that the pitch at Stamford Bridge was in. It had become unplayable and that was frustrating as we were a footballing side and that pitch didn't help.

That game at Wolves (7 May 1977; Wolverhampton Wanderers 1-1 Chelsea, Langley) was probably the most bizarre game I ever played in. First of all though, Chelsea supporters were banned so we were not looking forward to that. We walked out on the pitch and literally thousands of Chelsea scarves appeared from nowhere!

Ban? What ban? It was amazing. It gave the whole team a real lift. We scored first which was what we wanted to do but Wolves scored a late equaliser with about 10-minutes to go. Bobby Gould, was playing up front for Wolves and, after they equalised, he said to a few of us we both had what we wanted by way of getting promoted so why don't both teams just pass the ball around for the last 10-minutes which we did – it was the most bizarre end to a game I have ever played in! Eddie had arranged for all the wives and girlfriends who'd travelled up to the game to come back on the players' coach. We saw Chelsea supporters driving back to London all the way back home and there were probably some who never even got into the game but went up to Wolves so they could be there. Eddie had booked Barberellas – the club next to Stamford Bridge – and when we got back to London, some of us went back there and partied into the night.

I remember being at Stamford Bridge the day I was told that Eddie had left and being in total shock. I went into the club that day and Christine Matthews said to me, "Have you heard the news?" I replied, "What news?" and she told me what happened. Several of the players had Eddie's telephone number so we called him and asked him why he was leaving. He said, "I have taken this club back to where it belongs and I just needed to be treated with some respect."

Eddie would have been a very averagely paid manager in the First Division so I don't think it was the money, I understand he wanted a car. I don't know how he would have fared in the First Division but the only person who could have replaced him and taken over was Ken Shellito. We all had respect for him. He was like a driving instructor and he taught us how to play. The only way the club could have defused the situation with the players with Eddie leaving was to bring in Ken Shellito. It was very clever. The right move.

I always thought the Chelsea support was fantastic and they were invaluable to the club at the time. When Chelsea played away from home we never felt lonely although when I went to QPR there were a few games you might say when I felt lonely. The following away from home was always better then the home support. Chelsea supporters away from home are a different breed. Then, if Chelsea were allocated 3,000 tickets for an away game, it would be guaranteed that double that would be there in other parts of the ground.

It was such a different time back then. You had this group of lads absolutely dedicated to Chelsea Football Club and getting them back to Division One. It was not about the money. Our bonus was £69 per game. When get got promoted it was a Labour Government in power and by the time we paid the tax we each got £3,000 for winning promotion.

I'll always remember Ian Hutchinson from my time at Chelsea – he was my hero and one of the nicest people one could ever meet. He had his own problems but always looked out for others. He was a good laugh in the dressing room but an iconic man.

I got on well with Ray Lewington and Ray Wilkins due to the fact we'd known each other for years and had come up through the ranks together and I was good friends with Ian Britton and Gary Locke. I never understood why he never got a chance to play for England. He was unlucky and had his share of injuries but when he was playing he never had a bad game. I also had a lot of sympathy for Graham Wilkins when he went through a bad patch at Chelsea and I known it wasn't easy for him.

It was a real tight-knit group and that had built up over the years. There are a lot of clichés in football but when we shook hands with each other to wish each other luck we meant it and we took that spirit on to the field together. Take Jock Finnieston for example. A great goal scorer and, when he scored, he would sometimes kiss the badge to celebrate. For me he earned the right to do that. Some of the modern-day footballers kiss the badge but are then off to another club at the drop of hat.

I left Chelsea at the end of Chelsea's second season back in the First Division. Danny Blanchflower had taken over when Chelsea were lying at the bottom of the table following Ken Shellito's departure. That was the start of everyone leaving. Kenny Swain had gone for £100,000 and Garry Stanley, Ray Lewington and Ray Wilkins followed at the end of the season. The administrators were in complete control and it did not matter what the bid was, they were selling the players.

Even after those players were sold, Chelsea still had money problems. I got a surprise 'phone-call saying that the club had agreed a fee with Derby County and could I be in Derby by 5pm that evening. I went home, picked up my wife and we drove up to Derby. They offered me three times the amount of money I was on at Chelsea, a brand new SAAB car and a fantastic signing-on fee but I didn't want to go there.

I didn't and I returned to Stamford Bridge. I met with Brian Mears and said, "I don't want to leave, please don't make me!" He replied, "I need to put you on the 'phone to someone you need to listen to about what is being said…" He passed the telephone to me and Martin Spencer was at the other end of the line. He told me, "If you don't sign for Derby by the end of this week, this club (Chelsea) will be here no longer. That's how bad things are here!" I asked him what about the money from the other players we had sold. He said, "It doesn't even pay off the interest on what we owe." I called Brian Mears the next day and signed for Derby the day after that. I was in tears when I left.

Not long after I arrived at Derby, their manager Tommy Docherty got the sack – I felt like I'd gone from the frying pan into the fire. Derby were rebuilding but Roy McFarland was still there who was, for me at least, the best player in that position I'd seen. The trouble was, he was a left sided centre-half, as I was, so I had to play on the right-hand side of defence which I didn't like. At the time, there was a lot of animosity from certain players towards Doc and to some of the players he brought in. He left at the end of season and then took over at QPR and I followed him there soon after. QPR had a good side back then. It was going well in my first season at Loftus Rd but Doc was beaten up one night by some football fans and, after that, the team lost its momentum and we eventually missed out on promotion.

He was sacked and soon after they brought in Terry Venables to join the backroom staff and he then became the manager. Terry was a great coach and we got promotion with him and we'd won the league by Easter. The biggest thing I could never understand is why Chelsea never asked him to be their manager. Terry's biggest dream was to one day be manager of Chelsea. He loved the club and I can't understand why they never at any stage made a move for him.

I know people talk about his business side but I never met a more professional person to deal with. His coaching was unbelievable and you would sit down with him and just talk football. He once said to me that the problem with England was that they make loads of players who can carry a piano but don't produce enough players who can play it!

Terry was very different to Eddie McCreadie and he placed great emphasis on the coaching side and studying the opposition and had more experience.

Eddie though was strong on motivational side and always was very attack minded. He always put a team out with the view of 'don't worry about them – let them worry about us'. Eddie was a strong motivator and encouraged his teams to just go out and play. The Doc was very similar to Eddie as well.

I'd been at QPR for nearly two-years and I'd won a few U21 caps and Spurs came in for me. I thought if I joined them, I'd improve my chances of playing for England. I sat down with QPR's Chairman Jim Gregory and told me that that he'd also had a bid for me from Newcastle. He said, "Tottenham are our neighbours. I'm not selling you to them so you can go to Newcastle. You've four-years on your contract and, if you don't like it, you can graze in a field for all I care!"

But then, suddenly, Crystal Palace came in for me. I asked them for a ridiculous contract for silly money which I thought they would never agree to in a million years but they said yes, which was something I didn't expect. I was at Selhurst Park for less than a year because Terry Venables took me back to Loftus Road and QPR. However, he left to take over at Barcelona and, by then, Jim Gregory had a 'no over 30s' policy and decided to sell me again.

I had a good final season at QPR and played some of my best football in 1986 and got in to Bobby Robson's initial 40-man World Cup squad. My problem was that Bobby Robson loved Terry Butcher, but if Terry Venables had been England manager then I am sure I would have made the final squad.

I was 29 at the time and there was interest in me from Sheffield Wednesday, Watford and West Ham. I was at home one day and Jim Gregory rang me to say he had accepted a bid for me. I said, "I suppose you've sent me off to the most far off place – Yorkshire..." but he said, "No, I've accepted a bid from Chelsea!"

The worst thing about my time at QPR was playing on that plastic pitch and I'm sure that I'm still feeling the effects of it now. When I returned to Chelsea, the first day of training saw us travel to Bangor in Wales. We had to piggy-back someone of equal weight up and down a hill and I got Eddie Niedzwicki. Suffice to say, Eddie had enjoyed a good summer and had piled on a few pounds. I got to the top and was about to turn and go down when I felt something go in my back. I had to drop Eddie and I collapsed to the ground. I played in agony for most of that year and had regular cortizone injections in my back.

I was bought by Chelsea because I think they thought that Joe McLaughlin was limited as a central defender but I played on the left side of the defence, as did Colin Pates. Neither of us liked playing on the right so we didn't get much chance to play together. They even played Patsey at left back in one game with me.

The Chelsea dressing room I had left a number of years ago had become a very different place to the one I returned to. It was the worst dressing room atmosphere I had ever known and much of it stemmed back to the previous season when Chelsea won the Full Members Cup. The players were mad at Ken Bates for not paying out the bonuses he had promised them.

The dressing room was also divided into cliques. There were the players who lived in Hertfordshire, the Scottish players and then there were the players who'd come through the youth team together like John Bumstead and Patesy. It was a dressing room divided.

It was toxic at times. I've never seen so many fights in training during my career. Some of the players thought they were superstars and they simply weren't. I loved the Chelsea when I was there first time around but not Ken Bates' Chelsea.

I wasn't at the club at the time but I was told that Bates took over from Brian Mears, he made everyone turn every photo of the Mears family upside down. If that happened that was disrespectful. The Mears family founded Chelsea and Joe Mears for me was the greatest chairman ever for Chelsea and, what ever happened, there was no need for that.

Brian Mears was visionary but he was also naive. He let his heart rule his head. The whole ground redevelopment project had been set up about finishing on time but he'd never put in any break clauses or penalties in the contract so he had to keep paying the contractors when they went way over deadline. It cost a lot more money as a result. But Brian had a vision of wanting to build the type of stadium that Chelsea now have, long before others thought about it.

He was the most honest chairman I ever worked for and he had a dream to have Chelsea as the best team in the country with the best stadium. It was a shame that it didn't work out for him.

My penultimate game for Chelsea was the first leg of the play-off game with Middlesbrough (23 May 1988; Middlesbrough 2-0). I remember it well. One of the goals we let in was a goalkeeping error by Kevin Hitchcock. Kerry Dixon also had three one-on-ones with the Boro keeper and, if one of those had gone in, we'd have lost 2-1. In the return at Stamford Bridge (28 May 1988; Chelsea 1-0, Durie), we scored an early goal and we threw everything at them for the rest of the game but only won 1-0. That must have been the unluckiest relegation ever. We were something like 11 points clear of the third place team below us at the bottom. We shouldn't have got sucked into it.

It was a full house at Stamford Bridge with a tremendous atmosphere and the Chelsea supporters were amazing that day. Batesy had been giving me loads of stick about my bad back but, despite the constant pain I was suffering, I think that was probably my best game for Chelsea.

My son Matthew supports Chelsea and bleeds blue. He loves the club and has supported them from day-one. I took him to Cobham which is a fantastic place with 47 pitches, all with brilliant surfaces – it's such a difference from where used to train at Mitcham! All credit to Mr Abramovich for what he's done. We met John Terry when we were there and he was absolutely brilliant. JT is for me a fantastic footballer, a great leader of men.

My first contract when in the youth-team was for £6.43 a week and £10 was sent home to our parents. Nowadays, youth-team players are driving home in BMWs and they're on £1m a year. I think they need to feel the 'hunger', the 'eye of the tiger' but, if they're given too much at an early age, they won't be hungry.

When Dave Sexton was manager he came to every youth-team game. He always made sure that once Easter was over, he'd blood one or two youngsters in the first-team. Johnny Sparrow was a good example. He was the best young left-back I ever saw. Dave Sexton gave him a run in the side of about six games at end of the season before he was 17! These days, a manager can rarely afford to play a young player for six games.

Once I finished playing, I went into management at Scarborough. Their Chairman at the time was Geoffrey Richmond. They were bottom of the league with 11 points when I took over and he gave me £50k to spend on three players. I brought in Shaun Murray from Portsmouth and I got Jason White from Scunthorpe. Jason White got 10 goals and Shaun Murray chipped in half a dozen and we rose up the table and finished in 9th place. I got the 'Manager of the Month' award a couple of times and things were going well.

However, Geoffrey Richmond sold-up and bought Bradford, and a guy called John Russell came in as Chairman. This was a guy who later went to prison later for fraud after he went to Exeter City. In his first game as

Chairman, we were playing Bradford City and we were losing 2-0 at half-time. We were in the dressing room during the break when Russell came in and started having a go at the players. I said, "Excuse me Mr Chairman, but this isn't your domain, it's mine, so please leave!" I told the lads they needed to play a lot better in the second-half as I could be struggling to keep my job. They did play better in the second '45' but we still lost 2-1. On the way home after the match, I was told that there would be a Board meeting to discuss my future. I received a call the next day to say I'd been sacked and they made Billy Aird manager instead. They were relegated that season. Shaun Murray was sold for £450k and Jason White went to York for £110k.

I then went to Lincoln who had a guy running the place who was every bit as bad as John Russell. I was there for 8 weeks until I said to him, "You know what? You run the team!" and I quit.

I went out to Singapore and then I was offered a job with Selangor FA. I didn't know much about Malaysian Football but I met with them and they offered me a fantastic contract, agreed to pay all my taxes and provided a house and a car. Their Shah Alam stadium was magnificent, holding 89,000. They were the Manchester United of the region. The average gate there was 63,000. We won the Treble of the Malaysian Cup, the League Title and the Malaysian FA Cup. But then, halfway through the following season, it went horribly wrong.

The club was run by huge sponsorship deals but the country suffered a recession and all the main sponsors pulled out, leaving the club with financial problems. I met with the chairmen and told him that he cannot afford to pay the team and pay me so I would go. It was very hot out there and my wife had had enough by then so was a good time to come home. I used to lose about 8 pounds just in a half-hour five-a-side session. Nowadays, I work for Liz Hobbs, the former British water ski champion. She has lots of contacts in the sport and entertainment industry and has a company based in Newark in Nottinghamshire.

Finally though, I'd like to thank all the supporters who sang "Chelsea reject!" at me and gave me so much grief when I played against them. I never wanted to leave Chelsea in the first place. Actually, I should say I'll never forget walking out at Stamford Bridge and playing for Chelsea and the supporters as long as I live. It was the greatest thing that's ever happened to me. It was the best time ever – we didn't win any trophies but we got Chelsea back where they belonged and saved the club as a result.

GRAHAM WILKINS

I signed my first contract for Chelsea in 1970 and started on £6, 19 shillings and sixpence. I got my first taste of being in the senior squad when Chelsea played against Spurs at White Hart Lane in 1972 (21 October 1972; Tottenham Hotspur 0-1 Chelsea, Hollins). I was the Chelsea substitute (in those days, there was only one) but I didn't get a game. I made my debut on Boxing Day that year at Ipswich (26 December 1972; Ipswich Town 3-0 Chelsea). I played my first game for Chelsea at Stamford Bridge against Norwich (26 October 1973; Chelsea 3-0 Norwich City, Baldwin (2), Kember) and it was nice for me to get a win under my belt and, as well as the victory, it was made more memorable for me because my brother Ray made his Chelsea debut.

I was picked to play the following week against Manchester United at Old Trafford (3 November 1973; Manchester United 2-2 Chelsea, Baldwin, Osgood) but the game ended badly for me. Chelsea were winning 2-0 when I broke my leg in a challenge on Willie Morgan. I'd managed to knock the ball out for a corner but I was lying on the ground in agony when Lou Macari came over and started to drag me by my shirt to get me off the pitch and, as he was doing so, my leg was bouncing up and down off the turf. Having already come on as a substitute for Chris Garland, my brother Ray ran over and pushed Macari away from me so I could get the attention I needed.

I don't think that anybody at the time would have foreseen Eddie becoming the Chelsea manager and, being an honest sort of a guy, I think he'd have probably admitted that coaching wasn't one of his great strengths but I must say that he was probably one of the best managers I ever played for. He'd talk to the players, he'd listen to them and he'd also advise them. The good thing for me was that he understood completely the role I had to play in the side as we both played in the same position.

When he took charge of the club, I think that all the players could sense that he'd be good at the job. He was one of us, a player's manager. He did a lot for us and I think he could see that he had a group of players who really wanted to play for him.

However, I don't think that many of us realised that he was struggling with having the financial burden on his shoulders but, Eddie being Eddie, he did his best to protect us and ensure that we, as players, weren't affected by it. We had a good year in the 1976/77 season. Previously, we'd let ourselves down because our home form had been poor but, the year we won promotion, we turned it around. We started well and then started picking up good crowds. We clicked on the field from the first game away at Orient

I wasn't in the side that won the point that took us up at Molineux against Wolves (7 May 1977; Wolverhampton Wanderers 1-1 Chelsea, Langley). I'd been left out of the team along with Kenny Swain and Garry Stanley and Ron Harris, Charlie Cooke and Tommy Langley replaced us. I don't know why we were dropped as we'd played most of the season and we were doing well enough. That was Eddie though – he wasn't scared to make tough decisions.

As a team, the players got on really well with each other. Once we'd finished training, we'd have a few pints and a game of snooker. Sometimes, because of the drinking, we were lucky to make it to training the next day but we always turned up. Even if we'd had a late night, we had too much respect for Eddie not to and we would never have wanted to let him down.

My brother Steve joined Chelsea thanks to Eddie. Ray and I asked him whether Steve could come and train with us and Eddie said he could. He joined in when we played and he played unbelievably. He had a foot like a snake's tongue and Eddie thought he was great and he wanted to sign him on the spot. Unfortunately, Steve liked a beer and the girls too much so sadly it didn't work out for him at Chelsea and he ended up playing non-league football.

When we heard Eddie had left Chelsea, we were all really deflated. Ken Shellito came in and then Danny Blanchflower followed him. We knew Ken from the youth-team but having got him as the first-team manager, we didn't do well under him.

Ken was a great coach and there was no doubt about that. He knew the players and so he looked the perfect fit but, although his coaching was great, he couldn't handle being the manager – he was in way as good as Eddie. Danny Blanchflower was a strange one and I think that some of his ideas were mad. We used to have to train with two balls because he told us if we did that during the week, it would be easier for us on a Saturday because we only had to play with one!

With Danny, we always used to train at Stamford Bridge on a Friday and when we came out of the tunnel, we used to drop all the balls and have a kick about and leave all the nets on the ground. One day, there was a crowd watching us and, as Danny walked out of the tunnel and onto the pitch, they started singing his name. Danny turned round and waved to them and walked backwards, tripped over the nets and went flying.

I left Chelsea in 1982 to join Brentford and I followed Ron Harris to Griffin Park but, looking back, I should never have left. I had the worst time of my life at Brentford. I dislocated my shoulder, I had my front teeth kicked out and then I had to pack in playing in 1983. I tried to carry on but physically I was finished. I played for Southall briefly when Les Ferdinand was there. I knew the manager and turned out a few times for them but my leg was too bad and I couldn't carry on playing. I had 17 operations on one knee and the last one I had was a knee replacement.

Nowadays, I'm employed by British Airways at Heathrow Airport where I work at the arrival services in Terminal 5. If passengers have any problems, they come and talk to me.

Recently, I've made the decision to go part-time and work for a couple of years more and then I plan to travel the world. I want to go to Mauritius as I've never been there. My wife Stephanie is an ex-stewardess and she's been everywhere but now we want to travel together.

I miss everything about being a professional footballer – the lads, the dressing room and the banter. For me, my days at Chelsea were great. My brother Ray and Charlie Cooke were the best two players I ever played with. Charlie was great to me when I was coming through the ranks at Chelsea. We needed a leader and Micky Droy was ours and, despite his size, he was a gentle giant.

Nowadays, I see Jock nearly every week and often see Clive Walker. Once or twice a week we try and have a round of golf. He's gambling mad but he managed to win enough over the years to pay for his house! When we were players, he used to queue up in the Barclays Bank at West Brompton to get brand new £1 notes. He'd ask the other players to get them and, for every £10 worth of new notes, he'd give you £11! I still don't know why he did that!

I did get a few own goals… I got one for Bolton (27 March 1976; Bolton Wanderers 2-1 Chelsea, Britton) but the one that David Hay scored in the same game was better than mine. I put through my own net again at Maine Road (26 November 1978; Manchester City 6-2 Chelsea, Britton, Wilkins R) and then again at Stamford Bridge against West Ham. (6 September 1980; Chelsea 0-1 West Ham United).

I know I came in for a lot of criticism from the Chelsea supporters and I suppose some of it was justified but plenty wasn't. However, I was mentally strong enough to take it. I felt although I was in the shadow of my brother Ray but, when I scored for Chelsea (21 April 1979; Chelsea 2-1 Middlesbrough, Stanley, Wilkins G), the only goal of my Stamford Bridge career, the supporters gave me a brilliant reception.

I had some really low points as a footballer and they came mainly as a result of the injuries I picked up. These days, players are more protected and better looked after than they were in my day. Then, the doctor would stick a cortisone injection into a player's leg and then give them the okay to get out onto the pitch and play a match.

I played against York in the last game of the 1976 season (24 April 1976; York City 2-2 Chelsea, Britton (P), Finnieston) and I made a block tackle and my leg seemed to rip but I straightened my leg and walked off. Unbeknown to me, I'd ruptured my cruciate ligament but I was told that I'd just sprained my knee and it was bandaged. We flew to Spain the next day but, as the aircraft took off and the higher it got, the more my knee hurt. By the end of the week I was in agony. I returned to England after a week and it was then the true extent of my injury became clear and I went straight into Hammersmith Hospital for an operation.

One of the highlights of my career were making my debut at Ipswich – the result wasn't great – but I'll always remember that Ron Suart came to our house on Christmas Day to ask if it would be alright if I travelled to

Portman Road with the first-team for the Boxing Day match and, suffice to say, my father George was over the moon. Another was playing against Liverpool in the FA Cup at Stamford Bridge when we beat them in the FA Cup (7 January 1978; Chelsea 4-2, Walker (2), Finnieston, Langley). It was an amazing victory for Chelsea because Liverpool were the European Cup holders. I thoroughly enjoyed that day. I was marking Steve Heighway that day and he didn't get a kick.

I went for the first time in 18 months to the Bradford City FA Cup game and it was the first game I'd been to since my brother was sacked by Chelsea. The side that Carlo Ancelotti had at Stamford Bridge was fantastic and I just couldn't understand why the club sacked him just a year after he led Chelsea to their first Double.

RAY WILKINS

My earliest memories of Chelsea are from the days when I joined as a schoolboy. My brother Graham and I joined at the same time. We were training there regularly and it's where I first met Ray Lewington who soon became a good pal and we're great friend still to this day. We both came from a similar background and we played together, starting in the kids' teams, the youth-team, the reserves and up to the first-team. We came from similar backgrounds and we clicked straight away.

I was 10-years old when I first went to Chelsea and I thoroughly enjoyed it, Frank Blunstone would take us coaching every Tuesday and Thursday evening and he was great at what he did. We then moved on to play under Ken Shellito who was in charge of the youth-team. He was fantastic. It was football, football with him and his emphasis was on teaching us technique – we learned so much from him.

We were a group of mates together and, when we played on a Saturday, we went out together after the game. We couldn't wait to get into training each day. It was just a group of mates together having fun doing something we loved and we still see each other today as much as we can.

The thing we had and still have is that we're all friends to this day – something that the current players won't have. With the cross-section of foreign players there are at Chelsea, that closeness won't be there.

Our dressing room was amazing and we couldn't wait to get into training every morning to give each other a loud of grief. Everyone gave as good as they got.

The moment I really sensed I was a footballer was not when I signed my first contract but when I went to Simpson's store at Piccadilly. I got my blue blazer, slacks and my shirt and tie, attire I had to wear to every game, every youth game and I thought, "This is the business!" The blazer had the club blazer with the CFC of Chelsea embroidered on your jacket pocket.

After playing for Ken Shellito in the youth-team, I started to play under Dario Gradi in the reserves. As a result, I didn't play as many games as I suppose I should have for the youth-team. Dario used to play me up front in the reserves, a position I didn't normally play but it was progression and I was playing with men and learning all the time.

I was very lucky playing in the reserves as I got to play with John Boyle. He really taught me about the positional sense of being a midfielder. We played 4-4-2 and I would hear John saying, "Ray go deep, Ray stay here, Ray get into the box, get out of the box." He taught me a lot. That was the great thing about playing in the Football Combination. What I liked about the reserves was, if the first team were at Arsenal, we'd play their reserves at Stamford Bridge and there would always be senior players in the team. They were our teachers. They taught us how to play. The pitches back then were often not that great, but you played your heart out for the reserves as it was the next step towards the first team.

When the senior players were in the side, if the ball was given away the players who lost it would get an ear-bashing. When I made my debut at home to Norwich (26 October 1973; Chelsea 3-0 Norwich City, Kember, Baldwin 2), I tried to play my brother Graham in behind the full-back and gave the ball away. I got absolutely lambasted by Ossie. I thought, "Wow!" and I made sure I didn't give the ball away after that!

The following week, Chelsea played away to Manchester United at Old Trafford (3 November 1973; Manchester United 2-2, Chelsea, Osgood, Baldwin) and I came off the bench to replace Chris Garland with about 20 minutes to go. Chelsea were winning 2-0 but United scored twice in injury-time and the game ended 2-2.

After Eddie McCreadie had been appointed manager, he took me out to lunch. We talked about Chelsea and he said, I'm going to make you the captain – how do you feel about that? My response was, "You've still got Ronny Harris and Johnny Hollins so are you sure you still want to do this? He replied, "Ray, we need to change – I want you to be captain."

To wear the Chelsea armband was an enormous honour for me but with it came enormous pressure. I didn't sleep the night before the Tottenham game. To be honest, I don't think I handled it well for the first six-months. I wasn't playing as well as I knew I could but people like Ron Harris, Peter Bonetti and the likes of David Hay and Micky Droy and some of the other senior lads helped me right the way through.

We had such as great blend of older players and younger players at the club at the time. Although we had a lot of young lads who made the first-team, the senior pros were great. Eddie brought us together so well as group. The other thing that came out of Eddie being there was I met my wife Jackie who, at the time, was working at the club as his secretary. She worked in the office with Christine Matthews who was a real unsung hero at the club.

My first game as captain was away at Tottenham (19 April 1975; Tottenham Hotspur 2-0 Chelsea) which was a high-stakes game. We were beaten and the game was played in a hostile but, nevertheless, a great atmosphere. I know there was fighting off the pitch but it didn't concern me too much to be honest as I was concentrating on playing. I missed a chance towards the end when it was 1-0 which could have got us a point but then Alfie Conn went up the other end and scored. ITV's 'The Big Match' played that miss in their opening credits the following season to remind me!

We drew both our remaining games at home with Sheffield United (23 April 1975; Chelsea 1-1 Sheffield United, Maybank) and Everton (30 April 1975; Chelsea 1-1 Everton; Wilkins R). My goal in the match against Everton put Chelsea into the lead but they equalised late on in the game but, by that time, it was too little too late and Chelsea were relegated. Relegation is tough. As a group we were really close and we felt and shared the pain of relegation between us. It's not just the players and the supporters who suffer though. There are also those behind the scenes that are affected.

As a manager, Eddie was innovative and, against Everton, he played me as a number 10 in the 'hole' behind the forwards. Following the relegation, during that first season in the Second Division, I had so much time and space on the pitch and I scored 12 goals. I remember the first goal I scored for Chelsea very well. It was at Stamford Bridge and I hit a left-footed volley into the corner of the goal at what is now the Matthew Harding end. However, I think my best goal for Chelsea was against Plymouth (1 November 1976; Chelsea 2-2 Plymouth Argyle, Britton, Wilkins R). I scored at The Shed end with a diving header after Bill Garner had put the ball across the area. We were winning 2-0 but somehow they came back to earn themselves a draw.

One of the memorable games for me from that period was when Chelsea played Palace in the FA Cup. (14 February 1976; Chelsea 2-3 Crystal Palace;

Wilkins R, Wicks) That year, I really thought that Chelsea would go all the way and it was a severe disappointment when we were knocked out. Chelsea had been losing 2-0, we came back to level but then Peter Taylor scored his second and the third for Crystal Palace who held out to win the game. The atmosphere that day was absolutely incredible that day. It was electric, especially when we equalised.

Collectively, we had a great group of players and, the football aside, we had a lot of fun together. I still remember coming back from Molineux when we played Wolves to get promoted (7 May 1977; Wolverhampton Wanderers 1-1 Chelsea, Langley) and, when we arrived back in London, some of us ended up in a pub between The Kings Rd and Fulham Road. Jock (Finnieston had broken his nose during the game and Ray Lewington kept twisting it on the coach all the way back from the game and carried on doing it once we were in the pub.

We were all friends together and it was fantastic. We had so many good times. The Hull City game was amazing (14 May 1977; Chelsea 4-0 Hull City 0, Britton, Finnieston 3 (1 P), Langley). The crowd kept running onto the pitch after every goal and there was Eddie – wearing dark tinted glasses and that silly sheepskin coat he liked to wear – shouting into a megaphone trying to get the supporters off the pitch.

I suppose the supporters did misbehave a bit back in those days but every club had their element who did. I always classed those who travelled away as the proper Chelsea supporters. Even to this day, they go week in, week out and it must cost them a fortune. It's more expensive now and it must be a tough for a dad to take his kids to football, but they go and I applaud every supporter that travels away every week – they're amazing! We were always well supported wherever we went.

Every club had their element of fans who liked to fight and it wasn't pleasant. People couldn't take their kids and it put a lot of people off going.

I still go to Chelsea myself. I have a couple of season tickets and when I've been away to watch them, I've sat amongst the travelling supporters. It's nice that a lot of the Chelsea supporters still remember me now. They've always been good to me and, in all my time both as a player and after I left, I only had trouble with a supporter once. That was when I missed a penalty at home to Bolton. (6 December 1975; Chelsea 0-1 Bolton Wanderers). I missed a penalty against Barry Siddall who was in goal and, as the teams came off the field at the end of the game and I walked down the tunnel, someone spat at me.

Chelsea were already in administration when Eddie left and the financial side of things were being handled by Martin Spencer, the club accountant. I couldn't believe it when I heard the news that he'd gone – it was unbelievable. Eddie had done a great job. He'd moulded us into something special and a side that was tough to beat and we were ready to take on the First Division and, if I'm being honest, I had high hopes for us in the top flight following our promotion.

Eddie was a great man. I'd played with him in the reserves and was in the first-team with him. As a manager, he was one of those blokes people wanted to run through a brick wall for. Before each game, all the players would shake hands with each other in the dressing room before went out. We looked each other in the eye and say to ourselves, "I want to run my socks off for him today! We're not going to lose today."

Once Eddie had gone, Ken Shellito took over. We all knew Ken from the youth-team and, playing for him in that side, it was football, football, football, pass, pass, pass. We had a pitch at the training ground at Mitcham that was in great condition and the first-team used to train on it but, on a Saturday when they were playing their game, the youth-team used it as their 'home' pitch. Playing on such a good surface definitely helped improve our individual skills and develop as footballers generally.

But, in the First Division, the points were more important than the football and sometimes during matches we played the long-ball game because winning was more important than the style of football we played.

After Ken left the club, Danny Blanchflower took over. He gave us two balls to train with on the training ground, his reason being that if we could play with two balls during the week, what would be like on a Saturday with only one ball to play with?

Some of the guys could not play the type of football Danny had in mind. We struggled under him and we went back down. One day, Danny came to me and said, "Ray, we've been offered £825.000 by Manchester United for you and we're selling you. The club is in debt and we need the money and you have to go." I replied, "Ultimately Danny, it's not your decision, it's mine!" But, having said that and after I'd had a chance to think about it, I left Chelsea in 1979 to go to Old Trafford. I didn't want to stay somewhere I didn't feel wanted.

I loved Chelsea Football Club then and I still do. I love the club so much. They needed the money badly so I had to leave but it hurt. I didn't want to go. I never wanted to leave. Such is life but, who knows where my career would have taken me if I had stayed?

I stayed at Manchester United for five-years and it was at a time when they were always competing with Liverpool. During my time at Old Trafford, we had the upper hand in games against each other but, at the end of the season, it was always Liverpool that won the league. We did win the FA Cup and I scored at Wembley in the final v Brighton in a game that was drawn (21 May 1983; Brighton & Hove Albion 2-2 Manchester United) but we went on to win the replay and lift the cup. I left Manchester Utd in 1984 to join AC Milan and joined the Italian side at the same time as Mark Hateley.

When I went to Italy, I found the change of culture incredible. The Italian league had sides which contained some of the top name players in the world such as Zico and Maradona. Although George Best was the best played I'd ever played against, Franco Baresi was probably the best player I have played with and, when I was there, Milan also had Paulo Rossi and Paulo Maldini in their side.

The Italian league was quite something. There were just 30 league games in a season with no matches over both Christmas and Easter and none on any other religious holiday. Going to Italy was an adventure for my wife Jackie and I. Our son Ross was 2-years old when we went there but his younger sister Jade was born just outside Milan so I suppose we'll always have a little bit of Italy in our family. The Italians are of a different ilk. They're great, passionate people who love their football and my family and I had a great time there.

After I'd been there for 3-years, I left to join Paris St Germain but only stayed there for a short time before Graham Souness who was the Rangers manager came in for me and I moved to Glasgow. Rangers are a great club who know how to look after their players – I couldn't wait to get to training every morning I was there!

I left Scotland in 1989 and moved back to London to join QPR. After staying there for 5-years, I accepted an offer to join Crystal Palace in 1994 as their player-manager but, in my first game, I broke my foot and it was the only time I ever pulled on a Palace shirt. I then had an offer from QPR to return to them as player/manager and I took the position.

During my time in charge, Ken Bates asked me if I wanted to come back to Chelsea. This was when John Hollins was coach. I asked Ken whether John Hollins – Chelsea's manager – knew that he was talking to me and Ken said, "No – why should he?" I told Ken that as far as I was concerned John was the manager and if he wanted me to come then we should talk. He thought about for about 10-seconds and just said, "Alright Wilky, I'm off!" and, off he went…

When I came back to Stamford Bridge in 1998 in a coaching role, I found the Chelsea that I'd rejoined was a very different club to the one I'd left back in 1979.

Before his court case and subsequent imprisonment, Graham Rix put Gianluca Vialli in touch with me. Although I had played against Luca when I was in Italy, I didn't know him. I came back for the Newcastle United game (22 August 1998; Chelsea 1-1, Babayaro) and it felt great to be back at Stamford Bridge.

I didn't want to mess around with contracts. It wasn't a time of agents and I had always negotiated my own contracts so I said to Chelsea I would take over Graham's contract. I stayed with Luca for 2-years and, when Graham returned to Chelsea, I was retained as a European scout. While I was there with Luca, Chelsea won the FA Cup in 2000 which was magnificent. I'll never forget the celebrations in the dressing room after the game. When Luca left and Claudio Ranieri arrived, I was moved aside and I followed Luca to Watford and then went to work with Dennis Wise at Millwall. Then, Luiz Felipe Scolari brought me back to Chelsea to help him.

Chelsea were playing Bordeaux at Stamford Bridge in the Champions League and Phil sat down with me and said, "I've looked at your CV and I'd like you to come and work with me." I loved working with Phil because he was a lovely bloke and he is one of the nicest human beings to have ever worked within football. The staff he had working for him were all good people. They were fantastic.

The thing was however, I think Phil forgot the training methods in day-to-day management compared to international football. We started so well and everybody got on like a house on fire. We worked and trained hard

379

Monday, Tuesday and Wednesday and harder on Thursday and then spent Friday coming back down. But, what with chopping and changing with Saturday and Sunday football, I think Phil got some weeks mixed up and we probably over trained players.

I remember the day that Scolari was sacked. Glenn Hoddle brought his academy over from Spain to Cobham to play the Chelsea youngsters. I was working that game and a helicopter appeared overhead and Mr Abramovich arrived. Usually, when the helicopter arrives, there's 'something' on the agenda. My phone rang. It was Eugene Tenenbaum who wanted me to meet with him and the owner. He said, "We've had to make a change Ray. It's not working out. It is breaking out hearts to do so as he's such a lovely guy." They asked me to take charge of the first team against Watford in the FA Cup 5th round. We beat Watford (14 February 2009; Watford 1-3 Chelsea, Anelka 3) and it is nice to be told I have a 100% record as a Chelsea manager but it was only one game!

Guus Hiddink came in to replace Scolari and he was a delight, a joy to work with and, as a man, he was just exceptional. He has seen it done it and worn the t-shirt. He's probably the best man manager I have ever come across – a real pro. He handled that dressing room group of players so well and it was a strong dressing room that Guus came into with some very senior players and he handled them so well.

When we won the FA Cup against Everton in the final (30 May 2009; Chelsea 2-1 Everton, Drogba Lampard), we went a goal down after 35 seconds. When the goal went in, Guus – very calmly – said, "That's not in the script!" I replied, "No Guus, but at least we have eighty-nine minutes to go!"

I love the FA Cup and the scenes in our dressing room after the game were incredible! Some people say that the foreign players just don't 'get' the FA Cup but everyone was going mad that day. Guus was smoking the biggest cigar ever and all the lads were singing and dancing.

After Guus left, Carlo Ancelotti came in from AC Milan and, initially, he wanted to bring Paulo Maldini with him. Paulo did come over but decided not to join Chelsea so Carlo asked me if I would stay and assist him. I did and rest is history and we won the Double. Carlo was similar to Guus in that he had his own way of wanting to play. He changed our style of play slightly. For him, it was about possession and keeping the ball. The only blot on the season was losing to Inter Milan in the Champions League.

Then, in November, I was asked to leave and although I was sorry to go, that's football. All good things come to an end. Winning the Double with those players was a massive feat. It was a privilege working with them. They gave us everything.

Nowadays, I'm working for Sky Sports, BT Sport and I do the Alan Brazil breakfast show which means an early 3.50am start for me. I love it and I enjoy it very much. If one can't be a player or a coach, being a broadcaster – for me at least – is the next best thing. When I appear in the media, I just give my opinion and, if people don't like it, I'm okay with that but it's nice to hear fans saying they like what I do.

I still come down to Stamford Bridge when I'm not working in the media – I'm Chelsea and always will be. I remember the first time I came back, someone said to me, "What are you doing back here? You're a red!" I retorted, "I've never been a red, I am Chelsea!"

What I would like to see is more and more of our talented young players get a chance at Chelsea. We have got so many great young players. With all our world-class players we have in the first team, I would love to see at least two youngsters in the side and be given a six to eight-game run. If a young player is put into the first-team, he'll give an extra 10-percent straight away. The crowd will love him and give him extra support and will be on his side from the off.

These lads regularly train with the first-team so are used to regularly working with the big stars and they score goals against the likes of John Terry in training. The next step is to see some of them in the first-team.

I did find it strange last year when Chelsea signed Falcao and Pato. Why did we buy them? For the life of me I don't know, especially when they weren't fit and we have young guys like Tammy Abraham who runs like the wind and scores goals for fun.

I was so chuffed when 11 of us turned up to Ian Britton's funeral. What a fellow he was. He would run his socks off for Chelsea. He wasn't a world-class player but he made up for that with heart – he never stopped running and the guys in the first-team loved him to bits.

All the guys from the 70s get together as often as we can. It is always nice to see everyone and we have known each other now for over 40 years and we're all good friends still.

BIOGRAPHICAL ARTICLES

BRIAN BASON

After representing England at schoolboy international level, Brian made his Chelsea debut whilst still an apprentice on 16 September 1972, just 13 days after his seventeenth birthday.

In doing so, he became one of the youngest first-team players in the club's history. As a youth-team player Brian played as a right-winger and occasional centre-forward.

Injuries to Peter Osgood, Alan Hudson and Charlie Cooke elevated the young Bason to the first-team at Bramall Lane against Sheffield United. Despite the team suffering a 1-2 defeat, Brian had lined-up with some seasoned professionals in Peter Bonetti, Eddie McCreadie, Ron Harris, David Webb and John Hollins and relished the moment.

Brian's next appearance saw him again donning the number 7 shirt in a 1-0 success at White Hart Lane in front of a crowd of 47,429. A goal scored by John Hollins beat Spurs and sent Chelsea to third in the First Division.

After making another two appearances in season 1972/73 against Newcastle and Crystal Palace, Brian's first-team chances became limited due to the return to the squad of a rejuvenated Tommy Baldwin, after injury and the emergence of £100,000 signings Chris Garland and Bill Garner.

Indeed, Brian was denied any further first team appearances during the following two seasons but continued his progress in the reserve team and, with Eddie McCreadie being well aware of his talent, he would soon figure in the new manager's plans following Chelsea's relegation to the Second Division at the end of the 1974/75 season.

Brian returned to the side wearing the number 4 shirt in the first home fixture of the 1975/76 season, appearing against Carlisle United and scoring Chelsea's last goal in a 3-1 victory with a blistering 30-yard drive. The effort would figure in the ITV Big Match programme's 'Goal of the Season' at the end of that campaign.

Brian made eight league appearances, the last being at the Dell where the team suffered a 1-4 reverse to a Peter Osgood inspired Southampton side. Sadly an injury sustained in the game curtailed his season.

Upon returning to the squad at the start of the 1976/77 season, Brian found himself vying for a position upon the right hand side in a 4-4-2 formation with other youngsters such as Ian Britton and Garry Stanley.

Sadly for Brian, upon re-establishing himself in the first X1, he suffered a double-fracture of his right leg in a League Cup tie at Arsenal in front of 52,305 spectators on 26 October 1976.

Thereafter Brian would not appear for Chelsea again, eventually moving onto Plymouth Argyle and then also playing for Crystal Palace, Portsmouth and Reading before retiring from football to manage a public house and hotel in Truro.

Eddie McCreadie was quick to acclaim Brian's part in the successful promotion campaign along with other senior players Charlie Cooke, Micky Droy, John Phillips and the young Tommy Langley who also made similar contributions in terms of limited appearances due to injuries.

PETER BONETTI

Peter Bonetti is undoubtedly a Chelsea legend, making 729 appearances for Chelsea between 1959 and 1979. During his time at Chelsea, he collected a League Cup winners' medal in 1965 followed by FA Cup and European

Cup Winners Cup honours in 1970 and 1971.

Whist starting between the sticks in the relegation haunted season of 1974/75, and playing eight times, by the time of Eddie McCreadie's appointment Peter had departed to the USA to commence coaching duties. However, after a relatively poor start to the 1975/76 season Eddie was successful in luring "the Cat" back to the Bridge in October where some much needed stability was indeed added to the defence with 24 consecutive appearances being made.

Furthermore, Peter's experience would prove invaluable to the younger squad members with only Ron Harris, Charlie Cooke and Ian Hutchinson remaining from the successful trophy winning sides of the early Seventies.

When the successful promotion season of 1976/77 kicked-off, Peter had re-established himself as number-one in front of John Phillips, a Welsh international.

Chelsea's barnstorming performances, some coinciding with them leading the table, were also punctuated with some brilliant performances by Bonetti with man-of-the-match awards received at Blackpool, Cardiff, Oldham and Burnley.

In particular, one Welsh hack described an acrobatic save from Robin Friday, a Cardiff and Reading legend, at Ninian Park in March as, "absolutely world class – as good a save as any in his career".

When promotion was secured in May at Wolverhampton, Peter remarked that whilst he had been proud to have played in the successful trophy winning teams in the past, this achievement was more important to Chelsea Football Club given the ongoing parlous financial predicament.

Indeed, it was a tribute to Eddie McCreadie's football insight that he had identified the need to install an experienced keeper at a very difficult time and convince Bonetti that he could still perform at the highest level.

Peter once recounted that, despite his outstanding performances for Chelsea, in some camps he will always be remembered as "that bloke who let in three for England against Germany" – a reference to England's defeat in the quarter-final of the 1970 Mexico World Cup.

It was often reported that Peter commenced his career at Chelsea after his mother wrote to the club requesting a schoolboy trial in 1957. Modestly, Peter neither confirms or denies this.

Peter recalled that, after an epic FA Cup fourth round victory over Leeds United in 1966, the team visited the London Palladium the following night where Liverpudlian Jimmy Tarbuck, opened proceedings by asking him to stand to warm applause from the assembled audience in acknowledgement of his outstanding performance the previous day.

In a League Cup quarter-final at Carlisle in 1969, Peter was rendered unconscious after being hit by a slab of granite launched from the terrace behind his goal. However, upon regaining consciousness and despite Chelsea losing the tie, Peter later commented that he had received a "nice letter of apology" from the Brunton Park faithful!

Many football fans will vividly remember some of Peter's fantastic penalty saves from BBC's Match of the Day programmes such as those from Alan Ball and Tony Brown in the 1968/69 season and another from Kevin Keegan in front of Liverpool's 'Kop End' in 1973.

Peter recalled once that he was privileged to have played with some of the true greats of the game and singles out Bobby Charlton as the best player he ever faced and indeed, played with, when representing England. It was also well acknowledged that Peter was always a first class athlete and lead from the front in any cross country running as part of training.

Furthermore, many of his former colleagues have mentioned Peter's abilities as an outfield player when participating in training matches. Some remarked that if he had not been a goalkeeper, he could have become a professional elsewhere on the park.

Whilst never given the opportunity to play outfield in any first-class fixture, on 21 April 1969 Peter was called upon to take, and score, two penalties against Charlton Athletic in a testimonial match for Bobby Tambling played at Stamford Bridge.

BILL GARNER

To many Chelsea supporters, Bill Garner attained near cult-status during his six seasons at Stamford Bridge as a swashbuckling target man who lived life very much on 'the edge'.

After impressing for Third Division Southend United in a League Cup tie against Chelsea, Dave Sexton saw fit to invest £100,000 to secure his transfer to SW6 in September 1972. The brave buccaneer looked every part an able deputy for the well established Ian Hutchinson who had formed a formidable and legendary partnership with Peter Osgood.

Due to Hutch's honest endeavour and 'never say die' attitude, many serious injuries were unfortunately sustained resulting in many short and long-term lay-offs, as was the case at the time of Bill's arrival. Ironically, when Bill made his first appearance as a 10th minute substitute for Alan Hudson in a 1-3 home reverse to West Ham United on 9 September 1972, he didn't see the game out after sustaining a bad ankle injury.

Things were to look up however when he netted after just five-minutes of his first full start two weeks later at Highfield Rd against Coventry City in a

3-1 victory – a fixture where Chelsea sported the Hungarian Maygars' red, white and green strip for the first time in a league match. Again however, Bill did not finish the game due to a hamstring injury but still won the acclaim of the assembled hacks who chose him as their 'Man of the Match'.

By the turn of the year, the Chelsea supporters had become acclimatised to Bill's aggressive style and abilities. However, noticeably, whilst he was a proficient header of the ball and liked to take control upon his chest, his footwork perhaps needed some attention.

Bill made a notable contribution to the side's run to the FA Cup quarter-final in 1973. At Brighton in the third round, he netted in 11-seconds only for the effort to be ruled out due to a team-mate being offside. Despite the game being remembered for a series of wild tackles by both sides, culminating in a sending-off of Chelsea captain Ron Harris, Bill kept his composure as a 2-0 victory was secured by a brace from Peter Osgood.

Bill netted both goals in a fourth round 2-0 home win against a much fancied Ipswich Town side, the first being an audacious chip from some 25 yards and the second, a miss-hit shot which somehow found its way past several leaden footed defenders.

Garner then took centre-stage in the next round at Hillsborough where Sheffield Wednesday were beaten 2-1. After trailing to an early goal, Bill netted with a tap-in from a Peter Houseman cross just before the break and celebrated with a 'five-knuckled shuffle' gesture towards the home fans in their kop.

His actions were captured by many snappers of the national press and appeared on most back pages of the Sunday red-tops the next day. Indeed, the Chelsea programme printed it the following week accompanied with the caption "Two goal tango".

Throughout the game, Bill endured the attention of Owl's skipper Holsgrove who left many lasting impressions on his legs and in the 88th minute, both were dismissed for brawling.

Unfortunately, Bill was ruled out of the sixth-round classic at home to Arsenal due to another injury, a game that ended 2-2 but was 'patched-up' for the replay at Highbury and, from his knock-down, Peter Houseman gave Chelsea the lead. However, the Gunners went on to win 2-1 with the assistance of a dubious penalty decision.

The following two league campaigns saw Bill net 13 times in 38 appearances that were punctuated by many absences due to injuries. His last goal for Chelsea in that campaign came in a season which saw Chelsea relegated from the top flight coming in an embarrassing 1-7 reverse at Molineux.

Whilst season 75/76 is one Blues supporters will wish to forget, Bill did weigh-in with 7 more goals from 21 starts including our first of the campaign at Roker Park from some 25 yards. However, it must be noted that he was again dismissed in a home draw with Bristol City after heading Chelsea in front, being cautioned for dissent upon the stroke of half-time and then receiving his marching orders for tripping the visiting goalkeeper!

In November 1975, Bill was again dismissed at Bristol Rovers after a similar altercation to that at Sheffield Wednesday. On this occasion, he appeared to attempt to return to the field of play in swirling fog – but was spotted by the officials and banished once more.

In a fixture with Luton Town at the Bridge on Good Friday 1976, Peter Bonetti sustained a dislocated finger with the score at 1-1 early in the second half and Bill agreed to become custodian of the gloves. A few minutes later, he saved bravely at the feet of Luton's Ron Futcher. Bill felt that the challenge he had sustained was not by fair means and in a moment of madness aimed a kick at his grounded opponent.

Whilst the crowd assumed that the the normal outcome would transpire, Bill remained on the pitch merely receiving a ticking off from the referee! Garner unfortunately did not play any part in the successful promotion season of 1976/77, again due to injury.

However, Bill wrote his name into Chelsea folklore when he netted the winner after only 90 seconds at Old Trafford on 17 September 1977 after 21 months out of the limelight.

He also made a marked contribution in the third round 4-2 FA Cup victory over Liverpool in January 1978 notably for two assists for Clive Walker. Bill's last appearance came in a 0-1 reverse at Derby on 7 October 1978 and shortly afterwards he was released by the club and joined Cambridge United, a very colourful contribution having been made in his time with Chelsea.

IAN HUTCHINSON

Ian 'Hutch' Hutchinson joined Chelsea from Cambridge United in the summer of 1968 for a bargain fee of £2,500, with an agreement that another £2,500 would be paid should he complete twelve first-team games.

Ian himself admitted that his progress to becoming a professional had been somewhat laboured as he did not join any football youth academy and had not even appeared consistently for his school sides and also when he did he played as a defender. Chelsea manager Dave Sexton handed Hutch his debut in a League Cup tie at Derby County on 2 October 1968.

Having grown up in Burton, Staffordshire – some 11-miles away from Derby's Baseball Ground – many of Ian's family and friends were witness to his first outing where, although the Blues were humbled 3-1, he gave a very good account of himself.

Derby were on the verge of greatness led by Scottish captain Dave Mackay who was quick to acknowledge that the youngster had given his defence a thorough examination. A crowd of over 34,000 provided record gate receipts of £10,116.

The following Saturday saw Ian appear at Stamford Bridge for the first time against Ipswich Town, who took an early lead through former England centre forward Ray Crawford. A few minutes, later Hutch retrieved the ball from the West Stand benches and launched the first of his legendary long throws.

The crowd were astounded by this effort as was Ipswich captain Bill Baxter who proceeded to head past his own keeper for the equaliser! Hutch was also prominent in the approach play resulting in further goals for John Hollins and Alan Birchenall securing a 3-1 victory.

Ian though, would have to bide his time before becoming a regular in the side as Tommy Baldwin returned from injury and began another spell of goal poaching, netting seven times in the next nine fixtures. However, injuries to team mates gave Hutch his first FA Cup outing in a fourth round replay against Preston North End at the Bridge on 29 January 1969.

Ian took his chance with gusto netting with a towering header in the first-half. Alan Birchenall added a second but, with some 12-minutes left, floodlight failure saw the match abandoned much to the disappointment of the 44,000 crowd.

Hutch watched on at the rearranged game the following Monday afternoon when 36,522 witnessed injury-time goals from David Webb and Charlie Cooke rescue a 2-1 win.

After a disappointing exit in the quarterfinal of the FA Cup to West Bromwich Albion, long-term injuries to strikers Baldwin and Birchenall saw Hutch given the number-nine shirt for the remaining 11 games with him netting on six occasions.

Notable feats among these games included scoring at Stamford Bridge in a 3-2 victory over reigning European Cup holders Manchester United and also giving the present England centre half, Brian Labone, a torrid evening when netting in a 2-1 win at Goodison Park.

Ian maintained the centre-forward berth at the start of the 1969/70 season, netting in a 1-4 reverse at Liverpool on the opening day. Hutch also netted the winner against Ipswich Town in Chelsea's first home fixture before sustaining an injury in the next match versus West Ham.

In the time Ian had been establishing himself as a bustling front runner, Peter Osgood had been excelling in the midfield wearing the number-four shirt.

When Hutch returned to action in November, Dave Sexton handed him the number-ten shirt alongside Ossie at nine. The rest as they say 'is history'.
A prolific partnership came into place culminating in Chelsea's first FA Cup.

Osgood netted in every round, a total of eight with Hutch weighing in with another six including the 86th minute equaliser in the Wembley final against Leeds United. However, Ian will be remembered by football fans worldwide for the immense throw that provided David Webb with the headed winner in the replay at Old Trafford. Indeed, well before this time Chelsea supporters had taken to anticipating any possible throw-ins within the attacking half of the field with chants of, "IAN-IAN HUTCHINSON!"

Ian began season 1970-71 where he had signed-off, netting with two headers in the opening game of the season against Derby County at Stamford Bridge.

Unfortunately, a series of injuries limited his appearances for the rest of the season and, after sustaining a twisted knee at Southampton at the end of February Hutch's season was brought to a premature end.

Ian had netted in both legs of Chelsea's 6-2 aggregate win over Aris Salonika in the first round of the European Cup Winners' Cup and returned to Greece with the team for the final in Athens in May.

Whilst obviously disappointed not to be involved in the final, Hutch delighted many of Chelsea's travelling supporters when spotted at many of the tourist attractions by posing for pictures and providing autographs.

Sadly, Ian did not make a first team appearance during the 1971/72 season and indeed did not return to the side until 9 December 1972 when bringing the house down with two strikes in a 3-1 win over Norwich City at the Bridge.

Alas, Hutch would only make two more appearances before succumbing to yet another long-term injury.

Similarly, in a further injury-plagued season 1973/74, Ian netted three times from ten league appearances. During this time, team-mates Peter Osgood and Alan Hudson departed the club after well documented disagreements with manager Dave Sexton.

Whilst Hutch started and finished the 1974/75 season which saw Chelsea relegated, his appearances numbered only 21 yielding seven goals.

Ian had really toiled alone upfront during this season unable to forge any partnership with either Chris Garland or Bill Garner, who themselves suffered long periods on the sidelines due to their own injuries.

Again, another injury ravaged season back in Division Two saw Hutch score three times in 18 appearances, with his last outing being at home to West Bromwich Albion on 31 January 1976.

The statistics make good reading, the striker scoring a total of 58 goals from 137 games in a career blighted by many serious injuries and brave comebacks. Often, during his periods of incapacity Hutch helped out in the club souvenir shop – a Portakabin in the Shed End forecourt. Many young supporters were in awe when receiving their merchandise from a true Chelsea hero.

Upon retirement from the game, Hutch put his culinary skills to the test at the The Union Inn, a public house which he had acquired with Peter Osgood.

It is well documented that this partnership was not as successful as that enjoyed upon the playing field but, nevertheless, many Chelsea supporters headed there to recount the many victories they had gladly witnessed over the years and drink with the boys.

The statistics will never bear out Hutch's bravery. When recounting his time with Chelsea FC for the purposes of this book, a former teammate of Hutch – Graham Wilkins – remembered an afternoon reserve encounter at the Dell, Southampton where Ian was endeavouring to return to full fitness. Wilkins said, "Hutch told me to put in a good cross near their keeper as he felt he had the beating of him in any aerial challenge" He continued, "I duly obliged but the keeper bludgeoned into Hutch breaking his nose. We took one look at him and told him he had better get off to hospital" Hutch apparently refused saying he would only leave after obtaining retribution for the challenge on him.

Hutchinson told Wilkins, "Put another one in and I'll have him!" This time after a mid-air collision Hutch fell to the ground – and sustained a broken elbow!

There was never a braver player who wore the Chelsea Blue and left us all too early when passing away in 2002.

COMPENDIUM OF RESULTS
Eddie McCreadie Chelsea manager

1974-75 SEASON

Tottenham Hotspur (0) 2 Chelsea (0) 0

Date:	Saturday, 19 April 1975
Competition:	Football League Division 1 Position 21
Venue:	White Hart Lane
Attendance:	51,064
Referee:	Jack K Taylor (Wolverhampton)
Spurs	Jennings, Kinnear, Knowles, Beal, Osgood, Naylor, Conn, Perryman, Jones, Duncan, Neighbour
Scorers	Perryman 57, Conn 74
Booked	Knowles
Sub Not Used	Chivers
Manager	Terry Neill
Chelsea	1 John Phillips, 2 Gary Locke, 3 John Sparrow, 4 Ian Britton, 5 Micky Droy, 6 Ron Harris, 7 David Hay, 8 Ray Wilkins, 9 Teddy Maybank, 10 Ian Hutchinson, 11 Charlie Cooke
Booked	Locke 4
Sub Not Used	12 Steve Kember
Debut Players	Teddy Maybank

Chelsea (1) 1 Sheffield United (0) 1

Date:	Wednesday, 23 April 1975
Competition:	Football League Division 1 Position 21
Venue:	Stamford Bridge
Attendance:	23,380
Referee:	Ron Crabb (Exeter)
Chelsea	1 John Phillips, 2 Gary Locke (12 Bill Garner 67), 3 John Sparrow, 4 Ian Britton, 5 Micky Droy, 6 Ron Harris, 7 David Hay, 8 Ray Wilkins, 9 Teddy Maybank, 10 Ian Hutchinson, 11 Charlie Cooke
Scorer	Maybank 6
Sheffield United	Brown, Badger, Bradford, Eddy, Colquhoun, Flynn, Woodward, Speight, Dearden (Garbett 75), Currie, Field
Scorer	Eddy 76
Manager	Ken Furphy

Chelsea (0) 1 Everton (0) 1

Date:	Saturday, 26 April 1975
Competition:	Football League Division 1 Position 20
Venue:	Stamford Bridge
Attendance:	28,432
Referee:	Peter Reeves (Leicester)
Chelsea	1 John Phillips, 2 David Hay, 3 John Sparrow, 4 Ian Britton, 5 Marvin Hinton, 6 Ron Harris, 7 Steve Kember, 8 Ray Wilkins, 9 Teddy Maybank, 10 Ian Hutchinson, 11 Charlie Cooke
Scorer	Wilkins 65
Sub Not Used	12 Bill Garner
Final Appearances	Marvin Hinton, Steve Kember
Everton	Davies, Bernard, Clements, Buckley, Kenyon, Hurst, Jones, Lyons, Latchford, Smallman, Pearson
Scorer	Latchford 70
Sub Not Used	Telfer
Manager	Billy Bingham

1975-76 SEASON

Sunderland (1) 2 Chelsea (1) 1

Date:	Saturday, 16 August 1975
Competition:	Football League Division 2 Position 16
Venue:	Roker Park
Attendance:	28,689
Referee:	Jack Rice (Leyland)
Sunderland	Swinburne, Ashurst, Bolton, Longhorn, Clarke, Moncur, Kerr, Gibb (Holden 46), Halom, Robson, Porterfield
Scorers	Robson 44, Longhorn 65
Booked	Halom
Manager	Bob Stokoe
Chelsea	1 Steve Sherwood, 2 Graham Wilkins, 3 John Sparrow, 4 Garry Stanley, 5 Micky Droy, 6 John Dempsey, 7 Ian Britton, 8 Ray Wilkins, 9 Teddy Maybank, 10 Bill Garner, 11 Charlie Cooke
Scorer	Garner 27
Booked	Garner
Sub Not Used	12 Ken Swain
Debut Players	Garry Stanley
Manager	Eddie McCreadie

West Bromwich Albion (0) 0 Chelsea (0) 0

Date:	Wednesday, 20 August 1975
Competition:	Football League Division 2 Position 14
Venue:	The Hawthorns
Attendance:	18,014
Referee:	Tony R Glasson (Salisbury)
WBA	Osborne, Nisbet, Wilson, Cantello, Wile, Robertson, Trewick, Brown, Hurst, Giles, Johnston
Sent Off	Cantello 16
Manager	Johnny Giles
Chelsea	1 Steve Sherwood, 2 Graham Wilkins, 3 John Sparrow, 4 Garry Stanley, 5 Micky Droy, 6 John Dempsey, 7 Ian Britton, 8 Ray Wilkins, 9 Teddy Maybank, 10 Bill Garner (12 Ken Swain 71), 11 Charlie Cooke
Booked	Graham Wilkins 75

Chelsea (1) 3 Carlisle United (0) 1

Date:	Saturday, 23 August 1975
Competition:	Football League Division 2 Position 9
Venue:	Stamford Bridge
Attendance:	19,165
Referee:	Alex R Lees (Street)
Chelsea	1 Steve Sherwood, 2 Graham Wilkins, 3 John Sparrow, 4 Brian Bason, 5 Micky Droy, 6 John Dempsey, 7 Ian Britton (12 Ron Harris), 8 Ray Wilkins, 9 Teddy Maybank, 10 Ken Swain, 11 Charlie Cooke
Scorers	Maybank 27, Maybank 54, Bason 69
Carlisle United	Burleigh, Carr, Gorman, O'Neill, Green, Parker, Martin, Train, Owen, Laidlaw, Clarke (Barry)
Scorer	Barry 70
Booked	Carr
Manager	Alan Ashman

Chelsea (2) 3 Oxford United (1) 1

Date:	Wednesday, 27 August 1975
Competition:	Football League Division 2 Position 2
Venue:	Stamford Bridge
Attendance:	22,841
Referee:	Bert Newsome (Broseley)
Chelsea	1 Steve Sherwood, 2 Graham Wilkins, 3 John Sparrow, 4 Brian Bason, 5 Micky Droy, 6 John Dempsey, 7 Ron Harris, 8 Ray Wilkins, 9 Teddy Maybank, 10 Ken Swain, 11 Charlie Cooke
Scorers	Ray Wilkins 9, Ray Wilkins 23, Swain 76
Sub Not Used	12 Ray Lewington
Oxford United	Burton, Aylott, Shuker, Lowe, C Clarke, Jeffrey, Houseman, Tait, D Clarke (McGrogan), Gibbons, Heron
Scorer	McGrogan 3
Manager	Gerry Summers

Luton Town (1) 3 Chelsea (0) 0

Date:	Saturday, 30 August 1975
Competition:	Football League Division 2 Position 6
Venue:	Kenilworth Road
Attendance:	19,024
Referee:	Eric A Read
Luton Town	Barber, John Ryan, Buckley, Anderson, Faulkner, P Futcher, King, Alston, R Futcher, West (Chambers), Aston
Scorers	Anderson 27, Buckley 46 (Pen), R Futcher 57
Booked	Buckley
Sent Off	Aston 72
Manager	Harry Haslam
Chelsea	1 Steve Sherwood, 2 Graham Wilkins (12 Ron Harris 62), 3 John Sparrow, 4 Brian Bason, 5 Micky Droy, 6 John Dempsey, 7 Ian Britton, 8 Ray Wilkins, 9 Teddy Maybank, 10 Ken Swain, 11 Charlie Cooke
Booked	Cooke 6, Droy 54, Britton 72

Chelsea (0) 0 Nottingham Forest (0) 0

Date:	Saturday, 6 September 1975
Competition:	Football League Division 2 Position 8
Venue:	Stamford Bridge
Attendance:	21,023
Referee:	William J Gow (Swansea)
Chelsea	1 Steve Sherwood, 2 David Hay, 3 John Sparrow, 4 Garry Stanley, 5 Micky Droy, 6 John Dempsey, 7 Ron Harris, 8 Ray Wilkins, 9 Teddy Maybank, 10 Ken Swain, 11 Charlie Cooke
Sub Not Used	12 Brian Bason
Notts Forest	Middleton, Anderson, Gunn, Clark, Chapman, Richardson, Curran, McGovern, O'Hare, Bowyer, Robertson
Manager	Brian Clough

Crewe Alexandra (1) 1 Chelsea (0) 0

Date: Wednesday, 10 September 1975
Competition: League Cup Round 2
Venue: Gresty Road
Attendance: 6,723
Referee: Harold Davey (Mansfield)
Crewe Alexandra   Crudgington, Lowry, Evans, Lugg, Bowles, Nicholls, Davies, Bevan, Purdie, Nelson, Humphreys
Scorer   Humphreys 37 (Pen)
Manager   Harry Gregg
Chelsea   1 Steve Sherwood, 2 Ron Harris, 3 John Sparrow, 4 David Hay, 5 Micky Droy, 6 John Dempsey, 7 Ian Britton, 8 Ray Wilkins, 9 Garry Stanley, 10 Ken Swain (12 Brian Bason), 11 Bill Garner

Oldham Athletic (1) 2 Chelsea (1) 1

Date: Saturday, 13 September 1975
Competition: Football League Division 2 Position 11
Venue: Boundary Park
Attendance: 10,406
Referee: Colin Seel (Carlisle)
Oldham Athletic   Ogden, Branaghan, Whittle, Blair (Robins), Hicks, Holt, Bell, Chapman, Jones, Wood, Groves
Scorers   Wood 14, Jones 50
Manager   Jimmy Frizzell
Chelsea   1 Steve Sherwood, 2 Ron Harris, 3 David Hay, 4 Garry Stanley, 5 Micky Droy, 6 John Dempsey, 7 Ian Britton, 8 Ray Wilkins, 9 Tommy Langley, 10 Ken Swain, 11 Bill Garner
Scorer   Wilkins 15
Sub Not Used   12 Brian Bason

Chelsea (1) 1 Bristol City (1) 1

Date:	Saturday, 20 September 1975
Competition:	Football League Division 2 Position 9
Venue:	Stamford Bridge
Attendance:	17,661
Referee:	Gordon C Kew (Amersham)
Chelsea	1 Steve Sherwood, 2 Ron Harris, 3 David Hay, 4 Garry Stanley, 5 Micky Droy, 6 John Dempsey, 7 Ian Britton, 8 Ray Wilkins, 9 Brian Bason, 10 Ian Hutchinson, 11 Bill Garner
Scorer	Garner 25
Booked	Droy, Hay, Hutchinson, Garner 44
Sent Off	Garner 72
Sub Not Used	12 Tommy Langley
Manager	Eddie McCreadie
Bristol City	Cashley, Gillies, Drysdale, Gow, Collier, Merrick, Tainton, Ritchie, Mann, Cheeseley, Brolly
Scorer	Cheeseley 42
Booked	Merrick 84
Manager	Alan Dicks

Portsmouth (1) 1 Chelsea (1) 1

Date:	Tuesday, 23 September 1975
Competition:	Football League Division 2 Position 8
Venue:	Fratton Park
Attendance:	16,144
Portsmouth	Lloyd, Roberts, Cahill, Piper, Went, Hand, McGuinness (Marinello 57), Reynolds, Graham, Wilson, Mellows
Scorer	Reynolds 24
Manager	Ian St John
Chelsea	1 Steve Sherwood, 2 Ron Harris, 3 David Hay, 4 Garry Stanley, 5 Micky Droy, 6 John Dempsey, 7 Ian Britton, 8 Ray Wilkins, 9 Brian Bason, 10 Tommy Langley, 11 Bill Garner
Scorer	Garner 37
Sub Not Used	12 Steve Finnieston

EDDIE MCCREADIE'S BLUE AND WHITE ARMY

Fulham (0) 2 Chelsea (0) 0

Date:	Saturday, 27 September 1975
Competition:	Football League Division 2 Position 14
Venue:	Craven Cottage
Attendance:	22,986
Referee:	Michael Lowe (Sheffield)
Fulham	Mellor, Cutbush, Strong, Mullery, Howe, Moore, Lloyd, Conway, Busby, Slough, Barrett
Scorers	Howe 48, Conway 71
Manager	Alec Stock
Chelsea	1 Steve Sherwood, 2 Ron Harris, 3 David Hay, 4 Garry Stanley, 5 Micky Droy, 6 John Dempsey, 7 Ian Britton, 8 Ray Wilkins, 9 Brian Bason (12 Steve Wicks), 10 Ian Hutchinson, 11 Tommy Langley
Booked	Bason, Harris, Hay, Stanley

Chelsea (0) 0 York City (0) 0

Date:	Saturday, 4 October 1975
Competition:	Football League Division 2 Position 11
Venue:	Stamford Bridge
Attendance:	15,323
Referee:	Alan Robinson (Portsmouth)
Chelsea	1 Steve Sherwood, 2 Ron Harris, 3 John Sparrow, 4 David Hay, 5 Micky Droy, 6 John Dempsey, 7 Ian Britton, 8 Ray Wilkins, 9 Brian Bason, 10 Ian Hutchinson, 11 Tommy Langley
Sub Not Used	12 Teddy Maybank
Penalty Missed	Wilkins 36 (Saved)
York City	Crawford, Stone, Downing, Cave, Swallow, Topping, Pollard, Wann, Seal, Jones, McMordie
Manager	Wilf McGuinness

Southampton (1) 4 Chelsea (0) 1

Date:	Saturday, 11 October 1975
Competition:	Football League Division 2 Position 12
Venue:	The Dell
Attendance:	21,227
Referee:	Ray Toseland (Kettering)
Southampton	Middleton, Rodrigues, Peach, Holmes, Bennett, Blyth, Fisher, Channon, Osgood, McCalliog, Stokes
Scorers	Channon 20 (Pen), Stokes 73, Holmes 76, Channon 89
Manager	Lawrie McMenemy
Chelsea	1 Steve Sherwood, 2 Gary Locke, 3 Ron Harris, 4 David Hay, 5 Micky Droy, 6 John Dempsey, 7 Ian Britton, 8 Ray Wilkins, 9 Brian Bason (12 Tommy Langley 74), 10 Ian Hutchinson, 11 Bill Garner
Scorer	Wilkins 90
Booked	Hay 79
Final Appearances	Steve Sherwood

Chelsea (0) 2 Blackpool (0) 0

Date:	Saturday, 18 October 1975
Competition:	Football League Division 2 Position 12
Venue:	Stamford Bridge
Attendance:	16,924
Referee:	Tom H Reynolds (Swansea)
Chelsea	1 Peter Bonetti, 2 Gary Locke, 3 Ron Harris, 4 David Hay, 5 Micky Droy, 6 John Dempsey, 7 Ian Britton, 8 Ray Wilkins, 9 Teddy Maybank (12 Tommy Langley 78), 10 Ian Hutchinson, 11 Ken Swain
Scorers	Wilkins 78 (Pen), Langley 90
Blackpool	Wood, Curtis, Harrison, Hart, Alcock, Hatton, Walsh, Suddick, Ainscow, Moore, Bentley
Manager	Harry Potts

Blackburn Rovers (0) 1 Chelsea (1) 1

Date:	Saturday, 25 October 1975
Competition:	Football League Division 2 Position 12
Venue:	Ewood Park
Attendance:	12,128
Referee:	Jack K Taylor (Wolverhampton)
Blackburn Rovers	Jones, Wilkinson, Wood, Metcalfe, Waddington, Fazackerley, Beamish, Oates, Hindson, Svarc, Parkes
Scorer	Metcalfe 58
Manager	Jim Smith
Chelsea	1 Peter Bonetti, 2 Gary Locke (12 Tommy Langley 67), 3 Ron Harris, 4 David Hay, 5 Micky Droy, 6 John Dempsey, 7 Ian Britton, 8 Ray Wilkins, 9 Teddy Maybank, 10 Ian Hutchinson, 11 Bill Garner
Scorer	Hutchinson 32
Booked	Droy 10

Chelsea (1) 2 Plymouth Argyle (0) 2

Date:	Saturday, 1 November 1975
Competition:	Football League Division 2 Position 14
Venue:	Stamford Bridge
Attendance:	20,096
Referee:	Derek W Civil (Birmingham)
Chelsea	1 Peter Bonetti, 2 Gary Locke, 3 Ron Harris, 4 Garry Stanley, 5 Micky Droy, 6 John Dempsey, 7 Ian Britton, 8 Ray Wilkins, 9 Teddy Maybank, 10 Ian Hutchinson, 11 Bill Garner
Scorers	Britton 4, Wilkins 58
Sub Not Used	12 Tommy Langley
Plymouth Argyle	Aleksic, Darke, Burrows, Green, Rioch, Delve, Randall, Johnson, Mariner, Rafferty, McAuley
Scorers	Mariner 70, Mariner 75
Sub Not Used	Foster
Manager	Tony Waiters

Hull City (1) 1 Chelsea (1) 2

Date:	Saturday, 8 November 1975
Competition:	Football League Division 2 Position 12
Venue:	Boothferry Park
Attendance:	9,097
Referee:	Roy Capey (Madeley Heath)
Hull City	Wealands, Banks, DeVries, Galvin, Croft, Haigh, Grimes, Gibson, Stewart, Wagstaff, Greenwood
Scorer	Grimes 17
Sub Not Used	Wood
Manager	John Kaye
Chelsea	1 Peter Bonetti, 2 Gary Locke, 3 Ron Harris, 4 Garry Stanley, 5 Micky Droy, 6 John Dempsey, 7 Ian Britton, 8 Ray Wilkins, 9 Teddy Maybank, 10 Ian Hutchinson, 11 Bill Garner
Scorers	Britton 44, Hutchinson 57
Booked	Garner
Sub Not Used	12 David Hay

Chelsea (0) 2 Notts County (0) 0

Date:	Saturday, 15 November 1975
Competition:	Football League Division 2 Position 10
Venue:	Stamford Bridge
Attendance:	18,229
Referee:	Peter Walters (Bridgwater)
Chelsea	1 Peter Bonetti, 2 Gary Locke, 3 Ron Harris, 4 Garry Stanley, 5 Micky Droy, 6 John Dempsey, 7 Ian Britton, 8 Ray Wilkins, 9 Teddy Maybank, 10 Bill Garner, 11 Ian Hutchinson
Scorers	Garner 47, Wilkins 59 (Pen)
Sub Not Used	12 David Hay
Notts County	McManus, Richards, O'Brien, Probert, Needham, Stubbs, Carter, McVay, Bradd, Mann, Scanlon
Manager	Ron Fenton

Blackpool (0) 0 Chelsea (1) 2

Date:	Saturday, 22 November 1975
Competition:	Football League Division 2 Position 9
Venue:	Bloomfield Road
Attendance:	8,595
Referee:	Peter N Willis (Newfield)
Blackpool	Wood, Hatton, Harrison, Hart, Suddaby, Moore, Ronson (Alcock 68), Suddick, Walsh, Ainscow, Tong
Booked	Walsh
Manager	Harry Potts
Chelsea	1 Peter Bonetti, 2 Gary Locke, 3 Ron Harris, 4 Garry Stanley, 5 Micky Droy, 6 John Dempsey, 7 Ian Britton, 8 Ray Wilkins, 9 Teddy Maybank, 10 Ian Hutchinson, 11 Bill Garner (12 David Hay)
Scorers	Droy 44, Maybank 80
Booked	Britton, Garner, Stanley

Bristol Rovers (0) 1 Chelsea (0) 2

Date:	Saturday, 29 November 1975
Competition:	Football League Division 2 Position 8
Venue:	Eastville
Attendance:	16,277
Referee:	George E Flint (Derby)
Bristol Rovers	Eadie, Williams, Parsons, Day, Taylor, Smith, Stanton, Prince, Warboys (Stephens 26), Bannister, Fearnley
Scorer	Williams 74
Booked	Parsons 89
Manager	Don Megson
Chelsea	1 Peter Bonetti, 2 Gary Locke, 3 Ron Harris, 4 Garry Stanley, 5 Micky Droy, 6 John Dempsey, 7 Ian Britton, 8 Ray Wilkins, 9 Teddy Maybank, 10 Ian Hutchinson, 11 Bill Garner
Scorers	Maybank 49, Hutchinson 55
Booked	Stanley 47, Garner 77, Hutchinson 88
Sent Off	Garner 90
Sub Not Used	12 David Hay

Chelsea (0) 0 Bolton Wanderers (1) 1

Date:	Saturday, 6 December 1975
Competition:	Football League Division 2 Position 10
Venue:	Stamford Bridge
Attendance:	20,896
Referee:	Roger B Kirkpatrick (Leicester)
Chelsea	1 Peter Bonetti, 2 Gary Locke, 3 Ron Harris, 4 Garry Stanley, 5 Micky Droy, 6 John Dempsey, 7 Ian Britton, 8 Ray Wilkins, 9 Teddy Maybank, 10 Ian Hutchinson, 11 Charlie Cooke
Booked	Droy
Sub Not Used	12 David Hay
Penalty Missed	Wilkins 88 (Saved)
Bolton Wanderers	Siddall, Ritson, Dunne, Greaves, P Jones, Allardyce, Waldron, Whatmore, G Jones, Reid, Thompson
Scorer	Greaves 15
Manager	Ian Greaves

Carlisle United (1) 2 Chelsea (1) 1

Date:	Saturday, 13 December 1975
Competition:	Football League Division 2 Position 12
Venue:	Brunton Park
Attendance:	8,065
Referee:	Les Hayes (Doncaster)
Carlisle United	Ross, Carr, Gorman, Barry, Green, Parker, McVitie, Train, Clarke, McCartney, Martin
Scorers	McCartney 44, McCartney 73
Manager	Dick Young
Chelsea	1 Peter Bonetti, 2 Gary Locke, 3 Ron Harris, 4 David Hay, 5 Micky Droy, 6 John Dempsey, 7 Ian Britton, 8 Ray Wilkins, 9 Teddy Maybank, 10 Ian Hutchinson, 11 Charlie Cooke
Scorer	Wilkins 16
Booked	Hay
Sub Not Used	12 Ken Swain

Chelsea (0) 1 Sunderland (0) 0

Date:	Saturday, 20 December 1975
Competition:	Football League Division 2 Position 11
Venue:	Stamford Bridge
Attendance:	22,806
Referee:	Lester C Shapter (Paignton)
Chelsea	1 Peter Bonetti, 2 Gary Locke, 3 Ron Harris, 4 Garry Stanley, 5 Micky Droy, 6 John Dempsey, 7 Ian Britton, 8 Ray Wilkins, 9 Teddy Maybank, 10 Ian Hutchinson (12 Tommy Langley 80), 11 Ken Swain
Scorer	Britton 64
Booked	Harris 90
Sunderland	Montgomery, Malone, Bolton, Towers, Clarke, Moncur, Kerr, Finney, Halom, Robson, Porterfield (Holden 65)
Manager	Bob Stokoe

Orient (1) 3 Chelsea (0) 1

Date:	Friday, 26 December 1975
Competition:	Football League Division 2 Position 11
Venue:	Brisbane Road
Attendance:	15,509
Referee:	Alf Grey (Great Yarmouth)
Orient	Jackson, Fisher, Grealish, Bennett, Hoadley, Walley, Cunningham, Roeder, Bullock, Possee, Queen
Scorers	Possee 38, Bennett 82, Cunningham 87
Manager	George Petchey
Chelsea	1 Peter Bonetti, 2 Gary Locke, 3 Ron Harris, 4 Garry Stanley, 5 Micky Droy, 6 John Dempsey, 7 Ian Britton, 8 Ray Wilkins, 9 Teddy Maybank, 10 Ian Hutchinson (12 John Sparrow), 11 Ken Swain
Scorer	Maybank 72

Chelsea (0) 2 Charlton Athletic (2) 3

Date:	Saturday, 27 December 1975
Competition:	Football League Division 2 Position 13
Venue:	Stamford Bridge
Attendance:	25,367
Referee:	Ron Crabb (Exeter)
Chelsea	1 Peter Bonetti, 2 Gary Locke, 3 Ron Harris, 4 Garry Stanley, 5 Micky Droy, 6 John Dempsey (12 Tommy Langley), 7 Ian Britton, 8 Ray Wilkins, 9 Teddy Maybank, 10 Charlie Cooke, 11 Ken Swain
Scorers	Swain 48, Britton 66
Final Appearances	John Dempsey
Charlton Athletic	Tutt, Curtis, Warman, Bowman, Giles, Young, Powell, Hales, Flanagan, Hunt, Peacock
Scorers	Warman 29, Hales 44, Hales 70
Manager	Andy Nelson

Chelsea (1) 1 Bristol Rovers (1) 1

Date:	Thursday, 1 January 1976
Competition:	F.A. Cup Round 3
Venue:	Stamford Bridge
Attendance:	35,226
Referee:	William J Gow (Swansea)
Chelsea	1 Peter Bonetti, 2 Gary Locke, 3 Ron Harris, 4 Garry Stanley, 5 Micky Droy, 6 Steve Wicks, 7 Ian Britton, 8 Ray Wilkins, 9 Teddy Maybank (12 Charlie Cooke 82), 10 Bill Garner, 11 Ken Swain
Scorer	Garner 35
Bristol Rovers	Eadie, Jacobs, Parsons, Bater, Day, Smith (Staniforth 10), Stephens, Williams, Warboys, Bannister, Evans
Scorer	Warboys 18
Manager	Don Megson

Bristol Rovers (0) 0 Chelsea (0) 1

Date:	Saturday, 3 January 1976
Competition:	F.A. Cup Round 3 (replay)
Venue:	Eastville
Attendance:	13,939
Referee:	William J Gow (Swansea)
Bristol Rovers	Eadie, Bater, Parsons, Aitken, Day, Williams, Stephens, Fearnley, Warboys (Staniforth 65), Bannister, Stanton
Manager	Don Megson
Chelsea	1 Peter Bonetti, 2 Gary Locke, 3 Ron Harris, 4 Garry Stanley (12 Bill Garner), 5 Micky Droy, 6 Steve Wicks, 7 Ian Britton, 8 Ray Wilkins, 9 Teddy Maybank, 10 David Hay, 11 Ken Swain
Scorer	Swain 77

Chelsea (0) 0 Oldham Athletic (1) 3

Date:	Saturday, 10 January 1976
Competition:	Football League Division 2 Position 15
Venue:	Stamford Bridge
Attendance:	16,464
Referee:	Terry P Bosi (Wolverhampton)
Chelsea	1 Peter Bonetti, 2 Gary Locke, 3 Ron Harris, 4 David Hay, 5 Micky Droy, 6 Steve Wicks (12 Charlie Cooke), 7 Ian Britton, 8 Ray Wilkins, 9 Teddy Maybank, 10 Ian Hutchinson, 11 Bill Garner
Booked	Harris
Oldham Athletic	Platt, Wood, Whittle, Bell, Edwards, Hicks, Blair, Shaw, Young, Chapman, Groves
Scorers	Young 44, Shaw 51, Young 70
Manager	Jimmy Frizzell

Nottingham Forest (1) 1 Chelsea (1) 3

Date:	Saturday, 17 January 1976
Competition:	Football League Division 2 Position 12
Venue:	City Ground
Attendance:	14,172
Referee:	Robert Matthewson (Bolton)
Notts Forest	Wells, O'Kane, Gunn, Clark, Cottam, Richardson, Curran, Bowyer, O'Hare, Butlin, Robertson
Scorer	Bowyer 12
Manager	Brian Clough
Chelsea	1 Peter Bonetti, 2 Gary Locke, 3 Ron Harris, 4 Charlie Cooke, 5 Steve Wicks, 6 David Hay, 7 Ian Britton, 8 Ray Wilkins, 9 Teddy Maybank, 10 Ian Hutchinson, 11 Bill Garner
Scorers	Garner 15, Wilkins 80, Hutchinson 87
Sub Not Used	12 Graham Wilkins

York City (0) 0 Chelsea (1) 2

Date:	Saturday, 24 January 1976
Competition:	F.A. Cup Round 4
Venue:	Bootham Crescent
Attendance:	9,591
Referee:	Ken W Baker (Rugby)
York City	Crawford, Scott, Woodward, Cave, Swallow, Topping, Hosker, Hunter, Seal, Hinch (McMordie), Pollard
Manager	Wilf McGuinness
Chelsea	1 Peter Bonetti, 2 Gary Locke, 3 Ron Harris, 4 Charlie Cooke, 5 Steve Wicks, 6 David Hay, 7 Ian Britton, 8 Ray Wilkins, 9 Teddy Maybank, 10 Ian Hutchinson, 11 Bill Garner
Scorers	Garner 15, Hutchinson 67
Sub Not Used	12 Graham Wilkins

Chelsea (1) 1 West Bromwich Albion (1) 2

Date:	Saturday, 31 January 1976
Competition:	Football League Division 2 Position 14
Venue:	Stamford Bridge
Attendance:	15,896
Referee:	PJ Richardson (Lincoln)
Chelsea	1 Peter Bonetti, 2 Gary Locke, 3 Ron Harris, 4 Charlie Cooke, 5 Steve Wicks, 6 David Hay, 7 Ian Britton, 8 Ray Wilkins, 9 Teddy Maybank, 10 Ian Hutchinson, 11 Bill Garner
Scorer	Britton 2
Sub Not Used	12 Ken Swain
Final Appearances	Ian Hutchinson
WBA	Osborne, Mulligan, Mayo, Robson, Wile, Robertson, T Brown, Martin, A Brown, Giles, Johnston
Scorers	Martin 27, T Brown 83
Manager	Johnny Giles

Oxford United (0) 1 Chelsea (0) 1

Date:	Saturday, 7 February 1976
Competition:	Football League Division 2 Position 12
Venue:	Manor Ground
Attendance:	11,162
Referee:	Brian Martin (Keyworth)
Oxford United	Burton, Taylor, Shuker, Lowe, C Clarke, Briggs, Houseman, Foley, D Clarke, McCulloch, Tait
Scorer	Tait 72
Manager	Mike Brown
Chelsea	1 Peter Bonetti, 2 Gary Locke, 3 Graham Wilkins, 4 Charlie Cooke, 5 Steve Wicks, 6 Ron Harris, 7 Ian Britton, 8 Ray Wilkins, 9 Teddy Maybank, 10 Ken Swain, 11 Bill Garner
Scorer	Garner 57
Booked	Harris 72
Sub Not Used	12 Garry Stanley

Chelsea (0) 2 Crystal Palace (2) 3

Date:	Saturday, 14 February 1976
Competition:	F.A. Cup Round 5
Venue:	Stamford Bridge
Attendance:	54,407
Referee:	Pat Partridge (Middlesbrough)
Chelsea	1 Peter Bonetti, 2 Gary Locke, 3 Ron Harris, 4 Charlie Cooke, 5 Micky Droy (12 David Hay 56), 6 Steve Wicks, 7 Ian Britton, 8 Ray Wilkins, 9 Teddy Maybank, 10 Ken Swain, 11 Bill Garner
Scorers	Wilkins 62, Wicks 71
Booked	Droy 42
Crystal Palace	Hammond, Wall, Cannon, Jeffries, Jump, Evans, Chatterton, Hinshelwood, Whittle, Swindlehurst, Taylor
Scorers	Chatterton 37, Taylor 40, Taylor 76
Sub Not Used	Holder
Manager	Malcolm Allison

Chelsea (0) 0 Hull City (0) 0

Date:	Wednesday, 18 February 1976
Competition:	Football League Division 2 Position 11
Venue:	Stamford Bridge
Attendance:	10,254
Referee:	Ken H Burns (Stourbridge)
Chelsea	1 Peter Bonetti, 2 Gary Locke, 3 Ron Harris, 4 Charlie Cooke, 5 Steve Wicks, 6 David Hay, 7 Ian Britton, 8 Ray Wilkins, 9 Steve Finnieston, 10 Ken Swain, 11 Bill Garner
Hull City	Wealands, Daniels, DeVries, Galvin, Croft, Roberts, Grimes, Lyall, Wood, Fletcher, Staniforth (Sunley)
Manager	John Kaye

Notts County (1) 3 Chelsea (2) 2

Date:	Saturday, 21 February 1976
Competition:	Football League Division 2 Position 15
Venue:	Meadow Lane
Attendance:	14,528
Referee:	George Courtney (Spenneymoor)
Notts County	McManus, Richards, O'Brien, Probert, Needham, Stubbs, Vinter, Sims, Bradd (Carter), Mann, Scanlon
Scorers	Scanlon 25 (Pen), Sims 59, Bradd 73
Manager	Ron Fenton
Chelsea	1 Peter Bonetti, 2 Gary Locke, 3 Ron Harris, 4 Garry Stanley (12 Ray Lewington), 5 Steve Wicks, 6 David Hay, 7 Ian Britton, 8 Ray Wilkins, 9 Steve Finnieston, 10 Ken Swain, 11 Charlie Cooke
Scorers	Stanley 13, Finnieston 39
Debut Players	Ray Lewington

Chelsea (2) 2 Portsmouth (0) 0

Date:	Wednesday, 25 February 1976
Competition:	Football League Division 2 Position 14
Venue:	Stamford Bridge
Attendance:	12,709
Referee:	Alan Porter (Bolton)
Chelsea	1 Peter Bonetti, 2 Gary Locke, 3 Ron Harris, 4 Garry Stanley, 5 Steve Wicks, 6 David Hay, 7 Ian Britton, 8 Ray Wilkins, 9 Steve Finnieston, 10 Ken Swain, 11 Charlie Cooke
Scorers	Cooke 26, Locke 35
Sub Not Used	12 Ray Lewington
Portsmouth	Lloyd, Lawler, Wilson, Macken, Went, Cahill, McGuinness, Piper, Busby, Graham, Mellows
Manager	Ian St John

415

Chelsea (1) 3 Blackburn Rovers (1) 1

Date:	Saturday, 28 February 1976
Competition:	Football League Division 2 Position 11
Venue:	Stamford Bridge
Attendance:	14,855
Referee:	Harold Davey (Mansfield)
Chelsea	1 Peter Bonetti, 2 Gary Locke, 3 Ron Harris, 4 Garry Stanley, 5 Steve Wicks, 6 David Hay, 7 Ian Britton, 8 Ray Wilkins (12 Tommy Langley 80), 9 Steve Finnieston, 10 Ken Swain, 11 Charlie Cooke
Scorers	Wilkins 34, Finnieston 49, Wilkins 62
Blackburn Rovers	Jones, Wilkinson, Bailey, Metcalfe, Fazackerley, Hawkins, Hird, Hoy (Kenyon), Oates, Parkes, Beamish
Scorer	Oates 13
Manager	Jim Smith

Plymouth Argyle (0) 0 Chelsea (1) 3

Date:	Saturday, 6 March 1976
Competition:	Football League Division 2 Position 9
Venue:	Home Park
Attendance:	20,638
Referee:	Alex J Hamil (Wolverhampton)
Plymouth Argyle	Furnell, Darke, Burrows, Sutton, Green, Horswill, Foster, Johnson, Pearson (Hardcastle 75), Rafferty, McAuley
Manager	Tony Waiters
Chelsea	1 Peter Bonetti, 2 Gary Locke, 3 Ron Harris, 4 Garry Stanley, 5 Steve Wicks, 6 David Hay, 7 Ian Britton, 8 Ray Wilkins, 9 Steve Finnieston, 10 Ken Swain, 11 Ray Lewington
Scorers	Stanley 24, Britton 46, Swain 56
Sub Not Used	12 John Sparrow

Chelsea (0) 1 Southampton (0) 1

Date:	Saturday, 13 March 1976
Competition:	Football League Division 2 Position 9
Venue:	Stamford Bridge
Attendance:	29,011
Referee:	Malcolm V Sinclair (Guildford)
Chelsea	1 Peter Bonetti, 2 Gary Locke (12 Bill Garner 6), 3 Ron Harris, 4 Garry Stanley, 5 Steve Wicks, 6 David Hay, 7 Ian Britton, 8 Ray Wilkins, 9 Steve Finnieston, 10 Ken Swain, 11 Ray Lewington
Scorer	Finnieston 62
Southampton	Turner, Rodrigues, Peach, Gilchrist, Blyth, Steele, Fisher, Channon, Osgood, McCalliog, Stokes
Scorer	Channon 61
Manager	Lawrie McMenemy

Chelsea (0) 0 Bristol Rovers (0) 0

Date:	Saturday, 20 March 1976
Competition:	Football League Division 2 Position 9
Venue:	Stamford Bridge
Attendance:	16,132
Referee:	HR Robinson (Norwich)
Chelsea	1 Peter Bonetti, 2 Ron Harris, 3 John Sparrow, 4 Garry Stanley, 5 Steve Wicks, 6 David Hay, 7 Ian Britton, 8 Ray Wilkins, 9 Steve Finnieston, 10 Ken Swain (12 Bill Garner 73), 11 Ray Lewington
Bristol Rovers	Eadie, Jacobs, Parsons, Day, Taylor, Smith (Evans), Stephens, Staniforth, Warboys, Bannister, Williams
Manager	Don Megson

Bolton Wanderers (0) 2 Chelsea (0) 1

Date:	Saturday, 27 March 1976
Competition:	Football League Division 2 Position 11
Venue:	Burnden Park
Attendance:	20,817
Referee:	Ray Tinkler (Boston)
Bolton Wanderers	Siddall, Nicholson, Dunne, Greaves, P Jones, Allardyce, Morgan, Whatmore, Byrom, Reid, Thompson
Scorers	Hay (O.G) 63, G Wilkins (O.G) 85
Manager	Ian Greaves
Chelsea	1 Peter Bonetti, 2 Graham Wilkins, 3 Ron Harris, 4 Garry Stanley, 5 Steve Wicks, 6 David Hay, 7 Ian Britton, 8 Ray Wilkins, 9 Bill Garner, 10 Ken Swain, 11 Ray Lewington
Scorer	Britton 50
Booked	Graham Wilkins, Wicks
Sub Not Used	12 John Dempsey

Chelsea (0) 0 Fulham (0) 0

Date:	Tuesday, 6 April 1976
Competition:	Football League Division 2 Position 12
Venue:	Stamford Bridge
Attendance:	23,605
Referee:	Tony R Glasson (Salisbury)
Chelsea	1 Peter Bonetti, 2 Ron Harris, 3 Graham Wilkins, 4 Garry Stanley, 5 Steve Wicks, 6 David Hay, 7 Ian Britton, 8 Ray Wilkins, 9 Bill Garner, 10 Ken Swain, 11 Ray Lewington
Sub Not Used	12 Steve Finnieston
Fulham	Mellor, James, Strong, Mullery, Lacy, Howe, Mitchell, Busby, Conway, Lloyd, Slough
Manager	Alec Stock

Bristol City (1) 2 Chelsea (1) 2

Date:	Saturday, 10 April 1976
Competition:	Football League Division 2 Position 11
Venue:	Ashton Gate
Attendance:	24,710
Referee:	John Hunting (Leicester)
Bristol City	Cashley, Sweeney, Drysdale, Gow, Collier, Merrick, Tainton, Ritchie, Gillies, Cheeseley, Whitehead (Mann 70)
Scorers	Ritchie 6, Ritchie 74
Manager	Alan Dicks
Chelsea	1 Peter Bonetti, 2 Graham Wilkins, 3 Ron Harris, 4 Garry Stanley, 5 Steve Wicks, 6 David Hay, 7 Ian Britton, 8 Ray Wilkins, 9 Steve Finnieston, 10 Ken Swain, 11 Ray Lewington
Scorers	Swain 43, Stanley 75
Sub Not Used	12 John Dempsey

Chelsea (1) 2 Luton Town (1) 2

Date:	Friday, 16 April 1976
Competition:	Football League Division 2 Position 11
Venue:	Stamford Bridge
Attendance:	19,878
Referee:	Lester C Shapter (Torquay)
Chelsea	1 Peter Bonetti (12 Bill Garner 40), 2 Ron Harris, 3 Graham Wilkins, 4 Garry Stanley, 5 Steve Wicks, 6 David Hay, 7 Ian Britton, 8 Ray Wilkins, 9 Steve Finnieston, 10 Ken Swain, 11 Ray Lewington
Scorers	Finnieston 32, Hay 53
Luton Town	Barber, Ryan, Buckley, Chambers, Price, P Futcher, Husband, Fuccillo, R Futcher, West, Aston
Scorers	Husband 12, Chambers 75
Manager	Harry Haslam

Chelsea (0) 0 Orient (1) 2

Date:	Saturday, 17 April 1976
Competition:	Football League Division 2 Position 11
Venue:	Stamford Bridge
Attendance:	17,679
Referee:	Clive Thomas (Treorchy)
Chelsea	1 John Phillips, 2 Ron Harris, 3 Graham Wilkins, 4 Garry Stanley, 5 Steve Wicks, 6 David Hay, 7 Ian Britton, 8 Ray Wilkins, 9 Steve Finnieston, 10 Ken Swain, 11 Ray Lewington (12 Bill Garner)
Orient	Jackson, Fisher, Payne, Allder (Bennett), Hoadley, Walley, Cunningham, Grealish, Queen, Heppolette, Possee
Scorers	Possee 38, Cunningham 66
Manager	George Petchey

Charlton Athletic (0) 1 Chelsea (0) 1

Date:	Monday, 19 April 1976
Competition:	Football League Division 2 Position 11
Venue:	The Valley
Attendance:	23,263
Charlton Athletic	Wood, D Young, Berry, T Young, Giles, Curtis, Powell, Hales, Flanagan, Hunt, Peacock
Scorer	Curtis 47
Booked	T Young
Manager	Andy Nelson
Chelsea	1 John Phillips, 2 Ron Harris, 3 Graham Wilkins, 4 Garry Stanley, 5 Steve Wicks, 6 David Hay, 7 Ian Britton, 8 Ray Wilkins, 9 Steve Finnieston, 10 Ken Swain, 11 Bill Garner
Scorer	Berry (O.G) 79
Booked	Wicks

420

York City (1) 2 Chelsea (0) 2

Date:	Saturday, 24 April 1976
Competition:	Football League Division 2 Position 12
Venue:	Bootham Crescent
Attendance:	4,914
Referee:	Anthony E Morrissey (Bramhall)
York City	Crawford, Scott, Downing, James, Topping, Woodward, Pollard, Holmes, Hinch, Cave, Seal
Scorers	Seal 27, Cave 68
Booked	Woodward
Sub Not Used	McMordie
Manager	Wilf McGuinness
Chelsea	1 John Phillips, 2 Ron Harris, 3 Graham Wilkins (12 Brian Bason), 4 Garry Stanley, 5 Steve Wicks, 6 David Hay, 7 Ian Britton, 8 Ray Wilkins, 9 Steve Finnieston, 10 Ken Swain, 11 Bill Garner
Scorers	Britton 64 (Pen), Finnieston 86
Booked	Britton, Ray Wilkins

EDDIE MAC EDDIE MAC

1976-77 SEASON

Orient (0) 0 Chelsea (0) 1

Date:	Saturday, 21 August 1976
Competition:	Football League Division 2 Position 8
Venue:	Brisbane Road
Attendance:	11,456
Referee:	Brian James (Selsdon)
Orient	Jackson, Payne, Fisher, Allen, Hoadley, Roeder, Cunningham, Heppolette, Queen, Possee, Allder
Booked	Heppolette
Manager	George Petchey
Chelsea	1 Peter Bonetti, 2 Gary Locke, 3 Graham Wilkins, 4 Garry Stanley, 5 Steve Wicks, 6 David Hay, 7 Ian Britton, 8 Ray Wilkins, 9 Steve Finnieston, 10 Ray Lewington, 11 Ken Swain
Scorer	Finnieston 87
Booked	Hay, Lewington, Stanley
Sub Not Used	12 Ron Harris

Chelsea (0) 1 Notts County (1) 1

Date:	Wednesday, 25 August 1976
Competition:	Football League Division 2 Position 5
Venue:	Stamford Bridge
Attendance:	17,426
Referee:	Trevor D Spencer (Salisbury)
Chelsea	1 Peter Bonetti, 2 Gary Locke, 3 Graham Wilkins, 4 Brian Bason, 5 Steve Wicks, 6 David Hay, 7 Ian Britton, 8 Ray Wilkins, 9 Steve Finnieston, 10 Ray Lewington, 11 Ken Swain
Scorer	Britton 78
Sub Not Used	12 Ron Harris
Notts County	McManus, Richards, O'Brien, Probert, Needham, Mann, McVay, Vinter, Bradd (Benjamin 30), Smith, Scanlon
Scorer	Probert 34
Booked	McVay 57, O'Brien 70, Mann 89
Manager	Ron Fenton

Chelsea (1) 2 Carlisle United (0) 1

Date:	Saturday, 28 August 1976
Competition:	Football League Division 2 Position 1
Venue:	Stamford Bridge
Attendance:	18,681
Referee:	Alan Robinson (Portsmouth)
Chelsea	1 Peter Bonetti, 2 Gary Locke, 3 Graham Wilkins, 4 Garry Stanley, 5 Steve Wicks, 6 David Hay, 7 Ian Britton, 8 Ray Wilkins, 9 Steve Finnieston, 10 Ray Lewington, 11 Ken Swain
Scorers	Swain 25, Finnieston 51
Sub Not Used	12 Ron Harris
Carlisle United	Ross, Carr, Gorman, Bonnyman, MacDonald, Parker, McVitie, McCartney, Owen, Rafferty, Martin
Scorer	McVitie 77
Manager	Dick Young

Chelsea (2) 3 Sheffield United (1) 1

Date:	Wednesday, 1 September 1976
Competition:	League Cup Round 2
Venue:	Stamford Bridge
Attendance:	16,883
Referee:	Jeff E Bent (Hemel Hempstead)
Chelsea	1 Peter Bonetti, 2 Gary Locke, 3 Graham Wilkins, 4 Garry Stanley, 5 Micky Droy, 6 David Hay, 7 Ian Britton, 8 Ray Wilkins, 9 Steve Finnieston, 10 Ray Lewington, 11 Ken Swain
Scorers	Swain 21, Ray Wilkins 30, Ray Wilkins 80
Sub Not Used	12 Ron Harris
Sheffield United	Brown, Franks, Garner, Flynn, Colquhoun, Kenworthy, Woodward, Edwards (Stainrod 46), Guthrie, Ludlam, Hamilton
Scorer	Franks 29
Manager	Jimmy Sirrel

Millwall (3) 3 Chelsea (0) 0

Date:	Saturday, 4 September 1976
Competition:	Football League Division 2 Position 9
Venue:	The Den
Attendance:	21,002
Referee:	Mike J Taylor (Walmer)
Millwall	Goddard, Evans, Donaldson, Brisley, Kitchener, Hazell, Lee, Seasman, Summerhill, Walker, Salvage
Scorers	Salvage 11, Evans 16, Brisley 32
Manager	Gordon Jago
Chelsea	1 Peter Bonetti, 2 Gary Locke, 3 Graham Wilkins, 4 Garry Stanley, 5 Micky Droy, 6 David Hay, 7 Ian Britton, 8 Ray Wilkins, 9 Steve Finnieston (12 Ron Harris 46), 10 Ray Lewington, 11 Ken Swain

Plymouth Argyle (0) 2 Chelsea (0) 3

Date:	Saturday, 11 September 1976
Competition:	Football League Division 2 Position 5
Venue:	Home Park
Attendance:	18,356
Referee:	Derek Lloyd (Fernhill Heath)
Plymouth Argyle	Ramsbottom, Randell, Horswill, Delve, Sutton, Green, Johnson, Hall, Mariner, Harrison (Hamilton 75), Rogers
Scorers	Hall 79, Mariner 82
Booked	Delve 90
Manager	Tony Waiters
Chelsea	1 Peter Bonetti, 2 Gary Locke, 3 Graham Wilkins, 4 Garry Stanley, 5 Steve Wicks, 6 David Hay, 7 Ian Britton, 8 Ray Wilkins, 9 Steve Finnieston, 10 Ray Lewington, 11 Ken Swain
Scorers	Britton 52 (Pen), Swain 78, Finnieston 83
Booked	Graham Wilkins, Stanley, Swain 88
Sub Not Used	12 Ron Harris

424

Chelsea (1) 2 Bolton Wanderers (0) 1

Date:	Saturday, 18 September 1976
Competition:	Football League Division 2 Position 2
Venue:	Stamford Bridge
Attendance:	24,835
Referee:	William J Gow (Swansea)
Chelsea	1 Peter Bonetti, 2 Gary Locke, 3 Graham Wilkins, 4 Garry Stanley, 5 Steve Wicks, 6 David Hay, 7 Ian Britton (12 Ron Harris 40), 8 Ray Wilkins, 9 Steve Finnieston, 10 Ray Lewington, 11 Ken Swain
Scorers	Hay 44, Stanley 63
Bolton Wanderers	Siddall, Ritson, Dunne, Greaves, Jones, Allardyce, Morgan, Whatmore, Taylor, Reid, Thompson
Scorer	Taylor 90
Booked	Jones 63
Manager	Ian Greaves

Chelsea (1) 2 Huddersfield Town (0) 0

Date:	Monday, 20 September 1976
Competition:	League Cup Round 3
Venue:	Stamford Bridge
Attendance:	19,860
Referee:	Alan Turvey (Basingstoke)
Chelsea	1 Peter Bonetti, 2 Gary Locke, 3 Graham Wilkins, 4 Garry Stanley, 5 Steve Wicks, 6 David Hay, 7 Brian Bason, 8 Ray Wilkins, 9 Steve Finnieston, 10 Ray Lewington, 11 Ken Swain
Scorers	Finnieston 37, Finnieston 70
Sub Not Used	12 Ron Harris
Huddersfield	Poole, Hart, Oliver, Smith, Baines, Hague, Firth, Fowler, Newton, Jones, Maitland (Sidebottom)
Booked	Smith
Manager	Tom Johnston

Blackpool (0) 0 Chelsea (1) 1

Date:	Saturday, 25 September 1976
Competition:	Football League Division 2 Position 1
Venue:	Bloomfield Road
Attendance:	19,041
Referee:	Eric Garner (Maghull)
Blackpool	Wood, Gardner, Bentley, Ronson, Hart, Suddaby, Hockaday, Suddick, Walsh, Hatton, Moore (Harrison 80)
Manager	Allan Brown
Chelsea	1 Peter Bonetti, 2 Gary Locke, 3 Graham Wilkins, 4 Garry Stanley, 5 Steve Wicks, 6 David Hay, 7 Brian Bason, 8 Ray Wilkins, 9 Steve Finnieston, 10 Ray Lewington, 11 Ken Swain
Scorer	Finnieston 16
Sub Not Used	12 Ron Harris

Chelsea (1) 2 Cardiff City (0) 1

Date:	Saturday, 2 October 1976
Competition:	Football League Division 2 Position 1
Venue:	Stamford Bridge
Attendance:	28,409
Referee:	Brian H Daniels (Brentwood)
Chelsea	1 Peter Bonetti, 2 Gary Locke, 3 Graham Wilkins, 4 Charlie Cooke, 5 Steve Wicks, 6 David Hay, 7 Brian Bason, 8 Ray Wilkins, 9 Steve Finnieston, 10 Ray Lewington, 11 Ken Swain
Scorers	Swain 6, Lewington 55
Sub Not Used	12 Ron Harris
Cardiff City	Irwin, Attley, Charles, Buchanan, Dwyer, Larmour, Sayer, Livermore, Evans, Alston, Anderson
Scorer	Charles 85 (Pen)
Booked	Livermore
Sub Not Used	Campbell
Manager	Jimmy Andrews

Bristol Rovers (1) 2 Chelsea (0) 1

Date:	Tuesday, 5 October 1976
Competition:	Football League Division 2 Position 1
Venue:	Eastville
Attendance:	13,199
Referee:	Clive Thomas (Treorchy)
Bristol Rovers	Eadie, Aitken, Williams, Day, Taylor, Prince, Stephens, Fearnley, Warboys, Bannister, Staniforth
Scorers	Bannister 42, Staniforth 87
Manager	Don Megson
Chelsea	1 Peter Bonetti, 2 Gary Locke, 3 Graham Wilkins, 4 Charlie Cooke, 5 Steve Wicks (12 Ron Harris 50), 6 David Hay, 7 Brian Bason, 8 Ray Wilkins, 9 Steve Finnieston, 10 Ray Lewington, 11 Ken Swain
Scorer	Finnieston 75
Booked	Harris

Chelsea (4) 4 Oldham Athletic (2) 3

Date:	Saturday, 16 October 1976
Competition:	Football League Division 2 Position 1
Venue:	Stamford Bridge
Attendance:	25,825
Referee:	Leslie Burden (Corfe Mullen)
Chelsea	1 Peter Bonetti, 2 Gary Locke, 3 Graham Wilkins, 4 Garry Stanley, 5 Steve Wicks, 6 David Hay, 7 Brian Bason, 8 Ray Wilkins, 9 Steve Finnieston, 10 Ray Lewington, 11 Ken Swain
Scorers	Swain 2, Ray Wilkins 17, Wicks 40, Finnieston 44
Booked	Stanley
Sub Not Used	12 Ron Harris
Oldham Athletic	Platt, Wood, Blair, Bell, Hicks, Hurst, Chapman, Straw, Halom, Young, Robins
Scorers	Robins 24, Young 33, Shaw 65
Booked	Hicks
Manager	Jimmy Frizzell

Blackburn Rovers (0) 0 Chelsea (1) 2

Date:	Saturday, 23 October 1976
Competition:	Football League Division 2 Position 1
Venue:	Ewood Park
Attendance:	15,039
Referee:	Roy Capey (Madeley Heath)
Blackburn Rovers	Bradshaw, Fazackerley, Bailey, Metcalfe, Keeley, Hawkins, Hird, Silvester (Mitchell), Wagstaffe, Parkes, Svarc
Manager	Jim Smith
Chelsea	1 Peter Bonetti, 2 Gary Locke, 3 Graham Wilkins, 4 Garry Stanley, 5 Steve Wicks, 6 Ron Harris, 7 Brian Bason, 8 Ray Wilkins, 9 Steve Finnieston, 10 Ray Lewington, 11 Ken Swain
Scorers	Finnieston 20, Finnieston 68 (Pen)
Booked	Harris
Sub Not Used	12 John Sparrow

Arsenal (0) 2 Chelsea (0) 1

Date:	Tuesday, 26 October 1976
Competition:	League Cup Round 4
Venue:	Highbury
Attendance:	52,305
Referee:	Ray Toseland (Kettering)
Arsenal	Rimmer, Rice, Nelson, Ross, Simpson, Howard, Ball, Brady, MacDonald, Stapleton, Armstrong
Scorers	Ross 52, Stapleton 59
Booked	Ball, Nelson 79
Manager	Terry Neill
Chelsea	1 John Phillips, 2 Gary Locke, 3 Graham Wilkins, 4 Garry Stanley, 5 Steve Wicks, 6 David Hay, 7 Brian Bason (12 Ron Harris 19), 8 Ray Wilkins, 9 Steve Finnieston, 10 Ray Lewington, 11 Ken Swain
Scorer	Hay 58
Final Appearances	Brian Bason

428

Chelsea (0) 3 Southampton (0) 1

Date:	Saturday, 30 October 1976
Competition:	Football League Division 2 Position 1
Venue:	Stamford Bridge
Attendance:	42,654
Referee:	Cliff Maskell (Cambridge)
Chelsea	1 John Phillips, 2 Gary Locke, 3 Graham Wilkins, 4 Garry Stanley, 5 Steve Wicks, 6 David Hay, 7 Ian Britton, 8 Ray Wilkins, 9 Steve Finnieston, 10 Ray Lewington, 11 Ken Swain
Scorers	Swain 76, Finnieston 81, Ray Wilkins 88
Sub Not Used	12 Ron Harris
Southampton	Montgomery, Rodrigues, Peach, Holmes, Waldron, Blyth, Williams (Stokes 85), Channon, MacDougall, McCalliog, Fisher
Scorer	MacDougall 72
Manager	Lawrie McMenemy

Hereford United (1) 2 Chelsea (2) 2

Date:	Saturday, 6 November 1976
Competition:	Football League Division 2 Position 1
Venue:	Edgar Street
Attendance:	12,858
Referee:	Tom H Reynolds (Swansea)
Hereford United	Hughes, Walker (Goodchild), Ritchie, Layton, Jefferson, Lloyd, Paine, Spiring, Davey, McNeil, Briley
Scorers	Ritchie 29, Layton 70
Manager	John Sillett
Chelsea	1 Peter Bonetti, 2 Gary Locke, 3 Graham Wilkins, 4 Garry Stanley, 5 Steve Wicks, 6 David Hay, 7 Ian Britton, 8 Ray Wilkins, 9 Steve Finnieston, 10 Ray Lewington, 11 Ken Swain
Scorers	Finnieston 28, Finnieston 41 (Pen)
Booked	Locke, Stanley
Sub Not Used	12 Ron Harris

429

Chelsea (1) 2 Charlton Athletic (0) 1

Date:	Wednesday, 10 November 1976
Competition:	Football League Division 2 Position 1
Venue:	Stamford Bridge
Attendance:	38,879
Referee:	Eric A Read (Bristol)
Chelsea	1 Peter Bonetti, 2 Gary Locke, 3 Graham Wilkins, 4 Garry Stanley, 5 Steve Wicks (12 Ron Harris 75), 6 David Hay, 7 Ian Britton, 8 Ray Wilkins, 9 Steve Finnieston, 10 Ray Lewington, 11 Ken Swain
Scorers	Swain 20, Stanley 76
Charlton Athletic	Wood, Hammond, Berry, Hunt, Giles, Curtis, Powell, Hales, Flanagan, Bowman, Peacock
Scorer	Giles 72
Manager	Andy Nelson

Nottingham Forest (1) 1 Chelsea (1) 1

Date:	Saturday, 20 November 1976
Competition:	Football League Division 2 Position 1
Venue:	City Ground
Attendance:	27,089
Referee:	Dennis Turner (Cannock)
Notts Forest	Middleton, Anderson, Clark, McGovern, Chapman, Bowyer, Haslegrave, O'Neill, Withe, Woodcock, Robertson
Scorer	O'Neill 34
Booked	Haslegrave
Sub Not Used	O'Hare
Manager	Brian Clough
Chelsea	1 Peter Bonetti, 2 Gary Locke, 3 Graham Wilkins, 4 Garry Stanley, 5 Steve Wicks, 6 David Hay, 7 Ian Britton, 8 Ray Wilkins, 9 Steve Finnieston, 10 Ray Lewington, 11 Ken Swain
Scorer	Britton 38
Booked	Lewington 36
Sub Not Used	12 Ron Harris

Chelsea (2) 2 Burnley (0) 1

Date:	Saturday, 27 November 1976
Competition:	Football League Division 2 Position 1
Venue:	Stamford Bridge
Attendance:	28,595
Referee:	Alf Grey (Gorleston-On-Sea)
Chelsea	1 Peter Bonetti, 2 Gary Locke, 3 Graham Wilkins, 4 Garry Stanley, 5 Steve Wicks, 6 David Hay, 7 Ian Britton, 8 Ray Wilkins, 9 Steve Finnieston, 10 Ray Lewington, 11 Ken Swain
Scorers	Britton 15, Finnieston 44 (Pen)
Sub Not Used	12 Ron Harris
Burnley	Stevenson, Newton, Brennan, Noble, Thomson, Rodaway, Ingham, Smith, Fletcher (Morley 30), Flynn, Summerbee
Scorer	Noble 77
Manager	Joe Brown

Sheffield United (0) 1 Chelsea (0) 0

Date:	Friday, 3 December 1976
Competition:	Football League Division 2 Position 1
Venue:	Bramall Lane
Attendance:	23,393
Referee:	Brian Martin (Keyworth)
Sheffield United	Brown, Franks, Garner, Longhorn, Colquhoun, Kenworthy, Woodward, Edwards, Guthrie, Hamson, Hamilton
Scorer	Hamilton 68 (Pen)
Manager	Jimmy Sirrel
Chelsea	1 Peter Bonetti, 2 Gary Locke, 3 Graham Wilkins, 4 Garry Stanley, 5 Steve Wicks, 6 David Hay, 7 Ian Britton, 8 Ray Wilkins, 9 Steve Finnieston, 10 Ray Lewington, 11 Ken Swain
Booked	Graham Wilkins
Sub Not Used	12 Ron Harris

Southampton (1) 1 Chelsea (0) 1

Date:	Tuesday, 7 December 1976
Competition:	Football League Division 2 Position 1
Venue:	The Dell
Attendance:	19,909
Referee:	Alex R Lees (Bridgwater)
Southampton	Turner, Rodrigues, Peach, Holmes, Waldron, Blyth, Williams, Channon, MacDougall, McCalliog, Stokes
Scorer	MacDougall 2
Booked	Peach
Manager	Lawrie McMenemy
Chelsea	1 Peter Bonetti, 2 Gary Locke, 3 Graham Wilkins, 4 Garry Stanley, 5 Steve Wicks, 6 David Hay, 7 Ian Britton, 8 Ray Wilkins, 9 Steve Finnieston, 10 Ray Lewington, 11 Ken Swain
Scorer	Finnieston 65
Booked	Lewington
Sub Not Used	12 Ron Harris

Chelsea (1) 3 Wolverhampton Wanderers (2) 3

Date:	Saturday, 11 December 1976
Competition:	Football League Division 2 Position 1
Venue:	Stamford Bridge
Attendance:	36,137
Referee:	Ron Crabb (Exeter)
Chelsea	1 Peter Bonetti, 2 Gary Locke, 3 Graham Wilkins, 4 Garry Stanley, 5 Steve Wicks, 6 David Hay, 7 Ian Britton, 8 Ray Wilkins, 9 Steve Finnieston, 10 Ray Lewington, 11 Ken Swain
Scorers	Ray Wilkins 19, Britton 80, Finnieston 87
Sub Not Used	12 Ron Harris
Wolves	Pierce, Palmer, Parkin, Daley, Munro, McAlle, Hibbitt, Richards, Sunderland, Gould, Patching
Scorers	Richards 17, Gould 38, Richards 71
Sub Not Used	Farley
Manager	Sammy Chung

Hull City (1) 1 Chelsea (0) 1

Date:	Saturday, 18 December 1976
Competition:	Football League Division 2 Position 1
Venue:	Boothferry Park
Attendance:	11,774
Referee:	Gordon C Kew (Middlesbrough)
Hull City	Wealands, Daniel, DeVries, Bremner, Croft, Haigh, Nisbet, Lord, Sunley, Hemmerman, Hawley
Scorer	Hemmerman 41
Manager	John Kaye
Chelsea	1 Peter Bonetti, 2 Gary Locke, 3 Graham Wilkins, 4 Garry Stanley, 5 Steve Wicks, 6 David Hay, 7 Ian Britton, 8 Ray Wilkins, 9 Steve Finnieston, 10 Ray Lewington, 11 Ken Swain
Scorer	Britton 89
Booked	Hay, Locke, Ray Wilkins
Sub Not Used	12 Ron Harris

Chelsea (0) 2 Fulham (0) 0

Date:	Monday, 27 December 1976
Competition:	Football League Division 2 Position 1
Venue:	Stamford Bridge
Attendance:	55,003
Referee:	Bartley John Homewood (Sunbury-On-Thames)
Chelsea	1 Peter Bonetti, 2 Gary Locke, 3 Graham Wilkins, 4 Garry Stanley, 5 Micky Droy, 6 David Hay, 7 Ian Britton, 8 Ray Wilkins, 9 Steve Finnieston, 10 Ray Lewington, 11 Ken Swain
Scorers	Droy 75, Swain 89
Sub Not Used	12 Ron Harris
Fulham	Peyton, Howe, Strong, Slough, Lacy, Moore, Greenaway, Best, Mitchell, Evanson, Barrett
Booked	Evanson, Lacy, Strong 86, Best 90
Manager	Bobby Campbell

Luton Town (2) 4 Chelsea (0) 0

Date:	Wednesday, 29 December 1976
Competition:	Football League Division 2 Position 1
Venue:	Kenilworth Road
Attendance:	17,102
Referee:	Clive B White (Harrow)
Luton Town	Aleksic, Price, Buckley, Chambers, Faulkner, P Futcher, Husband, West, R Futcher, Fuccillo, Ryan
Scorers	Fuccillo 2, Chambers 13, Husband 57, Buckley 88 (Pen)
Manager	Harry Haslam
Chelsea	1 John Phillips, 2 Gary Locke, 3 Graham Wilkins, 4 Garry Stanley, 5 Micky Droy, 6 David Hay, 7 Ian Britton, 8 Ray Wilkins, 9 Steve Finnieston, 10 Ray Lewington, 11 Ken Swain
Sub Not Used	12 Ron Harris

Chelsea (3) 5 Hereford United (0) 1

Date:	Saturday, 1 January 1977
Competition:	Football League Division 2 Position 1
Venue:	Stamford Bridge
Attendance:	27,720
Referee:	Tony R Glasson (Salisbury)
Chelsea	1 John Phillips, 2 Gary Locke, 3 Ron Harris, 4 Garry Stanley (12 John Sparrow 85), 5 Micky Droy, 6 David Hay, 7 Ian Britton, 8 Ray Wilkins, 9 Steve Finnieston, 10 Ray Lewington, 11 Ken Swain
Scorers	Swain 3, Stanley 24, Wilkins 38, Finnieston 46, Galley (O.G) 90
Hereford United	Charlton, Spiring, Ritchie, Jefferson, Galley, Lindsay, Paine, Carter (Sinclair 73), Davey, Goodchild, Briley
Scorer	Paine 57
Manager	John Sillett

Southampton (0) 1 Chelsea (1) 1

Date:	Saturday, 8 January 1977
Competition:	F.A. Cup Round 3
Venue:	The Dell
Attendance:	26,041
Referee:	William J Gow (Swansea)
Southampton	Wells, Andruszewski, Peach, Holmes, Blyth, Steele, Ball, Channon, Osgood, McCalliog, MacDougall
Scorer	Channon 56
Booked	Steele 86
Manager	Lawrie McMenemy
Chelsea	1 John Phillips, 2 Gary Locke, 3 Ron Harris, 4 Garry Stanley, 5 Micky Droy, 6 David Hay, 7 Ian Britton, 8 Ray Wilkins, 9 Steve Finnieston, 10 Ray Lewington, 11 Ken Swain
Scorer	Locke 35
Sub Not Used	12 John Sparrow

Chelsea (0) 0 Southampton (0) 3

Date:	Wednesday 12 January 1977
Competition:	F.A. Cup Round 3 (replay)
Venue:	Stamford Bridge
Attendance:	42,868
Referee:	Jeff E Bent (Hemel Hempstead)
Chelsea	1 John Phillips, 2 Gary Locke, 3 Ron Harris, 4 Garry Stanley, 5 Micky Droy, 6 David Hay, 7 Ian Britton, 8 Ray Wilkins, 9 Steve Finnieston, 10 Ray Lewington, 11 Ken Swain
Sub Not Used	12 John Sparrow
Southampton	Wells, Andruszewski, Peach, Holmes, Blyth, Steele, Ball, Channon, Osgood, McCalliog, MacDougall
Scorers	MacDougall 107, Channon 115, Peach 120 (Pen)
Booked	Osgood, Steele
Manager	Lawrie McMenemy
	After extra time. Score at 90 minutes 0-0

Chelsea (1) 1 Orient (1) 1

Date:	Saturday, 22 January 1977
Competition:	Football League Division 2 Position 1
Venue:	Stamford Bridge
Attendance:	25,744
Referee:	Peter Reeves (Leicester)
Chelsea	1 John Phillips, 2 Gary Locke, 3 Ron Harris, 4 Garry Stanley, 5 Micky Droy, 6 David Hay, 7 Ian Britton, 8 Ray Wilkins, 9 Steve Finnieston, 10 Ray Lewington, 11 Ken Swain
Scorer	Stanley 32
Sub Not Used	12 John Sparrow
Orient	Jackson, Fisher, Allder, Bennett, Hoadley, Roeder, Cunningham (Roffey), Grealish, Allen, Queen, Whittle
Scorer	Whittle 15
Manager	George Petchey

Carlisle United (0) 0 Chelsea (0) 1

Date:	Saturday, 5 February 1977
Competition:	Football League Division 2 Position 1
Venue:	Brunton Park
Attendance:	11,356
Referee:	Harold Hackney (Barnsley)
Carlisle United	Burleigh, Hoolickin, Carr, Tait, MacDonald, Moncur, O'Neill, McVitie, Deans, Rafferty, Martin
Booked	Tait
Sub Not Used	Bonnyman
Manager	Bobby Moncur
Chelsea	1 John Phillips, 2 Gary Locke, 3 Ron Harris, 4 Garry Stanley, 5 Micky Droy, 6 David Hay, 7 Ian Britton, 8 Ray Wilkins, 9 Steve Finnieston (12 John Sparrow 17), 10 Ray Lewington, 11 Ken Swain
Scorer	Swain 83

Chelsea (0) 1 Millwall (0) 1

Date:	Saturday, 12 February 1977
Competition:	Football League Division 2 Position 1
Venue:	Stamford Bridge
Attendance:	34,857
Referee:	Derek Nippard (Christchurch)
Chelsea	1 John Phillips, 2 Gary Locke, 3 Ron Harris, 4 Garry Stanley, 5 Micky Droy, 6 David Hay, 7 Ian Britton, 8 Ray Wilkins, 9 Teddy Maybank, 10 Ray Lewington, 11 Ken Swain
Scorer	Stanley 72
Sub Not Used	12 John Sparrow
Millwall	Goddard, Evans, Moore, Brisley, Kitchener, Hazell, Donaldson, Seasman, Summerhill, Walker, Salvage
Scorer	Brisley 51
Booked	Hazell 85
Manager	Gordon Jago

Notts County (2) 2 Chelsea (1) 1

Date:	Tuesday, 15 February 1977
Competition:	Football League Division 2 Position 1
Venue:	Meadow Lane
Attendance:	11,902
Referee:	Alan Porter (Bolton)
Notts County	McManus, Richards, O'Brien, Busby, Needham, Stubbs, Carter, Vinter, Bradd, Mann, Smith
Scorers	Stubbs 11, Carter 24 (Pen)
Manager	Ron Fenton
Chelsea	1 John Phillips, 2 Gary Locke, 3 Graham Wilkins, 4 Garry Stanley, 5 Micky Droy, 6 David Hay, 7 Ian Britton, 8 Ray Wilkins, 9 Teddy Maybank, 10 Ray Lewington, 11 Ken Swain
Scorer	Ray Wilkins 31
Sub Not Used	12 Ron Harris

Chelsea (1) 2 Plymouth Argyle (0) 2

Date:	Saturday, 19 February 1977
Competition:	Football League Division 2 Position 1
Venue:	Stamford Bridge
Attendance:	22,154
Referee:	Jeff Sewell (Birstall)
Chelsea	1 John Phillips, 2 Gary Locke, 3 Graham Wilkins, 4 Garry Stanley, 5 Steve Wicks, 6 David Hay, 7 Ian Britton, 8 Ray Wilkins, 9 Teddy Maybank, 10 Ray Lewington, 11 Ken Swain
Scorers	Swain 2, Britton 62 (Pen)
Booked	Maybank
Sub Not Used	12 Ron Harris
Final Appearances	Teddy Maybank
Plymouth Argyle	Ramsbottom, Randell, Horswill, Delve, Green, Peddelty, Hall, Craven, Austin, Bannister, Rogers
Scorers	Austin 52, Bannister 65 (Pen)
Booked	Craven, Delve, Green
Sub Not Used	Collins
Manager	Tony Waiters

Bolton Wanderers (2) 2 Chelsea (0) 2

Date:	Saturday, 26 February 1977
Competition:	Football League Division 2 Position 1
Venue:	Burnden Park
Attendance:	31,600
Referee:	CN Steel (Carlisle)
Bolton Wanderers	McDonagh, Nicholson, Dunne, Greaves, P Jones, Allardyce, Morgan, Whatmore, G Jones, Reid, Waldron
Scorers	Whatmore 22, G Jones 30
Booked	Nicholson
Manager	Ian Greaves
Chelsea	1 John Phillips, 2 Gary Locke, 3 Graham Wilkins, 4 Garry Stanley, 5 Steve Wicks, 6 David Hay, 7 Ian Britton, 8 Ray Wilkins, 9 Steve Finnieston, 10 Ray Lewington, 11 Ken Swain
Scorers	Finnieston 67, Swain 72
Booked	Graham Wilkins
Sub Not Used	12 Ron Harris

Chelsea (1) 2 Blackpool (1) 2

Date:	Saturday, 5 March 1977
Competition:	Football League Division 2 Position 1
Venue:	Stamford Bridge
Attendance:	27,412
Referee:	Alan Robinson (Portsmouth)
Chelsea	1 John Phillips, 2 Gary Locke, 3 Graham Wilkins, 4 Garry Stanley, 5 Steve Wicks, 6 David Hay, 7 Ian Britton, 8 Ray Wilkins, 9 Steve Finnieston, 10 Ray Lewington, 11 Ken Swain
Scorers	Swain 37, Wicks 47
Sub Not Used	12 Ron Harris
Blackpool	Wood, Curtis, Harrison, Ronson, Hart, Suddaby, Ainscow, Spence, Walsh, Hatton, Bentley
Scorers	Ronson 35, Spence 52
Booked	Suddaby
Sub Not Used	Summerbee
Manager	Allan Brown

Cardiff City (0) 1 Chelsea (0) 3

Date:	Saturday, 12 March 1977
Competition:	Football League Division 2 Position 1
Venue:	Ninian Park
Attendance:	20,194
Referee:	Derek W Civil (Birmingham)
Cardiff City	Healey, Dwyer, Charles, Giles, Went, Larmour, Grapes, Livermore, Evans, Friday, Sayer
Scorer	Dwyer 83
Manager	Jimmy Andrews
Chelsea	1 Peter Bonetti, 2 Gary Locke, 3 John Sparrow, 4 Garry Stanley, 5 Steve Wicks, 6 David Hay, 7 Ian Britton, 8 Ray Wilkins, 9 Steve Finnieston, 10 Ray Lewington, 11 Ken Swain
Scorers	Britton 60, Swain 79, Stanley 90
Booked	Wicks 40
Sub Not Used	12 Ron Harris

Chelsea (0) 2 Bristol Rovers (0) 0

Date:	Saturday, 19 March 1977
Competition:	Football League Division 2 Position 1
Venue:	Stamford Bridge
Attendance:	26,196
Referee:	Mike J Taylor (Walmer)
Chelsea	1 Peter Bonetti, 2 Gary Locke, 3 John Sparrow, 4 Garry Stanley, 5 Steve Wicks, 6 David Hay, 7 Ian Britton, 8 Ray Wilkins, 9 Steve Finnieston, 10 Ray Lewington, 11 Ken Swain
Scorers	Aitken (O.G) 63, Wicks 81
Sub Not Used	12 Ron Harris
Bristol Rovers	Eadie, Williams, Parsons, Prince, Taylor, Aitken, Stephens, Fearnley, Staniforth, Hamilton, Evans
Manager	Don Megson

Chelsea (2) 3 Blackburn Rovers (0) 1

Date:	Saturday, 2 April 1977
Competition:	Football League Division 2 Position 1
Venue:	Stamford Bridge
Attendance:	20,769
Referee:	Ray Toseland (Kettering)
Chelsea	1 Peter Bonetti, 2 Gary Locke, 3 John Sparrow, 4 Garry Stanley, 5 Steve Wicks, 6 Ron Harris, 7 Ian Britton, 8 Ray Wilkins, 9 Steve Finnieston, 10 Ray Lewington, 11 Ken Swain
Scorers	Wicks 15, Finnieston 30, Finnieston 60
Sub Not Used	12 John Dempsey
Blackburn Rovers	Bradshaw, Fazackerley, Wood, Hird, Waddington, Hawkins, Metcalfe, Round (Bailey), Svarc, Parkes, Wagstaffe
Scorer	Waddington 52
Manager	Jim Smith

Fulham (2) 3 Chelsea (0) 1

Date:	Friday, 8 April 1977
Competition:	Football League Division 2 Position 2
Venue:	Craven Cottage
Attendance:	29,690
Referee:	Tom Bune (Billinghurst)
Fulham	Peyton, Evans, Strong, Storey, Lacy, Moore, Best, Maybank, Warboys, Mitchell, Slough
Scorers	Warboys 11, Best 20, Mitchell 47
Booked	Storey 2
Manager	Bobby Campbell
Chelsea	1 Peter Bonetti, 2 Gary Locke, 3 John Sparrow, 4 Garry Stanley, 5 Steve Wicks, 6 Ron Harris, 7 Ian Britton, 8 Ray Wilkins, 9 Steve Finnieston, 10 Ray Lewington, 11 Ken Swain
Scorer	Wilkins 75
Sub Not Used	12 John Dempsey

Chelsea (2) 2 Luton Town (0) 0

Date:	Saturday, 9 April 1977
Competition:	Football League Division 2 Position 1
Venue:	Stamford Bridge
Attendance:	31,911
Referee:	Jack K Taylor (Wolverhampton)
Chelsea	1 Peter Bonetti, 2 Gary Locke, 3 John Sparrow, 4 Garry Stanley, 5 Steve Wicks, 6 Ron Harris, 7 Ian Britton, 8 Ray Wilkins, 9 Steve Finnieston, 10 Ray Lewington, 11 Ken Swain
Scorers	Finnieston 14, Sparrow 38
Sub Not Used	12 John Dempsey
Luton Town	Aleksic, Price (Jones 30), Buckley, Chambers, Faulkner, P Futcher, Husband, West, Geddis, Fuccillo, Aston
Manager	Harry Haslam

Charlton Athletic (2) 4 Chelsea (0) 0

Date:	Monday, 11 April 1977
Competition:	Football League Division 2 Position 2
Venue:	The Valley
Attendance:	25,757
Referee:	Ron Crabb (Exeter)
Charlton Athletic	Wood, Curtis, Warman, Tydeman, Giles, Berry, Powell, Hunt, Flanagan, Peacock, McAuley
Scorers	Flanagan 32, Flanagan 43, McAuley 55, Flanagan 67
Manager	Andy Nelson
Chelsea	1 John Phillips, 2 Gary Locke, 3 John Sparrow, 4 Garry Stanley, 5 Steve Wicks, 6 Ron Harris, 7 Ian Britton, 8 Ray Wilkins, 9 Steve Finnieston, 10 Ray Lewington, 11 Ken Swain
Sub Not Used	12 John Dempsey

Chelsea (0) 2 Nottingham Forest (1) 1

Date:	Saturday, 16 April 1977
Competition:	Football League Division 2 Position 2
Venue:	Stamford Bridge
Attendance:	36,499
Referee:	Ron Challis (Tonbridge)
Chelsea	1 Peter Bonetti, 2 Gary Locke, 3 John Sparrow, 4 Charlie Cooke, 5 Steve Wicks, 6 Ron Harris, 7 Ian Britton, 8 Ray Wilkins, 9 Steve Finnieston, 10 Ray Lewington, 11 Tommy Langley
Scorers	Britton 63, Finnieston 87
Sub Not Used	12 Clive Walker
Notts Forest	Middleton, Anderson, Clark, Chapman, Lloyd, Bowyer, McGovern, O'Neill, Withe, Woodcock, Robertson
Scorer	O'Neill 42
Manager	Brian Clough

Oldham Athletic (0) 0 Chelsea (0) 0

Date:	Tuesday, 19 April 1977
Competition:	Football League Division 2 Position 1
Venue:	Boundary Park
Attendance:	10,074
Referee:	Keith S Hackett (Sheffield)
Oldham Athletic	Ogden, Wood, Whittle, Bell, Holt, Hurst, Blair, Shaw, Robins, Chapman, Groves
Manager	Jimmy Frizzell
Chelsea	1 Peter Bonetti, 2 Gary Locke, 3 John Sparrow, 4 Charlie Cooke, 5 Steve Wicks, 6 Ron Harris, 7 Ian Britton, 8 Ray Wilkins, 9 Steve Finnieston, 10 Ray Lewington, 11 Tommy Langley (12 Clive Walker)
Booked	Locke, Britton 88
Debut Players	Clive Walker

Burnley (0) 1 Chelsea (0) 0

Date:	Saturday, 23 April 1977
Competition:	Football League Division 2 Position 2
Venue:	Turf Moor
Attendance:	14,927
Referee:	Terry Farley (Durham)
Burnley	Stevenson, Newton, Brennan, Noble, Robinson, Rodaway, Ingham, Smith, Fletcher, Flynn, Morley
Scorer	Ingham 85
Manager	Harry Potts
Chelsea	1 Peter Bonetti, 2 Gary Locke, 3 John Sparrow, 4 Charlie Cooke, 5 Steve Wicks, 6 Ron Harris, 7 Ian Britton, 8 Ray Wilkins, 9 Steve Finnieston, 10 Ray Lewington, 11 Tommy Langley
Sub Not Used	12 Clive Walker

Chelsea (2) 4 Sheffield United (0) 0

Date:	Saturday, 30 April 1977
Competition:	Football League Division 2 Position 2
Venue:	Stamford Bridge
Attendance:	28,158
Referee:	Tom H Reynolds (Bratton Westbury)
Chelsea	1 Peter Bonetti, 2 Gary Locke, 3 John Sparrow, 4 Charlie Cooke, 5 Steve Wicks, 6 Ron Harris, 7 Ian Britton, 8 Ray Wilkins, 9 Steve Finnieston, 10 Ray Lewington, 11 Tommy Langley
Scorers	Langley 15, Lewington 20, Wilkins 50, Finnieston 70
Sub Not Used	12 Clive Walker
Sheffield United	Brown, Cutbush, Garner, Longhorn, Franks, Kenworthy, Calvert, Stainrod, Edwards, Hamson, Hamilton
Sub Not Used	Flynn
Manager	Jimmy Sirrel

Wolverhampton Wanderers (0) 1 Chelsea (1) 1

Date:	Saturday, 7 May 1977
Competition:	Football League Division 2 Position 2
Venue:	Molineux
Attendance:	33,465
Referee:	Donald Biddle (Bristol)
Wolves	Pierce, Palmer, Parkin, Daley, Munro, Berry, Hibbitt, Richards, Sunderland (Gould 68), Patching, Carr
Scorer	Richards 79
Manager	Sammy Chung
Chelsea	1 Peter Bonetti, 2 Gary Locke, 3 John Sparrow, 4 Charlie Cooke, 5 Steve Wicks, 6 Ron Harris, 7 Ian Britton, 8 Ray Wilkins, 9 Steve Finnieston, 10 Ray Lewington, 11 Tommy Langley
Scorer	Langley 15
Sub Not Used	12 Clive Walker

Chelsea (1) 4 Hull City (0) 0

Date:	Saturday, 14 May 1977
Competition:	Football League Division 2 Position 2
Venue:	Stamford Bridge
Attendance:	43,718
Referee:	Reg Robinson (Norwich)
Chelsea	1 Peter Bonetti, 2 Gary Locke, 3 John Sparrow, 4 Charlie Cooke, 5 Steve Wicks, 6 Ron Harris, 7 Ian Britton, 8 Ray Wilkins, 9 Steve Finnieston, 10 Ray Lewington, 11 Tommy Langley
Scorers	Finnieston 16, Finnieston 59, Britton 82, Finnieston 88 (Pen)
Sub Not Used	12 Clive Walker
Hull City	Wealands, Daniel, DeVries, Haigh, Croft, Roberts, Nisbet, Lord, Sunley, McDonald, Galvin
Sub Not Used	Gibson
Manager	John Kaye

GATE 17
THE COMPLETE COLLECTION
(MAY 2017)

FOOTBALL
Over Land and Sea - Mark Worrall
Chelsea here, Chelsea There - Kelvin Barker, David Johnstone, Mark Worrall
Chelsea Football Fanzine - the best of cfcuk
One Man Went to Mow - Mark Worrall
Chelsea Chronicles (Five Volume Series) - Mark Worrall
Making History Not Reliving It - Kelvin Barker, David Johnstone, Mark Worrall
Celery! Representing Chelsea in the 1980s - Kelvin Barker
Stuck On You: a year in the life of a Chelsea supporter - Walter Otton
Palpable Discord: a year of drama and dissent at Chelsea - Clayton Beerman
Rhyme and Treason - Carol Ann Wood
The Italian Job: Antonio Conte Chelsea manager - Mark Worrall

FICTION
Blue Murder: Chelsea till I die - Mark Worrall
The Wrong Outfit - Al Gregg
The Red Hand Gang - Walter Otton
Coming Clean - Christopher Morgan
This Damnation - Mark Worrall
Poppy - Walter Otton

NON FICTION
Roe2Ro - Walter Otton
Shorts - Walter Otton

www.gate17.co.uk

Printed in Great Britain
by Amazon